HUMAN RIGHTS LAW

General Editors

Bríd Moriarty and Anne-Marie Mooney Cotter

OXFORD

UNIVERSITY PRESS

OXFORD
UNIVERSITY PRESS

Great Clarendon Street, Oxford OX2 6DP

Oxford University Press is a department of the University of Oxford.
It furthers the University's objective of excellence in research, scholarship,
and education by publishing worldwide in

Oxford New York

Auckland Bangkok Buenos Aires Cape Town Chennai
Dar es Salaam Delhi Hong Kong Istanbul Karachi Kolkata
Kuala Lumpur Madrid Melbourne Mexico City Mumbai Nairobi
São Paulo Shanghai Taipei Tokyo Toronto

Oxford is a registered trade mark of Oxford University Press
in the UK and in certain other countries

Published in the United States
by Oxford University Press Inc., New York

British Library Cataloguing in Publication Data
Data applied for

Library of Congress Cataloging in Publication Data
Data available
ISBN 0–19–925552–0

1 3 5 7 9 10 8 6 4 2

Typeset by RefineCatch Limited, Bungay, Suffolk
Printed in Great Britain by
Antony Rowe Limited, Chippenham, Wiltshire

Disclaimer

While every care has been taken in the production of this book,
no legal responsibility or liability is accepted, warranted or implied by the
authors, editors, publishers or the Law Society in respect of any
errors, omissions or mis-statements.

HUMAN RIGHTS LAW

PREFACE

This text is designed to support the teaching of human rights law on the Law Society's Professional Practice Course. It is an introduction to human rights law in Ireland. A significant development in human rights law in this jurisdiction, discussed in this text, is the European Convention on Human Rights Act, 2003 which incorporates the European Convention on Human Rights (ECHR) into Irish domestic law. It remains to be seen how the provisions of the Act will operate in practice.

The book covers:

Chapter 1: Three spheres of Human Rights Protection in Ireland: An overview of the Hierarchy (Bríd Moriarty); Chapter 2: Human Rights in the Irish Constitution and Irish Legislation (Hugh O'Donoghue); Chapter 3: The European Convention on Human Rights (Gráinne Mullan); Chapter 4: International Human Rights Law (Gráinne Mullan); Chapter 5: Human Rights in EC/EU Law (Bríd Moriarty); Chapter 6: Due Process and the Right to a Fair Trial (Dara Robinson); Chapter 7: Freedom of Expression (Michael Kealey); Chapter 8: Family and Child Law (Geoffrey Shannon); Chapter 9: The Right to Life and the Right to Bodily Integrity (Asim A. Sheikh); Chapter 10: Equality (Conor Power); Chapter 11: Civil Rights: The North American Experience (Dr. Anne-Marie Mooney Cotter); Chapter 12: Refugee Law (Noeline Blackwell).

I would like to thank Siobhán Gallagher for reading a draft of this book and making many helpful comments on it. I would also like to thank the following people who read various chapters and commented on them or who willingly engaged in discussions about specific aspects of chapters: Alma Clissmann, Caroline Cross, Professor Caroline Forder, Dr. Liz Heffernan, Kevin Kitching, TP Kennedy, Antoinette Moriarty, Leesha O' Driscoll, Claire Waterson and the UNHCR in Dublin. Special thanks to Catherine Byrne, Rachel D'Alton, Anthony Griffin and Sinéad Freeman for their assistance in formatting and proofreading the text.

While every effort has been made to ensure the text is accurate neither the authors, the editors, nor the Law Society of Ireland accept legal liability for any errors, omissions or mis-statements of law. Any comments or queries on this book should be sent to the general editors at the Law Society.

Bríd Moriarty
March 2004

CONTENTS

CONTENTS

CONTENTS

CONTENTS

TABLE OF CASES

TABLE OF CASES

TABLE OF CASES

TABLE OF LEGISLATION

European Union legislation

Foreign legislation

International Treaties and Conventions

Secondary legislation

AUTHORS

Noeline Blackwell is a solicitor practising in Dublin. Noeline is a member of the Law Society's Family Law and Civil Legal Aid Committee and of its European Convention of Human Rights Task Force. She is a former chairperson of the Irish section of Amnesty International. She is a trustee of Front Line, the international Foundation for the Protection of Human Rights Defenders and a member of the steering Committee of the Immigrant Council of Ireland.

Dr Anne-Marie Mooney Cotter earned her Bachelors degree from McGill University at age 18, her Juris Doctor law degree from one of the leading Civil Rights Institutions, Howard University School of Law, and her Doctorate degree (PhD) from Concordia University in Political Economy International Law on the issue of equality. Her work experience has been extensive, acting as Chief Advisor and later Administrative Law Judge appointed by the Prime Minister to the Veterans Review and Appeals Tribunal in Canada; Supervising Attorney in Alaska for the Legal Services Corporation in the United States and later Executive Director; National Director for an Environmental Network in Canada; and now Course Co-ordinator for Business Law at the Law Society of Ireland.

Michael Kealey is a solicitor with an established reputation in defamation, privacy and media law. Michael advises newspapers, television companies and individuals. He has written and lectured extensively on media law and Article 10 of the European Convention on Human Rights. He is a member of the Law Society's European Convention on Human Rights Task Force.

Bríd Moriarty is a barrister and Course Co-ordinator at the Law Society with responsibility for courses in European Law, Human Rights Law and Legal Research. Prior to joining the Law Society Bríd worked as Senior Judicial Research Assistant in the Judges' Library. Previously she taught at Portobello College and the University of Limerick, where she completed an LLM in European Law.

Gráinne Mullan is a practising barrister and part-time lecturer in the Law School, Trinity College Dublin, where she lectures Human Rights on the LLM course. Gráinne also lectures Human Rights in the Law Society of Ireland and has written a number of articles in the areas of human rights and criminal procedure.

Hugh O'Donoghue is a partner in the Cork based firm of HV O'Donoghue, Solicitors. Hugh is a specialist in international laws as well as being affiliated to OHIM (EU) as a Community Trade Mark Attorney. He lectures on International Human Rights. Hugh is an associate faculty member of the Law School and a member of the EU and International Affairs Committee of the Law Society. He presently serves as the current Law Society representative to Union Internationale du Notariat Latin (UINL).

AUTHORS

Conor Power is a barrister, who practises in the areas of human rights and employment law. Conor is also a contributor to the Law Society on these topics.

Dara Robinson was admitted as a solicitor in London in 1988. He has practised in Dublin since 1992 and is a partner with the firm of Garrett Sheehan & Company, Solicitors. Dara is a member of the Criminal Law Committee of the Law Society and lectures and tutors regularly in the Law School on Criminal Law and Human Rights.

Geoffrey Shannon is a solicitor and Deputy Director of Education with the Law Society of Ireland. Geoffrey is editor of the *Irish Journal of Family Law* and is the Irish expert on the *Commission on European Family Law*. Geoffrey is a member of the Law Society of Ireland's Family Law and Civil Legal Aid Committee and has written extensively on family law.

Asim A. Sheikh is a Lecturer in Legal Medicine with the Division of Legal Medicine, Faculty of Medicine, University College Dublin and a practising barrister. Asim lectures and has published widely on aspects of medical law, legal medicine and Genetics and Law He is a member of the Irish Council for Bioethics and is a member of the Research Ethics Committee (REC) of the Health Research Board. He is currently editor-in-chief of the Medico-legal Journal of Ireland. He is the author of the report *Genetic Research and Human Biological Samples: The Legal and Ethical Considerations* which was commissioned and published by the Health Research Board in February 2002, and is a contributing author to the text *Risk Manager for GPs* (Roundhall, Sweet & Maxwell, Dublin, 2002).

CHAPTER 1

THREE SPHERES OF HUMAN RIGHTS PROTECTION IN IRELAND: AN OVERVIEW OF THE HIERARCHY

1.1   Introduction

There are three spheres of human rights law in Ireland. Irish domestic law, European Community (EC) law and international law all contain guarantees of human rights that Ireland seeks to uphold. In Irish domestic law Bunreacht na hÉireann, the Irish constitution is the chief source of such guarantees. Other sources include legislation and case-law.

As Ireland is a strict dualist state international human rights obligations that are not incorporated into domestic law only bind the State under international law and do not create rights or duties that are enforceable in domestic courts. The European Union, of which Ireland is a member is increasingly concerned with human rights protection and EC law is enforceable in domestic courts. The rights that are protected in each of these spheres are discussed in the following chapters.

This chapter is concerned with the relationship between domestic and the international law and between the domestic and EC law. The relationship between international law and EC law is beyond the scope of this text, although the relationship between the European Convention on Human Rights and Fundamental Freedoms (the ECHR) is discussed in **chapter 5**.

1.2   The First Sphere of Human Rights Protection: The Constitution and Domestic Legislation

The Constitution, Bunreacht na hÉireann, contains a catalogue of human rights protections. These rights are at the apex of domestic human rights protection and are discussed in **chapter 2**. Domestic legislation concerning human rights is also considered in **chapter 2**.

In the first place the Constitution prohibits the Irish legislature from enacting laws which conflict with the provisions of the Constitution, including it's human rights guarantees.

Article 15.4 of Bunreacht na hÉireann provides:

> *'1° The Oireachtas shall not enact any law which is in any respect repugnant to the Constitution or any provision thereof.*
>
> *2° Every law enacted by the Oireachtas which is in any respect repugnant to this Constitution or any provision thereof, shall but to the extent only of the repugnancy, be invalid.'*

In the case of a conflict between constitutionally protected rights, it is the responsibility of the courts to balance those rights. In the *People (DPP) v Shaw* [1982] IR 1, the Supreme Court held that because of 'extraordinary excusing circumstances' evidence obtained in deliberate violation of an accused's constitutional rights was admissible in a murder trial. The police had detained the accused beyond permissible period but had been motivated by the possibility of saving the victim's life. The court held that the right to life ranked higher than the right to liberty.

1.3 The Second Sphere of Human Rights Protection: International Law

The domestic impact of international treaties has traditionally been a subject determined in accordance with the constitutional law of the signatory state. In international law there are two theories of incorporation of international obligations into the legal systems of states. These are the monist and the dualist theories. When monist obligations are assumed by a monist state they automatically become part of the legal system of that state, individuals can plead provisions of international law in their domestic courts and international law is considered superior. Dualism binds the state in the international sphere but international treaties do not become part of domestic law on ratification. There must be the additional step of incorporation. Without incorporation, individuals cannot rely on provisions of international law in the domestic courts of dualist states. Difficulties arise when international obligations conflict with domestic legal rules.

Many human rights protections stem from international treaties (see **chapters 3** and **4**). For that reason, it is necessary to consider the relationship between international law and Irish law when considering the hierarchy of human rights norms in this jurisdiction.

1.3.1 BUNREACHT NA hÉIREANN'S APPROACH TO INTERNATIONAL LAW

The Constitution adopts a rigid dualist stance to international law. Article 29.6 of Bunreacht na hÉireann provides:

> *'No international agreement shall be part of the domestic law of the State save as may be determined by the Oireachtas.'*

International laws that are ratified by the Irish State are binding on the State under international law and enforceable by other states in accordance with their terms. However they only become binding on the State under domestic law following incorporation into domestic law as determined by the Oireachtas. This stance has a significant impact on the practice of human rights law as many human rights protections originate as international treaties.

1.3.2 DUALISM AND THE ECHR PRIOR TO THE EUROPEAN CONVENTION ON HUMAN RIGHTS ACT, 2003

The most significant international human rights treaty from an Irish perspective is the ECHR. Ireland ratified the ECHR in the early 1950s but it has only been incorporated into Irish law as a consequence of the European Convention on Human Rights Act, 2003 (see **1.3.3**)

It is proposed to look at the status of the ECHR in Irish domestic law prior to the European Convention on Human Rights Act, 2003. Initially, the Irish courts adopted a rigid dualist approach to the ECHR. More recently, they seem to have accepted that the ECHR had some persuasive value. In *Re Ó Laighléis* [1960] IR 93, the Supreme Court stated *per* Maguire CJ:

'The insuperable obstacle to importing the provisions of the convention . . . into the domestic law of Ireland – if they be at variance with that law – is, however the terms of the constitution of Ireland. . . .

The Oireachtas has not determined that the Convention for the Protection of Human Rights and Fundamental Freedoms is part of the domestic law of the State, and accordingly this Court cannot give effect to the convention if it be contrary to domestic law or purports to grant rights or impose obligations additional to those of domestic law.

No argument can prevail against the express command of section 6 of Article 29 of the Constitution before judges whose declared duty it is to uphold the Constitution and the laws.

The Court accordingly cannot accept the idea that the primacy of domestic legislation is displaced by the State becoming party to the Convention for the Protection of Human Rights and Fundamental Freedoms. . . .'

This stance severely limited the individual's ability to rely on the ECHR in domestic courts. In *Norris v AG* [1984] IR 36, the plaintiff challenged legislative provisions which criminalised homosexual activities on two principal grounds: (i) the legislation was inconsistent with the ECHR and (ii) as Ireland had ratified the ECHR there was a presumption of compatibility of the Constitution with the ECHR. The European Court of Human Rights (ECt.HR) in *Dudgeon v UK* (1982) 4 EHRR 149 had previously held that the legislation at issue in *Norris* was incompatible with Article 8 ECHR (the privacy guarantee). Norris also sought to rely on this judgment before the Irish courts. The Supreme Court rejected these arguments on the basis of the Irish dualist stance. *Per* O'Higgins CJ:

'. . . acceptance of [counsel's] view would be contrary to the provisions of the Constitution itself and would accord to the Government the power, by an executive act, to change both the Constitution and the law. The [ECHR] is an international agreement to which Ireland is a subscribing party. As such, however it does not and cannot form part of our domestic law nor affect in any way questions which arise thereunder. This is made quite clear by Article 29, s. 6, of the Constitution. . . .'

Per Henchy J:

'. . . the constitutional question that calls for resolution is unaffected by the fact that the precise statutory provisions in this case were held by the European Court of Human Rights in *Dudgeon v United Kingdom* (1982) 4 EHRR 149 to be in breach of article 8 of the European Convention for the Protection of Human Rights and Fundamental Freedoms. That Convention, as has been held by this Court, although it has by its terms a binding force on the Government of this State as one of its signatories, forms no part of the domestic law of the State.'

Pre-incorporation, the ECHR was not however without domestic impact. Judgments of the ECt.HR are binding under international law on the Irish State albeit indirectly and in compliance with the dualist requirements of the Constitution. Where Ireland is found to be in breach of the ECHR, the State is obliged to amend its domestic law. Subsequent to the Supreme Court ruling, Norris took a case (*Norris v Ireland* (1991) 13 EHRR 360) to the ECt.HR which held that the impugned provisions were in breach of Art 8 ECHR. It took five years after that, however, before the Oireachtas enacted legislation giving effect to the judgment (Criminal Law (Sexual Offences) Act, 1993).

There were some judgments before the incorporation of the ECHR where the Irish courts seemed to recognise that the ECHR had some persuasive value. An example is the High Court decision in *Desmond v Glackin* [1992] ILRM 490. At issue in the case was whether comments made during the course of a radio interview by the Minister for Tourism, Transport and Communications concerning judicial review proceedings, amounted to contempt of court. O'Hanlon J, at 513, considered that judgments of the ECt.HR would have persuasive value:

> 'As Ireland has ratified the [ECHR] and is a party to it, and as the law of contempt of court is based . . . on public policy, I think it is legitimate to assume that our public policy is in accord with the convention or at least that the provisions of the convention can be considered when determining issues of public policy. The Convention itself is not a code of legal principles which are enforceable in the domestic courts, as was made clear in *In re Ó Laighleis* [1960] IR 93, but this does not prevent the judgment of the European Court from having a persuasive effect when considering the common law regarding the contempt of court in the light of constitutional guarantees of freedom of expression contained in our Constitution of 1937. Henchy J expressed the view in *State (Director of Public Prosecutions) v Walsh* [1981] IR 412 at 440, that there was a presumption that our law on contempt is in conformity with the convention, particularly Articles 5 and 10(2).'

The persuasive value of the ECHR is also apparent from the partly dissenting judgment of Denham J in *O' Brien v Mirror Group Newspapers* [2001] 1 IR 1. The facts concerned an appeal against the quantum of damages awarded in a libel case. Keane CJ at page 18 (for the majority) stated that the appeal on quantum should be dealt with on the basis of the law as stated in *de Rossa v Independent Newspapers plc.* [1999] 4 IR 432. Denham J opined that as ECHR jurisprudence was of persuasive value, a cogent argument that there was an error in the interpretation of an ECt.HR judgment, was a compelling reason to reconsider precedent.

> '. . . In light of the current practice whereby decisions of the European Court of Human Rights may have persuasive authority on issues where the Convention and Constitution are similar, in light of the fact that Ireland was one of the original states which ratified the Convention (with the consequent effect on policy), and in light of the declared intention of the Irish Government to incorporate the Convention into the domestic law of Ireland, the law of the Convention has a persuasive relevance. Consequently a cogent argument that there was error in part in its interpretation is significant and a compelling reason to reconsider the issue.'

According to O' Connell, '. . . it is clear that the prevailing orthodoxy – that the Convention is of no more than persuasive value in domestic proceedings – remains unpenetrated.' (O' Connell 'Ireland' in Blackburn and Polakiewicz (eds.) 'Fundamental Rights in Europe: The ECHR and its Member States, 1952–2000' 2001, OUP, 423, 435).

A useful summary of the pre-incorporation position of the ECHR in Irish law may be found in a dicta of Barrington J in *Doyle v Commissioner of An Garda Síochána* [1999] 1 IR 249. The case arose out of the car bomb explosions that took place in Dublin and Monaghan in 1974 which killed thirty-three people including the plaintiff's daughter and two granddaughters. The plaintiff sought discovery of files relating to these atrocities which were in the possession of An Garda Síochána to use them as evidence in proceedings instituted by him before the ECt.HR. The Supreme Court in considering the ECHR guarantee of the right of individual petition held that the duty imposed by this obligation appears to be a negative duty to refrain from frustrating the individual's right of petition. The Supreme Court also held that as the ECHR (prior to incorporation) was an external Treaty obligation, the domestic courts were not in a position to enforce it. In the course of his judgment Barrington J stated at 268:

> 'Ireland is a signatory of the European Convention on Human Rights and accepts the right of individual petition. But Ireland takes the dualistic approach to its international obligations and the European Convention is not part of the domestic law of Ireland. The Convention may overlap with certain provisions of Irish constitutional law and it may be helpful to an Irish court to look at the Convention when it is attempting to identify unspecified rights guaranteed by Article 40.3 of the Constitution. Alternatively, the Convention may, in certain circumstances influence Irish law through European

community law. But the Convention is not part of Irish domestic law and the Irish court has no part in its enforcement. So far as Ireland is concerned the institutions to enforce the provisions of the Convention are the European Court of Human Rights and its Commission.'

One issue mentioned by Barrington J in this paragraph, which has not yet been addressed, is the influence of EC law on the impact of the ECHR in Irish law. It is discussed at **1.4.7.**

The lack of binding force of the ECHR in domestic law, was of practical concern when advising clients. It was not possible to rely directly on the ECHR guarantees before the Irish Courts. Irish Courts were however influenced by the persuasive value of the ECHR. Until the ECHR was incorporated, it was necessary to pursue a case to the ECt.HR to secure an ECHR guarantee. Even after incorporation, it will still be necessary in some cases to go to the ECt.HR to secure human rights protections. (See **1.3.3**)

1.3.3   THE EUROPEAN CONVENTION ON HUMAN RIGHTS ACT, 2003

The European Convention on Human Rights Act, 2003 was signed on 30 June 2003, and came into force on 31 December 2003. The Act incorporates the ECHR into domestic law, making it applicable and enforceable by Irish courts. The incorporation of the ECHR has the potential to alter the human rights protection within this jurisdiction. The provisions of the Act and the possible effects of incorporation are discussed in **chapter 3**. The ECHR is discussed in **3.5.3** and **3.5.4**. For the purposes of this chapter it is important to consider the implications of incorporation on the hierarchy of laws in this jurisdiction.

According to the explanatory memorandum which accompanied the European Convention on Human Rights Bill, 2001, the current position would be fundamentally altered. The Bill was 'designed to facilitate the bringing of cases involving alleged breaches of rights under the Convention in Irish courts. In other words, it will make rights in the Convention enforceable in Irish courts and this means that cases of this type will be able to be processed much more expeditiously than under the present arrangements.'

Irish courts are required to interpret all statutory provisions or rules of law whether they pre-date or post-date the Act, in accordance with the ECHR in *'so far as possible'*. To the extent that it is not possible to apply or interpret a provision in accordance with the State's obligations under the ECHR provisions, the statutory provision or rule of law at issue prevails. The High Court and the Supreme Court, where there is no other adequate or available remedy, may make a declaration that a statutory provision or rule of law is incompatible with the State's obligations under the ECHR. However, the Act does not provide for the striking down of legislation or rules of law on the basis of incompatibility with the ECHR, so the incompatible domestic provision continues in force. In such circumstances, proceedings against the State in the ECt.HR may still be necessary to bring rules in line with the ECHR provisions, although the Act also provides for an ex gratia compensation payment following a declaration of incompatability.

The ECHR has been incorporated at sub-constitutional level. The explanatory memorandum provides that the Act 'will ensure that there are two complementary systems in place in Ireland for the protection of fundamental rights and freedoms, with the superior rules under the Constitution taking precedence . . .'. The rationale for incorporating the ECHR at sub-constitutional level is that there is a considerable overlap between the protection of rights in the Constitution, and the ECHR. Consequently, if the ECHR had been incorporated directly into the Constitution it was feared that this would lead to a diminution in some rights as protected in the Constitution. (See the Constitutional Review Group Report and the Explanatory Memorandum to the ECHR, Bill 2001). The question of sub-constitutional incorporation has been the subject of much debate in this jurisdiction. It is problematic because while the Irish Constitution might often offer a higher protection of a right than the protection at ECHR level, this is not always the case. This is evidenced by the fact that the ECt.HR has on a number of occasions found Ireland to be in breach of the ECHR standard of human rights protection in situations where the Irish courts had found the law at issue not to be in breach of the Constitution. For example the Supreme Court in *Norris v AG* [1984] IR 36 held that the legislation at issue was not unconstitutional, where the ECt.HR found a breach of the ECHR in *Norris v Ireland* 13 EHRR 360, see **3.7**.

The co-existence of two systems of human rights leaves open the possibility of complementary or conflicting standards of human rights protections. Given that in the Irish Constitution some rights are protected at a higher standard and that in the ECHR some rights are protected at a higher standard the systems are difficult to reconcile. This is especially true because the protection of human rights often involves a balance of competing rights (a stark example is the balancing of the right to life of the mother and unborn child in Article 40.3.3° of Bunreacht na hÉireann) and a standard which prefers one right, of necessity, diminishes another. For example, while the Irish Constitution prefers the right of the family over the rights of its constituent members, on occasion the rights of individual members may be better protected by the ECHR. (See **8.2**, **8.4** and **8.5**). In a case where an unmarried father had not been consulted prior to the placing of his child for adoption, the Irish courts *In Re SW, K v W* [1990] 2 IR 437 found no breach of constitutional rights whereas the ECt.HR in *Keegan v Ireland* (1994) 18 EHRR 342 found that Ireland had breached the applicants' right to respect for family life under the ECHR.

The complementary systems allow the possibility of redress under one system where it is not available under the other. However, this approach is open to the criticism that this very flexibility renders the protection of human rights uncertain. Litigation is required to determine which of the complementary systems applies in a particular factual situation.

Neither *Norris* nor *Keegan* is an example of a direct conflict between the Constitution and the ECHR. Rather, each is an example of a case where legislation found not to breach the Constitution, was found to breach the ECHR. As a result, legislative changes to bring about compliance with the ECHR do not breach the Constitution.

In the case of a direct conflict between the Constitution and the ECHR, Ireland would be in breach of its international obligations under the ECHR. As a matter of domestic law, even after the coming into force of the European Convention on Human Rights Act, 2003 the Constitution is superior. As a matter of international law the ECHR ranks higher. A constitutional amendment would be required to ensure compliance with Ireland's international obligations.

To date, of the Irish cases before the ECt.HR (discussed at **3.7**), there is one example of a direct conflict. In *Attorney General (SPUC) v Open Door Counselling Ltd and Dublin Well Woman Centre Ltd* [1989] ILRM 19, an issue arose as to the constitutionality of non-directive counselling to pregnant women that included information about abortion clinics in another jurisdiction. The Irish courts found that there could be no constitutional right to information about the availability of the service of abortion outside the State, as this would conflict with the constitutional right to life of the unborn and granted an injunction restraining the defendants from providing this information. In proceedings challenging the injunction, *Open Door Counselling and Dublin Well Woman v Ireland* (1993) 15 EHRR 244, the ECt.HR took a radically contrasting view and held that the injunction breached the freedom of expression guarantee in Art 10, ECHR. A subsequent constitutional referendum brought Ireland into line with its international obligations.

An area of potential conflict concerns the definition of the family. In Irish constitutional terms this is defined as being based on marriage, but the ECt.HR recognises a broader definition of the family (see **8.2**, **8.4** and **8.5**). Another area of potential conflict concerns freedom of expression (see **chapter 7**).

1.3.4 DUALISM AND OTHER INTERNATIONAL HUMAN RIGHTS INSTRUMENTS TO WHICH IRELAND IS PARTY

The dualist stance set out in Article 29.6 applies to all international agreements and not just the ECHR. In *Application of Woods* [1970] IR 154, a *habeas corpus* application, the applicant argued that his sentence of penal servitude was contrary to Art 4(1) of the Universal Declaration of Human Rights, 1948, ratified by the Irish Government in 1953. The Supreme Court held *per* Ó Dálaigh CJ at 161 that:

> '... the United Nations' Universal Declaration of Human Rights is not part of the domestic law of Ireland: see Article 29, s. 6 of the Constitution and the judgment of this Court in In *Re Ó Laighléis* [1960] IR 93.'

More recently, a novel argument concerning the application of international human rights provisions was put forward in *Kavanagh v Governor of Mountjoy Prison* [2002] 3 IR 112. The facts involved an appeal against a refusal to grant leave for judicial review related to the applicant's conviction by the Special Criminal Court. He sought to rely on the UN International Covenant on Civil and Political Rights (ICCPR) and in particular a communication from the Human Rights Committee (HRC), the complaints mechanism established under the ICCPR, which stated that the applicant's trial was in violation of the ICCPR. The Director of Public Prosecutions had certified that the ordinary courts were inadequate to secure the effective administration of justice and consequently the applicant had been tried in the Special Criminal Court and not by the ordinary courts. Inequality of treatment, in that he was tried by a non-jury court, was at the core of his complaint.

The applicant argued that Art 29 'constitutionalises' general principles of international law including the principle of equal treatment and could be invoked in the domestic courts to invalidate a conviction or to render repugnant a statutory provision. The Supreme Court held that the applicant was not entitled to rely on the provisions of the ICCPR as the acceptance in Art 29.3 of the generally recognised obligations of international law only applied in the State's 'rule of conduct with other States' and did not confer, and could not be interpreted as expressing an intention to confer, rights capable of being invoked by individuals. Further, the Court opined *obiter* that to rely on the decision of the HRC which was not a legally binding decision in preference to the judgment of the Special Criminal Court would conflict with Article 34.1 of the Constitution which provides:

> *'Justice shall be administered in courts established by law by judges appointed in the manner provided by the Constitution, and, save in such special and limited cases as may be prescribed by law, shall be administered in public.'*

As already emphasised international law instruments are not automatically binding internally within the State. To determine the status of an international law instrument under Irish domestic law, it is first necessary to check whether it has been incorporated. If it has not been incorporated it is not binding internally within the State and cannot be enforced in the Irish courts. However, the courts might look to the persuasive value of the international law instrument. Irish courts will interpret domestic law in light of the State's international obligations – *Ó Domhnaill v Merrick* [1984] IR 151.

International law instruments are incorporated into domestic law by means of legislation which is also subject to the Constitution. According to the hierarchy of norms laid down by the Constitution, provisions of the Constitution trump provisions of international law that have been incorporated into domestic law by means of legislation, including provisions of human rights treaties.

This point may be more readily understood if one considers the UN Convention on the Rights of the Child, 1989, discussed at **8.3.2**. Ireland ratified this Convention but it has not yet been incorporated into domestic law. Even if it were to be incorporated by means of a legislative enactment, the Constitution would continue to trump the Convention. In domestic law, the Constitution prevails but in international law, the Convention prevails, leaving open the possibility in a case of conflict in standards of protection that, by complying with the constitutional standard the State breaches such international obligations. In domestic law also, legislation prevails over unincorporated international law instruments. Even if an international law instrument were implemented by means of ordinary domestic legislation, later domestic legislation would prevail in the case of conflict. Contrast however the position of the ECHR since incorporation. The ECHR Act, 2003 requires statutory provisions and rules of law to be applied and interpreted in accordance with the State's obligations under the Convention provisions 'in as far as possible'.

Like the pre-incorporation position of the ECHR, other international law instruments rank higher than domestic laws under international law. However, unlike the ECHR most international law instruments do not have a court structure to secure their enforcement (see **chapter 4**). These instruments are largely dependent on political embarrassment to secure change. Individuals can be disappointed to find that grand-sounding commitments in international agreements may be of little effect in securing the protection of rights.

1.4 The Third Sphere of Human Rights Protection: EC/EU Law

Human Rights are protected in a third legal sphere in this jurisdiction, the EC legal order. The evolution of human rights protection in the EC is discussed in **chapter 5**. For now, it is sufficient to note that although the founding Treaties of the European Communities contained no reference to human rights law, the European Court of Justice (ECJ) recognised an unwritten catalogue of human rights enshrined in the general principles of Community law. Sources of these rights included the constitutional traditions of the Member States and international treaties for the protection of human rights on which the Member States had collaborated. Treaty amendments subsequent to the ECJ's elaboration of a human rights policy approved the development. A Charter of Fundamental Rights for the EU was solemnly proclaimed in December 2000, although the Charter is not yet a legally binding text. This section is concerned with the interaction between EC Law and Irish constitutional law. First it examines the nature of EC law and the interaction between EC Law and Irish constitutional law and then goes on to examine the impact of the interaction on human rights law.

1.4.1 EUROPEAN COMMUNITY LAW AS A NEW LEGAL ORDER

European Community law is distinct from international law. It is 'supranational' in nature, in that it involves the transfer of competences from the Member States to the EC institutions and possesses unique characteristics, notably supremacy and direct effect. The treaties of the European Communities and European Union found a new legal system. '. . . those treaties have created not only institutions which have a separate legal personality . . . but also a system of law within which those institutions, the member states and their nationals have rights and duties' (Collins 'European Community Law in the United Kingdom' 4th edn. 1990, Butterworths, 2–3). The EC institutions enact legislation and the ECJ interprets and applies European law. The Treaties are the primary source of law. The EC institutions are empowered to enact secondary legislation.

As a consequence of the nature of EC law and its supra-constitutional incorporation into Irish law, EC law has much more far-reaching effects on the domestic Irish legal system than any international law instrument. The treaties, secondary legislation and judgments of the ECJ are binding internally within the domestic sphere and, within the scope of EC law, rank higher than all domestic laws.

The huge volume of legislation and case-law emanating from the European institutions, evidence the formidable and pervasive effect of EC law on the domestic system. European law is a layer of law lying over our domestic provisions, to be applied within the scope of EC law, in preference to domestic law.

1.4.1.1 Characteristics of EC Law

Direct effect and supremacy ensure that EC law is incorporated uniformly into the national legal orders of both monist and dualist states. An EC provision that gives individuals rights or obligations which can be relied on before their national courts is directly effective. The concept of direct effect was first espoused in Case 26/62 *Van Gend en Loos v Nederlandse Administratie der Belastingen* [1963] ECR 1.

> 'Independently of the legislation of the Member States, Community law therefore not only imposes obligations on individuals but is also intended to confer rights on them which become part of their legal heritage. These rights arise not only when they are expressly granted by the Treaty, but also by reason of obligations which the Treaty imposes in a clearly defined way upon individuals as well as upon Member States and upon the institutions of the Community.'

The operation of the doctrine of supremacy means that EC law takes precedence over national laws of the Member States in the domestic legal system.

In Case 6/64 *Costa v ENEL* [1964] ECR 585, the ECJ stated that:

> ' . . . law stemming from the Treaty an independent source of law, could not because of its special and original nature, be over-ridden by domestic legal provisions, however framed, without being deprived of its character of Community law and without the legal basis of the Community itself being called into question.'

The rule that EC law is superior to the national laws of the Member States and that it is the duty of national courts to enforce Community rules when they conflict with national laws applies irrespective of the nature of the Community provision. It is not just the Treaties that are superior to the national laws of the Member States but also validly adopted binding secondary legislation and binding agreements with non-Member States. The rule applies irrespective of whether the Community provision came before or after the national law and the rule applies irrespective of the nature of the national rule. In all situations, within the scope of EC law, EC law is superior to the national law.

The decisions in *Van Gend en Loos* and *Costa v ENEL* tell us much about the nature of Community law. Community law is an independent, autonomous legal system which is distinct from both the international sphere and the national legal sphere. Community legal measures are not always dependent on national incorporating measures to be part of the national legal order. Where there is a conflict between national law and EC law, EC law is superior. Binding legislation may in appropriate cases be relied on by individuals in their national courts.

The doctrine of direct effect has evolved since the *Van Gend en Loos* judgment. All binding EC legislation is capable of direct effect once the provision at issue satisfies a number of criteria. The provision must be clear, precise and unconditional and must not be dependent on further action [requiring choice] being taken by Community or national authorities (Case 2/74 *Reyners v Belgium* [1974] ECR 631). For a directive to be directly effective it must satisfy further criteria. Its date for implementation must have passed (Case 148/78 *Pubblicco Ministero v Ratti* [1979] ECR 1629) and the action must be against the State or an emanation of the State (Case 152/84 *Marshall v Southampton Area Health Authority* [1986] ECR 723). Emanation of the State is broadly interpreted (Case C-188/89 *Foster v British Gas* [1990] ECR I 3313). There is an obligation to interpret national law in the light of Community law. (Case 14/83 *Von Colson v Land Nordrhein Westfalen* [1984] ECR 1891 and Case 79/83 *Harz v Deutsche Tradax* [1984] ECR 1921. Also, a State may be liable in damages for non-implementation (Case C- 6 & 9/90 *Francovich and Bonifaci v Italy* [1991] I ECR 5357) or incorrect implementation of a directive (Case C-392/93 *R v HM Treasury ex parte British Telecommunications* [1996] 1 ECR 1631.)

The doctrine of supremacy has evolved since it was first espoused by the ECJ in *Costa v ENEL*. In Case 11/70 *Internationale Handelsgescellschaft* [1970] ECR 1125, the ECJ held that EC law is superior to the constitutional provisions of the Member States, including the human rights provisions. In Case 106/77 *Amministrazione delle Finanze dello Stato v Simmenthal SpA* [1978] ECR 629, the ECJ held that national courts are obliged to dissapply national laws which conflict with Community provisions. In case 167/73 *Commission v France* [1974] ECR 359, the ECJ held that in certain circumstances, there is a positive obligation on Member States to repeal conflicting national legislation. In Case C- 213/89 *R v Secretary of State for Transport, ex parte Factortame Ltd* [1990] ECR I 2433, the ECJ held that putative EC law rights are superior to clear provisions of national law. There is a limitation on the doctrine of supremacy. While national courts are required to dissapply a national measure which conflicts with an EC measure, it is not necessary for the national courts to render the national measure non-existent (Case C-10–22/97 *Ministero delle Finanze v IN.CO.GE. '90 Srl* [1998] ECR I 6307.)

The EC treaties have been amended on a number of occasions (see **1.4.2**). The Maastricht Treaty amended the EC Treaty but also established the European Union. The European Union has three pillars: the supranational EC pillar and two intergovernmental pillars (Common Foreign and Security Policy and Justice and Home Affairs (now Police and Judicial Co-operation in Criminal Matters.) The principle of direct effect and supremacy apply only to the EC pillar. Weatherill and Beaumont ('EU Law', 3rd edn, 1999, Penguin, 12) state:

> 'Outside the EC, in the pillars concerning foreign and security policy and justice and home affairs, the principle of direct effect and supremacy do not prevail. The domestic impact of non-EC EU law depends on the orthodox attitude taken to public international law in the State in question.'

The doctrine of supremacy emerged from the case-law of the ECJ and is accepted as a fundamental tenet of EC law. Certainly new Member States seem to have accepted it as part of the *acquis communautaire* (the body of EC law built up over time) as to date it has not been expressly included in the Treaties or Accession Agreements.

It is proposed that the doctrine will be given Treaty expression in the proposed Draft Treaty Establishing a Constitution for Europe (CONV 820/1/03 Brussels, 27 June 2003). Draft Article 9(1) provides:

> *'The Constitution, and law adopted by the Union Institutions in exercising competences conferred on it by the Constitution, shall have primacy over the law of the Member States'*

Throughout the development of the concept of supremacy the ECJ has made clear that it is necessary as a principle to ensure the effectiveness of Community law. However, the ECJ view of supremacy is only a portion of the picture, as the doctrine of supremacy is not merely a unilateral matter. The application of the principle is dependent on the attitude of the national courts and their willingness to dissapply national laws in favour of Community laws. While the ECJ is keen to impose a monist approach to supremacy, national courts often prefer to regard supremacy as a matter of national law. (See Craig and de Búrca, 'EU Law: Text, Cases and Materials', 3rd edn, 2003, OUP, chapter 7.) For a full picture of supremacy it is necessary to consider the principle both from the perspective of the ECJ and the Member State courts. Approaches to supremacy vary from Member State to Member State.

1.4.2 BUNREACHT NA hÉIREANN'S SUPRA-CONSTITUTIONAL APPROACH TO EC LAW

When Ireland became a member of the EEC, as it then was, the concepts of direct effect and supremacy were already well established. Ireland's traditional dualist approach necessitated a domestic measure to incorporate EC Law into Irish domestic law. The European Communities Act, 1972 was enacted. Section 2 of the European Communities Act, 1972 provides:

> '. . . the treaties governing the European Communities and the existing and future acts adopted by the institutions of those Communities shall be binding on the State and shall be part of the domestic law thereof under the conditions laid down by those treaties.'

Domestic legislation was insufficient for EC membership. Owing to the supranational nature of EC law, accession to the EC involved the transfer of a degree of legislative and judicial competence to the institutions of the Communities, which was clearly incompatible with the Constitution. To facilitate accession, the Constitution was amended through a general amending clause which would limit each constitutional provision. Ireland provided for the supremacy of EC law in this constitutional amendment as it joined the EEC after the *Costa v ENEL* judgment. De Witte states 'In Ireland, given the inability of the dualist constitutional tradition to cope with the demands of membership, a special EC clause was added to the Constitution (and adapted to later Treaty provisions) vouchsafing the direct effect and primacy of Community law.' (De Witte 'Direct Effect, Supremacy and the Nature of the Legal Order' in Craig and de Búrca (eds) 'The Evolution of EU Law', 1999, OUP, 177, 198.)

The amendment was inserted as Article 29.4.3° of the Constitution and consisted of only two sentences. The first is merely enabling, allowing the State to join the Communities, which it names, by ratifying the treaties. The second sentence protects from Constitutional challenge both domestic acts *'necessitated by the obligations of membership'* and lawful Community acts. The amendment is now found in Article 29.4.10°, the text of which is set out below.

The constitutional amendment and the 1972 Act had a far-reaching effect.

The constitutional amendment provides for supremacy of EC law. In the respect that European law has supremacy, the perspective of European law and the Irish Constitution are as one, as the Constitution affords primacy to European laws necessitated by our obligations of membership.

The EC Treaties became part of domestic law. Secondary EC legislation and judgments of the ECJ (existing and future) become part of the domestic law and are binding therein without requiring any constitutional amendment. Some EC secondary law is capable of being relied on in Irish courts through the operation of the doctrine of direct effect. Directly effective secondary law is superior to all domestic law, by operation of the doctrine of supremacy. Even if EC secondary legislation requires implementation, this does not imply that it suffers from the same legal inadequacies as the traditional dualist approach to an international law instrument because incorporation of secondary EC law is necessary to fulfil the obligations of membership. The Oireachtas has no choice over whether to implement EC secondary legislation. EC directives are an example of a form of EC secondary legislation which require implementing measures. While the Oireachtas has no choice regarding whether to implement a directive, it retains discretion as to the form and method of implementation (Art 249 EC (ex Art 189 EC)). In Ireland, pursuant to s 3(1) European Communities Act, 1972, secondary EC legislation that requires national implementing measures may be incorporated by statutory instrument. Pursuant to s 3(2) statutory instruments made under the s 3(1) may repeal, amend or apply laws exclusive of the European Communities Act, 1972. Such a statutory instrument may have the impact of amending, repealing or applying statutory instruments or legislation.

THREE SPHERES OF HUMAN RIGHTS PROTECTIONS IN IRELAND

The original amendment was very broad and granted constitutional immunity to many Community measures and measures adopted by the State to fulfil Community obligations. The amendment was limited to measures 'necessitated by the obligations' of Community law. 'This suggested that the constitutional immunity would only extend to those measures whose adoption was legally obligated as a matter of Community law.' (Hogan and Whyte, 'JM Kelly: The Irish Constitution', 4th edn, 2003, Butterworths, 515.)

The scope of measures, which were immune from Constitutional challenge, was unclear, particularly whether ratifications of amendments to the Community Treaties were covered by the original constitutional amendment or whether such changes would require further constitutional amendments. A significant revision to the Treaties was proposed in the form of the Single European Act, 1986 (SEA). Whether ratification of the SEA was necessitated by the obligations of EC membership was considered in *Crotty v An Taoiseach* [1987] IR 713. The case centred on the meaning of the amendment to the Constitution authorising membership of the Communities.

The Supreme Court decided that ratification of some Treaty amendments was licensed by the existing amendment but that ratification of amendments involving the transfer of new competences to the Communities would require further constitutional amendment This case challenged the right of the Irish government to acquiesce to the transfer of increased competences to the Communities without the consent of the people. The Supreme Court held at page 767, *per* Finlay CJ:

> 'It is the opinion of the court that [the amendment] must be construed as an authorisation given to the Sate not only to join the Communities as they stood in 1973, but also to join in amendments of the Treaties so long as such amendments do not alter the essential scope or objectives of the Communities. To hold that [the amendment] does not authorise any form of amendment of the Constitution would be too narrow a construction; to construe it as an open authority to agree, without further amendment to the Constitution, to any amendment to the treaties would be too broad.'

The Supreme Court held that the majority of the provisions of the SEA were covered by the constitutional amendment. However, the provisions relating to European Political Co-operation went beyond the scope of what was permissible and required a further constitutional amendment. In other words a referendum was required before the SEA could be ratified.

Subsequent to the SEA there was three further Treaty amendments: The Maastricht or Treaty on European Union (TEU) the Amsterdam Treaty and the Nice Treaty. A referendum has been held on the occasion of each subsequent Treaty amendment. For the purposes of this section it is necessary to highlight only some aspects of the amending Treaties. (For a full discussion see Craig and de Búrca ('EU Law: Text, Cases and Materials' 3rd edn, 2003, OUP, Chapter 1.)

The Maastricht Treaty established the European Union founded on three pillars. One of these pillars is the European Economic Community which became the European Community. Two new pillars were introduced: Common Foreign and Security Policy and Justice and Home Affairs. The two new pillars were essentially intergovernmental rather than supranational in nature. New competences were added to the Community pillar.

The Treaty of Amsterdam amended certain aspects of the three pillar structure. Some elements of the third pillar were incorporated into the first pillar and the remaining part of the third pillar now covers Police and Judicial Co-operation in Criminal Matters. The Treaty of Amsterdam introduced 'variable geometry' within the EU. This meant that Member States had more discretion to decide whether to participate in certain EU or EC measures.

There are new enhanced co-operation procedures in the Treaty of Nice that allow at least eight Member States, in certain circumstances, to use the EC institutions for the purpose of deeper integration.

The variable geometry provisions of the Amsterdam and Nice Treaties required a different type of constitutional amendment. As Hogan and Whyte ('JM Kelly: The Irish Constitution' 4th edn, 2003, Butterworths, 518) point out: 'the traditional "necessitated obligations" formula .... would no longer suffice in circumstances where Member States were increasingly obliged to take decisions which resulted from a voluntary act on their part and which decisions could not in any sense be described as "necessitated" by the obligations of membership.' The provision chosen enabled the State to exercise certain options and discretions contained in the Treaty of Amsterdam subject to the prior approval of both houses of the Oireachtas. The Nice Treaty amendment contains a similar formula.

The relevant parts of Article 29.4 provide in full:

'3° The State may become a member of the European Coal and Steel Community (established by Treaty signed at Paris on the 18th day of April, 1951), the European Economic Community (established by Treaty signed at Rome on the 25th day of March, 1957) and the European Atomic Energy Community (established by Treaty signed at Rome on the 25th day of March, 1957). The State may ratify the Single European Act (signed on behalf of the Member States of the Communities at Luxembourg on the 17th day of February, 1986, and at the Hague on the 28th day of February, 1986).

4° The State may ratify the Treaty on European Union signed at Maastricht on the 7th day of February, 1992, and may become a member of that Union.

5° The State may ratify the Treaty of Amsterdam amending the Treaty on European Union, the Treaties establishing the European Communities and certain related Acts signed at Amsterdam on the 2nd day of October, 1997.

6° The State may exercise the options or discretions provided by or under Articles 1.11, 2.5 and 2.15 of the Treaty referred to in subsection 5° of this section and the second and fourth Protocols set out in the said Treaty but any such exercise shall be subject to the prior approval of both Houses of the Oireachtas.

7° The State may ratify the Treaty of Nice amending the Treaty on European Union, the Treaties establishing the European Communities and certain related Acts signed at Nice on the 26th day of February, 2001.

8° The State may exercise the options or discretions provided by or under Articles 1.6, 1.9, 1.11, 1.12, 1.13 and 2.1 of the Treaty referred to in subsection 7° of this section but any such exercise shall be subject to the prior approval of both Houses of the Oireachtas.

9° The State shall not adopt a decision taken by the European Council to establish a common defence pursuant to Article 1.2 of the Treaty referred to in subsection 7° of this section where that common defence would include the State.

10° No provision of this Constitution invalidates laws enacted, acts done or measures adopted by the State which are necessitated by the obligations of membership of the European Union or of the Communities, or prevents laws enacted, acts done or measures adopted by the European Union or by the Communities or by institutions thereof, or by bodies competent under the Treaties establishing the Communities, from having the force of law in the State.

11° The State may ratify the Agreement relating to Community Patents drawn up between the Member States of the Communities and done at Luxembourg on the 15th day of December, 1989.'

1.4.3 JUDICIAL INTERPRETATION OF THE CONSTITUTIONAL AMENDMENTS

As discussed above an issue arose in *Crotty v An Taoiseach* [1987] IR 713 as to whether ratification of the Single European Act was necessitated by the obligations of EC membership and therefore free from constitutional attack. Subsequent cases considered the extent to which domestic measures implementing EC law are necessitated by the obligations of Community membership.

In *Meagher v Minister for Agriculture* [1994] 1 IR 329 and in *Maher v Minister for Agriculture* [2001] 2 IR 139, a question arose as to whether the implementation of EC law, requiring domestic implementation measures, by way of statutory instrument pursuant to s 3(1) European Communities Act, 1972 was necessitated by Ireland's obligations of membership (Art 29.4). The Supreme Court in these cases held that EC legislation, which requires implementation and which sets out principles and policies may be implemented by means of statutory instrument but EC legislation which requires implementation but which does not set out principles and policies should properly be implemented by legislation. Implementation is 'necessitated' by the obligations of membership but the mode of implementation is a matter of Irish law. The Constitution requires that where the principles and policies are not set out in EC law that EC law be implemented by means of statute. (See Tompkin, J. 'Implementing EC Directives into National Law: The Demands of a New Legal Order' (to be published shortly)). An example of EC legislation which is likely to require implementation into Irish law by means of a statute is a Framework Directive. Where the principles and policies are set out in parent EC law, whether it is a directive or another form of EC law requiring an implementation measure, it is permissible as a matter of Irish constitutional law for the implementing measure, to be a statutory instrument.

The facts of *Meagher* related to a farmer who was charged with possession of illegal veterinary medical products. At issue were statutory instruments implementing EC directives. The statutory instruments had the effect of amending existing laws by granting a power to the District Court to issues a search warrant and in providing for a two-year time limit to institute proceedings. The Supreme Court held that the regulations were not *ultra vires* the powers of the Minister as they were implementations of the principles and policies of the directives. *Per* Denham J in *Meagher* at 365–6:

> 'If the directive left to the national authority matters of principle or policy to be determined then the "choice" of the Minister would require legislation by the Oireachtas. But where there is no case made that principles or policies have to be determined by the national authority, where the situation is that the principles and policies were determined in the directive, then legislation by delegated form, be regulation, is a valid choice.'

Ordinarily, it would be unconstitutional to amend legislation by statutory instrument but these were saved because of their EC dimension. This case is an example of procedural rules in a criminal case being altered by virtue of a statutory instrument where the parent legislation is an EC Directive.

It must be emphasised that the parent law of such a statutory instrument is an EC law norm which ranks in hierarchical terms above the Constitution. This point has been made clearly by Tompkin J 'Implementing EC Directives into National Law: The Demands of a New Legal Order' (to be published shortly).

> ' . . . a further difficulty with the use of statutory instruments as a means of implementing [EC] legislation, is that it is paradoxical and may in certain circumstances undermine the status of European Community Law. If one considers the hierarchy of different forms of legislation in Ireland, it is evident that EC Law (in areas of community competence) would be at the top. At the other extreme are statutory instruments, which are the lowest and most subordinate form of law in the State. On a theoretical level, it is paradoxical for potentially the highest form of legislation in Ireland to be encased and published in the most subordinate form of legislation.'

In general, the principle of supremacy has been accepted by the Irish courts. In *Meaghar*, Blayney J commented at p. 360:

> 'It is well established that Community law takes precedence over our domestic law. Where they are in conflict it is Community law that prevails.'

When reading the Constitution, it is necessary to bear in mind the extent to which the document is qualified by membership of the Community and its incumbent obligations, particularly having regard to the doctrine of supremacy which declares EC law to be superior to all domestic laws even constitutional ones.

1.4.4 THE RELATIONSHIP BETWEEN EC LAW AND IRISH LAW

The relationship between EC law and national law differs from the relationship between international law and national law.

As discussed above, the impact of international law has traditionally been determined along a monist/dualist divide, where the law of the State party to the international law instrument determines its domestic impact. EC law prefers a monist approach, so in Ireland, EC law has much greater impact than international law. This is apparent from the case of *Tate v Minister for Social Welfare* [1995] 1 IR 418. The applicants were married women who sought equal treatment to married men in terms of social welfare payments. The Social Welfare Act, 1985 sought to remove differences in treatment between married men and married women. However, the Social Welfare (Preservation of Rights) Regulations (No. 2), 1986 introduced payments to compensate those married men who were no longer entitled to certain benefits as a result of the 1985 Act.

The plaintiffs sought to rely on an EC Directive that provided for equal treatment in social welfare and claimed that the State had failed to implement the Directive properly and that the 1986 Regulations were *ultra vires* the powers of the Minister. O' Carroll J held that in the absence of proper implementation of the Directive the plaintiffs were entitled to rely on it. It was directly effective from the date by which it should have been implemented and that married women were entitled to have the same rules applied to them as applied to married men. The EC rule was applied by the Irish court in preference to the domestic measure. This case demonstrates the effect of the doctrines of supremacy and direct effect.

The impact of EC law, as opposed to (unincorporated) international law is even more apparent when the *Norris* or *Keegan* judgments (discussed at **1.3.2** and **1.3.3**) are contrasted with *Tate*. In those judgments, the domestic measure was applied by the domestic court in preference to the international law obligation. Both plaintiffs brought successful cases to the ECt.HR but even then they were obliged to wait for domestic legislation to alter the domestic legal position.

This position is clearly stated in *Doyle v Commissioner of An Garda Síochána* [1999] 1 IR 249 by Barrington J.

> 'The position of the European Convention on Human Rights [which is an example of an international law instrument subject to the dualist approach] in Irish law contrasts sharply with that of the founding treaties of the European Union. They have become part of the domestic law of Ireland and have resulted in the formation of a European Community the laws of which bind both the member states and their citizens and may have direct effect in each of the member states. As a result, the national judge is a community judge and is obliged to give priority to community law in his court.'

The impact of EC law is also greater than the impact of the ECHR, even after incorporation into domestic law, as the ECHR has been incorporated at sub-constitutional level (European Convention on Human Rights Act, 2003, discussed at **1.3.3**) while EC law is incorporated at supra-constitutional level.

1.4.5 HUMAN RIGHTS PROTECTION UNDER EC/EU LAW

Protection of human rights in EC/EU law is discussed in more detail in **chapter 5**. For now, it is sufficient to note that the ECJ has recognised an unwritten catalogue of fundamental rights enshrined in the general principles of EC law. Sources of these rights include the constitutional traditions common to the Member States and international treaties to which the Member States are parties. While the EU Charter of Fundamental Rights is likely to become binding as part of the new EU Constitutional Treaty, (currently the Draft Treaty Establishing a Constitution for Europe (CONV 820/1/03 Brussels, 27 June 2003) it must be emphasised that the Charter is concerned with increasing the visibility of human rights protection within the EU legal order and not about creating new rights. (See **5.10.2**)

The ECJ has the power to review acts of the EC and acts of the Member States when acting within the scope of EC law. Member States are only bound by the EC human rights law when they act within the scope of EC law. The ECJ has no jurisdiction to review purely national measures for compatibility with the EC human rights standard (see **5.7.2**). For an overview of human rights protected in EC law, see **5.9** and **5.10.5**.

The rights protected in EC law are discussed at **5.9** and the standard of EC human rights protection is discussed at **5.8**. For the moment it is sufficient to note that the standard of protection at EC level is not identical to that in the Irish Constitution. The evolving nature of EC human rights means that it is not always readily apparent whether a right is protected at EC level or whether it is protected to the same standard as in a Member State's domestic law. When these differences are considered alongside the doctrine of supremacy, which declares Community law to be superior to all domestic laws, even constitutional ones (albeit within the scope of EC law) a potential clash is apparent.

1.4.6   SUPREMACY OF EC LAW AND HUMAN RIGHTS: A CONFLICT

This very issue, the clash between human rights protections and the doctrine of supremacy, gave rise to a well-known conflict between the ECJ and the German Courts.

1.4.6.1   Germany: the supremacy and human rights conflict

Case 11/70 *Internationale Handelsgesellschaft* [1970] ECR 1125 involved a conflict between the human rights provisions of the German Constitution and the EC Treaty. The applicants argued that a system of applying for agricultural licences which resulted in the forfeiture of a large deposit on the part of the licensee if he failed to export during the validity of the license violated the principle of proportionality and hence the German constitution. The ECJ pointed out that the validity of EC law measures could not be judged according to the national rules of the Member State. The ECJ emphasised that the validity of Community measures could not be judged even according to national constitutional provisions protecting human rights. From the perspective of the protection of human rights, the ECJ provided some consolation in that the measures at issue were held to be subject to review for compatibility with the EC standard of human rights protection.

Given the nascent stage of human rights protection in EC law, the German Constitutional Court refused to accept the absolute supremacy of EC law (*Internationale Handelsgesellschaft v Einfuhr-und Vorratsstelle fur Getreide und Futtermittel* [1974] CMLR 540 (decision of the German Constitutional Court).) The German Constitutional Court expressed concern about the impact on fundamental rights enshrined in the German Constitution of conflicting measures of EC law. Of concern to the German Constitutional Court was that at the time of this judgment the EC lacked both a democratically elected parliament and a codified catalogue of rights.

In a later judgment (*Re Wunshe Handelsgesellschaft*, decision of 22 October 1986, [1987] 3 CMLR 225, 265), following developments in the protection of fundamental rights in EC law, the German Constitutional Court seemed more willing to accept the doctrine of supremacy and stated that it would no longer review secondary European legislation by the standard of fundamental rights contained in the German Constitution. Relevant developments taken into account by the Court included the evolution of the ECJ's general principles case law, the accession of the remaining EC Member States to the ECHR and the direct election of the European Parliament.

A later judgment, *Brunner v The European Union Treaty* [1994] 1 CMLR 57 involved a constitutional challenge to the ratification of the Treaty on European Union (TEU). The German Constitutional Court emphasised, at paragraph 22, that given that the two new TEU pillars, Common Foreign and Security Policy and Justice and Home Affairs, were intergovernmental rather than supranational in nature, 'the protection of basic rights provided by the Constitution is not displaced by supranational law that could claim precedence ... In this respect the position is no different from that with a traditional international convention: in so far as its internal implementation would infringe constitutional rights it is prohibited by constitutional law.' EU activity in the intergovernmental sphere cannot restrict human rights protection by the German courts although the German Constitutional Court does seem willing to accept precedence of EC law and the EC standard of human rights protection in the supranational sphere, provided the EC acts within competences transferred to it. The German Constitutional Court (at paragraphs 49 and 99) also asserted the right to review acts of the institutions to ensure they act within the limits of the competences transferred to them. Craig and de Búrca point out that the German Constitutional court seems to be issuing a warning that "Germany's acceptance of the doctrine of supremacy is conditional" (Craig and de Búrca, 'EU Law: Text, Cases and Materials', 3rd edn, 2003, OUP, 294).

In a decision of the German Constitutional Court, 7 June 2000 (2 BvL 1/97 – the *Bananas* case), the German Constitutional Court confirmed its rulings in *Re Wunshe Handelsgesellschaft* and *Brunner* and indicated that it was satisfied that the standard of human rights protection in EC law was comparable to the level of protection in German law. (See Aziz, M. 'Sovereignty Lost, Sovereignty Regained? The European Integration Project and the Bundesverfassungsgericht', Robert Schuman Centre Working Paper, EUI 2001/3.)

From the perspective of hierarchy of laws, the key point is that EC law trumps the Constitution, including according to *Internationale Handelsgesellschaft*, the human rights provisions of the Constitution, within the scope of EC law. From the perspective of the standard of human rights protection, there is no guarantee that rights will be protected in a similar way or to the same standard that is protected at national level. Through the evolution of the protection of human rights at EC level, the ECJ and the political institutions have done much to reassure the Member States and the German Constitutional Court seems to have accepted that the standard of human rights protection at EC level is equivalent to the standard of protection afforded by the German Constitution. This general acceptance that human rights are protected to a sufficient standard does not address the issue of a direct conflict between EC Law and a constitutional human rights protection.

1.4.6.2   Ireland, supremacy and human rights

As discussed above, the Irish constitutional amendment at the time of accession provided for supremacy of EC Law. By the time of Ireland's accession some steps had been taken by the ECJ to secure the protection of human rights at EC level. However it was still unclear whether the Irish courts would accept the doctrine of supremacy in the case of a conflict with a fundamental human rights provision of Bunreacht na hÉireann. The Irish courts faced such an issue involving an apparent conflict between EC law and the constitutionally protected right to life of the unborn child.

In *SPUC v Grogan* [1989] IR 752, the Society for the Protection of Unborn Children (SPUC) took an action against officers of student associations seeking a declaration that distribution of information concerning abortion clinics in the UK was unlawful. As a matter of Irish law at the time it was not permissible to disseminate this type of information. The High Court made an Art 177 (now Art 234 EC) reference to the ECJ asking whether abortion could be regarded as a service within the meaning of EC law. Pending the ECJ's ruling, Carroll J declined to grant or refuse the interlocutory injunction seeking to restrain the defendants from distributing abortion information.

The High Court decision was appealed to the Supreme Court ([1989] IR 753.) As a matter of Irish law, *Campus Oil v Minister for Industry* [1983] IR 82, there is no appeal against a decision to refer a case to the ECJ. However the Supreme Court did allow the appeal to the extent of ordering an interlocutory injunction to protect the constitutional right pending the ECJ ruling. Finlay CJ deferred addressing the issue of the potential conflict of the Constitution and EC law pending the ECJ ruling. The judgment of Walsh J indicates that he would be reluctant to dissapply the constitutional right.

> 'any answer to the reference received from the [ECJ] will have to be considered in the light of our own constitutional provisions. In the last analysis only this Court can decide finally what are the effects of the interaction of the 8th Amendment of the Constitution [the Amendment protecting the right to life of the unborn] and the 3rd Amendment [the accession amendment] of the Constitution.'

Of the judgments delivered by the Supreme Court, only McCarthy J alluded to the supremacy of EC law.

> '[The EC accession amendment] may exclude from constitutional invalidation some provision of the Treaty of Rome the enforcement of which is necessitated by the obligations of membership of the European Communities; it may be that in enacting the 8th Amendment to the Constitution [the Amendment protecting the right to life of the unborn] . . . the People of Ireland did so in breach of the Treaty to which Ireland had acceded in 1973.'

In Case C-159/90 *SPUC v Grogan* [1991] I ECR 4685, the ECJ ruled that abortion could be regarded as a service within the meaning of EC law. Further questions sought to establish whether it was contrary to EC law for a Member State where abortion was forbidden to prohibit student associations from distributing information about clinics in another Member State where abortion was legal. The ECJ did not answer these questions directly but focused on the 'freedom to provide services' provisions of the Treaty, holding that there was no economic link between the student associations and the abortion clinics. The ECJ held that the link was too tenuous for the restriction on the provision of information to be capable of being a restriction on freedom to provide services. As the matter fell outside the scope of EC law, the ECJ had no jurisdiction to review the measure for compatibility with the EC human rights standard, specifically freedom of expression and the freedom to receive and impart information.

The interesting point to note however, is that if there had been an economic link, there would have been a clear conflict between the Irish Constitution and the Treaty. Given that EC law is superior, the freedom to provide services would prevail over the constitutional guarantee of the right to life of the unborn child as protected by the Irish Constitution. The Irish Courts would have been required to disapply a constitutionally protected right to give precedence to EC law.

Subsequent constitutional amendments in Ireland provided that the right to life of the unborn would not limit the freedom to travel between Ireland and another State and that the right to life of the unborn child would not limit freedom to obtain or make available services lawfully available in another state. These amendments have lessened the potential for direct conflict between EC law and the Irish Constitution.

In hierarchal terms, it is worth emphasising that constitutionally protected human rights are subject to EC law in the same manner as any other domestic provision. The entire body of domestic law is subject to the entire body of EC law. To this extent, it is not a matter of subjecting one right to another but subjecting the protection of a right to a superior body of law which may or may not protect the right at issue, although it must be emphasised that when applying EC law the domestic courts are bound by the standard of EC human rights protection. In addition, when implementing EC law, Irish constitutional law provides a safeguard of the protection of constitutional standard of human rights (see **1.4.6.3**).

1.4.6.3   **Obligation to have regard to the Irish standard of human rights protection, when implementing EC Law**

A safeguard of the protection of human rights is that when implementing EC law the Oireachtas is obliged to have regard to the EC standard of human rights protection but also, unless an implementing provision which breaches Irish constitutional human rights protections is 'necessitated by the obligations of membership', the Oireachtas is required to protect the Irish Constitutional standard of human rights protection. In *Maher v Minister for Agriculture* [2001] 2 IR 139, a case concerning the regulation of milk quotas in Ireland pursuant to a statutory instrument implementing an EC Regulation, Murray J. considered this issue at p. 227:

> '[W]here the State enacts a legislative measure in the exercise of a discretion conferred by community law it is not ipso facto absolved from ensuring that such legislation is compatible with the Constitution. This is self-evident from the terms of Article 29.4 which inter alia, provides that no provision of the Constitution invalidates laws enacted or measures adopted by the State which are "necessitated" by the obligations of membership of the European Union or the Communities. The discretion allowed to the member state maybe so circumscribed by Community law that the entire of any legislative measure taken by it or the exercise of such discretion is "necessitated". This could arise where the exercise of a discretion conferred by Community law was required to be exercised exclusively having regard to the policy considerations and objectives of the Community measure and where considerations of national law would distort the proper exercise of such a discretion.
>
> On the other hand, the discretion conferred by Community law on the State when implementing legislative measures maybe sufficiently wide to permit the State to have full regards to the constitutional protection afforded to fundamental rights without impinging on the full effect and uniform application of Community law. In such circumstances the State, in the exercise of such discretion, would be bound to respect personal and fundamental rights as guaranteed by the Constitution.'

This safeguard extends to judicial interpretations so that Irish courts interpreting EC obligations will interpret those obligations where possible in compliance with fundamental rights as guaranteed by the Constitution. This safeguard will not apply where there is a direct conflict between EC law and a constitutionally protected right.

1.4.6.4   **Dis-application of a constitutional right, where there is a direct conflict between the right and EC Law**

By virtue of the doctrine of supremacy, EC law may require a national court to dissapply a human rights protection if it is in direct conflict with EC law within the scope of EC Law. In doing so the national courts are bound by the EC standard of human rights protection, which standard has proved acceptable to the German Constitutional Court. (See **1.4.6.1**)

The potential conflict is not just one of human rights standards. There is also the possibility that protection of a human right may be limited by another objective of EC law (see **5.8.1**). This is apparent from the issues arising in Case C-159/90 *SPUC v Grogan* [1991] ECR I 4685. (See **1.4.6.2**) The issue, which fell outside the scope of EC law, was a conflict between freedom to provide services and a right to life of the unborn child. If the matter had fallen within the scope of EC law, the ECJ would have considered other rights which are protected in EC law such as freedom of expression and the freedom to receive and impart information.

In the case of a direct conflict between EC law and a constitutionally protected right, the Irish courts are required to dissapply a constitutional protection, to comply with their EC law obligations. This differs from a situation of conflict between international law and an Irish constitutional provision where in the Irish courts the Constitutional provision will trump the international right and the Irish courts have no authority to dissapply a constitutional provision in favour of an international law.

1.4.7 WHETHER THE ECHR IS PART OF IRISH DOMESTIC LAW BY VIRTUE OF EU LAW

The ECHR is a source of the general principles of EC human rights protections. As EC law is binding in domestic law a question arises as to whether the ECHR has been indirectly incorporated into Irish law via EC law.

The decision in *Kavanagh v Governor of Mountjoy Prison* [2002] 3 IR 112 was discussed above. The decision to try the applicant before the Special Criminal Court had previously been judicially reviewed unsuccessfully on different grounds in *Kavanagh v The Government of Ireland* [1996] 1 IR 348. On that occasion one of the arguments made by the applicant was that provisions of the ECHR form part of the domestic law by virtue of the ECHR's status within EC law. The applicant submitted that in considering the thrust of Art 40.1, Bunreacht na hÉireann, which guarantees equality before the law, account must be taken of the obligations of the State under the ECHR. The applicant argued that the ECHR was part of the domestic law of the State by virtue of Art 29.4.4, which enables Ireland to ratify the TEU, and Art F(2) (now Art 6(2)) TEU which provides:

> *'The Union shall respect fundamental rights, as guaranteed by the European Convention for the Protection of Human Rights and Fundamental Freedoms signed in Rome on 4 November 1950 and as they result from the constitutional traditions common to the Member States as general principles of Community law.'*

The respondents argued, relying on *In Re Ó Laighléis*, that the ECHR is not part of the domestic law. Further, they argued that no essential change was effected by the TEU, that the subject matter of the proceedings was not a matter coming within the scope, operation or competence of the EU and that the TEU did not change the essential adherence by the EC, reflected in the jurisprudence of the ECJ, to the basic rights reflected in the ECHR in the application and interpretation of EC law.

Laffoy J, at 345, considered it unnecessary to determine whether the ECHR had become part of the domestic law (as a result of the ECHR's status in EC law) as the applicant had not established any breach of the ECHR or Art 40.1 of the Constitution.

In my opinion the respondent's view is the better one and Ex Art F(2) (Now Art 6(2)) merely confirms the jurisprudence of the ECJ, that the ECJ will protect human rights as general principles of EC law, that the ECHR is one source of these general principles and that Member States are only bound by the EC standard of human rights protection when acting within the scope of EC law.

This view is consistent with the views of Barrington J in *Doyle v Commissioner of An Garda Síochána* [1999] 1 IR 249, 268. He emphasised that the ECHR in contrast to the EC Treaties, is not part of Irish domestic law but stated that 'the ECHR may in certain circumstances influence Irish law through European Community law.' One commentator has provided the following explanation. 'The [ECJ] has stressed that such general principles can be discerned from the [ECHR]. However, this is not a back door incorporation of the [ECHR] into national law since the [ECJ] has been keen to state that the national court can use these general principles of Community law only in matters where Community law is at issue. These general principles cannot be applied to matters which fall solely within the ambit of the national legislator . . .' (Burrows 'The European Union and the European Convention', in Dickson (ed) 'Human Rights and the European Convention: The Effects of the Convention on the United Kingdom and Ireland', 1997, Sweet and Maxwell. Within the scope of EC law the ECHR may be applied by the Irish courts.

1.5   Conclusion

There are three spheres of human rights protections in this jurisdiction. The first sphere encompasses the constitutional protection of fundamental rights which is at the apex of domestic law within the scope of national law. Within the domestic sphere, constitutional rights rank above all domestic legislation. However, constitutional rights do have to be balanced against one another.

The second sphere is the international sphere. These international and domestic spheres are entirely separate unless an international law instrument is incorporated into domestic law. Where there is a conflict between a right as protected by the Constitution and by an international instrument, the constitutional protection ranks higher in domestic law while the international obligation ranks higher in international law. A domestic court will apply the constitutional right over the international right and will not be required to dissapply a constitutional protection. An international court will apply an international right over a domestic provision. In the instance of a constitutional/international law clash of rights, Ireland would be required as a matter of international law to amend the Constitution to comply with the international obligation. If the clash is between a domestic legislative provision and an international law instrument arises, the situation will follow the constitutional/international clash scenario apart from the fact that it is only domestic legislation which will be required to bring Ireland into line with its international law obligations.

Where an international human rights obligation is incorporated into domestic law, its status will depend on how it has been incorporated. If it is incorporated as an ordinary statute it will have the status of legislation and will rank below the Constitution and later legislation. If it is incorporated on the basis of an interpretative model, courts will be required to interpret national law in accordance with it. If it is incorporated by constitutional amendment then it will have constitutional status and will rank above legislation. The ECHR has been incorporated on the basis of an interpretative model at sub-constitutional level.

The third sphere is the EC law sphere. At EC level, the ECJ will apply EC law, balancing rights against one another. The EC sphere and the domestic sphere apply concurrently in the Irish legal system, as there can be no dualist approach to EC law. EC law is superior to all domestic law, including the human rights protections in the Constitution within the scope of EC law. In the case of a conflict within the scope of EC law between EC law and a constitutional protection of a human right, EC law will prevail at both ECJ level and at domestic court level, although the ECJ and the domestic courts will be required to take account of the EC law standard of human rights protection. In the case of a direct conflict, national courts would have to dissapply national laws, including constitutionally protected human rights in favour of EC law. It is apparent from **5.8.1** that EC human rights protection can be limited by reference to other European law objectives such as the organisation of the common market.

However, it must be emphasised that the doctrine of supremacy of EC law operates only within the scope of EC law and in any case without an EC law dimension, it is the Constitutional protection which is at the top of the hierarchy. In addition, where there is a conflict between EC law and Irish law which is capable of being resolved in accordance with the Constitution this method will take precedence.

Within a sphere it is for the courts to balance rights with one another. Across the spheres it is a question of hierarchy of laws rather than a balancing of rights.

CHAPTER 2

HUMAN RIGHTS IN THE IRISH CONSTITUTION AND IRISH LEGISLATION

2.1 Introduction

2.1.1 THE SCOPE OF THE CHAPTER

This chapter considers how contemporary Irish law protects 'human rights'. The term 'human rights' is, of course, more or less interchangeable with mostly 'fundamental rights', a term employed in the constitutional text to describe the personal rights enjoyed mostly by Irish citizens. Yet the expression 'human rights' also suggests an international dimension, a nuance of meaning not traditionally contained in the phrase 'fundamental rights'. Furthermore, new legislation broadens the reach of human rights recognised by Irish law, from a narrower context of constitutional rights to one inclusive of universal standards.

For those reasons the Irish human rights régime is considered in this chapter not solely from a perspective of an isolated legal system but also as a constituent in a broader picture.

We begin in section one with a brief history. Section two looks at sources of rights. Section three examines the express freedoms listed in the Irish Constitution, organised by reference to a table, where the reader will find in a convenient form a summary list as well as the leading case-law associated with those guarantees. By way of contrast, in section four we focus on rights that though not explicitly stated are nevertheless recognised as being implicit in the text of the Constitution. Section five surveys the qualifications, restrictions and limitations associated with human rights in Ireland.

We go on to discuss the way international human rights are received into the *corpus* of Irish law in section 6 while human rights within the Irish statutory framework is the subject of section seven. There legislation that bears the imprint of international human rights instruments is highlighted, a selection that can be justified perhaps not simply by confines of space in this chapter but also by the slight difference in emphasis contained in the term human rights, mentioned above.

2.1.2 ORIGINS

The provenance of human rights is ancient. The precursors to human rights instruments occur in Mosaic Law (see for example Leviticus Ch 25) if not earlier still in Egyptian and Sumerian law codes like that of Hammurabi (c1760 BC). The much later *Enlightenment* (c.1680–1800) provides the immediate background in the development of the concept.

That epoch is associated especially with the theories of John Locke (1632–1704), the author best known perhaps for the slogan 'no taxation without representation', a phrase that figured so prominently in the American colonists' complaints. However, the *Enlightenment* also features Rousseau (1712–1778) and Voltaire (1694–1778), writers who sharpened a political edge for the variable, but not so incisive, philosophy of the natural law that was synonymous with that *milieu*. The French revolutionary war-cry of *'liberté, égalité et fraternité,* for instance, continues to resonate politically and juridically throughout modern Western civilisation in particular, providing a clearly recognised theme, as well as a basis for much contemporary legislation. In the Irish context, we can point to *'communautaire'* law (the law derived from the EU) as an example in that tradition, where the signature, especially of ideals of equality, is clearly discernible.

2.1.3 A NOVEL RÉGIME

Independent Ireland began life in the true sense in 1922 as Saorstát Éireann. At the same time the character of the jural order underwent a radical change. Three elements in the fledgling constitution set the stage for a human rights culture. First the preamble to the Constitution Act, 1922 and Art 2 of the Constitution itself promoted the idea of popular sovereignty (the sovereignty of the *people* as distinct from the Crown). It also introduced a theocratic element, and opened a door for natural law later, by the insistence that all government powers are derived from *God*. Thirdly the document also asserted a number of basic rights such as Art 6 that proclaimed 'the liberty of the person is inviolable, and no person shall be deprived of his liberty except in accordance with law'. This proved a significant advance as, up to 1945 international law was not concerned with the protection of individuals from State interference. The Irish Constitution was in the vanguard of charters protecting human rights by a constitutional 'Bill of Rights'. It followed in a sequence including pre-eminently, the reformed US Constitution of 1787, or closer to home, the Polish Constitution of 3 May 1791 and the 1848 French Constitution that is often considered the prototype of continental Constitutions. Later, Bunreacht na hÉireann (1937), fell into a similar pattern of republican Constitutions but greatly expanded on the number and complexity of rights listed in the 1922 Constitution.

2.2 Sources of Rights

2.2.1 NATURAL JUSTICE EMERGES AS ONE BASIS FOR IRISH JURISPRUDENCE

There was yet another innovation in the Free State Constitution in the form of an indirect reference to natural justice. This feature was related to and inferred from the theocratic features we noted in the previous paragraph. The concept is of course highly theoretical, but we must add, it had thoroughly practical implications for the way that Irish law developed a human rights régime. For this reason, the manner in which *The State (Ryan) v Lennon* [1935] IR 170 built upon these conceptual foundations of natural justice is now examined. The plaintiff had argued, in that case, that he was denied the constitutional guarantee to basic human rights and in particular, he said that the circumstances of his arrest were incompatible with Art 6 (quoted in **2.1.3**). He had been detained on the strength of a legal warrant that was issued, not by a judicial figure, but on the lesser authority of a State official. He argued that his treatment by the State was 'not in accordance with law' – an essential precondition for legitimacy under Art 6.

2.2.2 A LANDMARK DISSENTING JUDGMENT

Kennedy CJ, in a famous dissenting opinion, recognised in the phrase 'in accordance with law', authority for the proposal, that for law to be legitimate, it must conform to a *higher* law; a fundamental postulate of the Constitution, that he insisted, could not be amended.

His natural law approach is clearly evident in the following often quoted extract from the judgment (at page 204):

'. . . all lawful authority comes from God to the people, and it is declared by Article 2 of the Constitution that "all powers of government and all authority, legislative, executive and judicial, in Ireland are derived from the people of Ireland . . .". It follows; that every act, whether legislative, executive or judicial in order to be lawful under the Constitution, must be capable of being justified under the authority thereby declared to be derived from God. From this it seems clear that, if any legislation of the Oireachtas (including any purported amendment of the Constitution) were to offend against the acknowledged ultimate source from which the legislative authority has come through the people to the Oireachtas, as, for instance, if it were repugnant to Natural Law, such legislation would be necessarily unconstitutional and invalid . . .'.

2.2.3   OTHER SOURCES

Kennedy CJ's seminal analysis, the conviction that a source of law exists outside and beyond the constitutional text, became a principal epistemology in Irish constitutionalism. The reader should be mindful, however, that the theory never found universal acceptance. On the contrary, it is clear that there was a strand of judicial thinking that was ill at ease with this philosophy. The following extract from the decision in *Riordan v An Tánaiste* [1995] 3 IR 62 may be considered as typical of an alternative view. Here, the plaintiff questioned the constitutionality of both the Taoiseach and the Tánaiste being absent from the State at the same time. Budd J observes (at 124) that natural law 'permits reliance on standards which are often subjective and nebulous and which may not give reliable guidelines in dealing with actual constitutional problems'. Scepticism, on the other hand, if not outright rejection of the natural law is apparent from the following ruling of Hamilton CJ, in the watershed *Regulation of Information (Services outside the State for Termination of Pregnancies Bill) 1995* [1995] 1IR 1, 43.

'the Courts, as they were and are bound to, recognised the Constitution as the fundamental law of the State to which the organs of State were subject and at no stage recognised the provisions of the natural law as superior to the Constitution'.

2.2.4   THE PREAMBLE

Of course, along with the natural law, the courts have indicated other sources of rights. The preambular concepts, for example, of prudence, justice and charity, most notably discussed in *McGee v Attorney General* [1974] IR 284, have been referred to by the courts as signposts to rights. In *McGee*, Walsh J in the context of considering the nature and extent of duties that flow from natural law again stated (at 319) that it was the exclusive duty of judges to interpret the Constitution. He went on to explain though, that in doing so, the guidelines laid down in the Constitution, namely the classic virtues of prudence, justice and charity, represented values by which these rights may be evaluated. In particular he explained that these were indicators of moral standards that are superior to and situated outside the positive law. In the same case Walsh J also referred to the concept of the *common good* as a source of rights (at 319). Similar views were expressed by Hamilton CJ in the recent cases of *Lawlor v Flood* [1999] 3 IR 107 and in *Haughey v Moriarty* [1999] 3 IR 1. In *Lawlor* (at 88) Hamilton CJ stated, for instance, that 'the right to privacy is however not an absolute right. The exigencies of *the common good* may outweigh the constitutional right to privacy'.

2.2.5 CHRISTIAN AND DEMOCRATIC

The norms associated with the Christian and democratic nature of the State have also provided a set of criteria for the discovery of rights (see *Kennedy v Ireland* [1987] IR 587 and *Crotty v An Taoiseach* [1987] IR 713). Nevertheless some earlier jurists were sceptical particularly of the rôle of democracy. Hogan and Whyte, for instance, wondered how the right to marry could possibly be derived from the democratic nature of the State (Hogan and Whyte, 'JM Kelly: The Irish Constitution', 3rd edn, 1994, Butterworths, 335). In their view the discovery of this right was surely a consequence of the judges' view of the Christian nature of the State, a historical irony perhaps, in the light of the centrality of democracy in contemporary case-law both here and in Europe. In Ireland for a current example of where democracy is identified as a foundational concept, see *TD v Eastern Health Board* [2001] 4 IR 259. Here, quoting Chief Justice Barak of Israel (*United Mizrahi Bank Ltd v Migool Village* (1995) 49 (4) PD 221), Denham J stated at p. 35 of her judgment that:

> '. . . [D]emocracy also means the rule of basic values and human rights as expressed in the Constitution. Democracy is a delicate balance between the majority rule and the basic values of society. Indeed, democracy does not mean formal democracy alone, which is concerned with the electoral process in which the majority rules. Democracy also means substantive democracy, which is concerned with the defence of human rights in particular . . .'.

Henchy J, in *McGee* (at 326) had earlier discovered a source in the idea of the dignity and freedom of the individual a notion that is shared by the drafters of the Universal Declaration of Human Rights (1948) (Preamble; Art. 1).

Occasionally too, the courts had regard to the international standards of human rights in identifying particular rights, for example, in *Desmond v Glackin* [1993] 3 IR 1. Indeed, some judges have found inspiration for rights in the Social Directives that are listed in Art 45 but declared therein to be non-cognisable. For example in *Murtagh Properties v Cleary* [1972] IR 330, where against the background of a trade union objection to the employment of women as part-time bar staff, Kenny J granted an interlocutory injunction restraining members of the trade union from picketing certain public houses pending the outcome of the action. He explained (at 335–6) that although Art 45 prevented the Courts from questioning the application of the principles of social policy, it was permissible for the court to examine the provisions of that Article to discover whether they recognised any relevant 'personal rights' within the meaning of Art 40.3 of the Constitution.

2.3 A Programme of Human Rights in Ireland – Express Rights in the Irish Constitution

2.3.1 THREE GENERATIONS OF RIGHTS

We now turn our attention to those fundamental freedoms explicitly listed in Bunreacht na hÉireann, the present day Constitution at the heart of governance in Ireland since 29 December 1937. Those rights can be categorised, not only as being substantive or procedural, but also as to how they fit in with what writers commonly refer to as first, second or third generation rights.

The first generation consists of 'civil and political rights', rights derived from natural law philosophy of the eighteenth century (Rousseau and others), traditionally given priority by Western states. The second generation is made up of economic, social and cultural rights, (that attained recognition in the twentieth century, for example the right to form a trade union) while group or collective rights form the third. There is considerable overlap between these categories and that none of them is 'airtight'. In the Constitution, there are examples of all types including a pure socio-economic right in the form of Art 42.4 (free primary education) and even a third generation right (self-determination) in Art 1.

Conveniently for us Arts 40–44 catalogue most of the so-called fundamental rights, or *Bunchearta*. Nonetheless, it will become apparent from the following tables that not all human rights protected by Irish law are included in that grouping and many rights are not expressed by the Constitution at all. Express rights are listed in the first table. For the convenience of the reader the leading judgments pertaining to those rights are also indicated.

2.3.2   A CATALOGUE OF EXPRESS CONSTITUTIONAL RIGHTS

Right	*Article*	*Precedent*	*Character*
1. Self-determination.	1.	*Crotty v An Taoiseach* [1987] IR 713	Collective or third generation right. Substantive.
2. Equality of citizens.	40.1.	*Quinn Supermarket v Attorney General* [1972] IR 1 *Murtagh Properties v Cleary* [1972] IR 330 *O'B v S* [1984] IR 316	First generation. Political. Substantive.
3. Personal rights in particular life, person, good name and property rights.	40.3.	*Dillane v Attorney General* [1980] ILRM 167	Procedural & Substantive.
4. Personal liberty.	40.4.	*The People (Attorney General) v O'Callaghan* [1966] IR 501	Substantive. First generation. Political.
5. Rights of the family.	41. 41.1.1°. 41.1.2°.	*The State (Nicolaou) v An Bord Uchtála* [1966] IR 567 *G. v An Bord Uchtála* [1980] IR 32. *Murray v Ireland* [1991] ILRM 465 *BL v ML* [1992] 2 IR 77 *North Western Health Board v H W & C W* [2001] 3 IR 635. *Murphy v Attorney General* [1982] IR 241	Substantive. Second generation. Social and economic.
6. The State pledges to guard the institution of marriage.	41.3.1°.	*Mayo-Perrott v Mayo-Perrott* [1958] IR 336 *T F v Ireland* [1995] 1 IR 321	Substantive. Second generation. Social and economic.

7. The 'inalienable' right of parents to educate their child. The right of the child to be educated.	42.1.	*In re Article 26 of the Constitution and the School Attendance Bill 1942* [1943] IR 334 *Ryan v Attorney General* [1965] IR 294	Substantive. Second generation. Social and economic.
8. Free primary education.	42.4.	*Crowley v Ireland* [1980] IR 102 *O'Donoghue v Minister for Health* [1996] 2 IR 20	Substantive. Second generation. Social and economic.
9. The State guarantees to supply the place of the parents in exceptional cases.	42.5.	*C. W. v North Western Health Board* [2001] 3 IR 635	Substantive. Second generation. Social and economic.
10. The 'natural right, antecedent to positive law', to the private ownership of property.	43.1.1°.	*Pigs Marketing Board v Donnelly (Dublin) Ltd.* [1939] IR 413 *Dreher v Irish Land Commission* [1984] ILRM 94 *Blake v Attorney General* [1982] IR 117 *PMPS v Attorney General* [1983] IR 339	Substantive. First generation. Political.
11. The guarantee against the abolition of private property.	43.1.2°.	*Blake v Attorney General* [1982] IR 117 *Brennan v Attorney General* [1984] ILRM 355 *Gilligan v CAB* [1998] 3 IR 185	Substantive. First generation. Political.
12. Freedom of worship.	44.1.	*Quinn Supermarket Ltd. v Attorney General* [1972] IR 1 *Norris v Attorney General* [1984] IR. 36	Substantive. First generation. Political.
13. Freedom of conscience.	44.2.1°.	*McGee v Attorney General* [1974] IR 284 *Quinn Supermarket Ltd. v Attorney General* [1972] IR 1	Substantive. First generation. Political.
14. The State guarantees not to endow any religion.	44.2.2°.	*Campaign to separate Church and State v Minister for Education* [1998] 3 IR 343.	Substantive. First generation. Political.

Right	Article	Precedent	Character
15. Guarantee against discrimination in the funding of schools.	44.2.4°.	*O'Sheil v Minister for Education* [1999] 2 IR 321.	Substantive. First generation. Political.
16. The rights to *Habeas Corpus* and Judicial Review.	40.4.2°. 34.3.2°.	*McMahon v Leahy* [1984] IR 525 *Cahill v Sutton* [1980] IR 269	Procedural. First generation. Political.
17. Inviolability of dwellinghouses.	40.5.	*DPP v Corrigan* [1986] IR 290 *The People (DPP) v Lawless* (1985 3 Frewen 30 *DPP v Gaffney* [1987] IR 173	Substantive. First generation. Political.
18. Freedom to express convictions and opinions.	40.6.1° (i).		Substantive. First generation. Political.
19. The right of assembly.	40.6.1° (ii).	*Attorney General v Paperlink Ltd.* [1984] ILRM 373	Substantive. First generation. Political.
20. The right to form associations.	40.6.1° (ii). 40.6.1° (iii).	*Brendan Dunne Ltd. v Fitzpatrick* [1958] IR 29 *The People (DPP) v Kehoe* [1983] IR 136 *NUR v Sullivan* [1947] IR 77. *Education Company of Ireland Ltd. v Fitzpatrick* (No. 2) [1961] IR 345	Substantive. First generation. Political. Substantive. First generation.
21. The right to non-discrimination in the formation of associations.	40.6.2°.	*NUR v Sullivan* [1947] IR 77	Substantive. First generation. Political.
22. Guarantee against retrospective legislation.	15.5.	*Doyle v An Taoiseach* [1986] ILRM 693 *Magee v Culligan* [1992] 1 IR 223	Substantive. First generation. Political.
23. The right to the rule of law.	34.1.	*In re Solicitors Act, 1954* [1960] IR 239. *Geoghegan v Institute of Chartered Accountants.* [1995] 3 IR 86 *McDonald v Bord na gCon* [1965] IR 217	Substantive and Procedural. First generation. Political.

2.4 A Doctrine of Unenumerated Rights

2.4.1 THE LEADING CASE: *RYAN V ATTORNEY GENERAL* [1965] IR 294

We made reference earlier in this chapter to natural law as a source for constitutional rights and we saw that in *The State (Ryan) v Lennon*, [1935] IR 170, the cause of express rights in the context of the 1922 Constitution was first championed. However not long after the inauguration of the new Constitution, Bunreacht na hÉireann, in 1937 a similar theme was taken up by different judges in *Ryan v Attorney General* [1965] IR 294 (referred to as *Ryan v Attorney General* in this chapter). In this case, the plaintiff challenged the constitutionality of water fluoridation legislation, and argued that the general words of Art 40.3 assured her of an implied right to bodily integrity. Giving judgment in the High Court, Kenny J expressed a view (at 312) that the human rights, 'which may be invoked to invalidate legislation are not confined to those specified in Article 40, but include all those rights which result from the Christian and democratic nature of the State'. Further, he went on to compare the general wording of Article 40.3.1° to the rights protected by 40.3.2° and found therein (at 313) a reservoir of 'personal rights of the citizen outside those listed in the Constitution', that was not drained dry by specific references to the guarantees to life, person, good name and property in the second part of the Article. He also explained that the High and the Supreme Court have the duty of 'ascertaining' and 'declaring' those human rights guaranteed but not expressed by the Constitution. The Supreme Court on appeal later endorsed this doctrine of unspecified rights.

From then on there followed a procession of judgments in Irish law that, adopting the same conceptual building blocks as those used in *Ryan*, declared an array of 'unenumerated' rights, which are outlined below.

2.4.2 A CATALOGUE OF UNENUMERATED CONSTITUTIONAL RIGHTS

Right	Source	Case	Character
1. The right to bodily integrity as well as the right not to have one's health endangered by the State.	Natural law. Christian and democratic nature of the State.	*Ryan v Attorney General* [1965] IR 294 *State v Frawley* [1976] IR 365.	Substantive. Second generation.
2. The right to earn a living.	Art 40.3.1°. Christian and democratic nature of the State.	*Murtagh Properties v Cleary* [1972] IR 330 *Murphy v Stewart* [1973] IR 97	Substantive. First generation.
3. The right to marry and found a family.	Art 41. Art 40.3.1°. Natural law.	*Ryan v Attorney General* [1965] IR 294 *McGee v Attorney General* [1974] IR 284 *Murray v Attorney General* [1985] IR 532	Substantive. Second generation.

Right	Source	Case	Character
4. The right to marital privacy and the right to individual privacy.	Natural law. Art 41. Art 40.3.1°.	*McGee v Attorney General* [1974] IR 284 *Kennedy v Ireland* [1987] IR 587	Substantive. Second generation.
5. The right to travel within and outside the State.	Christian and democratic nature of the State. Art 40.3.1°. Art (40.3.3°.)	*Ryan v Attorney General* [1965] IR 294 *State (M) v Attorney General* [1979] IR 73 *Lennon v Ganley* [1981] ILRM 84	Substantive. Second generation.
6. The right of access to the courts.	40.3.1°. Christian and democratic nature of the State. 34.3.1°. Common law.	*MacAuley v Minister for Posts & Telegraphs* [1966] IR 345 *Murphy v Minister for Justice* [2001] 1 IR 95	Substantive and Procedural. First generation.
7. The right to strike.	Natural law.	*Educational Co. Ltd. v Fitzpatrick* (No. 2) [1961] IR 345	Substantive Second generation.
8. The right to cross-examine and confront witnesses.	Art 38.1. Common law. Natural law.	*In re Haughey* [1971] IR 217 *State (Healy) v Donoghue* [1976] IR 325 *White v Ireland* [1995] 2 IR 268.	Procedural. First generation.
9. Exclusion of unconstitutionally obtained evidence.	Art 40.3.1°.	*People (DPP) v Kenny* [1990] 2 IR 110	Procedural. First generation.
10. The right to legal representation.	ECHR (Art 6(3)(c). Art 38.1. Art 40.3.4°. Natural justice.	*State (Healy) v Donoghue* [1976] IR 325	Procedural and Substantive. Second generation.
11. The right to trial with reasonable speed.	Natural justice. Art 40.3.1°. Art 38.1.	*Cahalane v Murphy* [1994] 2 IR 262 *State (Healy) v Donoghue* [1976] IR 325 *State (O'Connell) v Judge Fawsitt* [1986] IR 362.	Procedural and Substantive. First generation.

12. The guarantee against vague and indefinite laws.	Concept of justice expressed in the Preamble. 34.1. Dignity of the Individual. 38.1. 40.4.1°.	*King v Attorney General* [1981] IR. 233	Substantive. First generation.
13. The presumption of innocence.	Art 38.1 Common law. Art 11: Universal Declaration of Human Rights 1948. American Convention on Human Rights 1969. Art 6(2) ECHR The African Charter on Human Rights.	*Hardy v Ireland* [1994] 2 IR 550 *O'Leary v Attorney General* [1993] 1 IR 102 (H.Ct.): [1995] 1 IR 254 (S.Ct.) *Citing X v UK* 5124/71 Dec. of European Commission on Human Rights. 4 Coll. of Dec. 42, 135.	Substantive and Procedural. First generation.
14. The right **not** to associate.	Art 40.6.1°. Art 40.3.	*Educational Co. Ltd. v Fitzpatrick* (No. 2) [1961] IR 345 *Mescall v CIE* [1973] IR 121	Substantive. First generation.
15. The right to fair procedures in decision making.	Natural law. Art 40.3.1°.	*In re Haughey* [1971] IR 217 *Garvey v Ireland* [1981] IR 75 *Dublin Wellwoman Centre Ltd. v Ireland.* [1995] 1 ILRM 408	Procedural and Substantive. First generation.
16. The right to know the identity of one's natural mother.	Natural law.	*O'T v B* [1998] 2 IR 321	Substantive. Second generation.
17. The right to independent domicile.	Art 40.3.	*CM v TM* [1991] ILRM 268	Substantive. Second generation.
18. The right to communicate.	Social policies seen in Art 45 Directives. 40.3. Common Good. Art 46.1.	*Attorney General v Paperlink Ltd.* [1984] ILRM 373 *Murphy v IRTC* [1999] 1 IR 12	Substantive. Second generation.

Right	Source	Case	Character
19. The right of a child to fully enjoy all the rights identified in Article 40.	Art 40.3. Art 41, 42, 43, 44.	*In re Article 26 and the Adoption (No. 2) Bill 1987* [1989] IR 656	Substantive. Second generation.
20. A right for a child to be placed and maintained in secure residential accommodation so as to ensure, so far as practicable, his or her appropriate religious and moral, intellectual, physical and social education.	Art 40.3. Art 42.5.	*F. N. v Minister for Education & Others.* [1995] 1 IR 409	Substantive. Second generation.

2.5   Limits, Qualifications and Restrictions

A general outline of the sources and the content, as well as the character and range of human rights both express and implied in the Irish Constitution has been traced. How and to what extent the courts actually apply these freedoms is a subject to which we now turn, an exercise that may be accomplished negatively, by examining the nature and scope of the restrictions accompanying these rights.

2.5.1   DEROGATIONS IN TIMES OF EMERGENCY

We start with the most radical provision, the power under Article 28.3° to suspend all or any human right. The provision states:

> '*Nothing in this Constitution shall be invoked to invalidate any law enacted by the Oireachtas which is expressed to be for the purpose of securing the public safety and preservation of the State in the time of war or armed rebellion . . .'.*

In the same vein, Art 40.4.6° provides for the suspension of *habeas corpus* during the existence of a state of war or armed rebellion. In the light of those extensive executive powers, we can accept Professor Casey's insight that: '[i]t would be difficult to over-emphasise the plenitude of power thus vested in the Oireachtas. In theory it could by invoking the Article 28.3.3° formula . . . re-write the Constitution'. (Casey, 'Constitutional Law in Ireland', 3rd edn, 2000, Roundhall, Sweet and Maxwell, 181).

2.5.2   THE *Ó'LÁIGHLÉIS* CASE

Those extreme measures envisaged in Arts 28.3.3° and 40.4.6.° have not been invoked often in the history of the State. However, a few cases during and shortly after the Second World War testify to the draconian potential of these provisions. For example, *In re Ó*

'In considering whether a restriction on the exercise of rights is permitted by the Constitution, the courts in this country and elsewhere have found it helpful to apply the test of proportionality, a test which contains the notions of minimal restraint on the exercise of potential rights and of the exigencies of the common good in a democratic society. . . . The objective of the impugned provision must be of sufficient importance to warrant overriding a constitutionally protected right. It must relate to concerns pressing and substantial in a free and democratic society. The means chosen must pass a proportionality test. They must:

(a)   be rationally connected to the objective and not be arbitrary, unfair or based on irrational considerations;

(b)   impair the right as little as possible, and

(c)   be such that their effects on rights are proportional to the objective'.

These guidelines were approved by the Supreme Court in *Rock v Ireland* [1997] 3 IR 484, 500 and *Murphy v IRTC* [1999] IR 12, 26.

2.6   International and Irish Constitutional Law

2.6.1   THE MONIST DUALIST DIALECTIC

There is an age-old academic controversy regarding how international law may become enforceable in national legal systems. This debate has been associated with protagonists such as Lauterpacht (a proponent of *monism*, that holds that international law becomes part of national law automatically) or Triepel (an advocate of *dualism*, the theory that limits the scope of international rules to those sanctioned by national legislation only). Now-adays an arcane dispute has been invested with relevance and a practicality that also extends to this chapter.

The reason for this is that Irish constitutional theory is dualist (sometimes referred to by writers as pluralist). Accordingly international law is blocked from entering the Irish legal sphere, unless hospitality is afforded in the form of national legislation (see **chapter 1**). This principle is given clear expression by Art 29.6 of the Constitution, which provides:

> 'No international agreement shall be part of domestic law of the State save as may be determined by the Oireachtas.'

Where it is sought to give domestic effect to an international law which is inconsistent with the Constitution, domestic legislation will not suffice. Rather a referendum will be required so that the people can approve the measure.

The requirement of Art 29.6 also explains why international treaties, including human rights instruments, like the ECHR, cannot be enforced in and by Irish law unless they have been incorporated into Irish domestic law (see *Horgan v An Taoiseach*, Kearns J, 28 April 2003, High Court (unreported) for a recent judicial application of Art 29.6).

In addition to the ECHR, the case-law of the ECt.HR in Strasbourg, is also prevented, in the light of similar considerations, from penetrating our jurisprudence. Although we should point out that the ECHR in particular has been called in aid by various Irish judges to justify the 'discovery' of so-called unenumerated rights (see **2.4.2**), for instance *State (Healy) v Donoghue* [1976] IR 325. The recent ruling in *Heaney v Ireland* follows the same pattern (already mentioned in **2.5.12**). In that case, Costello J invoked Art 6 ECHR to justify the right to silence as a latent constitutional guarantee. See also in this connection *Desmond v Glackin* (No. 1) [1993] 3 IR 1.

2.6.2 A NEW TREND

There may, however, be an unfolding judicial trend that could significantly alter the understanding of Irish law as being absolutely dualist. The possible change centres on the undertaking contained in Art. 29.3 that accepts for Ireland the 'generally recognised principles of international law' in its rule of conduct in relations with other states. In *ACT Shipping Limited v the Minister for the Marine* [1995] 3 IR 406 at 422 for instance, Barr J held that a private litigant may invoke Article 29.3 against the State, so as to assert that a particular international rule: 'has in time evolved into Irish domestic law from customary international law'. He did however qualify that general observation by pointing out that such a rule of international law must not be contrary to the Constitution, statute law or common law. (Please note customary international – including customary international human rights law – is a universally accepted principle of International Law. (see Brownlie, 'Principles of Public International Law', 5th edn, 1998, OUP, 42 *et seq* and *Horgan v An Taoiseach*, Kearns J., 28 April 2003, High Court (unreported), see **2.6.1.**)

2.6.3 THE CONSTITUTIONAL REVIEW GROUP

The Constitutional Review Group Report also recognised a similar trend towards giving effect, in national law, to the generally recognised principles of international law (see *Grúpa Aithbhreithnithe an Bhunreachta*, Baile Átha Cliath, 1996, 105). If this trend is realised and if a human right falls within the category of 'generally recognised principles of international law', referred to in Art 29, it too might enter Irish law directly, without the need for transposing national legislation. An example is the universal condemnation of torture, a clear example of customary international law. Moreover the prohibition on torture has acquired added force in that it has evolved into a peremptory norm of international law or *jus cogens*, as these *absolute* rules are called.

The absolute priority assigned to such a right at international level should be compared to the protection presently afforded to a similar right nationally, where as we have seen McCarthy J said, 'it is difficult to identify a constitutional right that is unqualified' in *Murray v Ireland* [1991] ILRM 465, 477 (see **2.5.4.** and **2.7.9.** which discusses recent legislation banning torture).

It is therefore possible, on the evidence of present trends, that international standards of human rights may enter Irish law directly, despite the blocking mechanism provided by Art 29 (see *Horgan v An Taoiseach*, Kearns J., 28 April 2003, High Court (unreported)).

2.7 Human Rights and Irish Legislation

We can now turn our attention to a short survey of human rights in Irish legislation. Again, so as not to pre-empt the specialised treatment of particular rights in other parts of the manual, we may confine our survey to general headings to which we can assign principal legislation.

2.7.1 HUMAN RIGHTS COMMISSION ACT, 2000

This Act addresses the protection of 'human rights' and introduces a novel dimension to the protection of human rights in Ireland, not least of which is a new meaning assigned to the term 'human rights', for the purpose of Irish law. This is defined as:

> '(a) the rights, liberties and freedoms conferred on, or guaranteed to, persons by the Constitution;
> (b) the rights, liberties or freedoms conferred on, or guaranteed to, persons by any agreement, treaty or convention to which the State is a party.'

This Act is a sequel to the political commitments assumed by the Irish Government, under 'The Good Friday Agreement'. The legislation is also in line with United Nations Policy and the recommendations for human rights institutions embodied in the *Paris Principles* of 1993.

The Irish Human Rights Commission (IHRC) is the centrepiece of this Act, endowed as it is 'with perpetual succession' (s 4). It is also assigned a statutory brief to keep under general review, the adequacy and effectiveness of law and practice in the State relating to the protection of human rights (s 8). The IHRC has also been given specialised functions for instance, the undertaking of human rights research, appearing before a superior court as *amicus curiae*, or providing legal assistance to suitable litigants and providing 'linkage' between national and international human rights agencies and bodies, and holding enquiries under s 9 of the Act. The power to hold enquiries, is wide ranging and gives rise to many unanswered questions about the operative role of the IHRC, including the precise contours of enquiries and the circumstances where the IHRC may choose to intervene. The power of enquiry is nonetheless an important development. Moreover, the Act envisages that these enquiries may be in public or private and are bolstered by the additional powers given to the IHRC to order discovery and to compel the attendance of witnesses (s 9(6)).

Of additional interest, the IHRC *must* refuse any request for an enquiry (or indeed to discontinue an enquiry already started), in conditions where it considers the complaint in question, is 'manifestly unfounded' s 9(3); a procedural hurdle common to the adjudication of international human rights generally, including the ECHR (See especially **chapters 3** and **4**). Equally, the rule that those seeking the assistance of the IHRC by way of enquiry may first have to exhaust any other remedies open to them (in contrast to proceedings started or likely to be commenced), may constitute a further obstacle for the individual hoping to use the machinery provided by the Act. Nevertheless, the importance of this legislation may lie in providing, outside the more usual constitutional framework of judicial review and presidential reference, a statutory structure for the review and perhaps the condemnation of laws and practices offensive to fundamental norms. In that connection, the extension of the definition of human rights in Irish law beyond the constitutional framework to international norms, is especially noteworthy. (See **chapter 4**.) The IHRC statutory power to 'double-guess' law and practice regarding human rights in Ireland is not, however, in any way co-extensive with the Supreme Court's paramount role as the final arbiter of all laws, 'having regard to the provisions' of the Constitution (see Art. 34). In the assessment of the IHRC role, particular attention must be paid nevertheless to the statutory obligation to construe human rights (under s 2), so as to include all international instruments to which the State is a party.

2.7.2   NEW HUMAN RIGHTS LEGISLATION

One recent accretion to the protection of human rights in Irish domestic law is the incorporation of the European Convention on Human Rights (ECHR) (see **chapters 1** and **3** and **2.7.3**). A potential accretion at EU level is the EU Charter of Fundamental Rights, if incorporated into the Draft Treaty Establishing a Constitution for Europe (Conv 820/1/03 Brussels, 27 June 2003) (see **chapter 5**).

2.7.3   THE EUROPEAN CONVENTION ON HUMAN RIGHTS ACT, 2003

The European Convention on Human Rights Act, 2003 which incorporates the ECHR into Irish domestic law commenced on 31 December 2003 (See **chapters 1** and **3**). The centrepiece of this legislation is s 2 (1) which provides:

> *'In interpreting and applying any statutory provision or rule of law, a court shall, in so far as possible, subject to the rules of law relating to such interpretation and application do so in a manner compatible with the State's obligations under the Convention provisions.'*

Furthermore the Act (s 3) enjoins every organ of the State to perform its functions in a manner compatible with the ECHR obligations. Section 1(1) defines 'organ of the State' as including:

> *'a tribunal or any other body (other than the President or the Oireachtas or either House of the Oireachtas or a Committee of either such House or a Joint Committee of both such houses or a Court) which is established by law or through which any of the legislative, executive or judicial powers of the state are exercised'.*

The Act has singularly excluded the provisions of the Constitution from its scope (see long title and s 2, quoted above) and it seems clear that the Act is subject to the precedence of Irish constitutional rules. We may question the extent to which the courts will be bound by the ECHR provisions when they conflict with or are incompatible with constitutional imperatives. There is also the related question concerning the legal status of existing case-law involving the interpretation of constitutional provisions. Will this body of precedent be subject also to review and possible modification in the light of the ECHR provisions, or will it be immune from challenge by virtue of Art 34 of the Constitution that allows the Supreme Court final say in all cases? Much will depend on how the Act is interpreted and applied by the courts.

Indeed an important feature of this legislation is the role of the Superior Courts in being able to declare incompatible a *statutory provision* or *rule of law* with the ECHR provisions. There is, nevertheless, a potential circularity built into the scheme of the Act in that the court must not only test the law in question for compatibility with the ECHR but must then test the overall result for compatibility with Irish law in the form of the Constitution. How the Supreme Court will square this circle remains to be seen.

2.7.4   EQUALITY LEGISLATION

The constitutional right to equality contained principally in Art 40.1 *'all citizens shall as human persons, be held equal before the law'* has not traditionally been associated with an expansive jurisprudence (see detailed discussion in Kelly, 712 and Casey, 450). The Courts have narrowed the scope of the section by confining the meaning of the words 'as human persons' to what they consider as the essential attributes of being persons, rather than, for example, the trades or professions that people pursue (see *MacAuley v Minister for Posts & Telegraphs* [1966] IR 345 and *Quinns Supermarket v Attorney General* [1972] IR 1). The guarantee has had little rôle in developing a culture of equality in the Irish legal order. Nonetheless, the legislature has attempted to provide focus to the guarantee of equality in the:

- Anti-Discrimination (Pay) Act, 1974

- Employment Equality Act, 1998

- Equal Status Act, 2000.

International human rights standards of equality are reflected in:

- Anti-Discrimination (Pay) Act, 1974

- Employment Equality Act, 1998

- Employment Equality Act, 1977.

2.7.5 WORK LEGISLATION

Freedom to work, or the right to earn a livelihood, is recognised as latent in the general guarantee of Art 40.3, a right that also has parallels in international human rights conventions. Ever since the Universal Declaration of Human Rights (1949), this right was projected onto the global plane by the International Labour Organisation (ILO) an offshoot of the League of Nations (a forerunner to the UN).

Those developments, together with International trade-unionism, generated empowering and ameliorating labour legislation at an early stage in Irish law. Before the dawn of the new State, for example, the Trade Dispute Act, of 1906 (which remained in force until supplanted by the Industrial Relations Act, 1990), allowed industrial action by the trades unions for the first time. Since then, a significant amount of legislation, protective also of the individual, (as opposed to collectives) has been enacted in Ireland, such as:

- Conditions of Employment Act, 1936
- Minimum Notice and Terms of Employment Act, 1973
- Anti-Discrimination (Pay) Act, 1974
- Unfair Dismissals Act, 1977
- Protection of Young Persons (Employment) Act, 1977
- Employment Equality Act, 1977
- Maternity Protection of Employees Act, 1981
- Safety, Health and Welfare at Work Act, 1989
- Employment Equality Act, 1998.

2.7.6 FAMILY AND CHILD RIGHTS

Article 41 of the Constitution contains the rights of the 'family' (a concept which is not defined by the Constitution) and Art 42 guarantees the right and duty of parents to provide, according to their means, for the education of their children. Much has happened in Irish legislation in recent years to modify Art 41, especially the introduction of divorce as well as the marked emancipation of women from the confines of a strict cultural straightjacket that was reflected in the words of Art 42.2.1°.

Legislation such as the Family Law (Divorce Act), 1996, the Family Home Protection Act, 1976 may be seen as a further expansion of basic human rights, protective, especially of women, within the institutional framework of the family. Other legislation along the same lines is:

- Married Women Status Act, 1957
- Guardianship of Infants Act, 1964
- Succession Act, 1965
- Civil Service (Employment of Married Women) Act, 1973.

The progress made with regard to the advancement of children's rights is obvious from the level of protection seen in the following acts:

- Age of Majority Act, 1985
- Status of Children Act, 1987
- Child Abduction Act, 1991
- Child Care Act, 1991

- Children Act, 1997

- Child Trafficking and Pornography Act, 1998

- Protection of Children (Hague Convention) Act, 2000

- Children Act, 2001

- Commission to Inquire into Child Abuse Act, 2000.

2.7.7 ADOPTION LEGISLATION

We should also note the:

- Adoption Act, 1988.

- Adoption Act, 1998. This was a response to the judgment of the European Court of Human Rights, in *Keegan v Ireland* (1994) 18 EHRR 342. In that case, the European Court of Human Rights condemned the Irish law that allowed a child to be placed for adoption without the knowledge or consent of its natural father. The court went on to hold our domestic legislation violated Arts 6 and 8 of the ECHR.

- Adoptive Leave Act, 1995.

- Maternity Protection of Employees Act, 1981.

- Parental Leave Act, 1998. This Act transposed Council Directive 96/34/EC, providing for unpaid leave to allow both men and women to care for children. The legislation also provides for paid leave in exceptional *'force majeure'* circumstances.

2.7.8 ASYLUM AND IMMIGRATION LAW

This is also a subject that has seen profound change since the State assumed the obligations of Community law. Much legislation has entered the statute book, on the free movement of workers and others, within the territory of the community. Allied to this is the right to European citizenship secured by Art 17 (ex Art 8) of the Treaty on European Union (Maastricht). Those rights are mostly confined to citizens of the Member States. Compare, however, substantial rights in Irish law that have been extended to 'aliens', ie persons with no connection to the State or the states of the European Community. The term 'aliens' has now become obsolete as a result of the Irish Nationality and Citizenship Act, 2001 (s 2) and has been replaced by the phrase 'non-national'. The leading legislation is as follows:

- Irish Nationality and Citizenship Act, 2001

- Immigration Act, 1999

- Refugee Act, 1996 (as amended) (see 12.1.3).

- Secondary legislation on the free movement and establishment of services.

The most important legislation is perhaps the Refugee Act, a measure that, as its long title states, is 'to give effect to the convention relating to the status of refugees, 1951, the so called Geneva Convention as well as the Dublin Convention of 1990'. The subjects of this legislation are persons who fall within the definition of refugees, and who are invested with rights, coextensive in large measure, with Irish citizens. These measures are considered in **chapter 12**.

2.7.9 CRIMINAL JUSTICE (UNITED NATIONS CONVENTION AGAINST TORTURE), ACT, 2000

The important and now universally accepted freedom from torture is now reflected in Irish statute law (see **2.6.5**). This Act became law on 14 June 2000. Its purpose is to give effect to the United Nations Convention Against Torture and Other Cruel Inhuman or Degrading Treatment. The Act creates a new statutory offence of torture that attracts a penalty of life imprisonment. The seriousness of the crime is evident in that jurisdiction is withheld from the District Court (s 8). Section 8 also provides that bail may only be granted by the High Court in the case of a person charged with an offence under the Act.

Torture, is defined in accordance with the United Nations Convention, as an act or omission by which severe pain or suffering, whether physical or mental, is intentionally inflicted on a person for the purpose of:

- obtaining information
- punishment
- intimidation and
- any reason that is based on any form of discrimination.

On the other hand, the now well recognised terminology of cruel inhuman or degrading treatment, normally associated with international human rights' condemnation and prohibitions (e.g. Art 3 of the ECHR) is not described in the Act.

2.7.10 HUMANITARIAN LAW – THE GENEVA CONVENTIONS

Humanitarian or Geneva law, often considered a facet of human rights law, is transposed into the Irish *corpus juris* by the Geneva Convention Act, 1962, the Red Cross Acts, 1938–1994 and the Prisoners of War and Enemy Aliens Act, 1956. The Geneva Convention aims to protect four categories of persons; that is the wounded and sick during land and sea warfare, prisoners of war and civilian populations under military occupation. The Geneva Conventions (Amendment) Act, 1998 enabled Ireland to ratify two protocols adopted in 1977, additional to the four Geneva Conventions of 1949.

The first additional protocol relates to the protection of victims of international armed conflicts. The second additional protocol provides the standards to be applied to non-international armed conflicts, such as civil war. Those standards concern the protection of civilians, while 'acts or threats of violence the primary purpose of which is to spread terror among the civilian populations' are specifically targeted and outlawed. In this protocol, like protocol one, there are also human rights safeguards as well as provisions for an amnesty at the end of the conflict for the protection of internees or detainees.

2.7.11 GENOCIDE ACT, 1973

The Genocide Act, 1973, gives effect to the Genocide Convention adopted by the General Assembly of the United Nations on the 9 December, 1948. Genocide is, according to the Convention, any of the following acts committed with intent to destroy, in whole or in part, a national, ethnical, racial or religious group, as such:

'(a) *killing members of the group;*

(b) *causing serious bodily or mental harm to members of the group;*

(c) *deliberately inflicting on a group conditions of life calculated to bring about its physical destruction in whole or in part;*

(d) *imposing measures intended to prevent birth within the group.*

(e) *forcibly transferring children of the group to another group.'*

2.8   Conclusion

Since 1922 the Irish courts have developed a considerable constitutional jurisprudence concerning human rights. We must note especially the doctrine of unenumerated rights, notable for its reliance on natural law foundations. It is as yet debatable whether natural law has been permanently eclipsed by other conceptual criteria. But should we keep faith with the concerns of this chapter, the following questions may have more relevance for us, (a) whether the Irish constitutional commitment to human rights remains and (b) at what level?

Our survey suggests a positive answer to the first question, reinforced by the deluge of human rights law springing from international sources (including the ECHR) that has added considerable weight to our established guarantees.

A possible answer to our second question may be that Irish law has become more human rights compatible, recently demonstrated by the openness of the courts to liberal models of interpretation, particularly those stemming from ECt.HR jurisprudence. Those recent trends lead us to predict that stock restraints, such as those contained in clauses like 'in accordance with law', may be applied more rigorously and explained with more precision than has been the case. This, together with an evident hospitality towards international standards, for example in the growing acceptance by the courts of international rulings as having some precedent value, presages an ever deepening engagement with human rights by Irish law.

CHAPTER 3

THE EUROPEAN CONVENTION ON HUMAN RIGHTS

3.1   Introduction

In 1949, a group of nations, appalled by the atrocities of World War II and concerned about the rise of Communism in central and eastern Europe, came together to form an organisation named the Council of Europe. In the statute establishing this organisation, the founding members pledged to uphold the principles of the rule of law and to protect the human rights and fundamental freedoms of all persons within their jurisdiction. However, it was recognised that to make this political promise a legal reality something more was needed: a document which would set out the minimum content of these protected rights and freedoms and, perhaps even more importantly, establish mechanisms to ensure the enforcement of these guarantees.

Hence, in 1950, the Council of Europe adopted the European Convention for the Protection of Human Rights and Fundamental Freedoms (usually known as the European Convention on Human Rights or the 'ECHR') although it did not in fact come into force until 3 September 1953. From that time onwards, the ECHR has become increasingly significant, to the extent that today it is often described as the single most successful international human rights instrument. Its influence can be seen from the fact that it is now a precondition to membership of the European Union that the applicant country has signed and ratified the ECHR.

The major achievement of the ECHR lies in the fact that it provided a mechanism whereby both *individuals* and *states* could make a complaint to the institutions established under the ECHR. Individuals could complain if they felt that their rights were being infringed by their own governments and states could complain if they felt that another state within the Council of Europe was abusing the rights of those within its own jurisdiction. A contracting state could be held to account by both an individual from within its jurisdiction and also another state concerned by its actions. As will be seen however, the ECHR has become something of a victim of its own success, in that increasing support for the ECHR has led to increasing strains being placed on its institutions. Radical procedural reform was introduced in 1998 in an attempt to remedy this, although it is too early to tell whether this has been sufficient. It should also be noted that there has not always been universal approval of the decisions of the institutions of the ECHR, with some arguing that these have been on the whole too conservative, others arguing they have been too liberal.

Ireland was one of the original signatory states to the ECHR but has only now, over 50 years later, passed legislation to bring it into domestic law.

3.2   The Scope of the ECHR

3.2.1   TYPE OF RIGHTS PROTECTED

The ECHR primarily covers what are sometimes referred to as 'first generation rights', ie civil and political rights. It does not, on the whole, protect 'second generation' or economic and social rights. The reason for this was essentially pragmatic. The original founding states knew that it would be much more difficult to get agreement on a text which included both types of rights. Instead, they pursued a short and non-controversial text that states could and would immediately accept, and agreed to consider at a later date the issue of economic and social rights.

The ECHR, as originally drafted, has since been supplemented by a number of protocols, some of which contain further substantive rights guarantees, others which deal with procedural matters. The protocols are separate treaties meaning that each individual state has a discretion whether or not to adopt them and that, with one exception, they bind only those states which have adopted them. (The exception being Protocol 11 which we shall look at later). The protocol mechanism has therefore been used for those most controversial issues such as the death penalty on which it was unlikely that there would be unanimous agreement.

3.2.2   TYPE OF PERSONS COVERED

In Article 1 of the ECHR, the state parties agree 'to secure to *everyone within their jurisdiction* the rights and freedoms defined in the ECHR and its substantive protocols'. It can be seen therefore that the rights contained in the ECHR are not confined to the citizens only of contracting states. Instead, these states agree to protect the ECHR rights of all those within their jurisdiction, regardless of whether they are nationals or non-nationals. This can be contrasted with the position under the Irish Constitution where it remains unclear to what extent non-nationals enjoy the guarantees contained in the fundamental rights provisions.

3.2.3   TEMPORAL SCOPE OF THE ECHR

The ECHR binds states only from the moment of ratification. It is not retrospective in its effect. Therefore, as a general rule a complaint can only be made in relation to an event which occurred after the state concerned ratified the ECHR, although where it is alleged that there has been a continuing abuse of rights, so that events prior to ratification are so closely bound up with events post-ratification that the two cannot be divorced, the ECHR institutions may consider matters that arose before the state involved had ratified the ECHR. However, such cases are highly unusual.

3.2.4   RESERVATIONS AND DEROGATIONS

Any state, when it signs up to the ECHR, can agree to be bound by all of its provisions. However, most of the contracting states have taken advantage of a concession in the ECHR that allows States at the time of signature or ratification to enter a *reservation* in respect of a provision of the ECHR if it considers that any law then in force in its jurisdiction is not in conformity with that particular provision. This prevents claims against that law being brought on the basis that it infringes the rights guaranteed by the particular provision. In other words, the law is given a certain immunity from challenge on ECHR grounds. However, such reservations cannot be vague, over-broad or of a general character. Although states can make these reservations, it must be clear to what they relate and they must be limited in nature.

A further type of restriction that can be made on the scope and application of the ECHR is the *derogation*. Article 15 of the ECHR allows states to derogate or opt out of its obligations under the ECHR but only in time of war or other public emergency and only to the extent strictly required to meet the exigencies of the situation. A number of states have invoked Article 15. For example, in the early 1990s, the UK government derogated from its obligations under the ECHR in relation to the length of time persons can be kept in custody without trial in respect of the holding of suspects in Northern Ireland. This derogation was challenged but the European Court of Human Rights accepted that the situation in the North at the time did constitute a public emergency so that Article 15 could be invoked. There is some scope for abuse of the Article 15 procedure but this is tempered by the requirement that states keep its use under review and the ability of the European Court of Human Rights to declare that the particular circumstances no longer justify derogation under Article 15.

3.3   Structures of the ECHR

As noted above, the ECHR has been very successful in terms of the number of state signatories and the number of important decisions it has generated. However, as time went on it became clear that the structures initially established by the ECHR did not have the time, money or other resources to deal with the increasing number of applications being made to them. A certain amount of piecemeal structural reform was achieved in an attempt to alleviate the situation but by the late 1980s, it was clear that nothing short of wholesale structural change would have the required effect. Therefore, the states embarked on an ambitious drafting project that eventually resulted in Protocol 11. Protocol 11 was opened for signature in 1994 and came into force on 1 November 1998.

Under the system before Protocol 11, there had been a two-tier system for applications, with the initial application being dealt with by a body known as the European Commission of Human Rights, which was composed of experts in the area. If the Commission did not consider that the case was admissible, the application would be dismissed at this stage. If the Commission considered that the application was admissible, it would form an opinion on the substantive merits of the case which would be sent on to the European Court of Human Rights, a body composed of judges. The Court would then give a determinative decision as to whether any or all of the complaints set out in the application were valid. However, both the Court and the Commission were part-time bodies and this two-tier system inevitably led to delay, particularly as the number of state signatories increased and knowledge of the ECHR became more widespread. Indeed, by the time Protocol 11 came into force there was a backlog of over 6,700 cases before the Court. The need for fundamental reform was evident, the aim being to produce a system which was relatively quick and cheap yet which would operate in a way that would produce quality case law and maintain confidence of all the participants in the system.

Protocol 11 attempted to achieve this primarily by abolishing the old Court and Commission and replacing these by a single, full-time Court. This Court would deal with *all* applications, at least to some extent, which has the merit that all applications will receive some level of judicial scrutiny.

The structures which now exist under Protocol 11 are as follows.

3.3.1 THE EUROPEAN COURT OF HUMAN RIGHTS (ECt.HR)

This new body, unlike its predecessor, is full-time and permanent. All contracting states *must* accept the jurisdiction of the ECt.HR in all cases and so it is an institution to which all individuals wishing to make a complaint will have access. The ECt.HR is now the first international court to which individuals have automatic direct access for alleged breaches of a State's international obligations. The ECt.HR is composed of judges who are elected by the Parliamentary Assembly of the Council of Europe from a list of three candidates supplied by the relevant state, although there is no necessity that such judges be nationals of the State nominating them. To make its operations more efficient, the ECt.HR has been divided into four *sections*, which are designed to be balanced in terms of regional and gender representation. These sections can then be sub-divided into the following:

3.3.1.1 Committees

These are composed of three judges who sift through the initial individual applications made to the ECt.HR and weed out any clearly unfounded cases at an early stage. The committees perform the 'filtering' role previously carried out by the old Commission, except for inter-state complaints, the admissibility of which must be considered by a chamber. Judges on committees are appointed for a twelve-month period.

3.3.1.2 Chambers

Chambers are the bodies which will decide the majority of cases and are composed of seven rotating judges. When a case is assigned to a particular section, the President of that section and the judge from the country against which the complaint has been made will always sit on the chamber. Chambers can consider both the admissibility of a case and the merits of a case.

3.3.1.3 Grand Chamber

This is composed of 17 judges and will decide the most important cases, namely those which raise a question of interpretation or application of the ECHR or those which raise a 'question of general importance'. Cases can end up before the Grand Chamber in two ways. First, a Chamber may decide that a case before it raises a question of interpretation of the ECHR or that the case is likely to prompt a departure from existing case-law, and so relinquish jurisdiction to the Grand Chamber. Secondly, if a Chamber has given judgment in a case any party to the case may in exceptional circumstances request that the case be referred to the Grand Chamber for re-hearing. The Grand Chamber shall accept the request if the case raises a serious question affecting the interpretation or application of the ECHR or a serious issue of general importance. The Grand Chamber will always contain the President of the ECt.HR, the two Vice-Presidents (who are also Presidents of sections), the Presidents of the other sections and the judge of the respondent state. This requirement that certain judges always sit on the Grand Chamber is designed to ensure that there is consistency in the decisions of the Grand Chamber, which is particularly desirable given that the Grand Chamber decides the most important cases.

3.3.1.4 Plenary court

Unlike under the old system, the full ECt.HR will only rarely sit and when it does, it decides purely procedural matters such as the composition of chambers, the appointment of Presidents of the chambers and the adoption of rules of procedure. The plenary ECt.HR sits only in an administrative capacity. It no longer sits in a judicial capacity.

3.3.2   THE COMMITTEE OF MINISTERS

This is the executive or political arm of the Council of Europe and is composed of the foreign ministers of each of the contracting states (although in fact the day-to-day business of the Committee of Ministers is performed by career diplomats who are the permanent representatives of the contracting states in Strasbourg). The principal role now of the Committee of Ministers is to ensure the enforcement of the judgments of the Court. For example, it can discuss cases on a six-monthly basis and the relevant national representative on the Committee must explain what steps have been taken by his or her government to enforce the particular decision. The Committee of Ministers however has lost the power it had under the old system to decide whether there had been a violation of the ECHR in those non-contentious cases which were not referred to the ECt.HR by the Commission. The now limited role of the Committee of Ministers is seen to enhance the credibility of the system as a *judicial* rather than political process.

3.3.3   SECRETARIAT OF THE COUNCIL OF EUROPE

Under the old system this was in fact the only full-time body. It remains a full-time body and is composed of nationals of all of the contracting states. The secretariat has a supervisory role in relation to reservations made by states and in relation to the ratification of the ECHR by potential contracting states. It also has the power to request reports from states to explain how their domestic law reflects the provisions of the ECHR.

3.3.4   PARLIAMENTARY ASSEMBLY OF THE COUNCIL OF EUROPE

This institution is composed of members of each of the national parliaments of the member states of the Council of Europe who are appointed by these parliaments to sit on the assembly. The main function of the parliamentary assembly is to examine whether the domestic law of countries applying for membership of the Council of Europe complies with the ECHR and to recommend individual states to the Committee of Ministers for membership of the Council of Europe.

3.4   Taking a Case to Strasbourg

There are two types of applications which can be made to the ECt.HR. These are individual applications and inter-state applications.

Previously, states had a discretion as to whether to accept the jurisdiction of the ECt.HR to hear individual petitions brought against them but since the entry into force of Protocol 11 all present and future parties to the ECHR must accept the right of individual application to the ECt.HR. The jurisdiction of the ECt.HR to hear inter-state complaints, ie a complaint brought by one state against another on the basis of the latter state's treatment of those within its borders, has always been compulsory.

Each of these forms of application will be examined in turn, followed by an examination of the admissibility criteria in respect of these applications.

3.4.1   INDIVIDUAL APPLICATIONS

Article 34 of the ECHR now provides that not only individuals but also groups of individuals and also non-governmental organisations (NGOs) claiming to be the victim of a violation of the ECHR can make an application to the ECt.HR. States are obliged to ensure that they do not hinder in any effective way the exercise of this right, so that for example, applicants and potential applicants must be able to communicate freely with the Strasbourg authorities in relation to their application. As mentioned earlier, this ability on the part of an individual to make a complaint against their government to an international court has been critical to the success of the Strasbourg system, not just in terms of public confidence in the process but also in producing a body of case-law which has been influential not just in the domestic legal systems of Europe but in other domestic legal systems and in international human rights jurisprudence generally.

3.4.2 INTER-STATE APPLICATIONS

Article 33 of the ECHR enables any state party to the ECHR to make a complaint against any other state party to the ECHR. This is an immediate right, ie all states enjoy this right and it is not dependent on any other act by any of the parties involved. The thinking behind such a mechanism is that every state party is one of the collective guarantors of the ECHR rights, so that every state party can take action designed to ensure the implementation of the ECHR and the protection of public order of Europe generally. For this reason, the right is not limited to cases involving nationals of the state bringing the action. Hence, a number of Scandinavian countries brought a case against Greece in the 1960s in relation to the treatment by the Greek government of its own nationals. In fact, for an application to be brought, there does not even have to be a threat to any particular individual, merely a danger that the ECHR is about to be breached.

However, this procedure has not been used that often, perhaps because states are aware of the political risks in bringing an action against another state. In fact under the old system, while approximately 15 inter-state complaints were made to the Commission, only one made it as far as the Court, this being the case brought by Ireland against the United Kingdom government in respect of the treatment of prisoners in Northern Ireland under emergency legislation introduced in the early 1970s (discussed below). Under the new procedure of course, all such applications will be dealt with by at least a chamber of the ECt.HR, but it remains to be seen whether this will have the effect of increasing the number of such applications.

3.4.3 MAKING AN APPLICATION

It is very easy to make an initial application to the Strasbourg authorities. All that is required is some sort of written complaint setting out the nature of the claim the person or state is making. This complaint should be sent to the Registrar of the ECt.HR who will then forward an official application form to the applicant. When the official application form is returned, the application will be assigned to a section whose President then appoints a 'judge-rapporteur'. The judge-rapporteur then decides whether the application will be dealt with by a committee or a chamber. The committee or chamber will then decide whether the application should get past this first stage in the process. To do so, it must satisfy a number of criteria known as 'admissibility criteria'.

3.4.3.1 Admissibility criteria

It is in fact quite difficult to get over the hurdle of admissibility and the vast majority of claims fall at this first stage. (Prior to the coming into force of Protocol 11 less than two per cent of claims were ultimately held to be admissible). The first two admissibility criteria relate to both individual and inter-state applications, the remaining four relate only to individual applications.

Exhaustion of local remedies

It is a cardinal procedural rule of international law that before a claim can be brought before an international court, all domestic remedies must be exhausted and this requirement is reiterated in Article 35 of the ECHR. This is consistent with the idea that domestic law, rather than international law, should be at the forefront in the protection of human rights. As a general rule therefore, potential Irish applicants must take their case to the highest possible court (which will usually be the Supreme Court) and lose there, before they can apply to Strasbourg. However, the ECt.HR has put something of a gloss on this requirement. It has held that Art 35 requires to be exhausted only those remedies which *relate to the breach alleged* and are *available and effective*. For example, in an Irish context, if the Supreme Court has already given judgment in a practically identical case and that judgment is unfavourable to a person who believes that their ECHR rights have been violated, that person will not be required to go all the way to the Supreme Court before they apply to Strasbourg where this would clearly be in vain.

Six-month rule

A complaint can only be considered by the ECt.HR if brought within six months of the date on which the final domestic decision is made. The reason for such a time limit is three-fold. First, it ensures a degree of legal certainty, secondly, it ensures that cases raising an ECHR point are examined within a reasonable time and thirdly, it ensures that the facts of the case can be established. The rule is usually strictly applied in relation to individual complaints (except for example in cases of ill-health) but there is more flexibility in relation to inter-state complaints, as these tend to relate to on-going situations of abuse and hence it is more difficult to identify an act or decision from which time should run. This six-month period is a relatively short period of time but the potential harshness of this rule is alleviated by the fact that any sort of communication with the Strasbourg authorities within this time frame will be enough to satisfy this condition.

Applicant must be a victim of the complained violation

As noted earlier, this criterion relates only to individual complaints. It does not relate to inter-state applications as the entire purpose of such applications is to enable claims to be brought on behalf of all the peoples of Europe. The Strasbourg authorities have drawn a distinction between those who are 'directly affected' and those who are 'indirectly affected' by a violation. As a general rule, only the former can claim to be 'victims' so as to satisfy this criterion. This distinction can be particularly important where there is a group that claims that its rights have been violated. For tactical reasons it is advisable to submit both a group application and an application on behalf an individual member of the group as the latter is more likely to be able to show he or she has been directly affected. In any case, what needs to be demonstrated is a clear link between the applicant and the treatment complained of, so that complaints of a very general nature from individuals who object simply to the existence of a law or government action will not satisfy this condition. Again however, the Strasbourg authorities have shown some flexibility here, for example allowing family members to lodge a complaint where the person most directly affected is physically not able to do so.

Application must not be anonymous

This requirement is designed to weed out frivolous or sinister claims. However, the condition relates only to the application when it is sent to Strasbourg; the Strasbourg authorities can decide to conceal the identity of an applicant from the public at large for reasons of security or confidentiality.

Matter must not have been examined already by the Strasbourg court or submitted to another international procedure

This condition ensures that there is no duplication of complaints either within the Strasbourg system or as between the Strasbourg system and another international procedure. An applicant cannot continuously apply to the ECt.HR to re-hear a complaint it has already decided upon. However, if circumstances have fundamentally altered since the matter was previously examined, the ECt.HR may decide that it will look afresh at the application.

Complaint must not be manifestly ill-founded, an abuse of the right of petition or incompatible with the convention

Again this condition is designed to eliminate entirely unmeritorious complaints. The ECt.HR is always concerned to ensure that its procedures are used in the manner intended. So for example, a complaint cannot be made if it is not in fact directed at the state or an arm of the state, because to allow such claims would be incompatible with the ECHR which is designed to protect individuals from the actions of the state. Further, the ECHR should not be used for political or propaganda reasons, so that applications which are made purely for these purposes will be inadmissible as an abuse of the right of petition.

If the complaint is declared inadmissible, it will go no further. If it is declared admissible by a committee, it will then be sent to a Chamber for a determination as to the merits of the case. As mentioned earlier, the Chamber can relinquish jurisdiction to the Grand Chamber if the case raises a serious question of interpretation of the ECHR or it may prompt a departure from existing case-law. If the Chamber does not relinquish jurisdiction, it will make a decision as to the merits of the case. Once it gives its decision, the parties have three months within which to request a referral of the case to the Grand Chamber. The Grand Chamber will only consider such a referral in cases of grave importance. If the parties do not make such a request within this three-month period, the decision of the Chamber becomes final.

3.4.4   PROCEDURES BEFORE THE ECt.HR

As a general rule, the admissibility stage is conducted on paper. However there is provision whereby oral hearings as to admissibility can take place but if this occurs the hearing as to the merits of the case will usually be conducted simultaneously.

If the application is declared admissible, the parties will be encouraged to reach a friendly settlement. If this cannot be achieved, then a date for the oral hearing will be set. Each side will submit written submissions before the hearing and the ECt.HR may also direct that briefs (known as *amicus curiae* or 'friends of the court' briefs) may be submitted by NGOs or other groups having expertise in the particular area involved.

The hearing itself is open to the public (unless the parties and the ECtHR agree otherwise). It is adversarial in nature but is more informal than proceedings before an Irish court. For this reason, applicants often represent themselves, though respondent states will always have legal representation. It is possible for an applicant to get *legal aid* but Council of Europe legal aid is low compared to domestic legal aid systems and usually consists only of a contribution to the travel and subsistence expenses of the applicant, together with a flat rate contribution to legal costs. It is most unlikely therefore that a lawyer would decide to represent an applicant for purely financial reasons. It also often occurs that legal academics rather than practitioners appear before the ECt.HR. The ECt.HR will decide on the order of oral submissions and usually prescribes a time-frame within which these are to be presented. Given the backlog of cases before it, the ECt.HR is always keen to ensure that hearings proceed in as speedy and efficient a manner as possible.

3.4.5 REMEDIES

The ECt.HR is limited in terms of the orders it can make. It cannot for example strike down a piece of legislation or order that the state take a particular course of action, such as reforming legislation or reviewing administrative practice.

However, it can:

(a) declare that a violation of the applicant's ECHR rights has occurred;

(b) award compensation (although this tends not to be a huge sum);

(c) order interim measures pursuant to a procedure known as a Rule 39 indication, which can be used in emergency situations where the applicant faces an immediate risk of irreparable harm, usually where the applicant's life is at risk or where there is a substantial risk of serious ill-treatment;

(d) award costs of the case to the applicant. Again these tend not to be the full measure of an applicant's costs.

As we have seen, the execution of the ECt.HR's decision will be policed by the Committee of Ministers who may take certain measures to ensure that the decision is given effect to. The ultimate sanction for failure to comply with a ECt.HR decision is, however, political rather than legal in nature in that the non-compliant state may be ordered to leave the Council of Europe, although this has never been done.

3.5 The ECHR in Irish Law

Ireland was one of the original signatories of the ECHR and its impact on both Irish domestic law and international human rights law has been significant. However, its impact in Irish law has not been as great as it perhaps could have been because of the fact that until very recently, legislation to incorporate the ECHR, ie make it part of domestic law, had not been passed. This meant that although the state had *international* obligations under the ECHR and had to answer before the ECt.HR in Strasbourg for any alleged breach of ECHR rights, it did not have to do so before the domestic court. The corollary of this was that an individual who felt aggrieved by any government action on ECHR grounds could not get a remedy before the Irish courts on this basis but was instead required to go all the way to Strasbourg to seek relief. However, this position has changed since incorporating legislation, the European Convention on Human Rights Act, 2003, came into force on 31 December 2003.

3.5.1 STATUS OF THE ECHR IN IRISH LAW

The need for separate incorporating legislation is a result of the *dualist* approach to international treaties, an approach to which Ireland subscribes by virtue of Arts 15 and 29 of the Constitution. Under this approach, an international treaty does not become part of Irish law unless and until it has been incorporated into Irish law by way of some constitutional or legislative act. This can be contrasted with the *monist* approach to international treaties which regards international law as automatically applicable in domestic law, without the need for a further domestic act. The vast majority of Member States of the Council of Europe adopt the monist approach to international law, with Ireland and the United Kingdom being the two exceptions. However, with the passage of the UK Human Rights Act 1998 the ECHR became part of the domestic law of the UK, meaning that Ireland was the only country in the Council of Europe not to have incorporated the ECHR into domestic law. As stated earlier, this position has finally changed with the passage of the 2003 Act, the primary impetus for which was the Good Friday Agreement, wherein the

Government agreed to bring forward measures to strengthen and underpin the constitutional protection of human rights, which proposals would draw upon the ECHR and other international human rights instruments. The Government also specifically agreed to examine further the question of the incorporation of the ECHR in this context. Moreover, the Government pledged that the measures brought forward would ensure at least an equivalent level of protection of human rights as would pertain in the North. It was in this context that legislation incorporating the ECHR was brought into force on 2 October 2000 in the North and there was an anticipation that similar legislation would be introduced in this State at that time. In fact, however, the Irish government only introduced draft legislation, the European Convention on Human Rights Bill, in 2001, which draft legislation, with only very minor amendments, was passed into law on 30 June 2003.

Prior to the passage of the 2003 Act, the courts had stated on a number of occasions that they were obliged to give effect to constitutional provisions and domestic legislation even where these were in clear conflict with provisions or case-law of the ECHR (see for example, *O'B v O'S* [1984] IR 316). This was in accordance with the principle of the primacy of domestic law which had been stressed by Irish courts from as early as 1960 in the case of *In re Ó Laighleis* [1960] IR 93. In recent years there did appear to have been a new willingness on the part of the Irish courts to at least listen to arguments based on the ECHR and to attempt to ensure that constitutional and legislative interpretation accorded with the ECHR (see for example, *Irish Times Ltd v Murphy* [1998] 2 ILRM 161) although of course they were not bound to do so. The courts seemed particularly willing to allow ECHR arguments to be raised when the existence of a claimed unenumerated constitutional right was under discussion. It is arguable that even though the 2003 Act is now in force, this position will remain relatively unchanged, as the terms of the legislation seem designed to protect the primacy of domestic law, particularly constitutional law. This issue is discussed further below.

3.5.2 INCORPORATION OF THE ECHR INTO IRISH LAW

Before examining the exact terms of the 2003 Act it is instructive to look briefly at the ways in which the ECHR *could* have been incorporated into Irish law, not least because many feel that the method actually adopted is unsatisfactory and may require amendment or repeal in the not too distant future.

Methods of incorporation can be classified under two broad headings 'direct' and 'indirect' incorporation. 'Direct' incorporation results in the ECHR being given the force of law in the State so that the obligations imposed on the State by the ECHR will be binding on a domestic level as well as an international level. Direct incorporation can be achieved through a variety of means and the method chosen will depend to a large extent on the nature of the relevant domestic legal order. For example, in those countries with written constitutions it may be decided to incorporate the ECHR into the constitution. This would then give the ECHR the same legal status as other human rights provisions in the constitution and mean that legislation which offends against the ECHR can be struck down on that basis. This method was considered in Ireland by the Constitutional Review Group (CRG), which ultimately recommended that only those provisions of the fundamental rights guarantees in the Constitution which were inferior, in terms of either content or linguistic style, to provisions of the ECHR should be replaced (and even here the CRG did not always recommend that the exact terms of the ECHR provisions be introduced into the Constitution – rather it recommended that text *drawn from* the ECHR be introduced). This 'partial' incorporation at a constitutional level can be contrasted with the approach in Sweden where the constitution was amended to provide that no law or regulation could be enacted which would be contrary to the obligations flowing from the ECHR. This approach is similar to the Irish constitutional provisions relating to membership of the European Union.

Alternatively, the ECHR could be given a status in domestic law which is lower than the

Constitution but higher than a piece of ordinary legislation. This 'intermediate' method has been used in France for example and has the effect that legislation may be struck down on the basis it is contrary to the ECHR, although constitutional provisions inconsistent with the ECHR will remain supreme. The third method of direct incorporation is to bring the ECHR into domestic law by way of either primary or subordinate legislation. By this method the statute incorporating the ECHR has the same status as any other piece of legislation, meaning that prior legislation can be struck down if it is contrary to the ECHR.

'Indirect' incorporation on the other hand involves the use of the ECHR as an interpretive tool (hence it is sometimes referred to as the 'interpretive model') so that the courts are obliged to interpret legislation in a manner which is consistent with the ECHR. However (although this depends on the exact terms of the incorporating measure) should this prove impossible, the court is not empowered to strike down the legislation; at best it is entitled to make a declaration to the effect that the legislation is incompatible with the ECHR and possibly to award damages on this basis. Likewise, if there is a written constitution, its provisions will not be struck down on the basis of incompatibility with the ECHR, so that the domestic primacy of the constitution remains intact. For these reasons, the interpretive model is often regarded as a weaker form of incorporation. However, its advocates argue that it is preferable to direct methods of incorporation which give too much power to the judiciary and result in the courts straying into area of law-making. This approach, for example, was favoured in the United Kingdom, not least because of the weight attached there to the doctrine of parliamentary sovereignty. The UK Human Rights Act 1998 provides that courts must interpret legislation in conformity with the ECHR, so far as this is possible, and where it is not possible the courts can make a declaration of incompatibility. However, it will then be left to the legislature to decide what, if any, action should be taken to remove this incompatibility. The UK Act allows the court to award damages for breach of ECHR rights by a 'public authority' (which is defined to include a court).

3.5.3   EUROPEAN CONVENTION ON HUMAN RIGHTS ACT, 2003

There has been much public debate about the form of incorporation to be adopted in Ireland and in particular, as to the resulting relationship between the ECHR and the Constitution. As stated earlier, draft legislation was finally published in 2001 which, despite considerable parliamentary debate, was passed into law, with only very minor amendments, as the European Convention on Human Rights Act, 2003 (an Act which has just nine sections). The 2003 Act appears to have been heavily influenced by the equivalent UK legislation, providing as it does that the courts shall, as far as is possible, interpret legislation in a manner compatible with the ECHR, and that superior courts (ie the High Court and the Supreme Court) may make declarations of incompatibility in relation to legislation and awards of damages against 'organs of the State' who act in a manner contrary to the State's obligations under the ECHR. The Act provides that such declarations of incompatibility can be made against 'a statutory provision or rule of law'. 'Rule of law' as defined includes the common law, and 'statutory provision' would seem to include legislation whenever enacted, meaning that *both* prior and subsequent legislation may be declared to be incompatible with the ECHR. Also, like the UK Act, the 2003 Act provides that a declaration of incompatibility does *not* affect the validity, continuing operation or enforcement of the relevant provision or rule of law.

The Act also provides that judicial notice shall be taken of the ECHR provisions and of decisions of the institutions of the ECHR and that a court shall 'take due account' of the principles established by these decisions when applying ECHR provisions.

However, there are some differences between the Irish legislation and the UK Human Rights Act. First, the Act provides that where a declaration of incompatibility is made, the Taoiseach shall cause such declaration to be brought before the Houses of the Oireachtas within 21 days. Secondly, where such declaration is made, a party to the proceedings concerned may apply to the Attorney General for compensation for any loss suffered by him as a result of the incompatibility concerned and the Government may then make an *ex gratia* payment in respect of such loss. Thirdly there is no Irish equivalent to s 19 of the UK Human Rights Act which provides that a Minister piloting proposed legislation through Parliament must make a statement to the effect either that the proposed legislation is compatible with the ECHR or to the effect that even though he cannot so state, the government still wishes to proceed with the relevant proposed legislation.

3.5.4 POSSIBLE EFFECTS OF INCORPORATION

By passing the 2003 Act into law, the legislature has chosen to incorporate the ECHR at a sub-constitutional level, so that the primacy of the Constitution will remain. In practice, therefore it would appear that plaintiffs will continue to rely on any constitutional right they might have as opposed to an ECHR right, and resort will be had to the ECHR only in limited circumstances. The converse of this is that in those areas where the Constitution offers little or no protection, the ECHR may have an important role to play. However there may be a number of difficulties in terms of the operation of the legislation.

- The 2003 Act provides that courts shall interpret legislation in conformity with the ECHR *'in so far as is possible* and *subject to the normal rules of interpretation'*. The normal rule that legislation is to be interpreted in a manner consistent with the Constitution will apply. This may give rise to a situation where a court would be obliged to interpret legislation so as to be in conformity with the Constitution even though this would have the result that the legislation could not be interpreted in a manner consistent with the ECHR. Applicants in such cases may ultimately decide that resort to Strasbourg is still necessary.

- The Act states that judges can make a declaration of incompatibility in respect of a law which is contrary to the ECHR but can provide no other remedy. Further, the Act states that such a declaration will not affect the continued operation of the law or rule in question. Judges will be placed in the uncomfortable position of knowing that a law is contrary to the ECHR, yet not being in a position to do anything about it other than make this declaration. Some commentators suggest that in such circumstances judges (of the superior courts) will prefer simply to declare the legislation unconstitutional, with the usual consequent effect that it would be struck down.

- The Act provides that after a declaration of incompatibility is made the applicant may apply to the Attorney General for compensation and the amount of such compensation is to be decided with reference to the principles applied by the ECt.HR in awarding just satisfaction. This mechanism has been criticised for focusing on compensation to the exclusion of other remedies. Also, it takes the decisions as to whether to award compensation and as to the amount of compensation out of the realm of those most used to making such decisions, the judiciary, and places them instead in the hands of a member of the Executive, the Attorney General. The level of awards is likely to be low, certainly lower than those paid out in other areas of law, which may undermine public confidence in the system as one which effectively protects human rights. Finally, there is no mechanism whereby the level of compensation awarded can be appealed and the possibility of a successful judicial review of such a decision would appear to be remote.

- The Act states only that Taoiseach is required to lay any declaration of incompatibility before the Oireachtas; it does not impose any further obligations on the Taoiseach, for example, to suggest to the Oireachtas what must be done to cure the incompatibility declared. In the absence of such government proposals, it might be difficult for the Oireachtas to provide a solution, certainly with any degree of speed. In the interim, the unsatisfactory position will be that a law which has been declared by the courts to be incompatible with the ECHR will remain in force, with others possibly being adversely affected by its continued operation. On an even more fundamental level, it is possible the legislature would decide to do nothing and leave the litigant the only option of taking his case to Strasbourg. If this becomes the norm, the impact of this type of incorporating measure will be minimal.

- Although the Act provides a remedy for those who claim their ECHR rights have been breached by an *'organ of the State'*, such proceedings can be brought only if no other remedy in damages is available. ECHR-based claims are only to be available as a last option with priority given to pre-existing causes of action. Presumably therefore, an ECHR-based claim could be defeated on the basis the applicant has not exhausted existing and available remedies. Further, the term *'organ of the State'* is narrowly defined and does not include, for example, the courts. Also, the limitation period for the commencement of such claims is extremely short, although this can be extended by the court if it is in the interests of justice so to do.

- The Act does not provide for legal aid to be available for those seeking declarations of incompatibility. Again, the effectiveness of the legislation may be undermined by the absence of such provision.

- The Act says nothing in relation to the need for training and education in the field of human rights for both judges and administrators. This is a crucial element if incorporation is to have any real effect, particularly in light of the traditional lack of awareness of, and recourse to, the provisions of the ECHR, especially in the lower courts. The failure to provide expressly for such training and education is a serious flaw in the legislation, which may lead to uncertainty and inconsistency in the interpretation and application of law.

However, the passage into law of the 2003 Act should have the effect of increasing popular awareness of the ECHR, at least to some extent. It will also oblige judges for the first time to listen to arguments based on the ECHR and have due regard to the decisions of the ECt.HR. This might then have the knock on effect of decisions from other legal systems, which have regard to ECHR jurisprudence, being considered by the Irish courts. Finally, the courts will be obliged as far as is possible to interpret legislation in a manner compatible with the ECHR so that points of ambiguity are resolved in a ECHR-friendly manner (provided there are no competing constitutional arguments).

Clearly, much will depend on the attitude of judges, lawyers, parliamentarians and administrators as to the effect the legislation will have. Of course, it may in time be viewed as unsatisfactory and new or amending legislation may always be drafted. In this sense, the use of the legislative model offers some flexibility. Ultimately, however, as some have suggested, this issue may have to be re-visited on a constitutional level if true, effective incorporation is to occur.

3.6   Rights Protected by the ECHR

As mentioned earlier, the rights covered by the ECHR are primarily civil and political rights, as no consensus existed at the time of the drafting of the ECHR as to either the content or the justiciability of economic and social rights. Any such rights as have been included in the ECHR have been introduced by means of an additional protocol rather than a substantive amendment to the main ECHR, leaving the decision to accept such rights to the individual contracting parties.

However, this is not to detract from the success of the ECHR system in respect of those rights which do come within its scope, although it must be acknowledged that some provisions have been more successful than others. For example, Article 14, the non-discrimination provision, has yielded little in terms of increased human rights protection. This is primarily due to the way in which the article is drafted, providing as it does that the right not to be discriminated against can only be claimed in conjunction with another article in the ECHR. In other words, there is no free-standing freedom from discrimination, let alone right to equality, provided by the ECHR. In this regard, the Irish Constitution can be said to offer more protection that the ECHR. However, this is due to change with the coming into force of Protocol 14 to the ECHR, which will introduce a much stronger equality guarantee.

Other rights protected by the ECHR include:

3.6.1   RIGHT TO LIFE

Article 2 of the ECHR provides that persons should not be intentionally deprived of their right to life by the forces of the State. However, this right will not be violated where death occurs as a result of the use of force in self-defence, to effect an arrest or to quell a riot or insurrection. Further, Article 2 does not prohibit the use of the death penalty. This is the subject of a separate protocol, Protocol 6, which provides, in respect of those states which have signed and ratified it, that the death penalty shall be abolished (save in times of war). The issue of abortion has not yet been dealt with by the court but the former Commission has suggested in the past that Article 2 may be relevant to such an issue, in the sense of providing a measure of protection to the foetus. However, this would have to be viewed in the light of the potentially competing rights of the mother and in light of the discretion which national authorities would have in relation to such a controversial issue (*Paton v UK* (1981) 3 EHRR 408).

3.6.2   FREEDOM FROM TORTURE

Article 3 provides that all persons are to be free from torture and inhuman or degrading treatment or punishment. No definition of these terms is given but the ECt.HR has made it clear that a 'sliding scale' of prohibited treatment is covered by the article, with torture being seen as the most serious form of such treatment but with other 'lesser' types of treatment covered too, including the use of corporal punishment in state schools in the UK (*Campbell and Cosans v UK* (1982) 4 EHRR 293). After a long period in which the ECt.HR failed to find that any state had committed torture contrary to Article 3, in a number of recent cases it has found Turkey guilty of a breach of the ECHR in this regard (see, eg *Aksoy v Turkey* (1997) 23 EHRR 533). Article 3 is also one of only a very small number of substantive rights provision in the ECHR from which no derogation is allowed, indicating the seriousness with which this type of treatment was regarded by the drafters of the ECHR.

3.6.3   RIGHT TO LIBERTY

Article 5 provides that no one shall be deprived of their liberty save in certain specified circumstances and even then this can only be done if the law in the individual country clearly provides for it. The type of circumstance in which deprivation of liberty can lawfully occur include detention:

(a)   of a person after conviction of an offence;

(b)   for the purposes of bringing a person before a court; and

(c)   for the purposes of preventing unlawful entry into a country or of facilitating lawful deportation from a country.

Article 5 also provides that persons who are deprived of their liberty by state authorities must be able to challenge the lawfulness of that detention and be released if such challenge is successful.

3.6.4 RIGHT TO A FAIR TRIAL

Article 6 provides that persons are entitled to a fair trial, before an independent and impartial tribunal. This right applies to both civil and criminal proceedings. Article 6 also provides that proceedings are to take place within a reasonable time and in fact the bulk of cases under this article have related to the length of time which has elapsed before a final domestic decision has been given. It also enshrines the principle that persons shall be presumed innocent until proven guilty, a provision which has been the subject of some litigation relating to domestic laws which penalise persons for or allow adverse inferences to be drawn from, their failure to answer questions or to produce documents. Certain other specific guarantees are provided for persons charged with criminal offences, such as the right to free legal aid if a person is not in a financial position to secure legal assistance.

3.6.5 RIGHT TO RESPECT FOR PRIVATE AND FAMILY LIFE

Article 8 of the ECHR has been one of the most successful provisions, not least because of the expansive view adopted by the ECt.HR towards its interpretation. It provides that persons are entitled to a right to respect for their private and family life, and home and correspondence, although such rights may lawfully be interfered with in certain specified circumstances, such as where this is necessary to prevent crime or protect the rights of others. Article 8 has been held to cover a wide range of interests, including:

(a) freedom from criminal prosecution for consenting adult homosexuals (*Dudgeon v UK* (1982) 4 EHRR 149);

(b) non-discrimination in succession laws as between marital and non-marital children (*Marckx v Belgium* (1980) 2 EHRR 330);

(c) freedom from unwarranted surveillance from state security forces (*Klass v Germany* (1980) 2 EHRR 214); and

(d) freedom from deportation where to do so would result in the break-up of the family unit (*Moustaquim v Belgium* (1991) 13 EHRR 802).

Indeed, it is in relation to the concept of 'family life' that the ECt.HR has been most expansive. From very early on, the ECt.HR indicated that the protection afforded by Art 8 did not depend on the existence of formal legal ties between the individuals involved. Instead, the ECt.HR would examine whether real and close personal ties exist between the parties and if they do, the ECtHR will hold that this is 'family life' within the meaning of Art 8. Family life has been held to exist between:

(a) engaged couples provided their relationship is sufficiently established (*Wakefield v UK*, Application No. 15817/89);

(b) non-marital fathers and their children (*Keegan v Ireland* (1994) 18 EHRR 342); and

(c) children and parents who are no longer co-habiting and whose relationship has broken down (*Berrehab v Netherlands* (1989) 11 EHRR 322).

This broad view of the notion of family life is in marked contrast to that traditionally taken by the Irish courts and it is not surprising that Article 8 has featured prominently in the Irish cases which have come before the ECt.HR.

3.6.6 FREEDOM OF THOUGHT, CONSCIENCE AND RELIGION

Article 9 protects the right to freedom of thought, conscience and religion which is stated to include the right to change one's religion etc, and to manifest one's religion in worship, teaching and practice. The exercise of this right to manifest one's religions is however, subject to certain restrictions if these are necessary for the protection of public safety, order, health or morals and the protection of the rights of others. Again, it is possible for states to prohibit public displays of worship if it can be objectively shown that this is required for example to prevent public disorder.

3.6.7   FREEDOM OF EXPRESSION

Article 10 has been one of the most significant articles of the ECHR, protecting as it does everyone's freedom of expression, which is stated to include the freedom to hold opinions and receive and impart information. Again however this freedom may be restricted if this is necessary to further some specified objective, such as the protection of the reputation or rights of others or the protection of morals. For example, a number of cases have come before the ECt.HR in which controversial books, paintings and films have been banned or subject to restrictions and these restrictions have been upheld by the ECt.HR on the grounds they were necessary to protect morals or the rights of others, especially young persons (see, eg *Muller v Switzerland* (1991) 13 EHRR 212). Also, Art 10 is unusual in that it stresses that the exercise of the right to freedom of expression carries with it duties and responsibilities. However, there is no doubt that this article has on the whole been interpreted in a way which is beneficial to the press, not least in the decision relating to the level of damages in libel awards in the UK, a decision with ramifications for Irish law (*Tolstoy Miloslavsky v UK* (1995) 20 EHRR 442). The ECt.HR has also stressed that comment on particular types of persons, especially those in politics and government, is vital in the interests of a democratic society and will receive a high degree of protection (see, eg *Lingens v Austria* (1986) 8 EHRR 407).

These are just some of the rights protected by the ECHR and include those most likely to be of relevance within the Irish system. We turn now to the cases which have come before the ECt.HR involving the Irish government.

3.7   Irish Cases Before the European Court of Human Rights

At the time of writing twelve cases involving the Irish government have been heard and determined by the ECt.HR. Eleven of these were taken by persons exercising the right of individual petition under the ECHR (a right, incidentally, that the Irish government was the first government to accept), and in nine of these the Government was found to have been in breach of the ECHR. One case was taken by the Irish government itself against another state party to the ECHR, using the inter-state application mechanism.

There have of course been other cases which have been accepted as admissible by the ECHR authorities but which have been settled by the Government before any decision was handed down by the ECt.HR. Some cases have even been settled before a decision as to admissibility has been made by the Strasbourg authorities. The advantages of such 'friendly settlements' can include, for the applicant, a greater financial award than he or she was likely to receive from the ECt.HR and for the State, the benefits of confidentiality and of avoiding a finding by an international court that it is in default of its human rights obligations. Usually, such settlements will involve some sort of undertaking on the part of the Government to introduce legislation to amend the law in question.

The cases which have reached the ECt.HR do not by any means tell the whole story of the Irish government's compliance with its international human rights obligations under the ECHR. They do however give an idea of the areas of most concern relating to the observance of these guarantees on a domestic level.

Lawless v Ireland ((1979) 1 EHRR 15) – This was in fact the first ever case to be decided by the ECt.HR and involved a claim by the applicant that his rights under Art 5 had been breached by the Irish government when he had been interned as a suspected member of the IRA pursuant to emergency legislation introduced in the late 1950s. The ECt.HR however, found that the Irish government had lawfully derogated from its obligations under Art 5 due to the existence of a public emergency threatening the life of the nation (due to increased IRA activity at the time) and hence it could not conduct any further investigation of the applicant's claims.

Airey v Ireland ((1979–80) 2 EHRR 305) – The applicant complained that the lack of legal aid in judicial separation proceedings violated her right of effective access to the courts under Art 6 and her right to private and family life under Art 8 (Mrs Airey argued that a judicial separation from her husband was necessary to ensure the peaceful enjoyment of the family life she enjoyed with her children). The ECt.HR agreed with her contentions and approved terms of compensation to be awarded to the applicant. The Government subsequently introduced a restricted, non-statutory scheme of civil legal aid and advice in 1980 (this being later replaced by the Civil Legal Aid Act, 1995).

Johnston v Ireland ((1987) 9 EHRR 203) – The applicants in this case were a couple who lived together but were unable to marry as one of them was already married and divorce was at that time prohibited in Ireland. They complained that their rights to private and family life under Art 8 and their right to marry and found a family under Art 12 of the ECHR had been breached by the prohibition on divorce in Irish law and the legal treatment of their child, especially for the purposes of succession rights. The Court found that there had been a violation of their family rights in respect of the inferior status given in Irish law to children born outside of marriage, but rejected their claims based on the prohibition on divorce. Following this decision, the Government introduced the Status of Children Act, 1987 which effectively abolished the legal status of illegitimacy.

Norris v Ireland ((1991) 13 EHRR 186) – The applicant was a practising homosexual who claimed that his right to respect for private life under Art 8 had been violated by the continued existence on the statute books of legislation criminalising homosexual activity between consenting male adults, even though the evidence indicated that it was unlikely this legislation would be invoked against the applicant. The ECt.HR found that the fact that the legislation existed and could in theory be used against the applicant constituted an interference with his right to respect for private life for which the Government had not forwarded any sufficient justification. The ECt.HR rejected the Government's contention that such legislation was necessary for the protection of health and morals (arguments which had met with some success before the Supreme Court which rejected Mr Norris's constitutional challenge to the legislation). This decision of the Court caused some controversy and it took five years for Irish law to be amended so as to be in line with the judgment in *Norris*, when the Criminal Law (Sexual Offences) Act, 1995 was passed, which decriminalized most forms of homosexual activity and provided for the same age of consent as for heterosexuals.

Pine Valley Developments Ltd v Ireland ((1992) 14 EHRR 319) – This case arose out of a complicated series of cases and legislative amendments relating to the grant of planning permission. The net result was that the first applicant company was not entitled to the benefit of legislation retrospectively validating decisions to grant planning permission which the Supreme Court had found to be void. (The first applicant company had sold on the relevant property to another company which was owned by one individual and this company and individual also were applicants to the case). The applicants claimed that their property rights under Art 1 of Protocol 1 had been breached and also that that had been discriminated against in the exercise of these property rights, contrary to Art 14. The ECt.HR upheld this latter claim and awarded substantial damages, in excess of £1m, to the applicants.

Open Door Counselling Ltd v Ireland ((1993) 15 EHRR 244) – This case related to an injunction which had been granted against the applicants prohibiting them from distributing information to pregnant women about the availability of abortion services in the United

Kingdom. The ECt.HR found that the extensive nature of the injunction constituted an unwarranted interference with the freedom of expression of the applicants under Art 10 and damages were awarded to the applicants. While the injunction was not immediately lifted, a subsequent constitutional referendum took place which resulted in an amendment to the Constitution allowing for such information to be distributed within the State.

Keegan v Ireland ((1994) 18 EHRR 342) – The applicant was the father of a non-marital child whose mother attempted to place the child for adoption without the consent of the applicant. The ECt.HR agreed with the applicant's claim that the Irish legislation which allowed this to occur was contrary to his right to respect for family life under Art 8. The ECt.HR also upheld his claim that the lack of procedures allowing him to challenge the mother's decision was a violation of his right of access to the courts pursuant to Art 6. As a result of this judgment the Adoption Act, 1998 was introduced which provides consultation procedures for natural fathers in the adoption process and sets out the circumstances in which such procedures do not need to be followed.

Heaney, McGuinness and Quinn v Ireland ((2001) 33 EHRR 264) – The applicants complained that s 52 of the Offences Against the State Act, 1939 which provides for the punishment or imprisonment of persons who fail to give certain information to the Gardaí constituted a breach of their right to silence pursuant to Art 6 and of their freedom not to express themselves pursuant to Art 10 of the ECHR. The ECt.HR found that there had been a violation of Art 6 (both of the right to silence and the presumption of innocence) and having held in this way, found that no separate issue arose under Art 10.

D.G. v Ireland ((2002) 35 EHRR 53) – The applicant who was a minor at the time of the impugned action, was the subject of High Court proceedings taken to vindicate his constitutional and statutory rights. In the course of these proceedings, the High Court ordered that he should be placed in St Patrick's Institution, a juvenile detention centre, even though he had not committed a crime, because his welfare and safety required him to be placed in secure accommodation, thus outweighing his right to liberty and there was no other secure facility in which he could be placed. The High Court also ordered that, while in St Patrick's Institution, he should be subject to a different regime to that experienced by juveniles detained there as a result of the criminal justice system. This action was upheld by the Supreme Court and the applicant applied to the ECt.HR on the basis that his right to liberty under Art 5 of the ECHR had been infringed. The ECt.HR found that while Art 5(1)(d) permits the detention of children *for the purpose of* educational supervision, on the facts of this case it could not be said that the detention of the applicant in St Patrick's Institution was sufficiently connected to the provision of education supervision. The ECt.HR found first that St Patrick's Institution did not of itself constitute 'educational supervision' for the purposes of the ECHR. It then noted that when the relevant detention orders were made no specific proposal for the secure and supervised education of the applicant was in place and even though the applicant was eventually placed in an educationally appropriate facility this did not occur until six months after his release from St Patrick's. Therefore, it could not be said that his detention in St Patrick's Institution constituted an 'interim custody' measure 'for the purpose' of an educational supervisory regime, which was followed speedily by the application of such a regime and a violation of the applicant's right to liberty had occurred.

Murphy v Ireland (judgment of 10 July 2003) – The applicant was a pastor with the Irish Faith Centre, a Christian ministry based in Dublin which sought to have an advertisement aired on a local radio station. However, the advertisement was prohibited pursuant to s 10(3) of the Radio and Television Act, 1988 which outlawed the broadcast of any advertisement directed towards any religious or political end. The applicant claimed that this ban violated his rights under Art 9 and 10 of the ECHR, although the ECt.HR examined his complaint under Art 10 only. The ECt.HR held that there were relevant and sufficient reasons for the measure, especially bearing in mind the religious sensitivities of the Irish people and that religion had been extremely divisive in Irish society in the past. The

ECt.HR also noted that, other than advertisements in the broadcast media, the applicant's religious expression was not restricted. Further, the ECt.HR accepted the Government's contention that to allow some form of religious advertising could result in unequal treatment between particular religions, or particular religious views could benefit a dominant religion and could result in unequal consequences for national and independent broadcasters. In all the circumstances the ECt.HR found there was no violation of Art 10.

Doran v Ireland (judgment of 31 July 2003) – This case related to the length of civil proceedings instituted by the applicants against a number of defendants, including two firms of solicitors, claiming, *inter alia*, negligence in relation to the purchase of a plot of land. The proceedings, which went all the way to the Supreme Court, were begun in July 1991 but did not finally end until December 1999 when the issue of costs was determined. The applicants claimed that their right to a fair hearing within a reasonable time under Art 6, and their right to an effective remedy under Art 13 of the ECHR had been violated. The ECt.HR found that despite the fact that the proceedings had not been administratively or factually complex they had lasted almost eight-and-a-half years and that the delay in the proceedings had been caused largely by the relevant authorities and had placed strain on the applicants. Therefore there had been a breach of Art 6. The ECt.HR also rejected the Government's argument that the applicants could have taken a constitutional action in relation to the delay as the Government had not cited a single example of a case where this had been successfully done. The ECt.HR found that no effective, adequate or accessible remedy had been available to the applicants and that accordingly Art 13 of the ECHR had also been violated. The ECt.HR awarded the applicants €25,000 in damages.

Ireland v United Kingdom ((1979–80) 2 EHRR 25) – This was in fact the first inter-state application to be decided by the ECt.HR. The Irish government complained about the treatment of detainees in detention centres in the North, primarily that the use of certain interrogation techniques known as the 'five techniques' constituted a violation of the prohibition on torture and inhuman or degrading treatment. The ECt.HR found that the treatment involved did constitute inhuman and degrading treatment but did not amount to torture. Interestingly the United Kingdom government had, prior to this decision being handed down, stated that it had ceased to use such methods in the North and that it would not use them again in the future. The case was significant not only in relation to its particular facts but also because it highlighted the impact which the threat of international scrutiny could have. However, it must be said that it has not been followed by a flurry of inter-state applications, presumably for the reasons given earlier.

So we can see that the number of cases in which the Irish government has appeared before the ECt.HR is relatively small. As stated earlier, this does not give the full picture of the level of compliance on the part of the Irish government with its obligations under the ECHR. A number of cases involving the Irish government have been settled before they reached the ECt.HR. Also a number of cases are currently making their way through the Strasbourg procedures or are pending before the ECt.HR (covering subjects such as the level of damages awarded in defamation cases (*Independent News and Media Plc v Ireland*, Application No. 55120/00) and the seizure of aircraft pursuant to international sanctions imposed on the Federal Republic of Yugoslavia (*Bosphorus v Ireland*, Application No. 45036/98)) and of course there must be a number of legitimate cases which never reach Strasbourg at all, due to lack of awareness of the remedies offered there.

3.8   Conclusion

It remains to be seen what impact the European Convention on Human Rights Act, 2003 will have in Irish law. At the very least it is hoped that it will generate increased awareness of the existence of a human rights document other than the Irish Constitution and provide another plank on which to mount human rights-based claims. However, given the form of incorporation chosen by parliament it is likely that the authorities in Strasbourg will continue to face cases brought by persons who claim that their rights under the ECHR have not been adequately protected under Irish law.

3.9 Checklist for Taking a Case to the European Court of Human Rights

CAN I TAKE A CASE TO THE EUROPEAN COURT OF HUMAN RIGHTS?

The following criteria all have to be satisfied before a person can take a case to the European Court of Human Rights.

- The complaint must be about a right or interest which is protected by the Convention, eg right to privacy, right to family life, right to a fair trial, freedom of speech.

- The complaint must be against some State body or relate to some act for which the State may be responsible.

- The action complained of must have occurred in the last six months.

- The person taking the case must be the person who is actually affected by the action or a person or group authorised to take the case on his/her behalf.

- The complaint must not have been submitted to any other international court or body for consideration.

- All possible domestic remedies must have been tried unless these are clearly not going to be effective or they are not available.

- The person making the complaint must not do so anonymously.

HOW DO I TAKE A CASE TO THE EUROPEAN COURT OF HUMAN RIGHTS?

The following steps should be taken to lodge a claim with the European Court of Human Rights.

- Action must be taken within *six months* of the date of the particular decision or conduct complained of.

- Depending on how much time is available one of the following steps should be taken:

  - If the six-month time limit is about to run out a short letter should be sent to the Registrar of the European Court of Human Rights in Strasbourg setting out brief details about the claim, including what right or interest it is claimed has been breached. The Registrar will then forward an official application form for the complainant to fill in.

  - If time is not about to run out, the complainant should write to the Registrar for an official application form.

- The complainant must fill in the application form and return it to the Registrar. Care must be taken not to include language which is insulting or tends to show that the complaint is political or personal rather than legal in nature.

Completed application forms should be sent to:

Registrar of the European Court of Human Rights,
Council of Europe,
F-67075 STRASBOURG CEDEX,
France

CHAPTER 4

INTERNATIONAL HUMAN RIGHTS LAW

4.1 Introduction

Ireland is a party to many international human rights instruments as well as being a member of a number of international organisations. As a result, it has a wide variety of international obligations in the area of human rights law, obligations which exist at both the regional and global levels. However, as has already been discussed, it has long been held (see *Re O' Laighleis* [1960] IR 93) that because Ireland is a dualist country these obligations are not binding on a domestic level, meaning that individuals cannot seek to enforce these obligations before national courts (unless of course the particular measure has been incorporated into Irish law, which some treaties have been). The status of international human rights law in Irish law has recently been confirmed in the case of *Kavanagh v Governor of Mountjoy Prison* [2002] 3 IR 97, in which the applicant sought to challenge the validity of his detention on foot of conviction by the Special Criminal Court (SCC) on the basis that his trial before the SCC had been found to be in breach of the International Covenant on Civil and Political Rights (ICCPR) by the UN Human Rights Committee. Both the High Court and Supreme Court confirmed that *Re O' Laighleis* remains the law and that the Constitution is clear and unambiguous in its terms in relation to the status of international agreements. It draws a clear distinction between domestic and international law until such time as the Oireachtas decides to pass legislation incorporating the particular piece of international law into Irish law. Until such incorporating legislation is passed, *neither* the terms of the ICCPR *nor* the views of the Human Rights Committee (HRC) could prevail over the legal effect of a domestic statute or a conviction by a duly constituted domestic court.

However this does not mean that the State's duties under international human rights law have no practical effect in the domestic sphere. A number of recent developments in domestic law and practice owe their origins to obligations arising by virtue of the State's acceptance of various international human rights measures. It is therefore important to examine the nature of some of these obligations. However, because it is not possible to look at every human rights measure to which Ireland is party, only the more significant of these measures will be discussed in this chapter.

It should be noted at the outset that in terms of deciding whether and when to accede to a human rights treaty, Ireland has stated that its practice is to accede to such a treaty only after it has taken all necessary domestic measures to ensure that the State is in compliance with the obligations set out in the particular treaty. This approach can be criticised from a factual perspective in that it is clear from the instances in which the State has been found to be in violation of a human rights treaty that the State has not in fact taken all necessary compliance measures before acceding to the treaty. Moreover, the approach can be criticised in that it fails to recognise the evolving nature of obligations under international human rights instruments, which generally require states to develop policies and practices designed to change societal attitudes, to promote a culture of human rights and, if necessary, to take positive steps to benefit persons and groups traditionally discriminated against. It is not sufficient for the State simply to say that it only accedes to a human rights treaty after it has taken all necessary steps for compliance, as this fails to understand that the act of accession itself gives rise to these ongoing obligations.

4.2   Universal Human Rights Law

The emergence of the notion that there are certain rights which are universal, ie enjoyed by everyone, no matter where in the world they live, and moreover that these rights might be enforced by international or domestic bodies, is one of the most significant legal developments of the twentieth century. The fact that the existence of such rights is almost taken for granted today belies the controversial beginnings of the concept. However, today, there are a variety of international instruments dealing with general and specific human rights issues and a number of international organisations whose task it is to ensure the implementation of these treaties.

4.2.1   UN CHARTER

The United Nations (UN) was founded in the wake of World War II with a view to preventing the sort of devastation wrought in the period before and during that war. Its founding document is the UN Charter of 1945 (the UN Charter), which, it has been said, 'internationalised' human rights. The UN Charter set out the purposes of the UN, one of which was to promote and encourage respect for human rights and fundamental freedoms for all, and required members to pledge that they would take both joint and separate action, in conjunction with the UN, to achieve this purpose. In this way, the state parties to the UN Charter, by signing up to it, accepted that human rights were the subject of *international* and not just domestic concern. Having said this, however, attempts to build more detailed human rights provisions into the UN Charter failed and it was to be some twenty years before such provisions were incorporated into an international treaty. Instead, the focus of the UN Charter was the establishment of institutions which could give effect to the statements of purpose and principle contained in the Charter. The most important body within the UN in terms of the protection of human rights is the Economic and Social Council (ECOSOC).

4.2.1.1   Economic and Social Council (ECOSOC)

Articles 62 and 68 of the UN Charter state that ECOSOC can, *inter alia*, make recommendations to promote respect for human rights and set up commissions in the economic and social fields for the protection of human rights. One of the first acts of ECOSOC was to establish the Commission on Human Rights in 1946. To an extent, the Commission is the most 'senior' human rights body in the UN system, although its importance and influence have been questioned through the years, not least because the members of the Commission sit as government representatives rather than independent experts and hence the usefulness of the Commission as a tool of independent scrutiny has been somewhat blunted. Nonetheless, it does have a number of potentially important functions, including those of setting standards in the area of human rights, increasing public awareness of human rights and investigating allegations of gross violations of human rights. The Commission also has the power to create whatever subsidiary mechanisms it considers necessary to enable it to carry out its functions under the Charter and a number of such mechanisms have been established over the years, for example, working groups on the suppression of apartheid and on disappearances and rapporteurs appointed to report on the human rights situation in specific countries. However, by far the most important mechanism established by the Commission on Human Rights has been the Sub-Commission on the Prevention of Discrimination and the Protection of Minorities.

The major mechanism used by the Commission to monitor the protection of human rights is the '1235' procedure, named after the Resolution establishing the mechanism. The resolution was adopted in 1967 and makes specific reference to human rights abuses in non-self-governing territories and apartheid, these being the factors which prompted the passing of the resolution. It authorises the Commission to undertake a thorough study of situations which reveal a consistent pattern of human rights violations. Hence, the power to initiate the process of investigation is left in the hands of the Commission itself, although it is possible that the initial impetus may come from a state or the Sub-Commission.

The Commission carries out two forms of activity under Resolution 1235. It can hold an annual public debate to discuss various violations, and following on from this, it may decide to investigate specific countries or cases. If the Commission does decide to conduct such an investigation, it will appoint a person or body to assist in this, although there has been criticism about the perceived lack of independence and expertise of some of these persons. In theory, such persons can conduct on-site interviews and visits to the state involved, but in practice, such visits will only occur if the state in question consents, so that, to an extent, the 1235 procedure is dependent on state co-operation, although it would appear that the level of co-operation has improved in recent years. When the investigation is complete, the investigator will report back to the Commission, which can then make a recommendation in relation to future action to ECOSOC, which can do likewise to the General Assembly.

In relation to those situations which are mentioned at annual public debate but where no formal investigation occurs, a number of options are available. First, the Commission may draft a resolution either condemning the activity or calling for all available information to be submitted to it. Secondly, the Commission may ask the government concerned to respond to the allegations in writing before its next session. Thirdly, the Commission may refer the matter to the Security Council with a view to the adoption of some sort of punitive measure. Finally, the mere fact of the matter being mentioned in public debate may cause political pressure to be brought on the government concerned and this pressure can be generated by other states, the media or, often, non-governmental organisations (NGOs). Indeed, one of the biggest advantages of the 1235 procedure is the fact that it is a public procedure and publicity of itself can equal pressure.

Another advantage is that the power of initiative is in the hands of the Commission itself so that it does not have to wait on any other person or body to start an investigation. However, it has been said that, since the members of the Commission are representatives of their countries, its choices in relation to which countries to investigate have been deeply political. For example, the Commission resisted calls in the 1980s to investigate Iraq, at a time when Iraq was doing business with a number of US and UK companies, but in 1991, in a move clearly prompted by the Iraqi invasion of Kuwait, the Commission appointed Special Rapporteurs for Iraq and Kuwait, with the latter being concerned only with human rights violations committed by Iraq in Kuwait and not with any violations by Kuwait either before or after the invasion. Therefore, the choice of states to be investigated is not necessarily a reflection of where the most reliably attested violations occur, but rather is, in part at least, the result of political manoeuvring, with the most influential states able to escape scrutiny. This has had the knock-on effect of undermining confidence in the Commission and led to calls for an enhanced role in the process for the Sub-Commission or some other non-political body. The 1235 procedure has also been criticised for being too cumbersome to respond to urgent situations where immediate action is required and that it appears to come into operation only in truly terrible situations of abuse, with less extreme cases slipping through the net.

4.2.1.2   Sub-Commission on the Prevention of Discrimination and the Protection of Minorities

In contrast to the Commission on Human Rights, the members of the Sub-Commission on the Prevention of Discrimination and the Protection of Minorities do sit in an independent capacity (although they are nominated by the Commission from lists provided by the states, so that in practice there has been a degree of politicisation of the Sub-Commission but not to the extent of that of the Commission). The activities of the Sub-Commission go far beyond what its name suggests and, in fact, it has become the main body of experts relating to human rights in the UN system, jealously guarding its own sphere of operations to such an extent that it has from-to-time come into conflict with its supposedly superior body, the Commission.

The major mechanism which the Sub-Commission utilises to supervise state respect for human rights is the '1503' procedure. This procedure, named after ECOSOC Resolution 1503, which brought it into being, enables the Sub-Commission to investigate allegations of gross violations of human rights. The Sub-Commission does not begin such investigations of its own initiative, but rather will only act on the basis of communications sent into it by persons or groups with reliable information about the alleged violations. In other words, communications do not have to be made by the actual victims of the alleged violations and it is common for the 1503 procedure to be initiated by NGOs (often using communications drafted by lawyers), providing a degree of flexibility to the procedure. There are, however, certain criteria which all communications must satisfy before they will be considered by the Sub-Commission, for example, the communication must not be vague in its terms, or manifestly political, and all relevant domestic remedies must have been exhausted by the complainant before sending in the communication to the Sub-Commission. It is also important to realise that the communication will only be considered if it tends to show a *consistent pattern* of gross human rights violations. In other words, the 1503 procedure is not designed to provide a remedy for an individual complaint relating to an isolated incident.

If the admissibility criteria have been satisfied, the Sub-Commission will establish a Working Group which examines the allegations in more detail and if the Working Group considers that the issue merits further attention, it places the matter on the agenda of the Sub-Commission. The Sub-Commission can then either refer the matter on to the Commission or decide to give the state concerned more time to redress the situation giving rise to the allegations.

If the matter does go on to the Commission, it has a number of options, including sending envoys out to the country involved to get information, entering into dialogue with the state to try to resolve the situation, keeping the matter 'under review' or, if the situation is sufficiently serious, referring it to the UN Security Council or the UN General Assembly. Finally, the Commission may decide to transfer the matter to the 1235 procedure.

A defining feature of the 1503 procedure is that all communications and discussions based thereon and all action taken on foot of such discussions are confidential. This has led to much criticism and the Commission has now adopted the practice of publicly announcing the names of those states which are currently under investigation, and also the names of those states which are no longer under investigation. It does not, however, give details of the allegations made or of any specific action taken by the Commission in respect of these. However, the cloak of confidentiality will be dropped if the Commission decides either to refer the case to the Security Council or General Assembly or to transfer the matter to the 1235 procedure, at which point the matter will become one of public record. Clearly most if not all states are anxious to keep allegations of human rights abuses quiet and seek to avoid either of these options being taken, primarily by being co-operative with the Commission. If this does not happen, states run the risk that the Commission will decide to invoke the sanction of publicity by resorting to the 1235 procedure or to the General Assembly, which it has done on a number of occasions. It would appear that more and more states are learning from this and, in general, are adopting a more co-operative approach in respect of the 1503 procedure

The confidential nature of the 1503 procedure can encourage both governments and individuals to participate in the process and this then increases the potential sources of information available to the Sub-Commission and Commission. However, the fact that what is done with this information is kept hidden from the public leads to accusations of partiality on the part of the Commission, and also makes it difficult to evaluate what standards the Commission uses in its decision-making. Too much confidentiality can lead to too little confidence in the process.

4.2.1.3 Thematic Studies

In answer to some of the criticisms levelled at the 1235 and 1503 processes, the Commission and Sub-Commission have, since the early 1980s, established what are known as thematic studies, which as the name suggests, are set up to investigate a particular type of human rights abuse, rather than a particular state. This mechanism has a number of advantages over the 1235 and 1503 procedures, namely that the persons appointed to carry out such studies are usually recognised human rights experts, the procedures involved tend to be more flexible, and because the studies are directed at a particular theme rather than a particular state, they are less dependent on the co-operation of any individual state. Also, such studies can be used in urgent cases and tend to be more victim-oriented, with Special Rapporteurs and Working Groups carrying out on-site investigations and hearing first-hand accounts of alleged abuses. These thematic studies, which have included subjects such as disappearances, extra-judicial executions, arbitrary detention and child prostitution, have tended to be very successful and have achieved results in places the 1235 and 1503 mechanisms have not even been able to reach, such as East Timor. Indeed, it appears that thematic studies have overtaken the 1235 and 1503 procedures as the favoured mechanism of the Commission and Sub-Commission for investigating alleged human rights abuses.

4.2.2 UNIVERSAL DECLARATION ON HUMAN RIGHTS

As mentioned earlier, the UN Charter focused more on the establishment of institutions which could supervise the enforcement of human rights rather than setting out in detail what such rights were. Efforts to draft an instrument which would contain a list of such rights continued, and in 1948 the Universal Declaration on Human Rights (the UN Declaration) was signed. The UN Declaration recognises two broad categories of human rights, civil and political rights and economic, social and cultural rights, and sets out a list of such rights. The rights protected are:

- The right to life, liberty, and security of the person

- Freedom from slavery

- Freedom from torture, inhuman or degrading treatment or punishment

- The right to recognition before the law

- The right to equality before the law and to equal protection from the law

- The right to an effective remedy for acts violating fundamental rights

- Freedom from arbitrary arrest, detention or exile

- The right to a fair trial

- The right to be presumed innocent until proven guilty and protection against retroactivity of the criminal law

- Freedom from arbitrary interference with privacy, family, home and correspondence and from attacks upon honour and reputation

- Freedom of movement within the borders of a state and the right to leave a country and return to one's own country

- The right to seek and enjoy asylum

- The right to a nationality

- The right to marry and found a family

- The right to own property

- Freedom of thought, conscience and religion

- Freedom of opinion and expression

- Freedom of peaceful assembly and association

- The right to participate in government of one's country

- The right to social security

- The right to work, to favourable conditions of work, the right to equal pay for equal remuneration and the right to form and join trade unions

- The right to rest and leisure

- The right to a standard of living adequate for oneself and one's family

- The right to education

- The right to participate freely in the cultural life of the community.

However, the Declaration is not a treaty. It was adopted by the General Assembly as a resolution having no force of law, its purpose being to set a standard, which states would strive in their domestic laws to achieve. However, as time has progressed, and particularly in the absence of binding international human rights treaties of universal effect, the status of the Declaration in international law has changed. It is now generally recognised that the Declaration does have some legal effect and that at least some of its provisions are legally binding. The difficulty lies in identifying which of the rights in the Declaration have this character, and to what extent. What is clear however is that the Declaration has been consistently relied on by the United Nations when applying the human rights provisions of the UN Charter, and by state governments and international organisations when invoking human rights norms. The Declaration has been extremely important in the development of the notion and content of international human rights law.

4.2.3 INTERNATIONAL COVENANT ON CIVIL AND POLITICAL RIGHTS

The International Covenant on Civil and Political Rights (ICCPR) was eventually signed in 1966, after a long period of negotiation which had originally been designed to produce a single, binding human rights treaty that would have universal effect as opposed to the non-binding Declaration. However, it became clear that agreement on a single treaty would not be achieved and so a compromise was reached that two treaties rather than one would be drawn up, with a clear distinction between civil and political rights on the one hand and economic, social and cultural rights on the other, and with different enforcement mechanisms for each. The products of this process were the ICCPR and the International Covenant on Economic, Social and Cultural Rights (ICESCR) which were both signed in 1966 but which did not come into force for another ten years, in 1976. Ireland signed the ICCPR in 1973 but it did not come into force in this country until December 1989.

The ICCPR contains a broad catalogue of rights, which have been supplemented by a number of additional protocols relating to matters too controversial to be included in the main treaty, for example a prohibition on the death penalty. The rights protected by the ICCPR are:

- The right to life
- Freedom from torture and inhuman treatment
- Freedom from slavery and forced labour
- The right to liberty and security
- The right of detained persons to be treated with humanity
- Freedom from imprisonment from debt
- Freedom of movement and of choice of residence
- Freedom of aliens from arbitrary expulsion
- The right to a fair trial
- Protection against retroactivity of the criminal law
- The right to recognition as a person before the law
- The right to privacy
- Freedom of thought, conscience and religion
- Freedom of expression and opinion
- Prohibition of propaganda for war and of incitement to national, racial or religious hatred
- The right of peaceful assembly
- Freedom of association
- The right to marry and found a family
- The rights of the child
- Political rights
- The right to equality before the law
- The rights of minorities to enjoy their own culture, to profess and practise their own religion or to use their own language.

Protocol 1 is also extremely important in that it provides for a right of *individual petition*, in other words, unlike the 1235 and 1503 procedures, the ICCPR provides a mechanism whereby an individual can complain to an international body about treatment they have received at the hands of the state and seek redress for this. In this way, as well as in relation to the rights enumerated, the ICCPR resembles quite closely the ECHR. However, while complaints under the ECHR are made to a court, under the ICCPR they are made to the Human Rights Committee (HRC).

4.2.2.1 Human Rights Committee (HRC)

The HRC has a number of functions relating to the supervision and enforcement of human rights in those states which are parties to the ICCPR. It consists of eighteen members who are elected by the states parties to the ICCPR, but all members have legal expertise. The HRC meets three times a year and proceedings are held in private.

Again, because of the dualist nature of Irish law, decisions of the HRC do not have the effect of overriding Irish law, but its recommendations are usually implemented by the

Government, not least because it is keen to avoid embarrassment in the General Assembly. However, since 1990, the HRC has appointed rapporteurs whose duty it is to monitor the progress of individual countries in implementing recommendations of the HRC.

The two main powers of the HRC are to receive individual complaints and to consider state reports.

Individual petitions

As mentioned earlier, the individual complaints procedure is not mandatory under the ICCPR, unlike the ECHR. Individual complaints can only be made against those state parties who have ratified the First Optional Protocol and thereby accepted the jurisdiction of the HRC to hear such complaints. Also, the respondent state must not have entered a reservation in relation to the particular provision relied on. However, the ICCPR procedure for individual complaints does have some advantages over the ECHR procedure, in that primarily the admissibility criteria for making such a complaint are less strict and the length of time for the complaint to be determined is much shorter (averaging about two years to the ECHR's five).

Since the entry into force of the Protocol in 1976, the HRC has dealt with quite a large number of individual communications, and in dealing with those communications it considered admissible, the HRC has been able to develop a valuable body of case-law interpreting and applying the ICCPR and Protocol, which is significant given the universal nature of the ICCPR. A number of these cases have involved Ireland, a recent example of which was the *Kavanagh v Ireland* (Communication No. 819/1998, decision of 4 April 2001). In this case, the HRC found that the State had failed to demonstrate that the decision to try Mr Kavanagh before the Special Criminal Court, as opposed to the ordinary courts, was based upon reasonable and objective grounds. In these circumstances, the HRC found that the applicant's rights under Art 26 of the ICCPR to equality before the law and to equal protection from the law had been violated. In the wake of this decision, the Government asked the Hederman Committee which had been established to examine the Offences Against the State Act, 1939 to provide it with an interim report to assist the Government in its response to the HRC's view in this case. The Government also offered the sum of £1,000 to Mr Kavanagh by way of satisfaction of the decision of the HRC, but this sum was refused. In its response to the HRC, the Government simply quoted the majority view of the Hederman Committee that the continued existence of the Special Criminal Court was justified in the current circumstances without even citing the existence of a minority, dissenting view.

Admissibility criteria

As mentioned earlier, before an individual can make a complaint to the HRC, the government concerned must have accepted the right of individual petition by ratifying the First Optional Protocol. The individual must also satisfy certain criteria before a complaint can be made, in particular they must have exhausted all domestic remedies available to them before making the complaint to the HRC. The complaint must relate to a 'victim' of an alleged violation of the ICCPR, although this term has been broadly interpreted so that a representative of such a person can make the complaint. Class actions are not allowed. Nor are applications seeking to prevent future events from occurring. A major advantage of the ICCPR system is that there is no time-limit for the making of complaints, unlike under the ECHR system where complaints have to be made within six months of the alleged violation. This makes the ICCPR system a very valuable alternative, particularly for persons who cannot make a complaint to Strasbourg because they are outside the six-month time-limit. However, as with the ECHR, an application will not be considered by the HRC if it is currently before another international human rights body.

Making a complaint

Complaints are initially sent to the secretariat for the HRC in Geneva which will send out a model form to be filled out concerning the case (although it is not essential that this be used to make the complaint). If the complaint is not considered frivolous, it will be assigned to a member of the HRC known as the Special Rapporteur on New Applications who will prepare the case for consideration as to whether the complaint satisfies the admissibility criteria. The case is then sent to the Working Group on Communications who will decide whether the application meets the admissibility criteria. The Working Group can take up to eighteen months to decide this issue, although there are procedures whereby the case can be expedited if both parties are in agreement. It is worth noting that even if an application is initially considered inadmissible, it can be re-considered in the light of changed circumstances.

If a case is declared admissible, the respondent state will be asked to furnish its views on the merits of the complaint and it must do this within six months. The state's reply will be sent to the complainant who is given six weeks to respond. As a general rule the HRC will accept any further written submissions the parties may wish to submit and each side will be given the opportunity to comment on such submissions. At the end of this process, the matter may be put to a working group or rapporteur, but ultimately the merits of the case will be considered by the plenary HRC sitting at one of its thrice-yearly sessions. The HRC will make a decision based on the written submissions and other documents only, as there is no provision for oral argument before the HRC in respect of individual complaints.

In terms of the burden of proof, the HRC has established that, in cases where allegations of severe abuse have been made, the burden of proof will not fall exclusively on the complainant, so that it will not be enough for the respondent state simply to refute the complaint in general terms.

The HRC will issue a single consensus report, although occasionally dissenting opinions may be included. If the HRC has decided that a violation of the ICCPR has occurred, it will give suggestions as to how the situation may be rectified and may include a suggestion that compensation be paid. Again, however, these suggestions are not legally binding and it is primarily a matter of conscience for the respondent state as to whether to follow these suggestions. The HRC will then appoint a special rapporteur to follow up on the case and observe the manner in which the state gives effect to the decision of the HRC, which may involve the rapporteur meeting with NGOs and independent lawyers to ascertain their views on the action taken by the state. The HRC will also give information on these follow-up missions in their annual report.

Once the HRC makes its decision, this will be communicated to the parties involved. It will also be published in the HRC's annual report to the UN General Assembly and is generally available to the public. Until this time, however, proceedings are strictly confidential. It should also be noted that there is no provision for legal aid under the ICCPR system.

State reports

Unlike the right of individual petition, the state reporting obligation is mandatory, so that all state parties to the ICCPR must submit such reports to the HRC. Given the optional nature of the individual petition process, the state reporting procedure is very significant, and the HRC has broadened its role in this process to maximum effect to encompass areas which are not likely ever to form the basis of an individual complaint.

Once a state has ratified the ICCPR, it must submit an initial report as to the human rights situation existing in its jurisdiction. This report is then followed up by periodic reports every three to five years. The reports fall into two parts, a general section which details the legal, political and constitutional background of the state and the legal framework within which human rights are protected in the state, followed by a section which examines the ICCPR article by article and relates how the state has given effect to the right contained in the particular article. The report should also indicate the manner in which human rights knowledge and in particular knowledge about the ICCPR itself is promoted at every level in the state. Periodic reports must also address the issues raised in previous reports and deal with any findings of the HRC in relation to breaches of the ICCPR.

Each report is examined at a session of the HRC, at which representatives of the state under investigation must attend to answer questions, and the HRC can request supplemental information at this stage. Periodic reports receive the attention of a pre-sessional working group, which meets in the week immediately preceding the meeting of the HRC. This group will prepare a list of questions to put to state representatives and it is usually possible for interested parties to get copies of this list. This can be useful in identifying the approach the HRC will take and enables such interested parties to adopt a successful lobbying strategy.

The HRC then sits in public session to scrutinise the report, usually over two to three meetings. The state representative will introduce the report and will then be questioned by members of the HRC in respect of the content of the report. At the end of the public sessions, the HRC will sit in private to draft its Comments, which are the HRC's critique of the report and the state representative's response to questioning by the HRC. The Comments will identify factors impeding implementation of the ICCPR and make recommendations as to what action the respondent state should take to enhance its compliance with the ICCPR. These Comments are issued as public documents and are included in the annual report of the HRC to the UN General Assembly. The respondent government must make copies of the report available to citizens and interested parties in their country. Tape-recordings and a written summary of the proceedings are also available.

The role of NGOs and other independent parties

The success of the reporting procedure depends to a large extent on the participation of non-governmental organisations (NGOs) or other independent parties who can provide the HRC with alternative sources of information in relation to the human rights situation in a country, and challenge the government's assessment of its compliance with the ICCPR. It is vital that NGOs are made aware of the reporting process, and indeed each state is required to inform such groups that a report is being prepared. However, it appears that some states, including Ireland, have not always fulfilled their obligation to do this, and so many state reports have been submitted without the critical input of such groups. This is significant, because NGOs have no formal right of audience before the HRC, so that the major way they can influence the state reporting procedure is in the drafting of the report itself. If NGOs are not involved, it can mean that many issues are not covered by the report and that the state is not questioned on these issues by the HRC.

However, NGOs can still have an impact, even if not consulted in the drafting of the report, as the HRC will accept written submissions from interested parties during the reporting procedure, and NGOs are able to lobby the HRC members during the examination procedure. Members of the pre-sessional working group also tend to be willing to meet informally with NGOs, and these encounters can be important in influencing the questions which are put to the state representatives. It is, therefore, always advisable for NGOs to send representatives to the HRC sessions for this to occur, as experience has shown that direct meetings with members serve to enhance the impact of submissions.

Lawyers can play a role in advising NGOs in preparing these submissions, particularly in challenging the government's analysis of the legal situation pertaining in the state and of its compliance with the Covenant. These submissions should be as clear and simple as possible, and should reflect the state report by dealing with issues on an article-by-article basis. This will make the submissions much easier for the HRC members to use in examining the state report. The submission should also be as concise as possible, as HRC members tend to be very busy during the thrice-yearly sessions and will not have time to read lengthy and elaborate submissions. Submissions should be sent at least seven weeks in advance to the Secretary of the Human Rights Committee, Palais des Nations, Geneva, CH 1211, Switzerland. NGOs should also remember the value of publicity and should use whatever contacts they have to ensure that the reporting process is widely covered by both domestic and international media.

Ireland's record

Ireland's first report to the Human Rights Committee was submitted in 1992 and covered a number of areas. The HRC questioned the government representatives closely on issues including emergency legislation, lack of divorce legislation, inadequacies in the legal aid system and the treatment of travellers, areas in which there have been considerable improvements in recent years. It seems clear that the State's obligations under the ICCPR, including the reporting obligation, were significant in bringing about those changes.

The government department responsible for preparing Ireland's reports is the Department of Foreign Affairs, in particular the Human Rights Unit. This unit has a broad range of responsibilities, including overseeing the State's ratification of international human rights treaties and the compilation of reports required under various human rights instruments. In preparing Ireland's report under the ICCPR, the Human Rights Unit will liaise with other government departments responsible for particular areas, for example, the Department of Justice. These departments will also keep the Human Rights Unit up-to-date in relation to any action taken to implement the HRC's recommendations. Ireland's second periodic report was submitted in 1998 and its third periodic report is due in July 2005.

Emergency reports

The HRC has also, since 1991, developed a procedure to respond to what it considers to be emergency situations. This allows the HRC to request a state to submit a report, usually within three months if it considers the situation to be sufficiently serious and these reports are then considered by the HRC as soon as possible. The HRC will make comments on the emergency report and can request the UN Secretary-General to bring the situation to the attention of the competent organs of the UN, including the Security Council. NGOs have an important role in bringing emergency situations to the attention of the HRC.

Inter-state complaints

The ICCPR also provides for an inter-state complaint machinery that allows one state party to bring a complaint against another state that it has violated the ICCPR. However this can only be done if both states have recognised the jurisdiction of the HRC to hear such complaints. The mechanism is further weakened by the fact that the HRC is not entitled to make an adjudication on the complaint, but rather provides only a conciliation process designed to encourage a friendly settlement between the parties. If this is not reached, the HRC will prepare a report setting out the facts and submissions of both parties and may decide to appoint an ad hoc conciliation commission. This commission can ultimately suggest its own solution to the dispute but neither party is required to accept this proposal. The inter-state procedure is a very weak mechanism, and has nowhere near the same importance as the individual complaint and state reporting procedures.

4.2.4   OTHER INTERNATIONAL HUMAN RIGHTS INSTRUMENTS

Ireland is a party to a number of other international human rights instruments under which it has a variety of obligations. Some of the most important of these are the International Covenant on Economic, Social and Cultural Rights and the United Nations Convention on the Rights of the Child (discussed in **chapter 8**). As well as having the general obligation to ensure that its laws and practices are in conformity with the rights contained therein, these conventions impose a specific reporting obligation on the State. It appears that participation in the reporting process has been significant in focusing domestic and international attention on areas where Irish law and practice is deficient, and in bringing about change in these areas.

It should also be noted that the State is a party to a variety of regional human rights treaties, including the European Convention on the Prevention of Torture, the European Social Charter as well as of course the European Convention on Human Rights.

4.2.4.1 International Covenant on Economic, Social and Cultural Rights

The sister covenant to the ICCPR, the International Covenant on Economic, Social and Cultural Rights (ICESCR) was also adopted by the United Nations in 1966. It contains a detailed list or economic, social and cultural rights, including the following:

- The right to work

- The right to enjoyment of just and favourable conditions of work

- The right to form and join trade unions

- The right to social security

- The right to the protection of the family

- The right to an adequate standard of living, including adequate food, clothing and housing

- The right to enjoyment of the highest attainable standard of physical and mental health

- The right to education

- The right to partake in cultural life.

The ICESCR in many cases also sets out steps which are to be taken by states to achieve the realisation of these rights. For example, Article 6, which guarantees the right to work, provides that the steps to be taken by states shall include technical and vocational guidance and training programmes, policies and techniques to ensure full and productive employment under conditions safeguarding fundamental political and economic freedoms to the individual. Article 7, which provides the right to the enjoyment of 'just and favourable conditions of work' is even more detailed, stipulating that such conditions should ensure, *inter alia*, fair remuneration for all workers, safe and healthy working conditions and equal opportunity for everyone to be promoted in their employment. However, it is clear that the obligations imposed on states under the ICESCR are *progressive* rather that immediate in nature. States are obliged to take steps 'to the maximum of their available resources' to achieve 'progressively the full realization' of the rights set out in the ICESCR. Unlike the ICCPR, states are not expected to be in a position to implement the ICESCR fully at the time of ratification. The traditional reason given for this difference in the nature of the obligations imposed by the two covenants is essentially resource-based: civil and political rights such as those set out in the ICCPR generally require little economic input to be protected; economic and social rights, on the other hand, require some expenditure of economic and technical resources and the gradual alteration of social priorities. This cannot be done by the simple act of signature of an international agreement and states must be given time to adopt the measures best suited to their own economic, social and cultural conditions to achieve the full enjoyment of the rights set out in the ICESCR. However, the body charged with supervising implementation of the ICESCR, the Committee on Economic, Social and Cultural Rights (see below) has stated that, at the very least, the ICESCR imposes a core obligation to ensure the satisfaction of minimum essential levels of each of the rights contained in the ICESCR. It is clear that states must make some effort toward the attainment of these minimum levels.

The ICESCR, unlike the ICCPR, does not proscribe a mechanism for the making of individual complaints. Nor does it provide for the establishment of a treaty body to monitor implementation of the ICESCR. Instead, many of the monitoring responsibilities were given to ECOSOC which, in 1985, established the Committee on Economic, Social and Cultural Rights, a body composed of experts who sit in an independent capacity. The primary function of the Committee is to examine the reports which state parties to the ICESCR are obliged to submit. Parties must submit an initial report within two years of the entry into force of the ICESCR for the state concerned and then periodic reports every five years thereafter. The Committee also has days of general discussion and can authorise individual members to undertake follow-up missions to states to ensure the proper implementation there of the ICESCR. As with the ICCPR, Ireland signed the ICESCR in 1973 but did not ratify it until 8 December 1989.

4.2.4.2 International Convention on the Elimination of all forms of Racial Discrimination

The International Convention on the Elimination of all forms of Racial Discrimination (ICERD) was passed by the UN in 1965 and obliges states, *inter alia*, to commit themselves to a policy of eliminating racial discrimination, to condemn racial segregation, to guarantee the enjoyment of a range of rights on a non-discriminatory basis, to provide effective remedies and to adopt educational measures to combat prejudices which lead to racial discrimination. The treaty is one of the most widely ratified international human rights instruments.

Responsibility for supervising its implementation is given to the Committee on the Elimination of Racial Discrimination (the Committee). States are required to submit an initial report to the Committee within one year and comprehensive periodic reports every four years thereafter on the measures they have taken to give effect to the provisions of the ICERD. States are also required to submit brief updating reports in the intervening two-year periods. Further, the Committee can request special reports on urgent cases. It is interesting to note that although the ICERD expressly states that it shall not apply to distinctions drawn between citizens and non-citizens, state parties have been questioned about situations which appear to indicate discrimination among non-citizens based on their country of origin.

The ICERD also provides a mechanism whereby any state party can bring an alleged violation of the Convention to the attention of the Committee and allows for the making of individual complaints to the Committee, although the latter is only possible if the relevant state party has accepted the competence of the Committee to receive such complaints. Only a small number of states have accepted the jurisdiction of the Committee in this regard, although Ireland is one of them. Despite its status as one of the most widely ratified international human rights documents, Ireland did not ratify the ICERD until 29 December 2000, some 22 years after it signed it.

4.2.4.3 International Convention on the Elimination of all forms of Discrimination Against Women

The International Convention on the Elimination of all forms of Discrimination Against Women (CEDAW) was adopted by the UN in 1979 and is the first universal instrument to deal with the issue of discrimination against women. Under CEDAW, state parties condemn discrimination against women in all its forms and agree to take a number of measures, including measures:

- To embody the principle of equality of men and women

- To ensure the full development and advancement of women

- To modify the social and cultural patterns of conduct of men and women with a view to achieving the elimination of prejudices and practices based on the idea of the inferiority of women

- To suppress all forms of traffic in women

- To ensure to women on equal terms with men, the right to vote in all elections and to be eligible for election to all publicly elected bodies and to participate in the formation of government policy

- To eliminate discrimination against women in the field of employment

- To eliminate discrimination against women in the field of health care in order to ensure, on the basis of equality, access to health care services, including those related to family planning

- To ensure equality before the law and to accord to women in civil matters a legal capacity identical to men.

It must be noted that despite the wide-ranging nature of the obligations set out in CEDAW, its effectiveness has been severely hindered by the number of reservations entered by state parties when ratifying it.

CEDAW also establishes a body, the Committee on the Elimination of Discrimination Against Women, to monitor implementation of the Convention. States are required to submit reports setting out the legislative, judicial, administrative and other measures they have adopted to give effect to CEDAW. Initial reports must be submitted within one year after entry into force of CEDAW for the state concerned and then at four-year intervals thereafter. The Committee can then make suggestions and recommendations based on examination of these reports and information received from state parties. It can also make General Recommendations which have covered a number of issues both procedural and substantive (for example, relating to violence against women, equal pay and female circumcision). For a number of years there was no mechanism whereby either inter-state or individual complaints could be considered by the Committee, but an optional protocol came into force in December 2000 which allows for the examination of individual complaints by the Committee if the state party concerned has accepted the competence of the Committee in this regard. Ireland acceded to CEDAW on 3 December 1985.

4.2.4.4 Convention against torture and other cruel, inhuman or degrading treatment or punishment

The Convention against Torture and Other Cruel, Inhuman or Degrading Treatment or Punishment (UNCAT) was adopted by the United Nations in 1984 and entered into force in 1987. UNCAT is composed of two parts, the first which sets out the substantive guarantees and the second which sets out a system for supervising implementation of UNCAT. Under UNCAT each state undertakes:

- To take measures to prevent acts of torture in its jurisdiction

- To make torture a criminal offence

- To prosecute or extradite persons charged with torture

- To make a prompt investigation into allegations of torture

- To provide a remedy for those who have been tortured

- Not to return people to countries where they may be subjected to torture.

UNCAT then creates a supervisory body, the Committee Against Torture, which is composed of independent experts and which has three main functions. First, state parties are required to submit reports to the Committee one year after the coming into force of UNCAT in the state concerned and thereafter every four years, and state parties are also required to submit any other reports the Committee may request. Secondly, the Committee can consider inter-state complaints and thirdly the Committee may receive complaints from individuals, although this latter competence is subject to state acceptance. The Committee has a further function which was innovative when first introduced. It has the power to act on its own initiative to begin an inquiry if it receives 'reliable information which appears to it to contain well-founded indications that torture is being systematically practiced in the territory of a State Party'. If this occurs, the Committee will invite the relevant state to co-operate in the examination of this information and submit observations in relation to it. Importantly, the Committee can decide not to disclose the source of the information to the state concerned. The Committee can also receive further information from NGOs, UN bodies, individuals and specialized agencies to assist in examining material it has received. If the Committee considers it necessary, it can then appoint one or more of its members to conduct a confidential inquiry relating to the information received and this inquiry can include a visit to the state concerned provided the state party agrees. The Committee member will then draw up a report on the situation which the Committee will examine and forward to the state concerned with its own comments and suggestions. The state will be given a period of time within which to respond to the report and recommendations. However, a weakness in this procedure is the lack of any sanction for failing to comply with the Committee's recommendations. More fundamentally, states may refuse to recognise the competence of the Committee to act in this way when ratifying the Convention although the majority of state parties have chosen not to do this. The procedure is also confidential although this is mitigated somewhat by the ability of the Committee to publish a summary of the results of the proceedings before it in its annual report. This power was first used by the Committee against Turkey in 1990. Ireland signed UNCAT on 28 September 1992 and ratified it on 4 April 2002.

4.2.4.5   European Convention for the Prevention of Torture

The European Convention for the Prevention of Torture and Inhuman or Degrading Treatment or Punishment (ECPT)is an interesting human rights instrument, in that its focus is less on the setting of substantive human rights standards and more on the creation of a supervisory body for the enforcement of standards already in existence. The central purpose of the Convention is to provide a procedure for supervising the treatment of persons who have been deprived of their liberty and to that end it creates the European Committee for the Prevention of Torture. The Committee is composed of experts in the area who act in an individual capacity and its powers are wide-ranging. The Committee can, for example, visit prisons and other places of detention, report on the facts found and make appropriate recommendations. The Committee does not, however, have any judicial role and is careful to adopt a co-operative rather than condemnatory approach. For this reason, the reports of the Committee in respect of its visits to places of detention are confidential. However, the Committee can make a public statement if any contracting party refuses to co-operate with it and it is also required to submit an annual report on its activities to the Council of Europe, under whose auspices it operates, so that there is some element of publicity to its operation. The ECPT has in fact been very active since its creation, exercising its powers both to make periodic visits, of which notice must be given, and ad hoc visits, which are not announced in advance. When making a visit, Committee members can speak privately with detainees and interview anyone they feel may have relevant information. The Committee, therefore, has direct access to anyone who may wish to complain about their conditions of detention and this has been a significant element in the success of the Committee. Ireland was visited by the Committee in 1993, 1998 and recently in May 2002. The report of the Committee on the 1998 visit is instructive in showing the different types of places of detention (garda stations, prisons, the Central Mental Hospital) and the breadth of recommendations it can make (for example, that members of the Gardaí be reminded to use only such force as is necessary when effecting an arrest, that appropriate action should be taken to guarantee detainees' right of access to a lawyer, that improvements be made to the condition of cells in certain garda stations, that a strategy be adopted to bring to an end over-crowding in detention centres).

However it is important to remember that the focus of the Committee's work is preventative rather than remedial in nature. Its purpose is not to provide a remedy for human rights violations but rather to encourage states to create conditions of detention which do not violate human rights standards in the first place. Ireland signed and ratified the ECPT on 13 March 1988.

4.2.4.6 European Social Charter

The European Social Charter (ESC) was drafted under the auspices of the Council of Europe and was designed to complement the European Convention on Human Rights, which protects only civil and political rights, by establishing a European system for the protection of economic and social rights. It must be acknowledged, however, that the ESC has not enjoyed anything like the success of the ECHR and indeed was revised in 1996 in an attempt to increase its effectiveness. The ESC, as initially drafted, outlines a number of principles which contracting parties agree to but then, somewhat unusually, lists a set of seven major articles, at least five of which contracting parties must agree to. States must also agree to a specified number of additional undertakings. The idea behind this unusual format was that it would encourage states to accept further commitments progressively, but this has not in fact happened and only a handful of states have fully accepted the Charter's provisions. The rights set out in the major articles as originally drafted are:

- The right to work

- The right to organise

- The right to bargain collectively

- The right to social security

- The right to social and medical assistance

- The right of the family to social, legal and medical protection

- The right of migrant workers and their families to protection and assistance.

The revised ESC follows this format but increases the obligations on state parties to the effect that they must accept six out of nine major articles. The major articles in the revised ESC are the above seven articles supplemented by:

- The right of children and young persons to protection

- The right to equal opportunities and equal treatment in matters of employment and occupation without discrimination on the grounds of sex.

The revised Charter also includes other new rights such as the right to protection against poverty and social exclusion, the right to housing and the right to protection against sexual harassment. It also improves gender equality in all fields covered by the Charter and provides better protection for employed children and handicapped people.

The ESC is implemented through a reporting mechanisms, with states required to submit reports every two years in relation to those provisions which they have accepted. The Committee of Ministers of the Council of Europe can also require a state to submit reports at specified intervals in relation to those provisions of the ESC which the state has not yet accepted. These reports must be submitted to national trade union organisations and employers' bodies for comment prior to submission and these comments must also be transmitted. The relevant report will then be examined by a number of bodies, including the Committee of Ministers, a Governmental Social Committee and Parliamentary Assembly of the Council of Europe. The report will also be initially reviewed by a Committee of Experts. However, the system of review is ultimately a weak one. The Committee of Ministers can only make recommendations and even these tend to be of a general nature rather than directed at any one state. Unlike the implementation system of the ECHR, the ESC does not provide for any judicial scrutiny of state action pursuant to the Charter and it has long been suggested that a complaint procedure relating to the ESC could be assigned to the social division of the European Court of Human Rights. In an attempt to address some of these criticisms, an amending protocol was drafted in 1991 which was designed to streamline the procedure for examining reports and to provide for the increased input of trade unions, employers' groups and NGOs. A further protocol allowing for the making of collective complaints was agreed in 1995.

Some efforts have been made to increase the effectiveness of the ESC, although more needs to be done if it is to have any chance of rivalling the success of its counterpart, the ECHR. Nevertheless, the ESC has been significant in providing a yardstick against which local laws and practices can be measured and in holding governments accountable, to some extent at least, for these laws and practices, through the reporting procedure. Ireland signed the ESC on 18 October 191 and ratified it on 7 December 1964. Ireland also ratified the revised ESC on 1 January 2001.

4.2.4.7   Rome Statute of the International Criminal Court

One of the most frequent criticisms of international law in general, and international human rights law in particular, is that it lacks an effective enforcement mechanism, whereby persons and governments who have breached international law can be brought to account. Although individual courts and tribunals have been established over the years to deal with specific situations, such as the Nuremberg trials and the international criminal tribunals for Rwanda and the former Yugoslavia, there was no permanent court with general jurisdiction to deal with breaches of international law, particularly, serious breaches of international human rights law by individuals, wherever they occurred.

In answer to this criticism, moves began as early as 1954 to establish an international criminal court which would have the jurisdiction to try those suspected of committing serious human rights abuses. After years of debate and deliberation, during which time many thought the project would never come to fruition, not least because of the opposition of some of the world's most powerful nations, the Rome Statute establishing the International Criminal Court was finally adopted by the UN in July 1998. Even then many doubted whether the Statute would be ratified by the requisite number of states to enable the International Criminal Court (ICC) to come into existence. These doubts were dispelled however on 1 July 2002 when the International Criminal Court came into force. Its establishment has been hailed as one of the most significant developments in international law in modern times, but whether in practice it fulfils this promise will depend on a number of factors, such as funding, staffing and, most importantly of all, state willingness to co-operate with the Court. Ireland ratified the Statute of the ICC on 11 April 2002 but has not yet, at the time of writing, passed incorporating legislation necessary to give full effect to the provisions of the Statute.

Jurisdiction of the ICC

Despite its name, the International Criminal Court does not have jurisdiction to try every offence under international law. The crimes over which it has jurisdiction are carefully drafted in the Statute and crucially the Court will only have jurisdiction in relation to those offences which are committed after the Court came into existence, ie 1 July 2002. The ICC does not have any retrospective jurisdiction. Moreover, the jurisdiction of the ICC is 'complementary' to national jurisdiction, so that if a state wishes to try an individual itself rather than hand that person over to the ICC it can do so. The ICC, will only exercise jurisdiction if the national courts are unwilling or unable to try those suspected of serious breaches of international law. The primacy of national jurisdiction remains, but the possibility of prosecution by the ICC may act as a spur to national authorities to prosecute both quickly and in a manner which conforms with international standards.

The crimes over which the Court has jurisdiction fall into three core categories and together can be described as the most serious crimes of concern to the international community. These are:

Genocide – this is generally regarded as the most serious of all the crimes over which the ICC has jurisdiction. It is defined in the Statute as the commission of any of the following acts with the intent to destroy, in whole or in part, a national, ethnic, racial or religious group, namely killing or causing serious bodily or mental harm to members of the group, deliberately inflicting on the group conditions of life calculated to bring about its destruction, imposing measures intended to prevent births within the group or forcibly transferring children of the group to another group (Art 6). While this definition may seem very comprehensive, it may in fact be difficult to satisfy because of the requirements of intent (which can be problematic in terms of proof) in relation to a group (as opposed to any particular individual). On the other hand, it is clear that genocide can be committed even if the group is not actually destroyed, as it is the intent along with any of the listed activities which is criminalised.

Crimes against humanity – the Statute sets out a number of acts which will constitute crimes against humanity, a list which clearly reflects developments in international law in this area. Crimes against humanity are defined as any of the following activities committed as part of a widespread or systematic attack directed against any civilian population, with knowledge of the attack: murder, extermination, enslavement, deportation or forcible transfer or population, imprisonment or other severe deprivation of liberty, torture, rape, sexual slavery, enforced prostitution, forced pregnancy, enforced sterilization and other forms of sexual violence of comparable gravity, persecution of an identifiable group, enforced disappearances, apartheid and other inhumane acts of a similar character intentionally causing great suffering or serious injury to body or to mental or physical health (Art 7).

The key aspects of this definition are the requirement that the activity be directed against a civilian population, as opposed to combatants and the lack of any requirement that the activities be committed during an armed conflict. In other words, crimes against humanity can be committed outside of the context of war, potentially covering the actions of a regime against its own citizens in so-called peacetime. Another striking feature of this definition is the inclusion of a number of what might be termed 'gender-related crimes', such as rape, which reflects international acceptance that such activities are now so objectionable as to be the subject of international criminal jurisdiction.

War crimes – these are defined as: wilful killing, torture or inhuman treatment including biological experiments, wilfully causing great suffering or serious bodily injury to body or health, extensive destruction or appropriation of property which is not justified by military necessity and is carried out wantonly and unlawfully, compelling a prisoner of war or other protected person to serve in the forces of a hostile power, wilfully depriving a prisoner of war or other protected person of the right to a fair and regular trial, unlawful deportation or transfer or unlawful confinement, taking of hostages, and other serious violations of the laws and customs applicable in international armed conflict, which may include some of the crimes against humanity already enumerated (Art 8). Unlike crimes against humanity, war crimes, as the name implies, will only be committed during times of armed conflict, whether this be international or internal armed conflict.

Note that the ICC does not as yet have jurisdiction in relation to crimes of aggression, as this crime has not been defined and the conditions for the exercise of jurisdiction have not been set out, although the Assembly of State Parties of the ICC may adopt such a provision at a review conference to be convened in 2009.

The ICC can exercise this jurisdiction over crimes committed in the territories of state parties, crimes committed by nationals of state parties and in situations where a non-state party agrees on an ad hoc basis to accept the ICC's jurisdiction over a crime committed in its territory or by one of its nationals. The ICC's jurisdiction does not extend to crimes committed against the national of a state party or crimes committed by a person who is in the custody of a state party. This position has been criticised by many as potentially reducing the effectiveness of the ICC, as it gives rise to the possibility of haven states existing to which war criminals can flee free from the threat of prosecution.

Challenges for the ICC

As stated above, the ICC will face many practical problems in the next few years. One of its biggest challenges will come from the US, which has voiced many concerns about its existence and operation, particularly in relation to whether US military personnel or even the US President himself could be indicted by the ICC prosecutor. To that end, the US has entered into a number of bilateral agreements with countries who have ratified the Statute to ensure that US military personnel who are serving in these countries will not be handed over to the ICC. While the legality of these agreements has not yet been tested, their very existence constitutes a challenge to the authority of the ICC on the part of the US, which, if replicated, could seriously undermine it. Other potential difficulties include securing adequate funding for the ICC and ensuring that it is staffed by persons of sufficient calibre who will command the respect of all those who come into contact with it. The office of prosecutor will also be crucial, particularly in light of some of the constraints placed on the role by the Statute itself. The prosecutor may need to be dynamic and courageous in the exercise of his role to ensure that the ICC operates in a meaningful and effective way. Some states may also be more willing than others to relinquish jurisdiction to the ICC, and it may be anticipated that some state parties will flout the prosecute or extradite requirement.

While the establishment of the ICC is to be welcomed, not least because of the message it sends out that from now on those who perpetrate massive human rights violations can be personally prosecuted by a permanent international court, it remains to be seen whether it will be as effective as those who worked so tirelessly for its establishment hope.

4.3   Conclusion

While Ireland has acceded to an impressive array of international human rights measures, the dualist nature of Irish law means that these measures are likely only to have a limited impact unless and until they are incorporated into domestic law. Incorporation requires a separate Act of Parliament and in this regard there has been a lag between action on the international plane and action in the domestic sphere. In this regard, the State is some-times accused of adopting a 'street angel, house devil' approach to its obligations under international human rights law. It is to be hoped that in the future any steps taken by the State in relation to existing or new international human rights obligations will be matched by simultaneous action in domestic law and practice, so that these obligations will have real meaning and effect.

CHAPTER 5

HUMAN RIGHTS IN EC/EU LAW

5.1 Introduction

This chapter aims to provide an overview of EC/EU human rights law. The history of human rights law in the EC/EU is explored. It will be noted that the method of development which resulted initially from judicial rather than Treaty sources impacts on the system of protection which exists today. The history of human rights law in the EC has significant consequences for issues such as the competence of the political institutions to legislate in the field of human rights, the scope of fundamental rights protection in the EC and the standard of human rights protection.

The human rights *acquis* is explored to indicate what substantive rights are protected. The sources of human rights include the Treaties, secondary legislation and case-law of the ECJ. While the human rights protection has developed on an ad hoc basis there now exists a considerable human rights *acquis*.

A Charter of Fundamental Rights for the EU was solemnly proclaimed at the Inter-Governmental Conference (IGC) in Nice in December, 2000. This chapter provides an overview of the contents of the Charter together with some of the issues concerning it which have arisen, for debate. These issues include the sources, scope and legal status of the Charter as well as questions as to who is to benefit from it and its relationship with the European Convention on Human Rights (ECHR).

The Convention on the Future of Europe debated whether the Charter of Fundamental Rights should be incorporated in the Draft Treaty establishing a Constitution for Europe and whether the EU should accede to the ECHR. A Draft Treaty Establishing a Constitution for Europe was submitted by the President of the Convention on the Future of Europe to the European Council meeting in Thessaloniki on 20 June 2003 (A corrected text is published at CONV 820/1/03 Brussels, 27 June 2003). The Draft Treaty proposes incorporation of the Charter and provides for accession of the EU to the ECHR. At the time of writing the Draft Treaty Establishing a Constitution for Europe is being debated.

5.2 The History of Human Rights Protection in the EC/EU

5.2.1 EXCLUSION OF A BILL OF RIGHTS FROM THE FOUNDING TREATIES

The Treaties establishing the European Economic Community (EEC), European Coal and Steel Community (ECSC) and the European Atomic Energy Community (EURATOM), as ratified in the 1950s, did not contain a catalogue of human rights. At first glance it may seem surprising that organisations established in the immediate aftermath of World War II and with the stated objective of preserving and strengthening peace did not state themselves bound by a bill of rights. This exclusion can be explained by the political failure of the European Defence Community Treaty and the consequent failure of the European Political Community Treaty (which was to include the application of the ECHR) which meant that a more cautious approach was taken when drafting the Community Treaties. Also, it may not have been so readily apparent at the time that a Community predominantly concerned with economics would impact on human rights.

5.2.2 THE EARLY APPROACH BY THE EUROPEAN COURT OF JUSTICE (ECJ)

In a series of early cases, the ECJ declined when invited to take human rights considerations into account. Examples of this former attitude can be seen in Case 1/58 *Stork v High Authority* [1959] ECR 17 and Joined Cases 16, 17 and 18/59 *Ruhr v High Authority* [1960] ECR 47.

In these cases, the ECJ decided that it did not have the competence to review a decision of the High Authority for compatibility with German basic law. The rationale for this decision was that the ECJ is only permitted to apply Community law and is not competent to apply the national laws of Member States.

5.2.3 A NEW APPROACH BY THE ECJ

With the emergence of the EC as a new supranational legal order based on the concepts of supremacy, as espoused by the ECJ in Case 6/64 *Costa v ENEL* [1964] ECR 585 and direct effect, as espoused by the ECJ in Case 26/62 *Van Gend en Loos v Nederlandse Administratie der Belastingen* [1963] ECR 1, it was no longer sufficient to leave the protection of fundamental human rights to the national courts. This was especially true when the ECJ in Case 11/70 *Internationale Handelsgescellschaft* [1970] ECR 1125 declared that Community law was superior even to the constitutional provisions of Member States.

5.2.4 THREAT OF CONSTITUTIONAL REBELLIONS IN THE MEMBER STATES

The ECJ's new approach to human rights may have resulted at least in part from a desire to head off threatened rebellions in certain Member States. The doctrine of supremacy of European law is a key method adopted by the ECJ to ensure the effectiveness and uniformity of EC law. In particular, German and Italian lawyers had difficulties with the possibility that the provisions of a supranational legal order might trump the constitutional provisions, and in particular, the fundamental rights provisions, of their respective legal orders as the EC system lacked *inter alia* a codified catalogue of fundamental human rights.

5.2.5 HUMAN RIGHTS AS GENERAL PRINCIPLES OF EC LAW

The ECJ responded by recognising an unwritten catalogue of fundamental human rights enshrined in the general principles of EC law and by holding that the ECJ had jurisdiction to review acts of the institutions to ensure compatibility with this human rights standard. The protection of fundamental rights in EC law, at least at the outset was a product of judicial activism. In this section, it is proposed to examine the early case law of the ECJ in which it espoused a Community concept of human rights protection.

The ECJ first recognised fundamental human rights as general principles of Community law requiring protection by the ECJ in Case 29/69 *Stauder v City of Ulm* [1969] ECR 419. The case concerned a European scheme to provide cheap butter to those on social welfare. The applicant was a social welfare recipient. He objected to the fact that he had to present a coupon bearing his name and address to obtain the cheap butter. He argued that the humiliation of revealing his identity was a breach of his fundamental human rights. He further argued that the Community decision was invalid in that it contained this requirement. The ECJ at paragraph 7 held that on a proper interpretation, the Community provision did not require the beneficiary's identity to appear on the coupon.

'Interpreted in this way the provision at issue contains nothing capable of prejudicing the fundamental rights enshrined in the general principles of Community law and protected by the Court.'

This decision is remarkable given the exclusion of the protection of fundamental rights from the ambit of the European Community Treaties by the Member States.

In Case 11/70 *Internationale Handelsgesellschaft* [1970] ECR 1125, the ECJ confirmed its view of human rights as general principles of EC law. The facts of the case concerned the Common Agricultural Policy. A system was in place whereby exporters of certain agricultural products had to obtain an export license. When applying for such a license the exporter had to pay a deposit. If he failed to export during the validity of the license, the sum was forfeit. The applicants argued that the system violated the principle of proportionality and hence the German Constitution.

Consistent with the judgment in *Stork*, the ECJ pointed out at paragraph 3 that the validity of EC law measures could not be judged according to national law rules.

'Recourse to the legal rules or concepts of national law in order to judge the validity of measures adopted by the institutions of the Community would have an adverse effect on the uniformity and efficacy of Community law. The validity of such measures can only be judged in the light of Community law. In fact, the law stemming from the Treaty, an independent source of law, cannot because of its very nature be overridden by rules of national law, however framed, without being deprived of its character as Community law and without the legal basis of the Community itself being called into question.'

The ECJ emphasised that the validity of Community measures could not be judged even according to national constitutional provisions protecting human rights.

Therefore the validity of a Community measure or its effect within a Member State cannot be affected by allegations that it runs counter to either fundamental rights as formulated by the constitution of that state or the principles of a national constitutional structure.

Hence, the doctrine of supremacy of EC law extends to supremacy over the fundamental rights provisions of the Member State Constitutions.

The measures at issue were however subject to review by the ECJ for compatibility with the Community standard of human rights protection. The fundamental human rights which the ECJ found itself obliged to protect could be inspired by the constitutional traditions of the member states. The ECJ stated at paragraph 4:

'However, an examination should be made as to whether or not any analogous guarantee inherent in community law has been disregarded. In fact, respect for fundamental rights forms an integral part of the general principles of law protected by the Court of Justice. The protection of such rights, whilst inspired by the Constitutional traditions common to the Member States, must be ensured within the framework of the structure and objectives of the Community.'

According to Hartley (Hartley, 'Foundations of European Community Law', 3rd edn, 1994, Clarendon Press, 142) this decision goes beyond that in *Stauder* – the concept of human rights applied by the ECJ while deriving its validity solely from Community law is nevertheless inspired by the Constitutional traditions of the Member States. On the facts, the ECJ concluded that the system did not violate any fundamental human rights.

The ECJ cited another source of inspiration for fundamental human rights in Case 4/73 *Nold v Commission* [1974] ECR 491 – International Treaties for the protection of human rights on which the Member States have collaborated or to which they are signatories. However, it is the general principle and not the Treaty, which is the source of law. The facts of this case related to a Commission decision under the ECSC Treaty which provided that coal wholesalers could not buy Rhur coal unless they agreed to purchase a specific quantity. Nold, who was not in a position to purchase the minimum quantity claimed the decision was a breach of his fundamental human rights for two reasons. First, he claimed that it was a violation of a property right and secondly, that it breached his right to the free pursuit of a business activity.

The ECJ seemed to recognise the two rights as general principles of EC law but held that they were not absolute rights. These rights were held to be subject to limitations justified by the overall objectives pursued by the Community. The ECJ held that no infringement had taken place. The ECJ in its judgment made the following pronouncement at paragraph 13.

> 'As the Court has already stated, fundamental rights form an integral part of the general principles of law, the observance of which it ensures.
>
> In safeguarding these rights, the Court is bound to draw inspiration from constitutional traditions common to Member States, and it cannot therefore uphold measures which are incompatible with fundamental rights recognised and protected by the Constitutions of those states.
>
> Similarly, international Treaties for the protection of human rights on which the Member States have collaborated or of which they are signatories, can supply guidelines which should be followed within the framework of Community law.'

This judgment is significant in that it makes clear that a Community measure in conflict with fundamental rights will be annulled.

A detailed discussion of human rights by the ECJ may be found in the decision in Case 44/79 *Hauer v Land Rheinland-Pfaltz* [1979] ECR 3727. The facts concerned a Regulation banning new plantings of vines. It was argued on behalf of the applicant that her right to property and her freedom to pursue a profession under German law were infringed. The ECJ rephrased the question asked and analysed the measure at issue in the light of the Community human rights standard. Again, the ECJ accepted these rights as general principles of Community law but pointed out that they were not absolute rights and were subject to the general interest exception.

The judgment is of interest in that the ECJ analysed provisions of the Irish, German and Italian Constitutions and the relevant provision (the first protocol) of the ECHR in order to establish that, in principle, it was permissible to restrict the rights at issue. The ECJ went on to consider whether the restrictions introduced by the measures at issue in fact corresponded to objectives of general interest pursued by the Community or whether the restrictions constituted a disproportionate and intolerable interference with those rights and found that the restrictions were justified.

The key points of these early judgments may be summarised as follows. It is possible to review the acts of the Community for compatibility with human rights protection but it is a Community standard of human rights protection. This standard is inspired by the constitutional traditions of the Member States and international human rights treaties to which the Member States are party. An act which is in breach of the human rights standard will be annulled. The rights protected are not absolute but subject to restrictions justified by the objectives pursued by the Community. These restrictions must be proportionate and must not constitute an intolerable interference with the right at issue.

In addition, it is worth noting that, in each of these four judgments, the ECJ recognised the existence of rights but went on to hold that the rights had not been violated.

5.3 Political Acceptance of Fundamental Human Rights as General Principles of Community Law

The ECJ's elaboration of fundamental human rights as general principles of Community law subsequently gained political acceptance. In 1977, the three political institutions issued a Joint Declaration on Fundamental Human Rights ([1977] OJ C103/1). This Declaration states:

'1.   The European Parliament, the Council and the Commission stress the prime importance they attach to the protection of fundamental human rights, as derived in particular from the Constitutions of the Member States and the European Convention on Human Rights and Fundamental Freedoms.

2.   In exercise of their powers and in pursuance of the aims of the European Communities, they respect and continue to respect these rights.'

The European Council endorsed the Joint Declaration the following year. Since the 1977 joint declaration, there have been a number of political initiatives, including a Joint Declaration by the institutions in 1986, a number of declarations and resolutions on racism and xenophobia by the European Council, a declaration of Fundamental Rights and Freedoms by the European Parliament ([1989] OJ C120/51) and a Charter of Fundamental Social Rights.

5.4 Treaty Amendments

Treaty amendments, subsequent to the ECJ's elaboration of a human rights policy approved the development. The Single European Act, 1987 contains the first explicit Treaty reference to human rights. In the preamble, the Member States determined

to work together to promote democracy on the basis of the fundamental rights recognised in the constitutions and laws of the Member states, in the Convention for the Protection of Human Rights and Fundamental Freedoms and the European Social Charter, notably freedom, equality and social justice.

Article F(2) of the Treaty on European Union (TEU) (the Maastricht Treaty) required the European Union to respect fundamental rights as general principles of Community law, as guaranteed by the ECHR and as they result from the constitutional traditions common to the Member States. However, pursuant to Article L TEU, this provision was originally not justiciable before the ECJ. A two-stage evolution is evident in the Treaty of Amsterdam amendments to the TEU. Article 6(1) TEU declares fundamental human rights as one of the basic principles on which the Union is founded and Article 6(2) TEU (ex Article F(2)), pursuant to the newly inserted paragraph (d) in Art 46 TEU (ex Art L), now comes within the jurisdiction of the ECJ.

Art 6 TEU provides:

'1.   The Union is founded on the principles of liberty, democracy, respect for human rights and fundamental freedoms and the rule of law, principles which are common to the Member States.

> 2. *The Union shall respect fundamental rights, as guaranteed by the European convention for the Protection of Human Rights and Fundamental freedoms signed in Rome on 4 November, 1950 and as they result from the constitutional traditions common to the Member States, as general principles of Community law.'*

Even after the Treaty of Amsterdam, Art 6(2) TEU (ex Art F(2)) goes no further than confirming the jurisprudence of the ECJ, that the ECJ will protect human rights as general principles of Community law. Rendering Art 6(2) justiciable does mean that the ECJ can review the actions of the EC institutions for compatibility with the human rights standard under provisions of the two intergovernmental pillars in the event that the ECJ has been given jurisdiction (see **5.7.1**).

The Maastricht Treaty did introduce one justiciable provision relating to human rights. Article 177(2) EC (ex Art 130u(2) EC) provides that 'Community policy in [the field of development co-operation] shall contribute to the general objective of developing and consolidating democracy and the rule of law, and to that of respecting human rights and fundamental freedoms.' The ECJ's interpretation of this provision in C-268/94 *Portugal v Council* [1996] ECR I 6177 is discussed at **5.6.2**.

In addition, the Treaty of Amsterdam introduced a political mechanism for sanctioning states guilty of a 'serious and persistent breach' of the principles on which the Union is founded, including respect for fundamental rights. Pursuant to Art 7 TEU, a 'serious and persistent breach' of fundamental rights may result in the suspension of rights, including voting rights, derived from the Treaty.

Article 7 has been amended by the Nice Treaty. A procedure was added allowing the Council to make recommendations to a Member State where there is a clear risk of a serious breach by a Member State of the principles mentioned in Art 6(1) (the basic principles on which the Union is founded including those of democracy, respect for human rights and fundamental freedoms, and the rule of law). This procedure will allow a more gradual response to a developing situation and the ECJ has jurisdiction over the procedures of Art 7.

Article I-2, 'The Union's Values' of the Draft Treaty Establishing a Constitution for Europe provides:

> *'The Union is founded on the values of respect for human dignity, liberty, democracy, equality, the rule of law and respect for human rights. These values are common to the Member States in a society of pluralism, tolerance, justice, solidarity and non-discrimination.'*

Article I-7, 'Fundamental rights', of the Draft Treaty Establishing a Constitution for Europe provides:

> *'1. The Union shall recognise the rights, freedoms and principles set out in the Charter of Fundamental Rights which constitutes Part II of this Constitution.*
> *2. The Union shall seek accession to the European Convention for the Protection of Human Rights and Fundamental Freedoms. Accession to the Convention shall not affect the Union's competences as defined in this Constitution.*
> *3. Fundamental rights, as guaranteed by the European Convention for the Protection of Human Rights and Fundamental freedoms, and as they result from the constitutional traditions common to the Member States, shall constitute general principles of the Union's law.'*

5.4.1 HUMAN RIGHTS AND THE FUTURE OF EUROPE

Post-Nice, it will be interesting to see how the protection of human rights within the EU develops. A Declaration on the Future of the Union was agreed at Nice. At Laeken, the European Council decided to convene a Convention on the Future of Europe, modelled on the body which drafted the EU Charter of Fundamental Rights (paragraphs 5.10.1 and 5.10.2), composed of the main parties involved in the debate, to prepare for the Intergovernmental Conference which commenced in 2003.

The Convention's task was to identify the key issues which would form the basis for the next ICG. More specifically, the Convention was charged with preparing a document, which together with national debates on the future of Europe, such as Ireland's National Forum on Europe, would form a basis for the next IGC ie the IGC which commenced in 2003. The Convention was composed of representatives of the Heads of State or Government of the Member States and accession States, members of national parliaments of the Member States and accession States, members of the European Parliament and members of the Commission. In the Nice (December 2000) and Laeken (December 2001) Declarations on the Future of Europe, it was agreed that consideration would be given to the status of the Charter of Fundamental Rights and whether it should be included in the EC Treaty. (See paragraph 5.10.10.)

The members of the Convention participated in working groups to look into particular issues more fully. In total, there were eleven Working Groups on the following subjects: Subsidiarity, Charter/ECHR, Legal Personality, National Parliaments, Complementary Competencies, Economic Governance, External Action, Defence, Simplification, Freedom, Security and Justice and Social Europe. After the Working Groups submitted their final reports, the Convention moved to the next stage of its work, the drafting of a Constitutional Treaty to replace the existing Treaties. The Working Group reports are available on the Convention website. The Working Group Report on Incorporation of the Charter and Accession of the EU to the ECHR (CONV 354/02 Final report of Working Group II 'Incorporation of the Charter/Accession to the ECHR' Brussels, 22 October 2002) is discussed later. (See paragraphs 5.6.5 and 5.10.10.)

The Draft Treaty establishing a Constitution for Europe was submitted by the President of the Convention to the European Council on 20 June 2003 (see **5.10.10**).

5.5 The Issue of EC Accession to the ECHR

The idea of EC accession to the ECHR has been mooted consistently since the late 1970s. The principal advantage of accession is that it would remedy an apparent *lacuna* in EC law. Currently, as the EC is not party to the ECHR, the EC institutions are not answerable to the European Court of Human Rights (ECt.HR) for possible violations of the ECHR.

The ECJ, in *Opinion 2/94* [1996] ECR I 1759, determined that the EC had no competence to accede to the ECHR. As a consequence of this judgment, accession can now only be brought about by means of an amendment to the EC Treaty. Currently, while the Member States are subject to the ECHR they have not amended the EC Treaty to subject the EC institutions to the possibility of review by the ECt.HR.

Recently, this issue has taken on renewed impetus as it was agreed by the European Council in the Laeken Declaration on the Future of the European Union, in December 2001, that consideration be given to whether the EC should accede to the ECHR and this issue was discussed by the Convention on the Future of Europe. The decision taken by the Convention on the Future of Europe is discussed later in this chapter. (See **5.10.10.**)

5.6 The Nature of Community Human Rights Law

The form of evolution of human rights protection within the Community legal order raises two issues. First, a question arises as to whether the EC political institutions have the competence to legislate in the field of human rights. Secondly, a question arises as to whether the Member States might be subject to review by an international legal order, specifically the ECt.HR, to ensure that the standard of human rights signed up to by the Member States is maintained. This issue arises in part as the Member States of the European Communities are all parties to the ECHR and subject to scrutiny by the ECt.HR. Difficulties may result from Member States transferring competences which might then be beyond the review of an international human rights standard to which the Member State is subject.

5.6.1   COMPETENCE

European Community law is distinct from international law. The ECSC was not established as a forum for intergovernmental decision-making. What was unique about the ECSC and the subsequent steps to European integration was the Member States' willingness to hand over their decision-making power to the institutions of these supranational Communities. Within defined areas, the Member States transferred competence to the political institutions of the European Communities. Article 5 EC (ex Article 3b) provides 'The Community shall act within the limits of the powers conferred upon it by this Treaty and of the objectives assigned to it therein.'

Consequently, while individual States clearly have competence to legislate in the domestic sphere and to conclude international agreements which will be binding on the State or both binding on the State and internally within the State, the European Communities only have competence where the Member States have chosen to transfer the requisite competence.

European integration is an ongoing process taking place incrementally. The first step was taken with the establishment of the European Coal and Steel Community. The process continued with the establishment of the European Atomic Energy Community and the European Economic Community. Further developments ensued when the Treaty establishing this latter Community was amended by the Single European Act, Maastricht Treaty, Treaty of Amsterdam and the Treaty of Nice. With each incremental step, further competences have been transferred from the Member States to the Communities.

Three types of legislative competence are conferred upon the EC/EU: exclusive, concurrent or shared. Currently, these terms are not defined in the Treaties but definitions are given in a discussion paper prepared by the Convention on the Future of Europe. (The European Convention *Discussion Paper on the Delimitation of Competence between the European Union and Member States* Brussels 15 May 2002 CONV 47/02, *6 et seq*). Unfortunately, it is not always clear whether a particular competence rests with the EC or with the Member States, although the discussion paper contains a very useful outline. In addition, the limit line between EC competence and national competence is changing all the time. It is necessary for lawyers to analyse the factual situation in a given case in the light of the division of competence at that time.

The Convention on the Future of Europe looked at establishing a more precise delimitation of competence between the EU and the Member States and a means of monitoring compliance with the delimitation of competence.

On 4 November 2002 the Convention on the Future of Europe Working Group on Complementary Competencies published its final report (CONV 375/1/02 REV 1) recommending a basic delimitation of EU competence in each policy area. The Draft Treaty establishing a Constitution for Europe (CONV 820/1/03) follows the recommendation of the Working Group. The Draft Treaty includes detailed provisions on competence in Volume I, Title III, Arts 9–17.

Article I-9 clarifies the delimitation of competences between the Union and the Member States and the use of competences by the Union.

'(1)   The limits of Union competences are governed by the principle of conferral. The use of Union
        competences is governed by the principles of subsidiarity and proportionality.

(2)   Under the principle of conferral, in areas which do not fall within its exclusive competence
        the Union shall act only if and insofar as the objectives of the intended action cannot be
        sufficiently achieved by the Member States, either at central level or at regional and local
        level, but can rather, by reason of the scale or effects of the proposed action, be better achieved
        at Union level.'

Article I-11 sets out the categories of competence. Three categories of competence are
provided for: exclusive competence, shared competence and a third category comprising
supporting, co-ordinating or complementary actions. Article I-12 sets out areas of
exclusive Union competence. Article I-13 sets out areas of shared competence. Article I-16
sets out areas of supporting, co-ordinating or complementary action. Specific provisions
are made in the areas of Common Foreign and Security Policy (Article I-15) and the
co-ordination of economic and employment policies (Article I-14) because of the difficulty
in neatly classifying these policies.

The advantage of delimiting competence is that the EU will be less open to the accusation
that it is encroaching on powers that have not been transferred by the Member States.

5.6.2   WHAT POWERS DO THE INSTITUTIONS HAVE TO ACT IN THE FIELD OF HUMAN RIGHTS?

In *Opinion 2/94* [1996] ECR I 1759 the ECJ commented on the EC's power to act in the field of
human rights. The ECJ examined the issue of whether the EC could accede to the ECHR.
The principal change which would be brought about by accession would be that the EC
institutions would be subject to scrutiny by the ECt.HR. The ECJ declined to rule on the
compatibility of accession with the EC Treaty on the basis that it did not have sufficient
information regarding the institutional systems which would operate. The ECJ went on to
consider whether the EC had competence to accede to the ECHR. The ECJ, in ruling that
the EC lacked competence to accede, opined at paragraph 27:

'No Treaty provision confers on the Community institutions any general power to enact
rules on human rights or to conclude international conventions in this field.'

The ECJ went on to consider whether Art 235 EC (now Art 308) could constitute a legal
basis for accession. Art 235 is designed to fill a gap where no specific provisions of
the Treaty confer on the Community institutions powers to act, if such powers appear
necessary to enable the EC to carry out its objectives. The ECJ stated at paragraph 30:

'. . . Article 235 cannot be used as a basis for the adoption of provisions whose effect
would, in substance be to amend the Treaty without following the procedure which it
provides for that purpose.'

Craig and de Búrca ('EU Law: Text, Cases and Materials', 3rd edn 2003, OUP, 353) have
explained the judgment in the following terms:

'In ruling that the Community lacked legislative competence under the Treaties to
become a party to the [ECHR], the ECJ gave some indication of the limits of human
rights as a legislative foundation for Community action, although without ruling more
specifically on the issue of what other, less fundamental kinds of legislation the [EC]
might be competent to adopt in the human rights field. Paragraph 27 is particularly
relevant in this respect, although it merely denies that the [EC] has any jurisdiction
under specific Treaty provisions to enact general rules on human rights.

The opinion however can be read as agreeing that Article 235 (now Article 308) may
form a basis for the adoption of specific Community measures for the protection of
human rights, so long as they do not amount to an amendment of the Treaty by going
beyond the scope of the Community's defined aims and activities.

... What appeared to place accession to the ECHR beyond the scope of [EC] competence was ... the fact that the agreement envisaged would bring with it fundamental institutional and constitutional changes which would actually require a Treaty amendment ...'

In a later case, the ECJ again discussed the issue of competence, specifically the external competence of the EC, in the field of human rights. In Case C-268/94 *Portugal v Council* [1996] ECR I 6177, Portugal challenged the legal basis of the EC's competence to conclude a development co-operation agreement with India. Portugal argued that that the acceptance of fundamental rights as general principles of Community law did not equate with a competence in the field, whether internal or external. Portugal submitted that the references to human rights in the Treaties were 'programmatic', that they defined a general objective of the EC but did not confer a specific power of action.

The agreement's legal basis was in Arts 113 and 130y EC (now Arts 133 and 181). In particular, Portugal objected to a provision in the agreement that respect for human rights and democratic principles was the basis for the co-operation and constituted an essential element of the agreement. In Portugal's view, the correct legal basis for the adoption of such human rights provisions was Art 235. The ECJ held that the correct legal basis had been utilised and pointed to the provision in Art 130u (now Art 177) which states that EC policy in the sphere of development co-operation shall contribute to respecting human rights and fundamental freedoms. The ECJ notes that the human rights clause in the agreement was an essential element and not a specific field of co-operation. According to Craig and De Búrca (p 354), the implication of this judgment is that the EC 'would not have had competence under Art 151 (ex Art 130y) to conclude a co-operation agreement principally on the subject of human rights, although it does have the power, under its development policy provisions, to insert a clause such as this one, making respect for human rights an essential element and basis for co-operation.' Article 181a, added by the Nice Treaty provides an express basis for human rights clauses in a co-operation policy.

In Case C-249/96 *Grant v South-West Trains Ltd* [1998] ECR I 621, at paragraph 5, the ECJ explained the limitation on the power to act in the field of human rights in the following terms:

> 'Although respect for the fundamental rights which form an integral part of those general principles of law is a condition of the legality of Community acts, those rights cannot in themselves have the effect of extending the scope of the Treaty provisions beyond the competences of the Community.'

It seems that the EC may act to protect human rights provided it acts within the scope of EC Law. (See Weiler, and Fries, 'A Human Rights Policy for the European Community and Union: The Question of Competences' in Alston, 'The EU and Human Rights', 1999, OUP, 147, 157). Craig and de Búrca ('EU Law: Text, Cases and Materials', 3rd edn, 2003, OUP, 357) submit that '[t]he institutional response to *Opinion 2/94* of the Court was a cautious one'. As evidence of this cautious approach, they cite, *inter alia*, Art 13, which, while creating a new EC power to combat discrimination, can be adopted only within the limits of the powers conferred on the EC by the Treaty and Art 51 of the Charter of Fundamental Rights, which emphasises that the Charter does not establish any new power for the Community. That no new competences would be conferred by virtue of incorporation of the Charter into the Draft Treaty establishing a Constitution for Europe (CONV 820/1/03) is apparent from the text of Art II 51(2) which provides:

> '*This Charter does not extend the field of application of Union law beyond the powers of the Union or establish any new power or task for the Union, or modify powers and tasks defined in the other parts of the Constitution.*'

5.6.3 MEMBER STATE COMPETENCE SUBJECT TO REVIEW BY AN INTERNATIONAL COURT

Another issue arises from the nature of EC law and the transferral of competences from the national to the supranational legal order. Member States are the primary protectors of human rights within their own territories but in fact the Member States are not completely independent in their application of human rights law.

All fifteen Member States are party to the ECHR, and consequently, have subjected themselves to review by an external international court (the ECt.HR) for compliance with a minimum standard of human rights protection as set out by the ECHR.

The question arises as to whether the Member States can transfer to a supranational legal order, competences, that at national level would be subject to review in accordance with human rights norms, when that supranational legal order is not (or at least was not) subject to review for compliance with human rights standards. This question is discussed in this chapter specifically in terms of the relationship between the EC and ECHR legal orders. It should be noted that the ECHR is not the only supervisory mechanism to which the EU Member States are party. A paragraph from the EU Annual Report on Human Rights, 2002, 13 (published on the europa website as 12747/02 Rev 1 COHOM 11. 16 October 2002, Brussels) illustrates this point.

'Protection and promotion of human rights within the member states of the Union are primarily a concern of the States themselves with due regard to their own judicial systems and international obligations. The member states are parties to a number of international instruments of legally binding as well as political character, and are therefore obliged to account for their actions within the field of human rights to a number of international organisations, including the Council of Europe, the Organisation for Security and co-operation in Europe and the United Nations.'

5.6.4 ARE EUROPEAN COMMUNITY ACTS SUBJECT TO SCRUTINY UNDER THE ECHR MACHINERY?

Article I 7(2) of the Draft Treaty establishing a Constitution for Europe (CONV 820/1/03 Brussels 27 June 2003) provides that the EU shall seek accession to the ECHR. As the draft Treaty has not yet been ratified, this section examines the current situation.

Previously, the EC refused to accede to the ECHR. This was a political decision taken by the Member States. Consequently it would seem that the EC institutions are not currently subject to review by the ECt.HR. Ironically, the Member States may find themselves accountable for breaches of the ECHR by the EC institutions. A recent ECt.HR decision illustrates this point.

The facts of *Matthews v United Kingdom* [1999] 28 EHRR 361 involved the applicant alleging a violation of the right to vote provision of the ECHR (Art 3, Protocol 1) by a Council decision and a Treaty. These European laws prevented the applicant, a national of Gibraltar, from voting in the direct elections to the European Parliament (EP). The ECt.HR held that the Community acts at issue were subject to review by the ECt.HR and held the Member States accountable for this breach. The ECt.HR held that the UK along with the other EU Member States, as contracting parties to the ECHR, could be held responsible for denying the inhabitants of Gibraltar the right to vote in the EP elections.

It should be emphasised however, that the acts at issue in *Matthews*, as primary laws are not capable of review by the ECJ. The ECt.HR stated at paragraph 33 of the decision in *Matthews* 'Indeed [the primary law at issue in *Matthews*] cannot be challenged before the European Court of Justice for the very reason that it is not a "normal" act of the Community, but is a Treaty within the Community legal order.'(ECJ jurisdiction is discussed at **5.7.1**) *Matthews* cannot be taken as clear authority for the proposition that all

Community or Union acts are subject to review by the ECt.HR. At the time of writing, there are a number of cases pending before the ECt.HR which will clarify this issue. (Application 45036/98 *Bosphorus Hava Yollari Turizm ve Ticaret AS v Ireland*, 13 September 2001, ECt.HR (unreported) admissibility decision, Case 56672/00 *DSR Senator Lines v Austria and Others*)

5.6.5 THE FUTURE OF EUROPE AND ACCESSION

The Future of Europe Working Group on the Charter/ECHR was asked to consider the question of whether the European Union should be able to accede to the European Convention on Human Rights.

The Working Group stressed that it was to decide only the issue of whether to introduce into the new Treaty a constitutional authorisation enabling the Union to accede to the ECHR. It would be for the Council of Ministers of the EU to decide unanimously when and how accession might take place.

All members of the Group either strongly supported or were willing to give favourable consideration to the creation of a constitutional authorisation enabling the EU to accede to the ECHR. The Working Group set out the main political and legal arguments in favour of accession:

> 'As the Union reaffirms its own values through its Charter, its accession to the ECHR would give a strong political signal of the coherence between the Union and the 'greater Europe', reflected in the Council of Europe and its pan-European human rights system.

> Accession to the ECHR would give citizens an analogous protection *vis à vis* all the Member States. This appears to be a question of credibility, given that Member States have transferred substantial competences to the Union and that adherence to the ECHR has been made a condition for membership of new States in the Union.

> Accession would be the ideal tool to ensure a harmonious development of the case law of the two European Courts in human rights matters; for some, this has even greater force in view of a possible incorporation of the Charter into the Treaties. In this connection, mention should also be made of the problems resulting from the present non-participation of the Union in the Strasbourg judicial system in cases where the Strasbourg Court is led to rule indirectly on Union law without the Union being able to defend itself before that Court or to have a judge in the court who would ensure the necessary expertise on Union law.'

The Working Group concluded that a legal basis to authorise accession of the EU to the ECHR should be inserted in the Constitutional Treaty but that accession should be on the basis of a unanimous decision of the Council and with the assent of the European Parliament.

The Working Group emphasised at p. 12 that after accession, the ECt.HR could not be regarded as a superior court but rather as a specialised court exercising external control over the international obligations of the EU resulting from accession to the ECHR. The Working Group indicated that incorporation of the Charter (see **5.10.10**) and accession should be viewed as complementary rather than as alternative steps.

The Working Group also clarified a number of issues surrounding the accession debate. First, accession will have effect only insofar as the law of the EU is concerned; no new EU competences will be created, the EU would not become a member of the Council of Europe, there would be an EU judge at the Strasbourg Court and the positions of the individual Member States with respect to the ECHR would not be affected.

Article I-7(2) of the Draft Treaty establishing a Constitution for Europe (CONV 820/1/03 Brussels 27 June 2003) provides:

'The Union shall seek accession to the European Convention for the Protection of Human Rights and Fundamental Freedoms. Accession to that Convention shall not affect the Union's competences as defined in this Constitution.'

5.6.6 IS THERE AN OBLIGATION ON THE ECJ TO ENSURE ADHERENCE TO THE ECHR?

The reference for a preliminary ruling in Case C-466/00 *Kaba v Secretary of State for the Home Department*, 6 March 2003 raises an interesting issue of whether there is an obligation on the ECJ to ensure adherence to the ECHR. The question asked by the UK Immigration Adjudicator was whether the procedure followed in a case before her, which had included an earlier preliminary reference to the ECJ, met the requirements of a fair hearing pursuant to Article 6, ECHR. However the ECJ was able to resolve the matter at issue without specifically answering this question.

5.7 Scope of Fundamental Human Rights Protection in the EU

Two questions arise concerning the scope of application of this EU human rights protection. First, over what activities of the Union does the ECJ have jurisdiction and secondly, who is bound by the EC standard of human rights protection?

5.7.1 ECJ JURISDICTION

Currently the ECJ does not have jurisdiction over all EU activity.

The Maastricht Treaty heralded the establishment of the European Union founded on three pillars. One of these pillars is the European Economic Community which became the European Community and over which the ECJ has jurisdiction. Common Foreign and Security Policy constitutes the second pillar and Justice and Home Affairs, the third pillar. These two new pillars were essentially intergovernmental rather than supranational in nature.

The Treaty of Amsterdam amended certain aspects of the EU's pillar structure. Some elements of the third pillar were incorporated into the European Community (first) pillar. The ECJ was given jurisdiction over certain measures under the third pillar but there are differences in some procedures. ECJ jurisdiction remained excluded from the second pillar. Article 46 TEU defines the scope of the ECJ's jurisdiction after the Amsterdam amendments. The Treaty of Nice did not significantly change the scope of the ECJ's jurisdiction but the procedures of Art 7 TEU were rendered justiciable (see **5.4**).

Certain areas of EU activity are currently outside the scope of ECJ human rights review as the ECJ does not have jurisdiction.

Pursuant to the Draft Treaty Establishing a Constitution for Europe (CONV 820/1/03 Brussels, 27 June 2003), the three pillar structure will almost cease to exist (see **5.10.7**). Within the limits of the powers conferred by the Draft Treaty Establishing a Constitution for Europe, it seems the ECJ will have jurisdiction over almost all EU activity (Articles I-18 and 28). ECJ jurisdiction will continue to be excluded in the areas of common foreign and security policy and the common security and defence policy (Article III 282).

5.7.2 ARE THE MEMBER STATES SUBJECT TO REVIEW BY THE ECJ FOR COMPLIANCE WITH THE EC HUMAN RIGHTS STANDARD?

It is clear from the case-law discussed above that the ECJ reviews the acts of the institutions for compatibility with human rights, as general principles of Community law. The issue also arises as to whether the Member States are subject to review for compliance with the human rights *acquis*. Are the Member States subject to review by the ECJ for compliance with the EC human rights standard within the field of EC law?

As the EC human rights standard is sourced in the constitutional traditions of the Member States and international human rights instruments to which the Member States are party, it might appear that the Member States would have no objection to complying with the EC human rights *acquis*. However, there are a number of reasons why the Member States might object. Rights protected may vary from Member State to Member State. The standard and/or scope of protection may also vary. Also, the ECJ's jurisdiction to review the acts of Member States is very limited. It is likely, at least at the outset of the European integration project, that the Member States would have been surprised to find themselves subject to review by the ECJ for compliance with a human rights standard to which they had not expressly agreed. The ECJ has however held the Member States subject to review for compliance with the EC human rights *acquis* when the Member States act in the context of Community law.

> '. . . it should be remembered that the requirements flowing from the protection of fundamental rights in the Community legal order are also binding on Member States when they implement Community rules. (Case C-2/92 *R v Ministry of Agriculture, ex parte Bostock* [1994] ECR I-955, paragraph 16 and Case C-292/97 *Karlsson*, paragraph 37).'

The reason why Member States are only subject to review for compliance with the European human rights *acquis* in limited instances results from the division of competences between the EC/EU and the Member States.

A number of specific categories in which the Member States are subject to review by the ECJ for compliance with the EC human rights *acquis* emerge from the case-law. (See Craig and De Búrca, 'EU Law: Text, Cases and Materials' (3rd ed) OUP, 2003, 338 *et seq*).

First, where Member States are applying provisions of Community law which are based on protection for human rights. A case within this category is the decision in Case 222/84 *Johnston v Chief Constable of the RUC* [1986] ECR 1651. The ECJ recognised the right to an effective remedy as a general principle of EC law. The ECJ held that Member States when applying the Equal Treatment Directive 76/207 are obliged to ensure the right to obtain an effective remedy in a competent court against measures which they consider to be contrary to the principle of equal treatment for men and women.

Secondly, when Member States are interpreting and enforcing Community provisions and thus acting as agents for the EC. Where the Community measures at issue do not specifically protect the right claimed, the ECJ has required the Member States to protect the right in their implementation processes. An example of a case within this category is the decision in Case 5/88 *Wachauf v Germany* [1989] ECR 2609. The applicant, a tenant farmer sought compensation for the discontinuance of milk production. A Community measure provided for such compensation. The German national implementing measure made the payment of compensation, conditional on the written consent of the lessor. The ECJ held that to deprive the tenant of the fruits of his labour, without compensation would be incompatible with the requirement of protection of fundamental rights within the EC legal order. The ECJ held that these requirements were also binding on Member States when they implement Community rules. An example in the Irish courts is the decision in *Maher v Minister for Agriculture* [2001] 2 IR 139. This case involved a challenge to the validity of a statutory instrument implementing an EC Regulation on milk quotas. The Supreme Court was bound by the interpretation of the extent to which a milk quota could be considered a property right in Case C-2/92 *R v Ministry of Agriculture, ex parte Bostock* [1994] ECR I-955.

Thirdly, when Member States derogate from Community Law requirements. An example of a case within this category is Case C-260/89 *Elliniki Radiophonia Tileorassi AE v Dimotiki Etairia Pliroforissis* [1991] ECR I 2925. The ECJ held that national measures derogating from the freedom to provide services would only be permissible where the derogations were compatible with the protection of fundamental rights, specifically in this case, freedom of expression.

Apart from these specific examples, it is difficult to define precisely the limits of the scope of EC law application and thus difficult to specify the limit of the ECJ's power to review Member State action for compliance with the EC human rights standard.

It is clear that cases which fall within the scope of national law and outside the scope of Community law will not be subject to review by the ECJ. An example is the ECJ decision in Case C-299/95 *Kremzow v Austria* [1997] ECR I 2629. The proceedings leading to Kremzow's conviction for murder were held by the ECt.HR to be in violation of the Article 6 ECHR right to a fair trial. Kremzow argued in the ECJ proceedings that his right to free movement had been infringed by his unlawful imprisonment. The ECJ held that there was no connection between his situation and any of the situations contemplated by the Treaty provisions on free movement of persons. Hence the circumstances of his case fell outside the scope of Community law. As such, the ECJ did not have jurisdiction to review national measures for compatibility with the EC human rights standard.

5.8   The Standard of Human Rights Protection

The ECJ applies a Community standard of human rights protection. The Community interest is different to the Member State interest. The ECJ does not apply the maximum standard of human rights protection, ie it does not impose the highest standard from one State on other Member States. Neither does the ECJ apply a minimum standard.

5.8.1   LIMITS OF EC HUMAN RIGHTS PROTECTION

Protection of human rights at EC level is not absolute (see **5.2.5**). To ascertain the standard of human rights protection it is beneficial to analyse some case-law and the limits imposed on the protection of human rights. Human rights are regularly used to challenge Community provisions. While the ECJ has often accepted that, in principle, a right is protected, there are only rare examples of broad Community legislation being struck down on the grounds of a violation of human rights. (See Weatherill and Beaumont 'EU Law', 3rd edn, 1999, Penguin, 287–8 and Craig and de Búrca, 'EU Law: Text, Cases and Materials', 3rd edn, 2003 OUP, 327–337). Craig and de Búrca point out that '[a] greater degree of success has been achieved in cases challenging specific administrative acts, rather than broad legislative measures, for breach of fundamental rights.' According to Weatherill and Beaumont '[o]ne of the reasons that fundamental rights pleas [in EC law] are rarely successful is that that rights are not absolute . . .'.

The approach of the ECJ to broad legislative measures is apparent in Case 4/73 *Nold v Commission* [1974] ECR 491 (see **5.2.5**). The applicant sought to annul a Commission decision authorising new trading rules, on the grounds, *inter alia*, that his fundamental rights had been violated. The applicant submitted that the effect of the decision was to deprive him of direct supplies for his business, thereby endangering both the profitability and the free development of business activity to such an extent as to endanger the existence of the business, thereby violating his proprietary rights and the right to free pursuit of a business. The ECJ stated that it was bound to ensure the observance of fundamental rights before indicating limitations on the protections of rights.

'If rights of ownership are protected by the constitutional laws of all the member states and if similar guarantees in respect of their right freely to choose and practise their trade or profession, the rights thereby guaranteed, far from constituting unfettered prerogatives, must be viewed in the light of the social function of the property and activities protected thereunder.

For this reason, rights of this nature are protected by law subject always to limitations laid down in accordance with the public interest.

Within the Community legal order it likewise seems legitimate that these rights should, if necessary, be subject to certain limits justified by the overall objectives pursued by the Community, on condition that the substance of these rights is left untouched.

As regards the guarantees accorded to a particular undertaking, they can in no respect be extended to mere commercial interests or opportunities, the uncertainties of which are part of the very essence of economic activity.

The disadvantages claimed by the applicant are in fact the result of economic change and not of the contested decision.'

In Case 5/88 *Wachauf v Germany* [1989] ECR 2609 (see **5.7.2**), a tenant farmer sought compensation pursuant to an EC regulation for the discontinuance of milk production. The German national implementing measure made the payment of compensation conditional on the written consent of the lessor. The ECJ held that to deprive the tenant of the fruits of his labour, without compensation, was incompatible with the requirement of protection of fundamental rights within the EC legal order. The ECJ stated that fundamental rights recognised by the court are not absolute.

'The fundamental rights recognised by the Court are not absolute, however but must be considered in relation to their social function. Consequently, restrictions may be imposed on the exercise of those rights, in particular in the context of a common organisation of the market, provided that those restrictions in fact correspond to the objectives of general interest, pursued by the Community and do not constitute, with regard to the aim pursued, a disproportionate and intolerable interference, impairing the very substance of those rights.'

The ECJ went on to hold that Regulation at issue did not breach fundamental rights as the Regulation afforded the competent national authority a sufficiently wide margin of appreciation to enable the rules to be applied in accordance with the requirement of fundamental human rights protection.

In Case 44/79 *Hauer v Rheinland-Pfalz* [1979] ECR 3727 (see **5.2.5**), the applicant submitted that a Regulation prohibiting the new planting of vines infringed, *inter alia*, her right to property. The ECJ conducted a survey of limits on the right to property contained in a number of Member State constitutions and in the ECHR, in determining that the Regulation at issue did not entail any undue limitation on the right to property and that the restriction was justified in the interest of the common organisation of the market.

In Case C-280/93 *Germany v Council* [1994] ECR 4973, a case involving the introduction of a quota and rules for its subdivision in the banana market resulting in alleged discrimination against traders in third country bananas, the ECJ again stated that the rights at issue, the rights to property and freedom to pursue a profession were not absolute but could be restricted in the context of a common organisation of the market.

The facts of Case C-84/95 *Bosphorus Hava Yolari Turizm ve Ticaret AS v Minister for Transport, Energy and Communications* [1996] ECR I 3953 involved the impounding, by the Irish Government, of an aircraft leased by the applicant, pursuant to EU sanctions against the Federal Republic of Yugoslavia (Serbia and Montenegro). The applicant alleged breaches of its right to peaceful enjoyment of its property and its freedom to pursue a commercial activity and of the principle of proportionality. The ECJ held that the impounding of the aircraft was not contrary to EC human rights law, stating that it was 'settled case-law that the fundamental rights invoked by [the applicant] are not absolute and their exercise may be subject to restrictions justified by objectives of general interest pursued by the Community'. In the view of the ECJ, the measure could not be disregarded as disproportionate in light of the objective of the international community to put an end to the state of war.

It is apparent from the cases cited that restrictions can be imposed on human rights protection. In *Wachauf, Hauer* and *Germany v Council* the ECJ justified restrictions on fundamental rights by reference to the common organisation of the market. In *Bosphorus Hava Yolari Turizm ve Ticaret AS* the ECJ justified restrictions by reference to the international situation at the time, namely a state of war.

It seems an interpretation of EC Law flowing from the Treaty may trump the protection of a right.

The facts of Case 263/02 P *Commission v Jégo-Quéré et Cie SA*, not yet decided, involve an appeal against a decision of the Court of First Instance (CFI) (Case T-177/01 *Jégo-Quéré v Commission* [2002] ECR II 2365) in which the CFI had proposed a new interpretation of the test for individual concern. Article 230(4) EC requires natural or legal persons to show direct and individual concern to establish standing to bring an application for annulment. Jégo-Quéré had been unable to show individual concern according to the traditional interpretation. The CFI held that the strictness of the traditional interpretation meant that in some circumstances Community Law would fail to guarantee to individuals access to an effective judicial remedy and went on to propose a new reading of individual concern.

Subsequent to the CFI decision the ECJ in Case C-50/00 P *Unión de Pequeños Agricultores* [2002] ECR I 6677 upheld the traditional interpretation of individual concern as an unavoidable condition for standing under Article 230(4) EC. The appeal in Case 263/02 P *Commission v Jégo-Quéré* falls to be decided in light of the ECJ decision in Case C-50/00 P *Unión de Pequeños Agricultores* [2002] ECR I 6677. The ECJ has not yet decided the case but Advocate General Jacobs delivered his opinion in July 2003.

> 'However, it clearly follows from the [ECJ's] judgment in *Unión de Pequeños Agricultores* [Case C-50/00 P [2002] ECR I 6677] that the traditional interpretation of individual concern, because it is understood to flow from the Treaty itself, must be applied regardless of its consequences for the right to an effective judicial remedy.
>
> Such an outcome is to my mind unsatisfactory, but is the unavoidable consequence of the limitations which the current formulation of the fourth paragraph of Article 230 is considered by the Court to impose. As the Court made clear in *Unión de Pequeños Agricultores* [Case C-50/00 P [2002] ECR I 6677], necessary reforms to the Community system of judicial review are therefore dependent upon action by the Member States to amend that provision of the Treaty. In my opinion, there are powerful arguments in favour of introducing a more liberal standing requirement in respect of individuals seeking to challenge generally applicable Community measures in order to ensure that full judicial protection is in all circumstances guaranteed.'

It is submitted that the real concern for human rights protection within the scope of EC law is that EC Law is superior to the human rights protections of the Member State constitutions whether EC Law protects human rights or not and regardless of the standard or limits of rights protection. On occasion the ECJ has been criticised for not taking human rights protections seriously. (Coppel and O' Neill *'The European Court of Justice: Taking Rights Seriously?'* (1992) 29 CMLR 669. But see also Weiler and Lockhart, ' *"Taking Rights Seriously" Seriously: The European Court and its Fundamental Rights Jurisprudence'* (1995) 32 CMLR 51 and 579.)

5.9 The Human Rights Acquis

5.9.1 WHAT RIGHTS ARE PROTECTED?

Whilst the protection of human rights by the ECJ is to be welcomed, it is open to the criticism that it is uncertain. Human rights protection by the ECJ has developed on an *ad hoc* basis in response to the issues raised. There is no guarantee that a right will be afforded protection by the ECJ if it is protected in the Constitutions of the Member States or in an international human rights treaty. The issue of whether a right is protected in European law is only determined when the ECJ makes a pronouncement on that right. This is hardly a satisfactory situation for an aggrieved litigant.

It is proposed to examine some of the rights protected in the European human rights *acquis* under three headings to provide example of the sources of human rights law. This discussion does not contain an exhaustive list of the rights protected nor the sources of rights in European law, but will serve as an indication of the human rights *acquis*.

5.9.2 THE TREATIES AS A SOURCE OF HUMAN RIGHTS

The omission of a bill of rights from the original Community Treaties was mentioned earlier. A number of provisions in the Treaty relate to human rights issues; for example Article 12 EC (ex Art 6) prohibits discrimination on the grounds of nationality and Article 141 EC (ex Art 119) provides for equal pay for equal work for men and women.

More recently, the Treaty of Amsterdam added two new legal bases in the field of human rights. Article 13 empowers the political institutions to take action to combat discrimination based on sex, racial or ethnic origin, religion or belief, disability, age or sexual orientation. Article 141 EC (ex Art 19) has been widened to apply the principle of equal opportunities and equal treatment of men and women in matter of employment and occupation as well as pay. In addition, Article 141(4) allows for affirmative action in favour of the under represented sex.

5.9.3 SECONDARY LEGISLATION AS A SOURCE OF HUMAN RIGHTS

Secondary EC legislation may also act as a source of human rights. It is beyond the ambit of this chapter to analyse all relevant secondary legislation. Instead it examines some important examples of secondary legislation.

On the basis of Art 13 EC, as inserted by the Treaty of Amsterdam, two Directives have recently been adopted relating to equal treatment. Council Directive 2000/43 on Race Discrimination is designed to prohibit discrimination on the grounds of race and ethnic origin. (Council Directive 2000/43 [2000] OJ L 180/22.) The Directive prohibits any direct or indirect discrimination on the grounds of race or ethnic origin in areas such as access to employment, access to vocational training, working conditions, membership of organisations, social protection, education and access to supply of goods and services. The Directive is applicable to both the public and private sectors. In cases where the facts establish a presumption of discrimination the burden shifts to the respondent to show that there has been no breach of the principle of equal treatment. Council Directive 2000/78 establishes a general framework to secure equal treatment in employment and occupation and is designed to prohibit discrimination on the grounds of religion, belief, disability, age and sexual orientation. (Council Directive 2000/78 [2000] OJ L303/16).

There are also a considerable number of directives relating to workers rights. These include Directive 89/391/EEC on the introduction of measures to encourage improvements in the safety and health of workers at work, Directive 80/987/EEC on the protection of employees in the event of the insolvency of their employer, Directive 93/104/EC concerning certain aspects of the organisation of working time, Directive 94/33/EC on the protection of young people at work and Council Directive 93/85/EEC on the introduction of measures to encourage improvements in the health and safety at work of pregnant workers and workers who have recently given birth or are breastfeeding.

5.9.4 RIGHTS RECOGNISED IN THE CASE-LAW OF THE ECJ

The early development of the protection of human rights by the ECJ was discussed at **5.2.5**. The ECJ indicated that the sources of rights included the constitutional traditions of Member States and international Treaties on which the Member States have collaborated.

There is a useful survey of the rights which the ECJ has ruled on in Lenaerts and Van Nuffel, 'Constitutional Law of The European Union', 1999, Sweet and Maxwell, 548. This list gives an indication of the breadth of rights protected by the ECJ. The rights recognised in the case-law of the ECJ are:

- The principle of equal treatment

- The right to a fair hearing and to an effective remedy

- The principle that provisions of criminal law may not have retroactive effect

- Respect for private life, family life, the home and correspondence, in particular respect for a person's physical integrity, the right to keep one's state of health private, medical confidentiality and the right to inviolability of one's home

- Freedom to manifest one's religion

- Freedom of expression

- Freedom of association, in particular the right to be a member of a trade union and to take part in trade union activities

- Rights of ownership or the rights to property

- Freedom to carry on an economic activity (trade or profession)

- The right of everyone lawfully within the territory of a state to liberty of movement therein.

5.10 The Charter of Fundamental Rights of the European Union

5.10.1 BACKGROUND TO THE CHARTER

The European Council in Cologne in June 1999 agreed that it was necessary to establish a Charter of Fundamental Rights 'in order to make their overriding importance and relevance more visible to the Union's citizens.' (Conclusions of the European Council, Cologne, 3 and 4 June 1999.) The Council agreed that the Charter should contain the fundamental rights and freedoms as well as the basic procedural rights guaranteed by the ECHR and derived from the constitutional traditions common to the Member States, as general principles of Community law, fundamental rights that pertain only to the Union's citizens and that the Charter should take account of the economic and social rights as contained in the European Social Charter and the Community Charter of the Fundamental Social

Rights of Workers (Article 136 TEU, insofar as they do not merely establish objectives for action by the Union). The Cologne European Council set up a timetable and a procedural framework for the drafting of the Charter.

5.10.2 INTRODUCTORY COMMENTS

At the meeting of the European Council in Nice on 7 December 2000, the European Parliament, the Council and the Commission solemnly proclaimed the Charter of Fundamental Rights of the European Union.

The stated objective of the Charter is to increase the visibility of human rights protection within the European Union legal order. Consequently, the Charter is confined to cataloguing existing rights. This point requires two clarifications. First (and more obviously) the purpose of the exercise was to increase the visibility of existing rights and not to create new rights. Second, that the task of the Charter is to catalogue existing rights might give rise to the supposition that all rights protected in EC law are to be found in the Charter. The Charter, however, affords a higher standard of protection than is actually protected (i.e. higher than the standard currently protected by ECJ case-law) but a lower standard than that which the ECJ is capable of protecting by reference to the constitutional traditions of the Member States and/or international human rights treaties to which the Member States are party.

Another interesting aspect of the Charter relates to the unusual manner of it's drafting. (See de Búrca, 'The Drafting of the European Union Charter of Fundamental Rights' (2001) 26 European LR 126.) The Charter was drafted by a unique body composed of 62 representatives of the Member State governments, the Commission, the European Parliament and the national parliaments. The openness of the deliberative process stands in marked contrast to the traditional IGC method of EU development. A multitude of submissions were made by other institutions, civil society, NGOs and applicant countries. Proceedings were generally in public and submissions and drafts were available on the Charter website. The Charter was drafted on a consensus-building basis. At least from the perspective of increased transparency, the process can be regarded as a success. In fact, the Convention for drafting the Charter was the model for the Convention on the Future of Europe which drafted the Draft Treaty establishing a Constitution for Europe in preparation for the next IGC (see **5.4.1** and **5.10.10**).

An explanatory text of the Charter has been published by the drafting body. The purpose of the explanatory text is purely to clarify the provisions of the Charter and it currently has no legal status.

5.10.3 CONTENTS OF THE CHARTER

This section provides an overview of the content of the Charter and the origins of the rights to be protected. The Charter is divided into a preamble and seven chapters: Dignity, Freedoms, Equality, Solidarity, Citizenship, Justice and General Provisions. The proposed form of the Charter in the Draft Treaty establishing a Constitution for Europe (CONV 820/1/03 Brussels, 27 June 2003) contains few amendments. One cosmetic change involves the Chapters of the Charter becoming Titles of Volume II of the Draft Treaty. Pending ratification of the Treaty (and the consequent incorporation of the Charter), this section will continue to refer to the Charter in its current form. The version of the Charter in the draft Treaty establishing a Constitution for Europe almost replicates the current Charter. Some changes, discussed below, have been incorporated into Title VII: General Provisions (currently Chapter VII).

Chapter I, *Dignity*, affirms the protection of the dignity of the person, the right to life (including freedom from the death penalty), right to integrity of the person, freedom from torture, inhuman or degrading treatment and punishment and prohibition of slavery and forced labour. The majority of the articles in this chapter correspond to rights protected by the ECHR but inspiration is also drawn from the Universal Declaration on Human Rights and the Convention on Human Rights and Biomedicine.

Chapter II, *Freedoms*, assures a right to liberty and security, respect for private and family life, protection of personal data, the right to marry and found a family, freedom of thought, conscience and religion, freedom of expression and information, freedom of assembly and association, freedom of the arts and sciences, a right to education, freedom to choose an occupation and a right to engage in work, freedom to conduct a business, a right to property, a right to asylum and protection in the event of removal, expulsion or extradition. Similarly, the articles in Chapter II correspond in large part to the freedoms guaranteed by the ECHR with additional inspiration from the constitutions of EU member states, Community secondary legislation, case-law of the ECJ and the Geneva Convention on Human Rights.

Chapter III, *Equality*, protects Equality before the Law, non-discrimination, cultural, religious and linguistic diversity, equality between men and women, rights of the child, rights of the elderly and integration of persons with disabilities. Chapter III is inspired by European constitutions, case-law of the ECJ, the ECHR, the Convention on Human Rights and Biomedicine, the EC Treaty, Community legislation, the European Social Charter and the New York Convention on the Rights of the Child.

Chapter IV, *Solidarity*, provides for workers' rights to information and consultation within the undertaking, a right of collective bargaining and action, a right of action to placement services, protection in the event of unjustified dismissal, fair and just working conditions, prohibition of child labour and protection of young people at work, reconciling family and professional life, social security and social assistance, health care, access to services of general economic interest, environmental protection and consumer protection. The rights in Chapter IV are predominantly drawn from the European Social Charter with additional inspiration from the ECHR and the EC Treaty.

Chapter V, *Citizenship*, assures a right to vote and to stand as a candidate in elections to the European Parliament, a right to vote and to stand as a candidate at municipal elections, a right to good administration, a right of access to documents, a right to refer to the Ombudsman, a right to petition the European Parliament, freedom of movement and of residence, diplomatic and consular protection. Rights accruing to EU citizens are drawn from the EC Treaty and ECJ case-law.

Chapter VI, *Justice*, guarantees a right to an effective remedy and a fair trial, presumption of innocence, a right of defence, principles of legality, proportionality of criminal offences and penalties and a right not to be tried or punished twice in criminal proceedings for the same criminal offence. The dominant source of Justice rights is the ECHR with further inspiration from the case-law of the ECJ and the ICCPR.

Chapter VII, *General Provisions*, sets out the scope of the provisions of the Charter, the scope of guaranteed rights, the level of protection and prohibits an abuse of rights. Chapter VII includes the 'horizontal clauses' whose objects are to explain the relationship of the Charter with the ECHR and to safeguard the position of the ECHR.

There are a number of changes to Chapter VII in the version of the charter to be incorporated in the Draft Treaty establishing a Constitution for Europe. Article 51 is amended to clarify that the Charter does not modify the allocation of competences between the EU and the Member States. A horizontal provision (Article II-52(4)) is added to ensure that where the Charter recognises rights which result from the common traditions of the Member States that those rights are interpreted in accordance with those traditions. A provision is added (Article II-52(5)) clarifying the meaning of the term 'principles' to confirm the distinction between rights and principles in the Charter. A provision is added (Article II-52(6)) to clarify that full account shall be taken of national laws and practices as specified in the Charter. These changes were suggested by the Working Group on the Incorporation of the Charter. The Working Group emphasised that its suggested amendments were not intended to alter the substance of the Charter but rather to render absolutely clear and legally watertight certain key elements of the overall consensus of the Charter as agreed by the previous Convention. (CONV 354/02 Final report of Working Group II 'Incorporation of the Charter/Accession to the ECHR' Brussels, 22 October 2002).

5.10.4   THE LEGAL STATUS OF THE CHARTER

A legally binding Charter would require a Treaty amendment. The Draft Treaty establishing a Constitution for Europe proposes the incorporation of the Charter. Even assuming there is agreement on the Draft Treaty establishing a Constitution for Europe it will be a number of years before it enters into force as it must be ratified by each Member State of the enlarged EU, according to each State's constitutional tradition. Pending incorporation, this section examines the current status of the Charter.

A decision was taken by the Member States at the Nice IGC that the Charter was to be declaratory rather than a legally binding text. The Member States decided not to incorporate the Charter into the Treaties, nor to refer to the Charter as a source of general principles of human rights law in Art 6 (ex Art F) TEU. In the Nice (December 2000) and Laeken (December 2001) Declarations on the Future of Europe, it was agreed that consideration would be given to the status of the Charter of Fundamental Rights and whether it would be included in the EC Treaty. These decisions will be taken at the IGC which commenced in 2003. (See **5.10.10**.)

The Charter is not binding and thus not a source of rights. However, some of the rights listed in the Charter are already legally binding within the EC legal order. The reason for this is that the Charter has disparate sources. Some of the articles are based on the Treaties, secondary EC legislation and the case-law of the ECJ while others stem from the ECHR, other international human rights instruments to which the EU Member States are party and the national constitutions of the EU Member States. The former are binding on the EC while the latter serve as guidelines to the general principles of EC human rights law.

Pursuant to Article 6(2) TEU (ex Art F), the ECJ already has jurisdiction to monitor the acts of the institutions to ensure compliance with rights found in the ECHR and constitutional traditions of the Member States.

To determine whether a right is binding it is necessary to look at its source.

5.10.5   WHAT FUNDAMENTAL RIGHTS IN THE CHARTER ARE ALREADY PROTECTED IN EUROPEAN LAW?

An analysis of the Charter will provide us with an overview of which of the rights enumerated in the Charter were previously (ie pre-Charter) protected in EC law. Those rights which have as their source the Treaties, EC secondary legislation or case-law of the ECJ are binding on the EU institutions either in the sense of requiring positive action to protect the rights or in the form of a negative prohibition on the breach of the rights.

However, not every right listed in the table setting out the rights is binding. Some of the sources are more ambiguous. An example is the European Social Charter, a document drafted under the aegis of the Council of Europe but now, since the Amsterdam Treaty, explicitly referred to in Art 136 EC as a possible source of the Community's Social Policy. The information contained in the table is taken from the Explanatory Text to the Charter.

Charter Guarantees Sourced in EC/EU Law

Chapter	Article	Guarantee	Source
Chapter I: Dignity	Article 5(3)	Prohibition on trafficking in human beings	Sourced in part in Chapter VI of the Convention Implementing the Schengen Agreement, which has been integrated into the *acquis communautaire*, in which the United Kingdom participates and Ireland has requested to participate.
Chapter II: Freedoms	Article 8	Right to protection of personal data	Sourced in part in Art 286 EC and Directive 95/46/EC on the protection of individuals with regard to the processing of personal data and on the free movement of such data.
	Article 11(2)	Freedom and pluralism of the media shall be respected	Sourced in ECJ case-law regarding television (particularly Case C-288/89 *Schichting Collectieve Antennevoorziening Gouda* [1991] ECR I 4007), the Protocol on the System of Broadcasting in the Member States annexed to the EC Treaty and on Council Directive 89/552/EC (particularly its seventeenth recital).
	Article 12(1)	Freedom of Assembly and Association	Sourced in part in Article 11 of the Community Charter of the Fundamental Social Rights of Workers.
	Article 12(2)	Political parties at Union level contribute to expressing the political will of the citizens of the Union	Corresponds to Article 191 EC.
	Article 14(1)	The extension of the right to education to include access to vocational and continuing training	Sourced in part in point 15 of the Community Charter of the Fundamental Social Rights of Workers.
	Article 15(1)	Freedom to choose an occupation	Sourced in the case-law of the ECJ, in *inter alia*, Case 4/73 *Nold* [1974] ECR 491 (paras 12–14) Case 44/79 *Hauer* [1979] ECR 3727 and Case 234/85 *Keller* [1986] ECR 2897 and in Art 1(2) of the European Social Charter and on point 4 of the Community Charter of the Fundamental Social Rights of Workers.
	Article 15(2)	Freedom of movement for workers, freedom of establishment and freedom to provide services	Sourced in Arts 39, 43 and 49 *et seq* EC.
	Article 15(3)	Entitles nationals of third countries authorised to work in the territories of the Member States to working conditions equivalent to those of citizens of the Union	Based on TEC Art 137(3) and on Art 19(4) of the European Social Charter.
	Article 16	Freedom to conduct a business	Sourced in ECJ case-law which has recognised a freedom to exercise an economic or commercial activity (Case 4/73 *Nold* [1974] ECR 491 (para 14) and Case 230/78 *SPA Eridiana* [1979] ECR 2749 (paras 20 and 31) and freedom of contract (*inter alia* Case 151/78 *Sukkerfabricken Nykøbing* [1979] ECR 1 (para 19) and Case C-240/97 *Spain v Commission* [1999] ECR I 6571 (para 19) and TEC Art 4(1) and (2) which recognises free competition.
	Article 17(1)	The right to property	Sourced in Art 1 of the Protocol to the ECHR but is a right which has been recognised on numerous occasions by the ECJ, initially in Case 44/79 *Hauer* [1979] ECR 3727.
	Article 18	Protects the right to asylum	Based on TEC Art 63. This article is in line with the Protocol on Asylum annexed to the EC Treaty.
Chapter III Equality	Article 20	Equality before the law	Recognised as a basic principle of Community law in the case-law of the ECJ (Case 283/83 *Racke* [1984] ECR 3791 and Case 15/95 *EARL* [1997] ECR I 1961 and Case 292/97 *Karlsson* [2000] ECR I 2737.
	Article 21(1)	The prohibition of discrimination on any ground such as sex, race, colour, ethnic or social origin, genetic features, language, religion or belief, political or any other opinion, membership of a national minority, property, birth, disability, age or sexual orientation	Sourced in part in Article 13 of the EC Treaty.
	Article 21(2)	Prohibits within the scope of application of the EC and EU treaties any discrimination on the grounds of nationality	Corresponds to Art 12 EC
	Article 22	Respect for cultural, religious and linguistic diversity	Sourced in Art 6 TEU, Art 151 (1) and (4) EC and Declaration No. 11 to the Final Act of the Treaty of Amsterdam.

	Article 23	The principle of equality between men and women	Sourced in Arts 2 EC, 3(2) EC and 141(3) EC, Art 20 of the revised European Social Charter, point 16 of the Community Charter on the Rights of Workers and Art 2(4) of Council Directive 76/207/EEC. Art 23(2) limits the equality guarantee in that it permits affirmative action in favour of the under-represented sex in accordance with Article 141(4) EC.
	Article 25	Rights of the elderly	Sourced in Art 23 of the revised social charter and Arts 24 and 25 of the Community Charter of the Fundamental Social Rights of Workers.
	Article 26	Promotes the integration of persons with disabilities	Sourced in Art 15 of the European Social Charter, Art 23 of the revised Social Charter and point 26 of the Community Charter of Fundamental Social Rights of Workers.
Chapter IV: Solidarity	Article 27	Workers' right to information and consultation within the undertaking	Sourced in Art 21 of the revised European Social Charter and in points 17 and 18 of the Community Charter on the Rights of Workers.
	Article 28	A right of collective bargaining and action	Sourced in Art 6 of the European Social Charter and on points 12–14 of the Community Charter of the Fundamental Social Rights of Workers.
	Article 29	A right of access to placement services	Based on Art 1(3) of the European Social Charter and point 13 Community Charter of the Fundamental Social Rights of Workers.
	Article 30	Protection in the event of unjustified dismissal	Sourced in Art 24 of the revised Social Charter and in Directive 77/187/EEC and Directive 80/987/EEC.
	Article 31(1)	For fair and just working conditions	Sourced in Directive 89/391/EEC, Article 3 of the Social Charter and point 19 of the Community Charter on the Rights of Workers and Article 26 of the revised Social Charter, The expression 'working conditions' must be understood in the sense of Art 140 of the Treaty.
	Article 31(2)	Relates to the organisation of working time	Sourced in Directive 93/104/EC, Article 2 of the European Social Charter and point 8 of the Community Charter on the Rights of Workers.
	Article 32	Prohibits child labour and protects young people at work	Based on Directive 94/33/EC, Article 7 of The European Social Charter and points 20–23 of the Community Charter of the Fundamental Social Rights of Workers.
	Article 33(1)	Protects family life	Sourced in Art 16 of the European Social Charter.
	Article 33(2)	Reconciles family and professional life	Sourced in Council Directive 92/85/EEC, Directive 96/34/EC, Art 8 of the European Social Charter and Art 27 of the revised Social Charter.
	Article 34(1)	Rrecognises the entitlement to social security and social assistance.	This principle is sourced in Arts 137 and 140 EC and in Art 12 of the European Social Charter and point ten of the Community Charter on the Rights of Workers. The Union must respect the principle when exercising the powers conferred on it by Art 140 EC.
	Article 34(2)	Provides that everyone residing and moving legally within the EU is entitled to Social Security benefits	This principle is sourced in Art 13(4) of the European Social Charter and point two of the Community Charter of Fundamental Social Rights of Workers and reflects the rules arising from Regulation 1408/71 and Regulation 1612/68.
	Article 34(3)	The right to Social and Housing Assistance	Sourced in Arts 30 and 31 of the revised Social Charter and point ten of the Community Charter. The Union must respect it in the context of policies based on Art 137(2) EC.
	Article 35	A Right of Access to Health Care	Sourced in Art 152 EC and Art 11 of the European Social Charter.
	Article 36	Access to services of general economic interest	Sourced in Art 16 of the EC Treaty.
	Article 37	Environmental Protection	Sourced in Arts 2, 6 and 174 EC.
	Article 38	Consumer Protection	Sourced in Art 153 EC.
Chapter V: Citizens' Rights	Article 39(1)	A right to vote and to stand as a candidate at elections to the European Parliament	sourced in Article 19(2) EC
	Article 39(2)	Provides that members of the European Parliament shall be elected by direct universal suffrage in a free and secret ballot	This guarantee is sourced in Article 190(1) EC.
	Article 40	A right to vote and stand as a candidate at municipal elections	Sourced in Art 19(1) EC.

Chapter	Article	Guarantee	Source
	Article 41(1) and (2)	A right to Good Administration	Sourced in the case-law of the European Court of Justice. (Case C-255/90 P, *Burban* [1992] ECR I 2253, Case T-167/94 *Nolle* [1995] ECR II 2589, Case T-231/97 New Europe Consulting [1999] ECR II 2403). The wording for this right in the first two paragraphs results from the case law of the European Court of Justice (Case 222/86 *Heylens* [1987] ECR 4097 (para 15), Case 374/87 *Orkem* [1989] ECR 3283, Case C-269/90 *TU Munchen* [1991] ECR I 5469, Case T-450/93 *Lisrestal* [1994] ECR II 1177 and Case T-167/94 *Nolle* [1995] ECR II 258 and the wording regarding the obligation to give reasons is sourced in Art 253 EC.
	Article 41(3)	Every person has a right to have the Community make good any damage caused by its institutions	Sourced in Art 288 EC.
	Article 41(4)	Every person may write to the institutions of the Union in one of the languages of the Treaties	Sourced in Art 21 EC.
	Article 42	Right of access to documents	Sourced in Art 255 EC.
	Article 43	For a right to refer to the Ombudsman	Sourced in Arts 21 and 195 EC.
	Article 44	A right to petition the European Parliament	Sourced in Arts 21 and 194 EC.
	Article 45(1)	Free movement and residence	Sourced in Art 18 EC. Article 45(2) provides this right of movement and residence to nationals of third countries legally resident in the territory of a member state and is sourced in Art 62(1) and (3) and Art 63(4) EC. Consequently, the granting of this right depends on the Institutions exercising that power.
	Article 46	Diplomatic and Consular Protection	Sourced in Art 20 EC.
Chapter VI: Justice	Article 47	A right to an effective remedy and to a fair trial	Sourced in Article 13 of the ECHR. However, in Community Law the protection is more extensive since it guarantees the right to an effective remedy before a Court. The ECJ enshrines this principle in its case-law. (Case 222/84 *Johnston* [1986] ECR 1651, Case 222/86 *Heylens* [1987] ECR 4097 and Case C-97/91 *Borelli* [1992] ECR I 6313).
	Article 47(2)	Everyone is entitled to a fair and public hearing	Sourced in Art 6(1) ECHR but the Community Law Right is more extensive as in Community Law the right to a fair hearing is not confined to disputes relating to Civil Law Rights and Obligations. This is a consequence of the fact that the Community is based on the Rule of Law (Case 294/83 *Les Verts v European Parliament* [1986] ECR 1339).
	Article 47(3)	Legal aid	It should be noted that there is a system of legal assistance for cases before the ECJ.
	Article 50	Right not to be tried or punished twice in criminal proceedings for the same criminal office	This right is sourced in Article 4 of Protocol 7 ECHR but is also sourced in ECJ case-law (Cases 18/65 and 35/65 *Gutmann v Commission* [1966] ECR 103 and joined cases T-305/94 *Limburgse Vinyl Maatschappij NV v Commission* [1999] ECR II 931). This principle applies not only within the jurisdiction of one state but also between the jurisdictions of several member states. This understanding is based on the *acquis* in Union Law and sourced also in Arts 54 to 58 of the Schengen Convention.

It is apparent from this table that in fact many of the rights enumerated in the Charter have legal sources which are legally binding. If the original source is legally binding, the simple restatement of that right in a new document (the Charter), whatever its legal status cannot deprive the underlying right if its binding legal status. The language used by the Court of First Instance (CFI) in recent judgments confirms this view. (These cases are discussed in **5.10.6**). The practitioner is required to conduct an analysis of the source of a particular right to determine its legal status. That the Charter is being regularly pleaded before the ECJ is evident from the following extract from the EU Annual Report on Human Rights, 2002, 19:

> 'Lawyers are also invoking the Charter more often before judicial bodies of the Union, and the advocates general at the Court of Justice of the Community regularly refer to it in their conclusions while underlining it must be admitted its lack of binding force.'

The Annual Report, at page 19, also makes reference to the increased currency of the Charter among EU citizens:

'Although the Charter is not legally binding, citizens are invoking it ever more frequently in their approaches to the institutions of the Union. Complaints, petitions and letters referring to the Charter are addressed in very large numbers to the European Parliament and to the Commission.'

In the wake of the Charter, it is necessary to remember that while the development of human rights protection has been on an *ad hoc* basis that there now exists a considerable human rights *acquis* that can be invoked in the courts.

5.10.6   ENFORCEMENT

Enforcement of the Charter is necessarily dependent on status. A declaratory Charter is not binding on the ECJ or the national courts of the Member States.

There is the possibility that the ECJ will rely on the Charter as a guide to the general principles of human rights. In this manner, the Charter may be given legally binding effect indirectly in the Member State courts as these courts are bound within the scope of Community law by decisions of the ECJ.

As Craig and de Búrca ('EU Law: Text, Cases and Materials', 3rd edn, 2003, OUP, 362) observe:

'Pending the decision on the legal status of the Charter to be taken by the IGC in 2004 . . . the Charter may be in something of a legal limbo, but is certainly not without any legal influence or effect.'

Indeed the Charter has already been cited in the Opinions of a number of Advocates General (see *inter alia* Advocate General Alber in Case C340/99 *TNT Traco SpA v Poste Italiane SpA*, 1 February, 2001, paragraph 94, Advocate General Tissano in Case C-173/99 *Broadcasting, Entertainment, Cinematographic and Theatre Union (BECTU) v Secretary of State for Trade and Industry*, Opinion of 8 February 2001, paragraph 28 and Advocate General Léger in Case C- 353/99P *Council v Hautala*, 10 July 2001, paragraph 80 *et seq)* and in judgments of the CFI, although not yet by the ECJ. The nature of the rights is evident from the language used. Two Advocate General Opinions and two decisions of the CFI serve as illustrations.

In a footnote to his Opinion in Case C-466/00 *Kaba v Secretary of State of the Home Department*, 11 July 2002, Advocate General Ruiz-Jarabo Colomer gives examples of how the Charter is being referred to by Advocates General of the ECJ (at footnote 74)

'As regards the Charter of Fundamental Rights of the European Union, proclaimed in Nice on 7 December 2000 (OJ 2000 C 364, p.1) which contains a more extensive and up-to-date list of rights and freedoms than the Convention, some Advocates General, within the Court of Justice and without ignoring the fact that the Charter does not have any *autonomous* binding effect, have nevertheless emphasised its clear purpose of serving as a substantive point of reference for all those concerned in the Community context . . . ,point out that it has placed the rights which it recognises at the highest level of the hierarchy of values common to the Member States and necessarily constitutes a privileged instrument for identifying fundamental rights . . . , or argue that it constitutes an invaluable source for the purpose of ascertaining the common denominator of the essential legal values prevailing in the Member States, from which the general principles of Community law in turn emanate. . . .' (Citations of Opinions omitted)

The significance of the Charter is also evident from the Opinion of Advocate General Mischo in Joined Cases C-20/00 and C-64/00 *Booker Aquaculture Ltd v The Scottish Ministers*,

20 September 2001. The facts involved a preliminary reference from a Scottish Court asking in essence whether the right of property, as recognised by EC Law requires that compensation to be paid to farmers whose fish have had to be destroyed under measures imposed by a Council Directive for the control of diseases. In reaching the opinion (at para 132) that the principles of EC Law concerning the protection of fundamental rights, in particular the right of property, are not to be interpreted as meaning that they require the payment of compensation to the owners concerned, Advocate General Mischo stated at paras 125-126:

'I note, lastly, that the European Union Charter of Fundamental Rights, proclaimed in December 2000 at the European Council of Nice, likewise does not encourage the conclusion that the protection of the right to private property requires that the owners of animals affected by an epidemic, or animal disease, have a right to compensation.

I know that the Charter is not legally binding, but it is worthwhile referring to it given that it constitutes an expression, at the highest level, of a democratically established political consensus on what must today be considered as the catalogue of fundamental rights guaranteed by the Community legal order. . . .'

Case T-54/99 *max.mobil Telekommunikation service GmbH v Commission*, 30 January 2002, a case involving competition in the telecommunications sector, involved an action for annulment against a rejection of a complaint. The CFI reasoned that the Charter was a confirmation of existing rights stating at paragraph 48:

'Since the present action is directed against a measure rejecting a complaint, it must be emphasised at the outset that the diligent and impartial treatment of a complaint is associated with the right to sound administration which is one of the general principles that are observed in a state governed by the rule of law and are common to the constitutional traditions of the member States. Article 41(1) of the Charter of Fundamental Rights of the European Union . . . *confirms* that "[e]very person has the right to have his or her affairs handled impartially, fairly and within a reasonable time by the institutions and bodies of the Union."' (Emphasis added)

The CFI also stated at paragraph 57:

'Such judicial review is also one of the general principles that are observed in a state governed by the rule of law and are common to the constitutional traditions of the Member States, as is *confirmed* by Article 47 of the Charter of Fundamental Rights, under which any person whose rights guaranteed by the law of the Union are violated has the right to an effective remedy before a tribunal.'

Case T-177/01 *Jégo-Quére et Cie SA v Commission* [2002] ECR II 2365, a fisheries case involved an argument that the inadmissibility of an action for annulment would deprive the applicant of a right to an effective remedy (see **5.10.6**). The CFI, in holding (at para 47), that the procedures did not guarantee the right to an effective remedy, relied on Arts 6 and 13 of the ECHR and Art 47 of the EU Charter of Fundamental Rights. The CFI opined at paras 41 and 42:

'. . . The Court of Justice bases the right to an effective remedy before a court of a competent jurisdiction on the constitutional traditions common to the Member States and on Articles 6 and 13 of the ECHR . . .

In addition, the right to an effective remedy for everyone whose rights and freedoms guaranteed by the law of the Union are violated has been *reaffirmed* by Article 47 of the Charter of Fundamental Rights of the European Union proclaimed at Nice on 7 December 2000.' (Emphasis added)

This decision is currently under appeal in Case 263/02 P *Commission v Jégo-Quéré* (see **5.8.1**).

The ECJ and CFI are unlikely to rely on the Charter as a source of rights given the decision by the Member States at the Nice IGC not to give binding status to the Charter. Since Nice, it seems that a consensus has emerged at least amongst the members of the Convention of the Future of Europe (who include representatives of the Member State Governments) that the Charter should be incorporated in the Draft Treaty establishing a Constitution for Europe and thus become a legally binding text.

5.10.7   SCOPE OF THE CHARTER

Article 51 deals with the scope of application of the Charter. It is clear from Art 51(1) that the institutions and bodies of the EU are the primary addressees of the Charter. The Charter is concerned with increasing the visibility of the limits on the actions of the EU institutions. The Charter is also addressed to Member States when implementing Union law. This latter point is both consistent with the case-law of the ECJ (see **5.7.2**) and logical in that when implementing Community law, the Member State are acting as agents of the EU.

It clear from Article 51(2) that the Charter does not increase the competence of the EU in the field of human rights. Lord Goldsmith answers the objections of some commentators who have criticised the Charter on the basis that the rights contained in the Charter go far beyond the competences transferred to the EU. (Lord Goldsmith, '*A Charter of Rights, Freedoms and Principles*' 38 CMLR (2001) 1201.) He states that the Charter must deal with the risk of touching fundamental rights with a side wind when an EU institution is exercising competence in another area. To illustrate this point, he gives the example that while the Charter enshrines the right to freedom of thought, conscience and religion, the EU has no competence to legislate in this field. However, if the EU is considering legislation on slaughterhouses, it cannot ignore the rituals of various religions in the area of animal slaughter as to do so would be to deny respect to religious freedom.

On this question of whether the Charter extends the powers of the Union, Mr Michel Petite, Director General Legal Service, European Commission has explained that '[t]he important thing here is to bear in mind the distinction between the powers of the Union (which are limited) and the duty of the institutions to respect fundamental rights when they act. This duty applies equally to rights such as the right to strike or the freedom of religion that the institutions could well affect indirectly by their measures, even if they cannot legislate on them.' He emphasised that review of Member States for compliance with the EC human rights standard is limited to circumstances where Member States are implementing Community law. He states: 'The fear that the Charter could have an impact on broad fields of the Member States' national legislation and that the slightest indirect link with Community law or powers would suffice to make it applicable therefore strikes me as unfounded.' (Working Document 13 of Working Group II 'Incorporation of the Charter/Accession to the ECHR', Brussels, 5 September 2002). The Working Group on Incorporation of the Charter emphasised that no modification in the allocation of competences between the EU and the Member States would result from the Charter and stated '[t]he fact that certain Charter rights concern areas in which the Union has little or no competence to act is not in contradiction to it, given that, although the Union's competences are limited, it must respect all fundamental rights wherever it acts and therefore avoid indirect interference also with such fundamental rights on which it would not have competence to legislate.' (CONV 354/02 Final report of Working Group II 'Incorporation of the Charter/Accession to the ECHR' Brussels, 22 October 2002, 5) The ECJ has no jurisdiction to review national measures for compatibility with the EC human rights standard. (See **5.7.2**.)

A final point to note is that the Charter, even in its current declaratory form, is not restricted to the European Community but applies to Union activity under all three pillars. Traditionally the ECJ power of review was largely restricted to the supranational pillar (see

5.7.1). If the Charter is given legally binding status or the ECJ chooses to rely on the Charter as a guide to the general principles of human rights (see **5.10.6**) the scope of Community human rights protection over the intergovernmental pillars will be extended. (See **5.4** and **5.7.1**.)

The distinction between the pillars may be abolished at the IGC which commenced in 2003. The Future of Europe Convention the Working Group on Legal Personality in its final report concluded that, in future, the EU should have its own explicit single legal personality. (Final Report of Working Group III on Legal Personality, Brussels, 1 October 2002, CONV 305/02). The Draft Treaty establishing a Constitution for Europe (CONV 820/1/03 Brussels 27 June 2003) follows the recommendation of the Working Group on Legal Personality. Article I-6 of the Draft Treaty provides '[t]he Union shall have legal personality.' On ratification of the draft treaty, the three pillar structure will be almost done away with and the EU's institutions will have a single structure. The Charter will apply to almost all EU activity.

Article 52 is concerned with the scope of the rights guaranteed in the Charter. It is accepted that rights are not absolute and that limitations may be imposed on rights but only to the extent that they are provided for by law and respect the essence of the rights and freedoms. Article 52(2) specifies that where a right is sourced in the EU/EC Treaties, the right must be exercised under the conditions and within the limits defined by those Treaties. This provision will be modified on ratification of the Draft Treaty establishing a Constitution for Europe to ensure a right sourced in the Constitution will be exercised under the conditions and within the limits defined by the Constitution. A number of amendments to Art 52 are proposed in the Draft Treaty establishing a Constitution for Europe. (See **5.10.3**.)

5.10.8 RELATIONSHIP OF THE CHARTER AND THE ECHR

Two European Courts applying different human rights codes implies the possibility of different standards.

It is important when considering the Charter to examine the wider picture of human rights in Europe. A key issue in drafting the Charter has been the relationship of the Charter to the ECHR. The rights and freedoms protected by the ECHR and interpreted by the ECt.HR are restated (although not replicated) in the Charter and could be interpreted by the ECJ.

However, it should be noted that the Charter is not the origin of this difficulty as the ECJ has used the ECHR as a source of inspiration for the general principles of EC human rights law since the late 1960s. Already the ECt.HR and the ECJ are both interpreting ECHR rights with the consequent possibility of divergent interpretations.

There is also a possibility of divergence between the case-law of the ECt.HR and the case-law of the Council of Europe Member States in that the latter are entitled to apply a higher standard through the operation of the margin of appreciation doctrine.

However, there are two crucial differences between the possible divergence between the national courts and the ECt.HR and the ECJ and the ECt.HR. First, in the case of the Council of Europe Contracting States, the ECt.HR retains ultimate authority to interpret the ECHR (See Lawson 'Confusion and Conflict? Diverging Interpretations of the European Convention on Human Rights in Strasbourg and Luxembourg' in Lawson and de Bloijs, (eds), 'The Dynamics of the Protection of Human Rights in Europe: Essays in Honour of Henry G. Schemers', 1994, Nijhoff, iii, 219, 229–230) while the ECJ does not consider itself bound by the ECt.HR interpretation of an ECHR right. (See the opinion of Advocate General Darmon in Case 374/87 *Orkem v Commission* [1989] ECR 3283, 3337–8.) Secondly, the Council of Europe Member States through the operation of the margin of appreciation doctrine are obliged to apply the ECHR as a minimum standard. No such obligation rests on the ECJ as the EC/EU is not a party to the ECHR.

Efforts to counteract these concerns are evident in the final chapter of the Charter. Article 52 is concerned with the scope of guaranteed rights and Art 53 with the level of human rights protection. Article 52(3), intended as a mechanism to ensure consistency between the Charter and the ECHR, provides:

> *'Insofar as this Charter contains rights which correspond to rights guaranteed by the Convention for the Protection of Human Rights and Fundamental Freedoms, the meaning and scope of those rights shall be the same as those laid down by the said Convention. This provision shall not prevent Union law providing more extensive protection.'*

Article 52(3) is designed to ensure consistency between the ECHR rights and the corresponding rights, in the Charter by stating that the meaning and scope including any limitations must comply with ECHR standards.

According to the explanatory text to the Charter, the reference to the ECHR in Art 52(3) is to be read as including the Protocols to the ECHR and when determining the meaning and scope of those rights, the case-law of both the ECt.HR and the ECJ is to be taken into account.

The explanations provide two lists of articles in the Charter covered by Art 52(3). One list details the articles which have both the same meaning and scope as the corresponding articles of the ECHR. The second list details the articles which have the same meaning as the corresponding articles of the ECHR but where their scope is wider.

Article 53 is entitled 'Levels of Protection' and provides:

> *'Nothing in this Charter shall be interpreted as restricting or adversely affecting human rights and fundamental freedoms as recognised in their respective fields of application, by Union law and international law and by international agreements to which the Union, the Community or all the Member States are party, including the European Convention for the Protection of Human Rights and Fundamental Freedoms, and by the Member States' constitutions.'*

Reading Articles 52(3) and 53 together it is apparent that when a right in the Charter corresponds to a right in the ECHR, the ECHR right serves as a minimum standard in determining the meaning and scope of the right but there is nothing to prevent the EU from adopting a more extensive standard.

Some rights are based on a combination of the ECHR and the EU or EC Treaty. Lenaerts and De Smijter (*'A "Bill of Rights" for the European Union'* 38 CMLR 273, 294) have explained the situation with regard to those rights as follows:

> 'Fundamental rights recognised by the Charter, corresponding to rights guaranteed by the ECHR and based on the EU or EC Treaty, should thus be exercised under the conditions and within the limits defined by the EU or EC Treaty to the extent only that these conditions and limits do not interfere with the meaning and scope of these rights as they are guaranteed by the ECHR. On the basis of a combined reading of Article 52(2) and (3) and Article 53 of the Charter we may thus conclude that the EU or EC Treaty as well as the ECHR (in fact, the norm offering the highest protection) serve as a reference to determine the minimal content of those fundamental rights contained in the Charter that are based on the EU or EC Treaty and correspond to a right guaranteed by the ECHR.'

5.10.9 BENEFICIARIES

The issue of beneficiaries is decided article by article. The rights and freedoms set out in Chapters I (Dignity), II (Freedoms), III (Equality) and VI (Justice) are for everyone. Within Chapter IV (Solidarity), some rights such as collective bargaining and the right to fair and just working conditions are for workers while other protections such as reconciliation of family and professional life and health care are for everyone. The title of Chapter V (Citizens' Rights) would seem to imply that the rights in this chapter accrue only to citizens of the European Union and this is generally true although Art 45(2) provides for a right of movement and residence to nationals of third countries legally resident in the territories of a member state.

5.10.10 THE CHARTER AND THE FUTURE OF EUROPE

Decisions regarding the status of the Charter and whether it should be included in the Draft Treaty establishing a Consitution will be taken at the IGC which commenced in 2003. As was discussed earlier (see **5.1** and **5.4.1**), the Draft Treaty establishing a Constitution for Europe, which was submitted by the President of the Convention on the future of Europe to the European Council meeting in Thessoloniki on 20 June 2003 (revised text published at CONV 820/1/03 Brussels 27 June 2003) incorporates the text of the Charter. If the Treaty is ratified in this form, the Charter will be legally binding.

Article I-7(1) of the Draft Treaty provides 'The Union shall recognise the rights, freedoms and principles set out in the Charter of Fundamental Rights which constitutes Part II of this Constitution.'

The Working Group on the Charter submitted its final report to the Convention on 22 October 2002. (CONV 354/02 Final report of Working Group II 'Incorporation of the Charter/Accession to the ECHR' Brussels, 22 October 2002.) The Working Group had been asked to answer the question; 'Should the Charter of Fundamental Rights of the European Union be incorporated into the Treaty?' The Working Group was also asked to consider a second questions; 'Should the European Union be able to Accede to the European Convention on Human Rights?' (See **5.6.5**.)

The question regarding incorporation of the Charter was answered resoundingly in the affirmative. The members of the Working Group indicated that they either strongly supported the incorporation of the Charter in a form which would make it legally binding and give it constitutional status or would not rule out giving favourable consideration to such incorporation. The Working Group stressed that the political decision on the possible incorporation of the Charter into the Treaty framework is reserved to the Convention.

The Working Group set out three basic incorporation options:

'(a) insertion of the text of the Charter articles at the beginning of the Constitutional Treaty, in a title or Chapter of that Treaty; or

(b) insertion of an appropriate reference to the Charter in one article of the Constitutional Treaty; such a reference could be combined with annexing or attaching the Charter to the Constitutional Treaty, either as a specific part of the Constitutional Treaty containing only the Charter or as a separate legal text (e.g. in the form of a Protocol);

(c) an "indirect reference" to the Charter could be used to make the Charter legally binding without giving it constitutional status.' (See document CONV 116/02, p. 7.)

The Report indicated that a large majority of the group favoured option (a), a smaller number option (b). Either option would 'serve to make the Charter a legally binding text of constitutional status.'

The Working Group also provided a series of supplementary conclusions and recommendations on legal and technical aspects of the Charter, which would be significant in ensuring the smooth incorporation of the Charter into the new Treaty architecture. The Working Group:

(a) concluded that the content of the Charter should be respected by the current Convention and should not be re-opened, apart from a number of drafting adjustments which would not alter the substance of the Charter;

(b) emphasised that no new competences would be conferred on the EU by virtue of incorporation of the Charter;

(c) proposed that a referral clause should be included in the Charter to ensure full compatibility between those fundamental rights which are already expressly enshrined in the EC Treaty and the Charter articles which restate them;

(d) reconfirmed Art 52(3) of the Charter and the explanation of this Article in the explanatory text which accompanies the Charter, that the rights in the Charter which correspond to ECHR have the same meaning as laid down in the ECHR but that the EU is not prevented from guaranteeing a higher level of protection for a particular right;

(d) proposed the addition of a paragraph to the General Provision on the scope of guaranteed rights (Art 52 EU Charter) to ensure an interpretation of fundamental rights in harmony with the common constitutional traditions of the Member States; and

(e) proposed the addition of an additional general principle to encapsulate the understanding of the concept of 'principles' as distinct from 'rights'.

These recommendations of the Working Group have been followed in the draft Treaty. See **5.10.3**.

The Group recommended that the Preamble to the Charter should be preserved in the future Constitutional Treaty framework and that the explanations (including explanations for the amendments to the Charter suggested by the Working Group) should be made more accessible to practitioners and should be more widely publicised.

The Working Group signalled to the Convention that it should consider whether, on incorporation of the Charter, the Constitutional Treaty should also contain a reference to the two external sources of inspiration for fundamental rights, currently found in Art 6(2) TEU, ie the ECHR and the common constitutional traditions of the Member States, and the procedure for the future amendment of the Charter.

Ultimately however, the decision as to whether the Charter will be legally binding is a political decision to be taken by the Member States at the IGC. There has been broad consensus among the Member States on the issue of incorporation of the Charter. It is unlikely that there will be significant movement from this position at the IGC

5.10.11 THE CHARTER'S IMPACT ON LEGISLATION

In the EU Annual Report on Human Rights, 2002, 19, the Commission indicated another significant impact of the Charter.

'The Commission also considers that it is necessary to draw practical lessons from the proclamation of the Charter and to guide its conduct by the rights contained in it. With this in mind, any proposal for a legislative or regulatory Act adopted by the Commission will now be subject to an *a priori* compatibility check with the Charter, attested by the inclusion of a standard recital and proposals which have a connection with fundamental rights.'

5.11   Conclusion

While the Charter of Fundamental Rights of the EU is a recent initiative human rights have been protected within the European legal order since the 1960s. The key points may be summarised as follows.

The protection of human rights was initially a product of judicial activism but now has a firm basis in the Treaties. The ECJ looks to the human rights provisions in the constitutions of the Member States and international agreements to which the Member States are parties for inspiration. The ECJ is entitled to annul an action which does not comply with the human rights standard.

The EC/EU institutions are bound by the European human rights standard. Member States are also bound but only when acting within the scope of EC law. Currently the Charter is not binding. However a decision will be taken at the IGC (currently under way) whether to incorporate the Charter into the text of the Draft Treaty establishing a Constitution for Europe (see **5.10.6**).

This is an exciting time for the development of human rights in the EC/EU. It remains to be seen whether the Member States at the IGC will accept the proposals on human rights included in the Draft Treaty Establishing a Constitution for Europe, namely the incorporation of the Charter (Part II of the Draft Treaty) and the inclusion of a legal basis to seek EU accession to the ECHR. (Article I-7(2) of the Draft Treaty, the text of which is set out at **5.4**).

CHAPTER 6

DUE PROCESS AND THE RIGHT TO A FAIR TRIAL

6.1   Introduction

For many years, the rights of citizens suspected or accused of criminal offences were protected by Article 38.1 of the Constitution, which provides that '. . . no person shall be tried on any criminal charge save in due course of law.' The Irish Courts were able to draw, in particular, on the jurisprudence of the 'due process' guarantees of the US Courts, while developing their own lines of authority.

The most trenchant expression of the concept in Irish jurisprudence is to be found in *Conroy v Attorney General* [1965] IR 411, where Kenny J observed that the phrase

> '. . . "due process of law" was adopted by those who drafted the fifth Amendment of the Constitution of the United States of America which prevents any person being deprived of life, liberty or property without due process of law. I think that section 1 of (Article 38) gives a constitutional right to every person to be tried in accordance with the law and in accordance with due course or due process of law . . .'

In its nature difficult to define, the idea was expanded upon in *State (Healy) v Donoghue* [1976] IR 325 by Gannon J as '. . . a phrase of very wide import which includes . . . the application of basic principles of justice which are inherent in the proper course of the exercise of the judicial function . . .'

However, in the period immediately after World War II, significant additional sources for the protection of rights became available in the two great political documents, the (United Nations) International Covenant on Civil and Political Rights (the Covenant) and the European Convention on Human Rights and Fundamental Freedoms (the ECHR).

The relevant provisions of the Irish Constitution are examined in this chapter. The Covenant is relatively little used in this jurisdiction and its provisions are in most instances almost identical to those of the ECHR. The ECHR has been the subject of considerable interest in recent times, as a result of Ireland's incorporation of the ECHR arising from international obligations under the Good Friday Agreement. The precise relationship between the Constitution and the ECHR is currently in flux. This is partly due to the very recent incorporation by way of the European Convention on Human Rights Act, 2003, but also to the apparent conflict between, on the one hand, the traditional Irish juristic approach to Constitutional sovereignty and, on the other, the European Court of Human Rights' (ECt.HR) role as, in effect, a court of final appeal on certain constitutional issues. In a nutshell, 'while the Convention applies *to* Ireland, it does not apply *within* Ireland', (O'Connell, 'Ireland' in Blackburn and Polakiewicz (eds) 'Fundamental Rights in Europe: The ECHR and its Member States, 1952–2000', 2001, OUP, 423, 425).

The Supreme Court has repeatedly rejected the notion of direct applicability of ECHR law, particularly if a case is being made that the Irish and ECHR jurisprudence are in conflict and the ECHR should prevail, as for example in *Norris v AG* [1984] IR 36. Here, the applicant was challenging the validity of criminal laws, which forbade certain homosexual acts, even between consenting adults in private, an argument which had already been accepted by the Strasbourg Court in *Dudgeon v UK* (1982) 4 EHRR 149. In the Supreme Court, the argument that the Court should take on board the *Dudgeon* judgment was dismissed by the Court, in clear terms. Henchy J remarked that '. . . [the European] Convention . . . although it has by its terms a binding force on the Government . . . as one of its signatories, forms no part of the domestic law of this State.' (at p. 68)

The European Convention on Human Rights Act, 2003 provides only (at s 2(1)) that courts shall, in so far as possible, interpret the laws of the State in a manner compatible with the State's obligations under the ECHR provisions, that judicial notice shall be taken of ECHR provisions and jurisprudence (at s 4), and that the High or Supreme Courts may make a 'Declaration of Incompatibility' as between the State's laws and the ECHR (at s 5). But the *Norris* position remains unaffected, and the operation of the 'Declaration of Incompatibility' leaves untouched the offending law, and in any event is only to come into play where no other legal remedy 'is adequate and available' (s 5(1)).

Further developments in relation to direct applicability are likely to arise due to the European Union proposals to legislate for a Charter of Fundamental Rights. This is dealt with in more detail at **6.7**.

6.2 Sources of the Available Protections

6.2.1 THE IRISH CONSTITUTION

Articles 34 to 37 provide in general for the administration of justice by the Courts. Article 38.1 is the key provision in relation to criminal charges, underpinned by Art 40.4.1, prohibiting detention save in accordance with law.

Article 38 provides:

'1. *No person shall be tried on any criminal charge save in due course of law.*

2. *Minor offences may be tried by courts of summary jurisdiction.*

3. *1° Special courts may be established by law for the trial of offences in cases where it may be determined in accordance with such law that the ordinary courts are inadequate to secure the effective administration of justice and the preservation of public peace and order.*

    2° The constitution, powers, jurisdiction and procedure of such special courts shall be prescribed by law.

4. *1° Military tribunals may be established for the trial of offences against military law alleged to have been committed by persons while subject to military law and also to deal with a state of war or armed rebellion.*

    2° A member of the Defence Forces not on active service shall not be tried by any court-martial or other military tribunal for an offence cognisable by the civil courts unless such offence is within the jurisdiction of any court-martial or other military tribunal under any law for the enforcement of military discipline.

5. *Save in the case of the trial of offences under section 2, section 3, or section 4 of this article, no person shall be tried on any criminal charge without a jury.*

6. *The provisions of Articles 34 and 35 of this Constitution shall not apply to any court or tribunal set up under section 3 or section 4 of this Article.'*

Article 40 provides, *inter alia*:

'1. *All citizens shall, as human persons, be held equal before the law . . .*

3. *1° The State guarantees in its laws to respect, and, as far as practicable, by its laws to defend and vindicate the personal rights of the citizen . . .*

4.   *1° No citizen shall be deprived of his personal liberty save in accordance with law . . .'*

6.2.2   THE EUROPEAN CONVENTION ON HUMAN RIGHTS AND FUNDAMENTAL FREEDOMS (ECHR)

The essential aspects, from the point of view of this chapter, are those contained in Articles 6 and 7 and the provisions of Protocol No 7, already signed, and soon to be ratified by Ireland.

Article 6 provides:

'Right to a fair trial:

1.   *In the determination of his civil rights and obligations or of any criminal charge against him, everyone is entitled to a fair and public hearing within a reasonable time by an independent and impartial tribunal established by law. Judgment shall be pronounced publicly, but the press and public may be excluded from all or part of the trial in the interests of morals, public order or national security in a democratic society, where the interests of juveniles or the protection of the private life of the parties so require, or to the extent strictly necessary in the opinion of the court in special circumstances where publicity would prejudice the interests of justice.*

2.   *Everyone charged with a criminal offence shall be presumed innocent until proved guilty according to law.*

3.   *Everyone charged with a criminal offence has the following minimum rights:*
       (a)   *to be informed promptly, in a language which he understands, and in detail, of the nature and cause of the accusation against him;*
       (b)   *to have adequate time and facilities for the preparation of his defence;*
       (c)   *to defend himself in person or through legal assistance of his own choosing or, if he has not sufficient means to pay for legal assistance, to be given it free when the interests of justice so require;*
       (d)   *to examine or have examined witnesses against him and to obtain the attendance and examination of witnesses on his behalf under the same conditions as witnesses against him;*
       (e)   *to have the free assistance of an interpreter if he cannot understand or speak the language used in court.'*

Article 7 provides:

'No punishment without law.
1.   *No one shall be held guilty of any criminal offence on account of any act or omission which did not constitute a criminal offence under national or international law at the time when it was committed. Nor shall a heavier penalty be imposed than the one which was applicable at the time the criminal offence was committed.*

2.   *This Article shall not prejudice the trial and punishment of any person for any act or omission which, at the time when it was committed, was criminal according to the general principles of law recognised by civilised nations.'*

Insofar as it is relevant to this chapter, Protocol 7 provides as follows:

'Article 2 – Right of appeal in criminal matters
1.   *Everyone convicted of a criminal offence by a tribunal shall have the right to have his conviction or sentence reviewed by a higher tribunal. The exercise of this right, including the grounds on which it may be exercised, shall be governed by law.*
2.   *This right may be subject to exceptions in regard to offences of a minor character, as prescribed by law, or in cases in which the person concerned was tried in the first instance by the highest tribunal or was convicted following an appeal against acquittal.*

Article 3 – Compensation for wrongful conviction
When a person has by a final decision been convicted of a criminal offence and when subsequently his conviction has been reversed, or he has been pardoned, on the ground that a new or newly discovered fact shows conclusively that there has been a miscarriage of justice, the person who has suffered punishment as a result of such conviction shall be compensated according to the law or the practice of the State concerned, unless it is proved that the non-disclosure of the unknown fact in time is wholly or partly attributable to him.

Article 4 – Right not to be tried or punished twice
1. *No one shall be liable to be tried or punished again in criminal proceedings under the jurisdiction of the same state for an offence for which he has already been finally acquitted or convicted in accordance with the law and penal procedure of that State.*
2. *The provisions of the preceding paragraph shall not prevent the reopening of the case in accordance with the law and penal procedure of the State concerned, if there is evidence of new or newly-discovered facts, or if there has been a fundamental defect in the previous proceedings, which could affect the outcome of the case.*
3. *No derogation from this Article shall be made under Article 15 of the Convention.'*

6.2.3   THE CONSTITUTION AND THE ECHR

The broad thrust of both the ECHR and the Constitution is similar, but the ECHR jurisprudence is both wider and more detailed in scope than the Irish equivalent. This is hardly surprising, given that all of the major western European countries have subscribed to the ECHR for many years, and have contributed law, lawyers and judges to the collective resolution of human rights issues for a generation, with an acknowledgement of the special character of human rights legislation, which calls for a generous approach to interpretation.

Both Irish and ECHR jurisprudence has tended, perhaps not surprisingly, to focus mainly on the 'due process' formalities of criminal procedure and trials, but it is clear from the authorities that the guarantees extend, as appropriate, to civil matters. In *Airey v Ireland* (1979-80) 2 EHRR 305, for example, the ECt.HR, sitting at Strasbourg, imposed on Ireland an obligation to institute a system of civil legal aid for separation proceedings, its absence being found by the ECt.HR as an interference with the applicant's right of effective access to the courts.

The Irish Supreme Court, while in many ways not an especially conservative institution, has suffered from the traditional restrictions placed on, or assumed by, judges in the common law tradition. In contrast, the ECHR jurisprudence is constantly developing and, unlike the traditional common law approach, the court is not bound by previous decisions. As a living instrument, which must be interpreted in the light of present day conditions, the ECHR has evolved significantly, particularly as regards the appearance of fairness in the administration of justice. In *Airey v Ireland*, the case referred to above, which effectively imposed a civil legal aid system on Ireland, it was said that the ECHR 'is intended to guarantee not rights that are theoretical and illusory but rights that are practical and effective.'

Many of the 'rights' conferred by the ECHR also contain limitations (see for example, Arts 8 to 11). Any interference with rights must be justified by the State in the context of the permissible restrictions contained in each Article. The onus will be on the State to show that the restrictions were, firstly, appropriately prescribed by law, and secondly, necessary in a democratic society. Exceptions to the rights 'must be narrowly interpreted' (*Sunday Times v UK* (1980) 2 EHRR 245).

Both of the Strasbourg institutions, that is the Court and the now-abolished Commission, as well as a number of common law countries, have to a greater extent than Ireland, acknowledged a guiding principle of human rights law interpretation, such as is suitable to give to individuals the full measure of the fundamental rights and freedoms referred to therein. New Zealand Courts, for example, have long acknowledged that human rights legislation has a 'special character' which calls for a 'broad and purposive approach to construction' (*R v Goodwin (No.1)* [1993] 2 NZL 153).

A further yardstick, the principle of proportionality, which the court considers in assessing the validity of any restriction of rights, involves balancing the demands of the community and the protection of the fundamental rights of individuals. Article 18 further prohibits States applying permissible restrictions to purposes outside those prescribed by the Convention. There is a margin of appreciation, that is, in the field of social and moral policy each State has or may have different standards, which will inform how states deal with particular issues of a human rights nature.

Domestic courts, which are signatories to the Convention, and which are considering questions that have arisen in relation to asserted ECHR Rights, are required to take into account decisions of the Strasbourg Court and the Commission, but the Irish Supreme Court, for technically sound reasons, has refused consistently to afford Convention law what observers would describe as full weight (see O'Connell 'Ireland' in Blackburn and Polakiewicz (eds) 'Fundamental Rights in Europe: The ECHR and its Member States 1952–2000', 2001, OUP, 423).

Among the general principles previously established by the Court and Commission are those that the Convention 'is an instrument designed to maintain and promote the ideals and values of a democratic society'. Critical features of such a society are 'pluralism, tolerance and broad mindedness' and 'respect for the rule of law' (see *Dudgeon v UK* (1982) 4 EHRR 149).

6.3   Specific Due Process Protections

6.3.1   WHAT PROCEEDINGS ARE PROTECTED?

The whole of Article 6 refers to the determination of criminal charges, but Art 6(1) also applies to civil rights and obligations. Put simply, Art 6(1) entitles everyone to a fair and public hearing within a reasonable time by an independent and impartial tribunal established by law. The court has traditionally interpreted this Article broadly on the grounds that it is of fundamental importance to the operation of democracy. When assessing if the rights of an applicant have been protected, the Court will have regard to the proceedings as a whole, including any appeal, and the extent to which such appeal may have corrected defects in the first instance proceedings (*Edwards v UK* (1993) 15 EHRR 417). Considering that the right to the fair administration of justice holds such a prominent place, the restrictive interpretation of Art 6(1) would not correspond to the aim and purpose of that provision (*Delcourt v Belgium* (1979) 1 EHRR 355).

When considering if any 'proceedings' are civil or criminal, the ECHR takes an 'autonomous approach'. It will disregard any categorisation of a matter as civil by the state, if the nature of the alleged offence and the severity of any penalty imply that the matter should properly be regarded as criminal. This is similar to the Irish approach, as exemplified in *Melling v O'Mathghamhna* [1962] IR 1 – the real question to be determined is whether at the conclusion of the proceedings, there is a punitive sanction.

Although criminal proceedings receive special and distinct due process protection under Art 38 of the Constitution, this is only to be expected given the special role of the State in the prosecution of criminal offences against individuals. However, Arts 34, 35 and 36 make clear the determination of the Irish State to provide for an independent and impartial judiciary, administering justice in public in all cases, civil and criminal.

6.3.2   EQUALITY OF ARMS

'Equality of Arms' is the most important principle of Article 6 as developed by the case-law. It postulates the idea that each party to a proceeding should have equal opportunity to present a side of the case and that neither should enjoy any substantial advantage over his opponent. Obviously, the right to legal representation in appropriate cases flows from this requirement. One of the most important Irish human rights cases, which is the authority for a number of human rights entitlements, arises from this issue. In *State (Healy) v Donoghue* [1976] IR 325, the Supreme Court formally acknowledged the right to legal assistance, and in the case under consideration, the right to State-funded Legal Aid, as being central to the concept of due course of law and a fair trial.

What Casey ('Constitutional Law in Ireland', 3rd edn, 2000, Roundhall, Sweet and Maxwell, 517) describes as 'the general overarching criterion of fairness' is the touchstone of Irish authorities in this area. Bearing in mind the overall discretion of trial judges, such discretion must be exercised 'within constitutional parameters' and in the light of overall fairness. Obviously, such a concept cannot be exhaustively defined, but in, for example, *DPP v Doyle* [1994] 2 IR 286, the Supreme Court found an obligation on the prosecution to disclose statements to the defence in summary trials of indictable offences, if the interests of justice demand it.

The ECt.HR has already held that it would be a breach of the principle where an expert witness appointed by the defence is not accorded the same facilities as one appointed by the prosecution (*Bonisch v Austria* (1987) 9 EHRR 191). Similar principles oblige prosecuting and investigating authorities to disclose any material in their possession which may assist the accused in exonerating himself or which may undermine the credibility of a prosecution witness (*Jespers v Belgium* (1981) 27 DR 61).

6.3.3   EVIDENCE AND FAIR TRIAL PROCEDURES

Broadly speaking, the rules of evidence are a matter for each contracting State, although the ECt.HR will exceptionally examine whether the proceedings as a whole were fair or assess the weight of the evidence before a national court. Perhaps surprisingly, the Court has held that Art 6 does not necessarily require the exclusion of illegally obtained evidence. This contrasts with States that operate a strict 'exclusionary rule', which prima facie rule out evidence obtained in consequence of breaches of rights.

The Supreme Court has dealt with this issue by establishing two categories of rights capable of being infringed in the collection of evidence, legal rights and constitutional rights. The two are not always readily distinguishable. In broad terms, the Courts will incline away from admitting evidence obtained in breach of a constitutional right, save in 'extraordinary excusing circumstances' (*People (AG) v O'Brien* [1965] IR 142). Where evidence is obtained in breach of a mere legal right, such evidence shall be admissible 'unless the Court in its discretion excludes it' (*per* the Supreme Court in *DPP v McMahon* [1986] IR 393).

6.3.4   PREJUDICIAL PUBLICITY

Particularly if a case is to be tried by a jury, 'a virulent press campaign against the accused' is capable of violating the right to a fair trial (*X v Austria* 11 CD 31 1963). However, the court will take account of the fact that some comment by the press on a trial involving a matter of public interest is inevitable and will also consider what steps the judge has taken to counter the effect of the prejudice in his charge to the jury.

The Irish judges have been very slow to prohibit cases from proceeding, because of adverse pre-trial publicity. In particular, in *Z v DPP* [1994] 2 IR 476, concerning the trial of the alleged rapist of a young girl who had been at the centre of *Attorney General v X* [1992] 1 IR 1 case which had attracted enormous national and international publicity, the Supreme Court permitted the trial to proceed subject to appropriate safeguards in the form of warnings to the jury. However, a temporary stay was afforded the defendant, a former Taoiseach, in *DPP v Haughey (No. 2)*, [2001] IR 162, for similar reasons, while the applicant in *Magee v O'Dea* [1994] 1 IR 500 succeeded in avoiding extradition to the UK because of adverse publicity in that jurisdiction.

6.3.5 REASONS FOR A DECISION

It is a basic requirement of a fair trial in both civil and criminal cases that courts should give reasons for their judgments. Common law decisions such as *Breen v Amalgamated Engineering Union* [1971] 2 QB 175 have been given ready acceptance in Ireland in such cases, as *Kinahan v Minister for Justice, Equality and Law Reform*, 21 February, 2001, Supreme Court, (unreported). In *McAlister v Minister for Justice, Equality and Law Reform* [2003] 1 ILRM 161, Finnegan P stated that '... it is important that justice should be seen to be done and this will very often require that a person affected by a decision should know why that particular decision has been taken ...' This does not apply to jury trials.

Where a submission to the court in the course of a trial would, if accepted, be decisive of the outcome of the case, it must be specifically and expressly addressed in a ruling by the court (*Hiro Bilani v Spain* (1995) 19 EHRR 566).

6.3.6 THE RIGHT TO A PUBLIC HEARING

The fundamental entitlement to a hearing in public is designed to protect litigants from 'the administration of justice in secret with no public scrutiny' and to maintain public confidence in the courts and in the administration of justice (*Pretto v Italy* (1984) 6 EHRR 182). For these reasons, only in exceptional circumstances can the press be excluded. This provision is mirrored in Art 34.1 of the Constitution, providing as it does for justice to 'be administered in public'. Article 34.1 actually limits this proviso to allow for private sittings of the Courts in circumstances prescribed by law, but those categories of cases which are so heard in private, mainly involving family law, tend to be heard out of the public gaze by general consent.

6.3.7 THE ENTITLEMENT TO TRIAL WITHIN A REASONABLE TIME

Of particular interest in Ireland is the right to trial within a reasonable time. There are frequent complaints from litigants, the media and indeed many of the judges, about the delays in getting cases on for trial in the higher criminal courts in particular. Deriving, again, in part from *State (Healy) v Donoghue* [1976] IR 325 where it was described as 'the right to trial with reasonable expedition', the question has repeatedly been brought before the appellate Courts over the last 20 or so years. One issue which has been addressed is the right to early trial of summary offences. The best discussion of this is to be found in the Supreme Court judgment in *DPP v Byrne* [1994] 2 IR 236, which without setting any time limits, imposed responsibility for all delays within both prosecution and Court systems on the State and obliged the prosecution to furnish explanations for any such delays.

Another issue which has arisen is the circumstances in which prosecutions should be prohibited where the offences were allegedly committed many years ago. In *B v DPP* [1997] 3 IR 140, the trial of alleged offences between 20 and 30 years old was allowed to continue, notwithstanding the Supreme Court finding '... an inordinate delay ...'. The Court found as highly relevant the fact that the alleged perpetrator was in a dominant position *vis-à-vis* the complainants, who felt unable to report the allegations of sexual offences for many years. This led the Court to emphasise the community's right to proceed with the prosecution.

However, in *O'C v DPP* [2000] 3 IR 87, another case dealing with sexual offences, the Court prohibited a case of similar age, on the basis that evidence which was, or may have been, available to the defence had the complaint been promptly made, and which might have helped to refute it, was by virtue of the delay no longer available.

In a European context, the entitlement to trial within a reasonable time is intended to prevent a person charged from remaining 'too long in a state of uncertainty about his fate' (*Stogmuller v Austria* (1979) 1 EHRR 155). The reasonable time guarantee runs from the time an individual is charged. What constitutes a 'reasonable time' is extremely flexible and there are no absolute time limits set by the ECHR or by ECt.HR jurisprudence. A more rigorous standard theoretically applies when the defendant is in custody.

ECHR law also makes the State responsible for delays attributable either to the prosecution or the court but suggests that understandable delays may arise from complex cases including numerous defendants or charges or where unusually difficult legal issues arise.

6.3.8 'BY AN INDEPENDENT TRIBUNAL'

Trial 'by an independent tribunal' is a fundamental tenet of Human Rights law. It is recognised in Article 6 ECHR, providing as it does for trial, either civil or criminal, by an independent and impartial tribunal established by law, in the Irish Constitution, as aforementioned (see **6.3.1** above), and in Common Law principles of natural justice, all of which contribute to this cornerstone of any legal system. In the leading Irish case, *People (AG) v Singer* [1975] IR 408, the foreman of the jury in a fraud trial had been a minor victim of the fraud. The conviction, not surprisingly, was set aside. As to the ECt.HR, in *Hauschildt v Denmark* (1990) 12 EHRR 266, the Court observed that:

> '. . . even appearances may be of a certain importance . . . what is at stake is (public confidence in the courts) . . . accordingly, any judge in respect of whom there is a legitimate reason to fear a lack of impartiality must withdraw . . .'

6.3.9 THE PROTECTION AGAINST SELF-INCRIMINATION AND THE RIGHT TO SILENCE

The Common law principle of the protection against self-incrimination and the right to silence, receives its most profound endorsement in the Fifth Amendment of the US Constitution. In Ireland, the Supreme Court held the right to be not only a common law right but also a constitutional right, which might, however, be validly limited by legislation (*O'Leary v AG* [1995] 1 IR 254).

There has, indeed, been a series of statutory encroachments, including the Criminal Justice Act, 1984, the Criminal Justice (Drug Trafficking) Act, 1998 and the Offences Against the State (Amendment) Act, 1998 all of which provide for adverse inferences to be drawn against a suspect who declines to answer questions while being questioned in Garda custody. In *Rock v Ireland* [1997] 3 IR 484, the Supreme Court affirmed a 'proportionality test', balancing the suspect's right to avoid self-incrimination with the State's right to protect life, person and the property of citizens. It is significant in the judgment that the inferences that may be drawn could not themselves form the basis for a conviction but were merely capable of corroborating other evidence. A similar approach has been maintained by the ECt.HR, in such cases as *Murray v UK* (1996) 22 EHRR 29.

A similar issue arose in a different form in the *Quinn v Ireland* (Application 36887/1997) and *Heaney & McGuinness v Ireland* (Application 34720/1997) cases. In both cases, the suspects had refused to answer questions when being questioned under s 52 of the

Offences Against the State Act, 1939, such a refusal constituting an offence in itself. The Supreme Court upheld the legislation as constitutionally valid, relying on the entitlement of the community to have crime properly investigated and/or detected.

The ECt.HR took a different view, holding that 'the right not to incriminate oneself, in particular, presupposes that the prosecution in a criminal case seeks to prove their case against the accused without resort to evidence by obtained methods of coercion or oppression 'in defiance of the will of the accused'.

Yet another related issue was considered in the Irish Courts in *In Re National Irish Bank* [1999] 1 ILRM 321, concerning ss 10 and 18 of the Companies Act, 1990. Here, officials of the Bank were compelled to answer questions under s 10, failure to do so being a criminal offence. Section 18 went on to provide that answers given under penalty by virtue of s 10 could then be used as evidence in a criminal prosecution of the same individual under s 18. Relying on the 'balancing of rights' argument, the Supreme Court found that bank officials could not invoke the privilege against self-incrimination to refuse to answer questions put under s 10. The separate, but obviously related, question, as to the admissibility of any s 10 admissions in any subsequent trial for an offence under s 18 was, in effect, reserved to a future trial judge, with a reminder from the Supreme Court that admissions could only be admitted against an accused if they were shown to be voluntary. This is presumably a difficult task for the prosecution if answers were extracted under threat of penalty, at the time of the making of the s 10 demand.

Similar UK legislation was impugned as a breach of Article 6, ECHR in *Saunders v UK* (1997) 23 EHRR 313. The Court found a violation of Article 6. In the case itself, a senior company executive was compelled by one government agency to furnish information about the way in which the company conducted its business, which resulted in him incriminating himself. The government then turned the information obtained over to prosecuting authorities to be used in criminal proceedings subsequently brought against him. In the domestic courts, he failed in his argument that the admissions should not be used against him. He appealed to the ECt.HR, where he was successful. The court has generally considered that the right to silence and the right not to incriminate oneself are universally recognised international standards lying at the heart of the idea of fair procedures. The right to a fair trial in a criminal case includes 'the right of anyone charged with a criminal offence . . . to remain silent and not to contribute to incriminating himself' (*Funke v France* (1993) 16 EHRR 297). In the *Saunders* case, the court held that the privilege against self-incrimination was 'closely linked' to the 'presumption of innocence'.

However, different considerations have been held by the court to apply to laws permitting the drawing of adverse inferences from the silence of suspects under interrogation who subsequently become accused at trial (see *Murray v UK* above). This is consistent with the Supreme Court's approach as considered above.

6.3.10 THE PRESUMPTION OF INNOCENCE

An absolute minimum requirement of the Common Law systems, the presumption of innocence is another fundamental guarantee of Art 6 ECHR. In the ECHR jurisprudence, it applies only to persons who are charged and has no application at the time of investigation into alleged offences. However, provided that the overall burden of proof of guilt remains on the prosecution, Art 6(2) does not prohibit rules, which transfer aspects of the burden of proof to the accused and presumptions of law or fact operating against the accused are permitted. However, such rules, either shifting the burden of proof or applying presumptions against the accused, must 'be confined within reasonable limits' (*Salabiaku v France* (1988) 13 EHRR 379).

In Irish Constitutional law, the existence of the right to the presumption of innocence has been stated. Deriving from the US Constitution, it received endorsement relatively late in

Irish law, in *People (AG) v O'Callaghan* [1966] IR 501, but has frequently been repeated since then in judicial pronouncements. As in the ECt.HR, the Irish Courts have permitted some limited evidential encroachments on the presumption, which are admitted in the relevant cases as shifting an evidential burden on to the accused (see for example *Hardy v Ireland*, 18 March 1993, Supreme Court, (unreported)). The Supreme Court has justified its approach by emphasising that at all times, the legal burden of proof remains with the prosecution.

6.4 Specific Guarantees to Ensure Fairness in Criminal Trials Provided by the ECHR

Specific guarantees to ensure fairness in criminal trials are of the utmost importance and are contained in Article 6(3) and Protocol 7. Most, if not all of these are mirrored by Irish constitutional provisions.

6.4.1 THE RIGHT TO KNOW THE DETAILS OF THE CHARGE

An accused person has a right to be informed of the charge against him, in a language he understands, and in detail. This principle is concerned with what the accused must be told at the time of charge, rather than with the disclosure of evidence in the course of the preparation for the trial itself (*Brozicek v Italy* (1990) 12 EHRR 371).

6.4.2 RIGHT TO REPRESENTATION AND TO LEGAL AID

The accused must be given adequate time and facilities for the preparation of a defence. Obviously, the adequacy of the time allowed will depend upon the complexity of the case. The Court has seen it as fundamental that a defence lawyer must be appointed in sufficient time to allow the case to be properly prepared (*X and Y v Austria* [1978] 12 DR 160). The requirement to afford adequate facilities for the preparation of the defence case obliges the state to adopt such measures as will place the defence on an equal footing with the prosecution (*Jespers v Belgium* (1981) 27 DR 61).

Article 6(3)(c) provides an accused with the right to represent himself in person or should he wish it, through legal assistance of his own choosing. It also provides that an accused may have legal assistance provided free of charge, if the interests of justice require it and he does not have sufficient means to pay for a lawyer. This is part of the 'equality of arms' set of rights discussed briefly above. States may however, place 'reasonable restrictions' on the right of an accused to counsel of his choice, although as a general rule, the accused's choice of lawyer should be respected (*Goddi v Italy* (1984) 6 EHRR 457). There must be good reason for excluding a lawyer from the court, such as a breach of professional ethics.

Irish constitutional law appears to go further. In *State (Freeman) v Connellan* [1986] IR 433, a Judge in the District Court refused to assign the applicant the Legal Aid solicitor of his own choosing. The High Court held that the applicant could only be refused the solicitor of choice if '. . . there is good and sufficient reason why the applicant should be deprived of . . . (the solicitor's . . .) services.' In order that the requirements of Art 6(3)(c) are met, representation provided by the State must be effective. The State will not generally be responsible for the inadequacies of a legal aid lawyer, but the authorities may be required to intervene where 'the failure to provide effective representation is manifest' and it has been brought to their attention. A lawyer appointed by the Court against the express wish of the accused will, generally, be '. . . incompatible with the notion of a fair trial . . . if it lacks relevant and sufficient justification . . .' (*Croissant v Germany* (1993) 16 EHRR 135).

In one specific instance however, Art 6 sits uneasily with the current state of the law in Ireland. *Lavery v The Member in Charge, Carrickmacross Garda Station* [1999] 2 IR 390, following on from a similar approach in *DPP v Pringle* (1981) 2 Frewen 57, expressly removed the entitlement for a solicitor to be present throughout detention or even during interviews in the investigative stages of a case. The Supreme Court may unwittingly have underestimated the significance, in terms of an investigation, of this period of detention. That significance was underlined in *DPP v Buck* [2002] 2 IR 268 where a suspect was arrested on a Sunday afternoon and requested a solicitor. Notwithstanding the difficulties in getting access to a solicitor, the suspect was questioned for a substantial period of time by relays of Gardaí before getting access to a solicitor. The Supreme Court found no violation of the applicant's constitutional rights, placing substantial reliance on the trial judge's findings that there were no conscious and deliberate violations of the applicant's right of access to a solicitor. The trial judge also found, and it was held to be significant, that there was no causative link between any breach of the applicant's constitutional rights and the making of the incriminating admissions.

Article 6(3)(c) ECHR has also been interpreted as requiring confidentiality of communications between detained persons and their lawyers, the ECt.HR citing such confidentiality as 'one of the basic requirements of a fair trial in a democratic society' (*S v Switzerland* (1992) 14 EHRR 670).

6.4.3 THE RIGHT TO CONFRONT PROSECUTION WITNESSES

Controversy in the area of the right to confront prosecution witnesses has tended to revolve around questions of hearsay and anonymity of witnesses. Broadly, hearsay evidence is not admissible, but the Strasbourg Court has allowed some flexibility in the admissibility of ordinarily prohibited hearsay evidence, where it is based on a statutory provision, which is accompanied by safeguards (see for example *Trivedi v UK* (Appliction No 31700/96, 27 May 1977). However, the Court will incline away from approving rules of evidence, which do not permit, at some stage, cross-examination (*Kostovski v Netherlands* 12 EHRR 434).

The Court has held that ordinarily witnesses should not remain anonymous, as ignorance of their identity may deprive the defence of particulars, which would enable them to demonstrate that the witness is prejudiced, hostile or unreliable. However, in exceptional circumstances, arrangements to preserve the anonymity of a witness could in principle be justified if there was an identifiable threat to the life or physical safety of the witness. Although such evidence is admissible in restrictive circumstances, the evidence should still be treated with 'extreme care' and a conviction should not be based 'solely or to a decisive extent' on evidence given anonymously (*Doorsen v Netherlands* (1996) 22 EHRR 330).

Ireland has stuck fairly resolutely to the hearsay rule, allowing, in the main, only the accepted common law exceptions. This is a regular feature of jurisdictions where the courtroom tradition of oral examination of witnesses and legal argument predominates. As to the anonymity of witnesses, this is extremely rare in Ireland. Recent legislation has provided for the taking of evidence by videolink, mainly in cases alleging sexual offences against young victims, but this is solely to remove the complainant from the oppressive atmosphere of the court and the witness is available for cross-examination in the ordinary way.

6.4.4 THE RIGHT TO FREE INTERPRETATION

The right to free interpretation is of increasing importance as the population of nonnationals residing in Ireland is growing. It is clearly an essential part of any system of justice that parties to the proceedings should be able to follow and properly participate in, those proceedings, if necessary through an interpreter. However the Supreme Court was proactive in its determination on this issue at an early stage, describing the right as '. . . one of the fundamental principles of the administration of . . . justice . . .', and to disregard it would mean that any conviction obtained in breach '. . . could not possibly stand in any court of law . . .' (*State (Buchan) v Coyne* 70 ILTR 185).

Likewise, Article 6(3)(e) ECHR provides that the accused has the right to the free assistance of an interpreter if he can not understand or speak the language used in Court. This is part of the State's obligation to run its judicial system fairly. The right is unqualified. A charged or convicted person cannot therefore be ordered to pay the costs of an interpreter. Although there is no recorded instance of an assertion of this right in civil proceedings, identical considerations will presumably apply, whether a case is taken in the Irish Courts or the Strasbourg Court, as to the entitlement of a litigant to free interpretation services in appropriate cases.

6.4.5   THE PROSECUTION'S DUTY OF DISCLOSURE

In the context of ECt.HR jurisprudence, there is much overlap between the specific guarantees of Art 6(3) ECHR and the principles of 'Equality of Arms'. An issue gaining increasing importance in Ireland, the duty of disclosure imposed on the prosecution, has already been adjudicated upon by the Commission in *Jespers v Belgium* (1981) 27 DR 61 (see **6.3.2** above). Here, it was decided that the authorities, whether investigating or prosecuting, must disclose to the defence any material in their possession, or to which they could gain access, which may assist the accused in exonerating himself or in obtaining a lighter sentence. This was extended in *Edwards v UK* (1993) 15 EHRR 417 to include material, which might be of assistance in undermining the credibility of a prosecution witness.

Recent Irish cases appear wholeheartedly to embrace the ECt.HR European standard. In *Braddish v DPP* [2001] 3 IR 127, Hardiman J prohibited a retrial from taking place when it emerged that a videotape purporting to have recorded a robbery in which the accused could be identified as a participant had in fact been returned to its owner, who had subsequently erased it. The prosecution were relying, instead, on a disputed confession statement. The Court reviewed the common law authorities and found that the Gardaí had a right to seize and preserve evidence, but that right carried with it the obligation to preserve and disclose to the defence all evidence obtained, whether or not helpful to the State's case. The Court referred to the 'unique investigative role . . . (of the Gardaí) . . .' and imposed a duty '. . . to seek out and preserve all evidence having a bearing or potential bearing on the issue of guilt or innocence . . .'

The Supreme Court appears to have extended this principle in *Dunne v DPP* [2002] 2 IR 305. Fennelly J, after reviewing the authorities extensively, found as '. . . the underlying principle . . .' that the accused should receive 'a fair trial'. In the course of evidence in the lower courts, it was unresolved as to whether a videotape of a robbery had either ever existed, or alternatively, had ever been handed to the Gardaí. The Court felt bound to resolve the issues in favour of the accused and Fennelly J observed that this approach, based as it was on *Braddish* (above) might seem a 'very significant new step in the law', imposing, as it did, a positive duty on the Gardaí, to collect evidence which has a potential bearing on the trial, with the possible sanction of a prohibition if they failed to comply with that duty.

6.5   Rights Arising on the Conclusion of Criminal Proceedings

6.5.1   THE RIGHT TO REVIEW A CRIMINAL CONVICTION OR SENTENCE

The right to review of a criminal conviction or sentence is guaranteed by Article 2 of the Protocol 7 ECHR subject only to exceptions in regard to offences of a minor character, as prescribed by law or to cases in which the person concerned was tried in the first instance by the highest tribunal or was convicted following an appeal against an acquittal.

The Irish judicial system provides comprehensive access to appeals. From the District Court, there is a full appeal, on law or fact, as of right, in every case. In all other Courts, the right of appeal is limited to issues of law and the court of first instance is effectively the finder of fact.

6.5.2 DOUBLE JEOPARDY

An obscure provision in Article 4(2) of Protocol 7 ECHR challenges the fundamental and seemingly immovably established principle of the common law, the prohibition on double jeopardy. Simply stated, a person once acquitted at trial of criminal offences could historically in the common law jurisdictions never be retried. Article 4(2) of Protocol 7 ECHR permits an exception to that situation 'if there is evidence of new or newly discovered facts, or if there has been a fundamental defect in the previous proceedings which could effect the outcome of the case'. There is as yet no recorded instance of the operation of this section.

In fact, even in the common law jurisdictions, this is not as immutable a principle as is commonly believed, and a series of Supreme Court decisions has left open the possibility of retrials for 'acquitted' accused, even, in appropriate cases, where an accused has been acquitted by a jury (see, for example, *DPP v O'Shea* [1982] IR 384, for contrasting judicial views of this topic. O'Higgins CJ and Henchy J took very different views of the matter, the former leaving open the idea that an acquitted accused might be susceptible to retrial, the latter roundly condemning the notion).

6.6 Freedom from Retrospective Criminal Legislation

Article 7 ECHR seeks to prohibit the retroactive application of criminal law resulting in a conviction or the imposition of a criminal penalty. It seeks to avoid the penalisation of conduct which was not criminal at the time when the relevant act occurred.

However, a major exception, contained in Art 7(2) ECHR, is intended to allow the application of national and international legislation enacted during and after World War II to punish war crimes and other lesser offences. This exception, when created was intended to allow the application of national and international legislation enacted expressly to deal with such offences as it became clear that such offences had occurred and that there was no specific legislation to deal with offences which had attracted universal abhorrence.

Article 15.5 of the Irish Constitution expressly prohibits retrospective criminal legislation. It is difficult to envisage a change in this position.

6.7 The Charter of Fundamental Rights of the EU

The Charter of Fundamental Rights of the EU was presented with considerable ceremony, signed and proclaimed by the Presidents of the European Parliament, Council of Ministers, and Commission, at the European Council meeting in Nice in December 2000. The Charter sets out the whole range of civil, political, economic and social rights of European Union citizens and residents. It is based, among other sources, on the ECHR and the constitutional traditions of the EU member states. Divided into 'Chapters', it contains provisions relating to 'Freedoms' and 'Justice', which contain broad aspirations similar, if not identical, to those contained in the ECHR.

The Charter's legal status is currently a matter for debate as part of the wider discussion on the future of the EU. The debate centres on whether the Charter should be a document which is legally binding or one which is merely declaratory. Obviously, the distinction is of huge significance, since a decision that the Charter is legally binding will not only allow access to the European Court of Justice (ECJ) to litigate its provisions but would also have the effect of implementing the Charter as part of domestic law, a point well settled in the Case 26/62 *Van Gend en Loos* [1963] ECR 1. This would have a profound effect in Ireland where judicial resistance to the importation of European Human Rights law is well documented (see **6.1** above). If, however it is determined that the Charter is to be merely declaratory, then it would have less direct effect but could still be used in ECJ cases as a guide to the general principles of EU law (see **chapter 5**).

There is unfortunately still a great deal of clarification needed, not only as to the status of the Charter, but also as to how, if at all, it will affect relations between citizens and their States, the ECJ, and the Strasbourg institutions. We also need to clarify how the relationship between the ECJ and the ECt.HR will be affected.

On this point, the ECJ has made it clear in a number of cases that there is considerable cross-fertilisation between its own jurisprudence and that of the ECt.HR. For example, in Case 222/84 *Johnston v Chief Constable of the RUC* [1986] ECR 1651, the ECJ reiterated the emphasis of the ECHR principles as cornerstones of EC law. The same case spelt out the EC demand that individual Member States provide access to an effective judicial remedy as provided for in Art 13 of the ECHR (in this instance for alleged sex discrimination).

At present, the predominant forum for the litigation of human rights issues is the ECt.HR. In a number of ways, creating access to a second Court might not be entirely desirable, as the applicable standards of human rights protection may begin to vary or diverge. However, it does appear that insularity in Irish human rights protection is a thing of the past, and future developments, however they may come, will in all likelihood bring Irish law ever closer to the European mainstream.

6.7.1 CIVIL AND CRIMINAL DUE PROCESS RIGHTS IN EC LAW

Certain due process protections are reflected in the Charter of Fundamental Rights of the EU. Again, it is necessary to emphasise that the legal status of the Charter is uncertain. It is a declaratory document but some elements may have legally binding sources if they confirm the existing *acquis*. It will be necessary to analyse the protections underlying the due process provisions of the Charter to determine whether the particular source is binding or not (see **5.10.5**). EC due process provisions are binding on the EU institutions and the Member States when acting within the scope of EC law.

The relevant Chapter of the Charter is Chapter VII: Justice, which contains Articles 47–50.

Article 47 provides for the right to an effective remedy and the right to a fair trial:

'Everyone whose rights and freedoms guaranteed by the law of the union are violated has the right to an effective remedy before a tribunal in compliance with the conditions laid down in this Article.

Everyone is entitled to a fair and public hearing within a reasonable time by an independent and impartial tribunal previously established by law. Everyone shall have the possibility of being advised, defended and represented.

Legal aid shall be made available to those who lack sufficient resources insofar as such aid is necessary to ensure effective access to justice.'

Article 47, paras 1 and 2 correspond to Art 13 ECHR and Art 6(1) ECHR respectively.

According to the explanatory text to the Charter, the right to an effective remedy in EC law 'is more extensive' than in ECt.HR jurisprudence 'since it guarantees the right to an effective remedy before a court'. The right to an effective remedy in a competent court is recognised as a general principle of EC law reflecting the constitutional traditions of the Member States and the ECHR in Case 222/84 *Johnston v Chief Constable* of the RUC [1986] ECR 1651, Case 222/86 *UNECTEF v Heylens* [1987] ECR 4097 and Case C-97/91 *Borelli v Commission* [1992] ECR 6313.

The issue of the right to an effective remedy arose in Johnston in the context of an equal treatment for men and women case. Mrs Johnston's employment contract was not renewed because of a new policy of the RUC that general police duties which frequently involved operations requiring the use of fire arms should no longer be assigned to women officers which had the consequence that fewer women officers were needed. In the proceedings before the national tribunal, Mrs Johnston alleged unlawful sex discrimination contrary to Directive 76/207 Equal Treatment for Men and Women. The Chief Constable of the RUC in those proceedings had produced a certificate which according to the provision of legislation at issue was required to be treated as conclusive evidence that the conditions for derogating from the principle of equal treatment had been fulfilled. In response to a preliminary reference, the ECJ held that to treat the national certificate as conclusive evidence would deprive the individual of the possibility of asserting by judicial process the rights conferred by the Directive. It was not permissible for such a national certificate to be treated as conclusive evidence so as to exclude the exercise of any power of review by the court.

In Case 222/86 *UNECTEF v Heylens* [1987] ECR 4097, the ECJ opined that the right to an effective remedy included an obligation to state reasons for a decision. The issue arose in the context of a freedom of establishment case where the decision not to recognise the equivalence of a diploma did not state the basis for the decision. Effective judicial review could only be secured where the court was aware of the reasons for the decision. The duty to state reasons is not however an absolute duty. In *UNECTEF* the ECJ, at para 16, limited the obligation to 'final decisions refusing to recognise equivalence and [does] not extend to opinions and other measures occurring in the preparation and investigation stage.'

In Case C-97/91 *Borelli SpA v Commission* [1992] ECR 6313, the ECJ held that an opinion of a Member State which forms part of the procedure leading to an EC decision is subject to the requirement of judicial control.

According to the explanatory text to Art 47(2) of the Charter, the right to a fair trial guarantee differs in scope to the analogous guarantee contained in Art 6(1) ECHR as it is not confined to disputes relating to civil rights and obligations.

Article 48 of the Charter provides for the presumption of innocence and the right of defence.

> '1. *Everyone who has been charged shall be presumed innocent until proved guilty according to law.*
> 2. *Respect for the rights of the defence of anyone who has been charged shall be guaranteed.'*

Article 48 is the same as Art 6(2) and (3) ECHR.

Article 49 provides for the principles of legality and proportionality of criminal offences and penalties.

> '1. *No one shall be held guilty of any criminal offence on account of any act or omission which did not constitute a criminal offence under national law or international law at the time when it was committed. Nor shall a heavier penalty be imposed than that which was applicable at the time the criminal offence was committed. If, subsequent to the commission of the criminal offence, the law provides for a lighter penalty, that penalty shall be applicable.*
> 2. *This Article shall not prejudice the trial and punishment of any person for any act or omission which, at the time when it was committed, was criminal according to the general principles recognised by the community of nations.*

> *3.   The severity of penalties must not be disproportionate to the criminal offence.'*

The principle reiterated in Art 49(3) confirms the case-law of the ECJ which has repeatedly held that the severity of the penalties must not be disproportionate to the offence. For example in Case C-193/94 *Criminal Proceedings against Skanavi* [1996] ECR I 929, the ECJ held that the criminal penalty imposed on a Greek national for failure to exchange her Greek driving license for a German driving license within one year of taking up normal residence in Germany was disproportionate to the gravity of the infringement.

Article 50 provides for the right not to be tried or punished twice in criminal proceedings for the same criminal offence.

> *'No one shall be liable to be tried or punished again in criminal proceedings for an offence for which he or she has already been finally acquitted or convicted within the Union in accordance with the law.'*

Article 50 corresponds to Art 4 of Protocol No. 7 ECHR.

The *non bis in idem* rule applies in EC law. An early authority is the decision in Cases 18/65 and 35/65 *Gutmann v Commission* [1966] ECR 103, involving internal disciplinary proceedings where the ECJ invoked the double jeopardy rule to prevent a second set of punishments being imposed in respect of a series of allegations that had already been the subject of a penalty. A more recent example is the decision in C-127/99 *Commission v Italy* [2001] ECR I 8305. The facts concerned an action for failure by Italy to adopt action programmes laid down in an environmental directive. Italy argued that the action was inadmissible on the grounds that it was contrary to the *non bis in idem* rule as the ECJ had earlier determined that Italy had failed to fulfill its obligations under the directive in Case C-195/97 *Commission v. Italy* [1999] ECR I 1169. The ECJ held that the *non bis in idem* rule was not violated as the earlier judgment related to specific provisions of the directive (Art 3(2) and 12(1)) whereas the current proceedings related to other provisions of the directive at issue (Arts 5, 6 and 10).

The explanatory text to Art 50 states that the *non bis in idem* principle in EC law applies not only within the jurisdiction of one Member State but also between the jurisdictions of several Member States, citing *inter alia* provisions of the Schengen Convention.

Article 54 of the Schengen Convention provides:

> *'A person whose trial has been finally disposed of in one Contracting Party may not be prosecuted in another Contracting Party for the same acts provided that, if a penalty has been imposed, it has been enforced, is actually in the process of being enforced or can no longer be enforced under the laws of the sentencing Contracting Party.'*

While to date there has not been a hugely significant amount of EC jurisprudence relating to civil and criminal due process rights, it is possible that this will soon change. Since the Amsterdam Treaty, the maintenance and development of the EU as an area of freedom security and justice has formed a key objective of the EU. Action areas falling under this title include asylum, immigration, judicial co-operation in criminal matters, judicial co-operation in civil matters, fundamental rights, police co-operation and citizenship. Some of these policy areas currently fall within the first pillar of the EU while others, notably police and judicial co-operation in the field of criminal matters fall within the third pillar. The jurisdiction of the ECJ with respect to the third pillar currently has limitations which do not apply to the first pillar. Recently, the Final Report of the European Convention on the Future of Europe Working Group on 'Freedom, Security and Justice' (CONV 426/02 Brussels 2 December 2002) took the view that the limited jurisdiction of the ECJ is no longer acceptable in areas which directly affect fundamental rights of individuals. The Working Group was of the view that the general system of jurisdiction of the ECJ should be extended to the area of freedom, security and justice. It is submitted that if this suggestion is adopted that there will be increased ECJ jurisprudence in the area of due process rights.

CHAPTER 7

FREEDOM OF EXPRESSION

7.1   Introduction

The right of freedom of expression has long been recognised as a cornerstone of any properly functioning democracy. It is only through receiving and imparting information and opinions that citizens can make properly informed political decisions. Freedom of expression is guaranteed under the Irish Constitution and the European Convention on Human Rights. It is also recognised and protected within European Union law. However, both Irish and European jurisprudence recognise that the right of free expression is not absolute. The need to balance often conflicting constitutional and human rights is well known to both the Irish courts and the European Court of Human Rights (ECt.HR) – indeed, it is a characteristic of the case-law of both that greater deliberation can be spent on the restrictions to the right of freedom of expression than on the right itself and, in more recent times, the European Court of Justice (ECJ) has undertaken this exercise as part of the increasing constitutionalisation of European Community Law.

7.2   Irish Constitution

The right to freedom of expression is expressly provided for in Article 40.6.1°(i) of the Irish Constitution of 1937. It is also recognised to be one of the personal unspecified rights of the citizen protected by Article 40.3.1°. Article 40.6.1°(i) states:

> '1°.   The State guarantees liberty for the exercise of the following rights, subject to public order and morality; —
> (i)   The right of the citizens to express freely their convictions and opinions.
>
> The education of public opinion being, however, a matter of such grave import to the common good, the State shall endeavour to ensure that organs of public opinion, such as the radio, the press, the cinema, while preserving their rightful liberty of expression, including criticism of Government policy, shall not be used to undermine public order or morality or the authority of the State.
>   The publication or utterance of blasphemous, seditious, or indecent matter is an offence which shall be punishable in accordance with law.'

In addition to the restrictions contained in the provisions of Article 40.6.1°(i) itself, the Constitution contains other explicit and implicit restrictions on the right to freedom of expression. The most significant of these is the constitutional right to one's good name, guaranteed as follows, in Article 40.3:

> '1°.   The State guarantees in its laws to respect, and, as far as practicable, by its laws to defend and vindicate the personal rights of the citizen.

> 2. *The State shall, in particular, by its laws protect as best it may from unjust attack and, in the case of injustice done, vindicate the life, person, good name, and property rights of every citizen.'*

Further, the right to privacy has been long recognised as an unenumerated right also guaranteed by Article 40.3 of the Constitution: see *Kennedy and Arnold v Ireland* [1988] ILRM 472. In appropriate cases, it also limits or balances the sometimes conflicting right of freedom of expression.

7.2.1 CONSTITUTIONAL GUARANTEE OF FREEDOM OF EXPRESSION

The freedom of expression guarantee has received comparatively little attention from the Irish courts. Both the parties to litigation and the judiciary tend to be more concerned about the practical limits on the exercise of the right rather than its intellectual or constitutional basis. There has been nothing like the volume of case-law on the First Amendment in the United States, which constitutionally guarantees freedom of expression. That does not mean that the right is not exercised. The media criticise and scrutinise Government policy and actions on a daily basis.

The guarantee applies equally to the media and individuals. It confers no special rights or privileges on the media.

Both the common law and statute law impose restrictions on free expression. Some limitations are in the interest of the administration of justice (contempt of court) or of protecting the rights of others (defamation). Others refer to public morality, eg controls on obscene material by the Censorship of Publications Acts, 1929–1967 and the Censorship of Films Acts, 1923–1992.

7.3 The European Convention on Human Rights (ECHR)

Article 10, ECHR states:

> '1. *Everyone has the right to freedom of expression. This right shall include freedom to hold opinions and to receive and impart information and ideas without interference by public authority and regardless of frontiers. This Article shall not prevent States from requiring the licensing of broadcasting, television or cinema enterprises.*
> 2. *The exercise of these freedoms, since it carries with it duties and responsibilities, may be subject to such formalities, conditions, restrictions or penalties as are prescribed by law and are necessary in a democratic society, in the interests of national security, territorial integrity or public safety, for the prevention of disorder or crime, for the protection of health or morals, for the protection of the reputation or rights of others, for preventing the disclosure of information received in confidence, or for maintaining the authority and impartiality of the judiciary'.*

The balancing right of an individual's reputation is explicitly recognised in para 2 of Art 10.

Unlike the Irish Constitution, the right to privacy is expressly protected in Art 8, which reads:

> *'Right to respect for private and family life*
> 1. *Everyone has the right to respect for his private and family life, his home and his correspondence.*

2.   *There shall be no interference by a public authority with the exercise of this right except such as is in accordance with the law and is necessary in a democratic society, in the interests of national security, public safety or the economic well-being of the country, for the prevention of disorder or crime, for the protection of health or morals, or for the protection of the rights and freedoms of others'.*

7.4   Comparison of the Irish Constitution and ECHR

At first sight, the protection afforded to freedom of expression by Article 10, ECHR appears wider than that under Article 40.6.1° of the Irish Constitution. The latter is circumscribed by 'public order (and) morality', while any interference with freedom of expression violates Article 10 unless it is 'prescribed by law' and is 'necessary in a democratic society'. As we shall see, in the jurisprudence of the ECt.HR, the word 'necessary' in this context implies both the existence of a pressing social need and that the interference with freedom of expression is no more than is proportionate to the legitimate aim pursued.

The view that Article 10 is stronger than its Irish constitutional equivalent is not universally held. The former Chief Justice, Hamilton C.J., stated his belief that: 'There does not appear to be any conflict between Article 10 and the common law or the (Irish) Constitution'. (*De Rossa v Independent* Newspapers [1999] 4 IR 432 at 450). Similar views were expressed by Geoghegan J in the earlier case of *Murphy v IRTC* [1997] 2 ILRM 467. (The Supreme Court judgment is at [1999] 1 IR 12.)

7.5   Incorporation of the ECHR into Irish Law

When the ECHR was adopted in 1950, Ireland was one of the original signatories. Under the Good Friday Agreement, the Irish Government committed itself to 'ensure at least an equivalent level of protection of human rights as will pertain in Northern Ireland' and agreed to incorporate the ECHR into Irish law. The Convention became law throughout the UK on 2 October 2000. The ECHR was incorporated into Irish law following the European Convention on Human Rights Act, 2003.

Even before incorporation, however, the Irish courts took cognisance of the ECHR. As Geoghegan J said in *Murphy v IRTC* [1997] 2 ILRM 467:

'Although the European Convention on Human Rights is not part of Irish municipal law, regard can be had to its provisions when considering the nature of a fundamental right and perhaps more particularly the reasonable limitations which can be placed on the exercise of that right.'

7.6   Case-Law of the European Court of Human Rights

7.6.1   THE IMPORTANCE OF FREEDOM OF EXPRESSION

The leading statement of the ECt.HR on the importance of freedom of expression is contained in *Handyside v UK* (1979–80) 1 EHRR 737, where it was stated:

'Freedom of expression constitutes one of the essential foundations of a democratic society, one of the basic conditions for its progress and for the development of every man. Subject to paragraph 2 of Article 10, it is applicable not only to 'information' or 'ideas' that are favourably received or regarded as offensive or as a matter of indifference, but also to those that offend, shock or disturb the State or any sector of the population. Such are the demands of that pluralism, tolerance and broadmindedness without which there is no 'democratic society'. This means that every formality, condition, restriction or penalty imposed in this sphere must be proportionate to the legitimate aim pursued.'

This ringing endorsement of the right and of its democratic theme recurs throughout the case law of the ECt.HR. It is supported by a conviction that the press has a vital role in underpinning democracy. For example, in *Observer and Guardian v UK* (1992) 14 EHRR 153, the ECt.HR stated:

'Freedom of expression constitutes one of the essential foundations of a democratic society, in particular freedom of political and public debate. This is of special importance for the free press which has a legitimate interest in reporting on and drawing the public's attention to deficiencies in the operation of Government services, including possible legal activities. It is incumbent on the press to impart information and ideas about such matters and the public has a right to receive them.'

7.6.2 RIGHT OF FREEDOM OF EXPRESSION IS NOT ABSOLUTE

However, the right to 'offend, shock or disturb, as so described in the *Handyside* case, is not unlimited. There are three fundamental restrictions contained in Art 10 itself:

(1) Under Art 10(2), as is the case with other freedoms protected under the Convention, restrictions on the protected right may be permitted provided that they are prescribed by law, that is that they have a basis in law that satisfies certain requirements of accessibility and foreseeability.

(2) That the restrictions pursue at least one of the aims defined by Art 10(2). As paragraph 2 of Art 10 specifies, the legitimate aims which may impact on freedom of expression include 'the prevention of disorder or crime, the protection of health or morals, the protection of the reputation and the rights of others' and 'maintaining the authority and impartiality of the judiciary'.

(3) That the restrictions are 'necessary in a democratic society to attain the legitimate aim or aims identified.'

Article 10(2) sets out the interests that may compete with freedom of expression and which have to be weighed in the balancing exercise to be carried out both by the national courts and in Strasbourg.

7.6.3 MARGIN OF APPRECIATION

The great majority of cases coming before the ECt.HR have turned not on the first two conditions, namely that the restrictions are prescribed by law and have a legitimate aim, but on the third one, the question of necessity in a democratic society. Here again, the *Handyside* case laid down the leading principles in this regard, particularly those relating to the application of a doctrine known as the margin of appreciation. The Court defined the concept of necessity as reflecting a 'pressing social need', but under the margin of appreciation allowed by the ECHR, it is for the national authorities to make the initial assessment of that pressing social need or, to put it another way, to balance the relevant competing interest against that of freedom of expression. Broadly speaking, the doctrine of the margin of appreciation recognises that the State authorities are in a better position than the international judges to give an opinion on the competing legitimate aims, because of their direct knowledge of their countries and the forces underpinning them. It is primarily for the national authorities to secure the rights and freedoms in the ECHR and the role of the ECt.HR is essentially a supervisory one.

The *Handyside* case concerned the publication in the early 1970s of the *'Little Red School Book'*, which contained sexual information primarily aimed at adolescents. Its publisher was convicted and fined for publishing an obscene book for gain as the material contained in it had, contrary to the UK obscenity laws, a tendency to deprave and corrupt. The ECt.HR, however, reached the conclusion that there had been no violation of Art 10, referring notably to the margin of appreciation left to the UK authorities and courts. It was for the UK initially to determine the balance between the need to protect adolescents from obscenity and freedom of expression and its decision fell within the latitude afforded by the ECHR.

7.6.4   INCITEMENT TO VIOLENCE

The 'right to offend, shock or disturb' enunciated in *Handyside* does not cover hate speech or incitement to violence. A case from Ireland in 1991 on this issue was decided by the European Commission of Human Rights, rather than the Court. *Purcell v Ireland* (1991) 12 HRLJ No 6–7 dealt with the ban on the broadcasting of interviews with members of proscribed organisations, in particular the IRA. Mr Purcell complained that the ban infringed the right to freedom of expression protected by Art 10. The Commission accepted however, that the restrictions were necessary to prevent representatives of known terrorist organisations and their political supporters from using the broadcast media as a platform for advocating their cause and thereby conveying an impression of legitimacy.

7.6.5   EXPRESSIONS OF OPINION

The right to offend is intended to guarantee participation in the democratic process through public debate on questions of general concern. The strength of the protection afforded by the ECHR will often be determined by the extent to which it can be linked to the direct functioning of a democratic society. The closer the link between the opinion expressed, however forthright, to a matter of public debate and interest, the more likely it is to be protected under Art 10.

The Irish common law and Constitution have long recognised a distinction between the protection afforded to factual statements and to expressions of opinion. If the opinion expressed was honestly held, based on facts which are shown to be true, it will be protected from an action for defamation. Such 'fair comment', as it is known, is not one which a judge and jury would necessarily make themselves or indeed consider reasonable. Extravagance of language and violence of opinion does not render the comment unfair and libellous.

This common law and constitutional protection for the expression of opinions is echoed at European level in two cases brought against Austria by a journalist, Mr Oberschlick. In the first action (*Oberschlick v Austria (No. 1)* (1995) 19 EHRR 389), Mr Oberschlick had argued in a newspaper that a proposal by a politician for a 50 per cent cut in family allowances by the State to immigrant mothers corresponded to the philosophy and aims of Nazism. The courts convicted Mr Oberschlick of defamation (in Austria, defamation is a crime, as well as a civil wrong). In doing so, the courts required him not only to establish the fact that the proposal for a cut in family allowance had been made but to prove the truth of his opinion or value judgment on it. The ECt.HR said that this infringed Art 10. Mr Oberschlick's opinion was expressed within the context of a public debate on a political question of general interest and his contribution to that debate was protected. In other words, he would not have to show that the proposal *in fact* corresponded to the philosophy and aims of Nazism, merely that he believed it did.

Some years later, Mr Oberschlick described Mr Haider, leader of the far right Austrian Freedom Party, as a trottel, which roughly translates as an idiot. The Austrian courts determined that the mere use of the word itself was sufficient to justify conviction for defamation. This lead to *Oberschlick v Austria* (No. 2) (1998) 25 EHRR 357 where again the ECt.HR overruled the national courts. Mr Haider was a controversial politician and Mr Oberschlick description of him followed a speech in which Mr Haider had stated that all the soldiers who served in World War II, whichever side they were on, had fought for peace and freedom and had contributed to founding Austria's democratic society. Mr Oberschlick's response to this was simply part of a political discussion provoked by the speech and amounted to an opinion, whose truth was not susceptible to proof. It was therefore protected by Art 10.

7.6.6 POLITICIANS

Another case brought against Austria appears to establish that the limits of acceptable criticism are wider as regards a politician than for a private individual. [In legal theory, at least, the Irish common law of defamation is more restrictive than European jurisprudence as no such distinction is drawn. In Irish defamation law, all citizens, politicians or not, are afforded equal protection from attacks on their reputation]. In *Lingens v Austria* (1986) 8 EHRR 407, a journalist had characterised the Austrian Chancellor as amoral and lacking in dignity because of an unduly accommodating attitude to former Nazis. The journalist was convicted of criminal defamation and fined. The ECHR determined that the restriction was not 'necessary in a democratic society'. In doing so, it stressed the crucial role of the press in imparting information, in the following terms:

> 'Freedom of the press affords the public one of the best means of discovering an opinion of the ideas and attitudes of political leaders.'

This crucial role of the media in imparting information was at the core of the concept of a democratic society, which is central to the ECHR. The fact that there was no defence of fair comment under Austrian law was a breach of Art 10.

7.6.7 THE FACTUAL BASIS FOR COMMENTS

In broad terms, the approach of the ECt.HR at least as far as politicians are concerned is that the expression in the press of an opinion, with a sufficient factual basis, where the opinion can be related to a matter of public concern, will normally attract the protection of Art 10, even where it entails strongly critical comments or language that can be regarded as insulting. This allows great latitude for exaggerated and provocative expressions of views, necessary for strident political debate.

At common law, the expression of opinions is protected once they are honestly made and are based upon facts shown to be true. The factual basis for the opinions can either be explicitly stated or be implicit in the opinion, provided it would be known to the audience. This approach is mirrored at European level as a case in July 2001, *Feldek v Slovakia* 12 July 2001, ECt.HR (unreported), shows.

In the Slovakian case, the applicant had accused a government minister of having a fascist past. The Minister had been a member of a fascist youth organisation in the early 1940s and had been enrolled on an SS training course towards the end of the World War II at the age of 17. He claimed that he had joined the youth organisation merely to participate in table tennis tournaments. Both the Slovakian court and the ECt.HR viewed what Mr Feldek had written as a statement of opinion. However, the local courts insisted that Mr Feldek should have explicitly indicated the facts upon which he had arrived at his opinion. The ECt.HR disagreed saying that the wider public would have already been aware of the information upon which the opinion was based. His value judgment was protected by Art 10.

7.6.8   STATEMENTS OF FACT

7.6.8.1   How has the ECt.HR approached statements of fact?

Under the common law, it is a complete defence to defamation that the words complained of were true in substance and in fact. However, once a plaintiff has shown that the words complained of are defamatory on their face, the burden of proof shifts to the defendant. The common law presumes the statements are false and the defendant must prove, on the balance of probabilities, that they are true. To succeed, the defendant must prove not only that the publication is true in its natural and ordinary meaning but in any innuendoes which are present. Where a defence of justification fails, aggravated damages may be awarded.

A significant recent European decision on statements of fact is *Bladet Tromso and Stensaas v Norway* (2000) 29 EHRR 125. A newspaper published details of a report by a seal-hunting inspector which contained allegations of cruelty against members of a particular ship. The inspector had not blamed the whole crew, only certain members, who were not named. The newspaper had relied solely upon the report by the official government inspector and had not carried out its own research into the allegations of cruelty. The report by the inspector had subsequently been largely discredited and the crew members successfully sued the newspaper for defamation.

The ECt.HR had to consider whether the circumstances of the case were such as to remove from the newspaper its general obligation to independently verify facts which were defamatory. Most importantly, the Court examined the statements complained of in light of the situation as presented to the newspaper at the time of publication rather than with the benefit of hindsight. It concluded that the newspaper could reasonably rely on the official report without being required to carry out its own research into the accuracy of the facts stated in it. The journalists had acted in good faith and according to the ethics of their profession. Therefore, a successful defamation action by the crew members of the seal hunting vessel infringed Art 10, even though the government report, published by the newspaper, was subsequently found to be largely inaccurate. The Court was not unanimous in its decision and it is unlikely that a newspaper here would, under existing Irish defamation law, be afforded such scope as the burden of proving the truthfulness of the statements of fact published rests at all stage with the defendants.

7.7   The Irish Experience of Article 10

As we have seen, the Irish courts have, in a number of cases, recognised the importance of the ECHR and have had regard to its provisions. The Irish courts have also, even prior to incorporation, shown a certain willingness to consider the case-law in relation to the interpretation and implementation of the ECHR. How then has the right to freedom of expression, as guaranteed by Art 10, impacted upon Irish law?

7.7.1   JURIES AND DAMAGES IN DEFAMATION CASES

The only method by which the Irish courts can vindicate the good name of a person who has been defamed is by awarding damages. Neither the court, nor any jury, can order a media defendant to apologise, to offer a right to reply or, indeed, to admit that they were wrong. The majority of defamation cases are heard by a jury in the High Court. The jury determines both liability and quantum. Further, at present, they decide the level of any award with only very limited guidance from the trial judge who cannot, for example, suggest financial parameters for any award or draw comparisons with personal injury damages. In effect the trial judge is limited to telling the jury to be fair to both sides in light of the evidence before them.

7.7.2   *DE ROSSA V INDEPENDENT NEWSPAPERS*

In July 1997, a jury awarded the former Government Minister, Proinsias de Rossa, damages of IR£300,000 (€380,921) for a libel in an Eamon Dunphy article published in the *Sunday Independent* in December 1992. The jury had decided that the article falsely alleged that Mr de Rossa was involved in, or tolerated, serious paramilitary crime, was anti-Semitic and supported violent communist oppression. The newspaper appealed on quantum only, arguing that the award was excessive and disproportionate to any damage done to Mr de Rossa's reputation.

Importantly, the *Sunday Independent* sought to challenge the system under Irish constitutional and defamation law whereby juries determine not only whether an article is libellous but also the size of the award without any realistic guidance by the trial judge. They alleged that this procedure in practice leads to erratic and often excessive awards. In 1997, the Supreme Court had held in *Dawson v Irish Brokers Association*, 27 February 1997, Supreme Court, (unreported) that:

> 'Unjustifiably large awards, as well as the costs attendant on long trials, deal a blow to the freedom of expression entitlement that is enshrined in the Constitution.'

The newspaper sought to rely on UK and European case-law on Art 10 of the ECHR in support of its challenge to Irish defamation practice.

Its arguments were as follows. In 1993, the Supreme Court had upheld an award given to a barrister, McDonagh, against the *Sun* newspaper for a very grave defamation. In *McDonagh v News Group Newspapaers Ltd*, 23 November 1993, Supreme Court, (unreported) the Supreme Court had determined, however, that the award of IR£90,000 (€114,276) was at 'the top of the permissible range'. The newspaper argued that it was wholly illogical that a jury should determine the award in the *de Rossa* case without having the benefit of this information. Only if they were armed with knowledge of the Supreme Court's views as to an appropriate award for a serious libel could the jury properly determine the level of compensation to which Mr de Rossa was entitled. The appellants also went on to argue that the jury should also be told the level of awards in personal injury actions so as to make appropriate comparisons with damage to reputation. If such guidelines and procedures were not in place, the legal system did not adequately protect the defendant's right to freedom of expression. The newspaper was supported in this view by two decisions on Art 10 at UK and European level.

In *Rantzen v Mirror Group Newspapers* [1993] 4 All ER 975, the Court of Appeal in England held that:

> 'to grant an almost unlimited discretion to a jury failed to provide a satisfactory measurement of deciding what was necessary in a democratic society for the purposes of Article 10.'

In the UK, juries were given, where appropriate, both financial guidance and comparisons with personal injury awards.

The ECt.HR endorsed this view in *Tolstoy Miloslavsky v UK* [1995] 20 EHRR 442. In that case, the Court considered a defamation award of £1.5m. It stressed that these damages had been awarded by a jury which had received no specific guidelines relating to its assessment of damages. The Court concluded that:

> 'Having regard to the size of the award in the appellant's case in conjunction with the lack of adequate and effective safeguards at the relevant time against a disproportionately large award, the court finds that there has been a violation of the applicant's rights under Article 10 of the Convention.'

In the event, the Supreme Court in *De Rossa v Independent Newspapers* [1999] 4 IR 432 (by a 4 to 1 majority) felt that, given the serious nature of the libel of Mr de Rossa, the jury were 'justified in going to the top of the bracket' and that the award was 'not disproportionate to the injury' suffered by Mr de Rossa. In the majority decision, the Chief Justice stated that the law must reflect a due balancing of the constitutional right to freedom of expression and the constitutional protection of every citizen's good name. He held that the obligations arising from the provisions of the Constitution and the ECHR were met by the existing law of the State which provides that the award must always be reasonable and fair and bear a due correspondence with the injuries suffered with the requirement that if it was disproportionately high, it would be set aside on appeal. On the issue of guidance to juries, accepted in the UK and endorsed at European level, the Chief Justice stated:

'While the aforesaid changes of practice were therein described as "modest" they are not only important but fundamental and radically alter the general practice with regard to the instructions or guidance to be given to a jury as to the manner in which they should approach the assessment of damages in a defamation action. It had been the invariable practice in the past that neither counsel nor the judge could make any suggestion to the jury as to what would be an appropriate award.'

While giving due consideration to the approach of the courts in the UK, he concluded that the giving of figures to a jury, even though by way of guidelines only, would constitute an unjustifiable invasion of the providence and domain of the jury, which would not be countenanced.

The dissenting judge, Denham J, would have reduced the award to Mr de Rossa to £150,000. She favoured giving guidelines to the jury and stated:

'In general, I favour the giving of guidelines to a jury on the level of damages. Information does not fetter discretion. If this is perceived as a more active approach by the judge I believe it is in the interests of justice. The legislature could legislate but in its absence more guidelines would, I believe, help juries in the administration of justice. Guidelines would assist in achieving consistent and comparable decisions, which would enhance public confidence in the administration of justice. There is a benefit to the administration of justice in such an approach. Whilst maintaining at all times the paramount position of the jury in determining the damages, specific information would aid decision making and the maintaining of an appropriate relationship to the awards of damages in other areas. Such information as is deemed appropriate could be given in more specific guidelines.'

The decision of the majority of the Supreme Court in *de Rossa* has been criticised. Eoin Quill of the University of Limerick stated in a paper entitled '*Jury Instructions on the Quantum of Damages in Defamation Cases in the wake of De Rossa*', delivered at a conference in Trinity College Dublin entitled '*Recent Developments in Defamation and Contempt of Court: A Practical Update*' 22 January 2000:

'The principles (upheld by the Supreme Court) are the traditional rules of defamation at common law and do not differ significantly from the principles applied by the European Courts in Tolstoy which were held to violate Article 10 of the Convention. The bare assertion of proportionality by Hamilton C.J. is surely inadequate if the substantive legal principles are largely the same as those which were held to lack such proportionality in Tolstoy. The constitutional gloss, by way of a backdrop in Irish law, is meaningless if there is no change in the substantive principles.'

The *Sunday Independent* newspaper has challenged the decision of the Supreme Court before the ECt.HR. The case was heard in November 2003 and it is expected that the Court's decision will be given in 2004.

In a case in the year following the *de Rossa* decision, the Supreme Court again upheld the practice of issuing jury instructions which leave the question of quantum at large; *O'Brien v MGN Limited* [2001] 1 IR 1. The court did, however, overturn an award of IR£250,000 (€317,435) as excessive and ordered a retrial on the level of damages.

7.8   The Right to Privacy

The right to privacy is explicitly recognised in Art 8 of the ECHR and is an unenumerated right protected by Art 40.3° of the Irish Constitution. There have been very few Irish decisions on the sometimes conflicting rights of free expression enjoyed by the media and of privacy. This may be due, to some extent, to a reticence on the part of media defendants to allow cases on the point to run to trial as this would give the Irish courts the opportunity to clarify, and perhaps extend, the ambit of the constitutional and ECHR right to privacy.

Some pointers on how the Irish courts might view Art 8 are contained in a number of recent decisions of the Court of Appeal in the UK.

7.8.1   CELEBRITY WEDDINGS

On 18 November 2000, the celebrity couple, Michael Douglas and Catherine Zeta-Jones, married in New York. *OK!* magazine paid approximately £1m for exclusive rights to cover the wedding. Shortly before publication, however, a rival magazine, *Hello!*, began printing an edition containing unauthorised photographs of the nuptials. An *ex parte* injunction was granted on 21 November but lifted by the Court of Appeal on 23 November 2000. In a judgment shortly before Christmas 2000, *Douglas v Hello!* [2001] QB 967, the Court of Appeal gave the reasons for its November decision.

The injunction was lifted, primarily on *American Cynamid Co. v Ethicon Ltd* [1975] AC 396 principles, on the grounds that the balance of convenience favoured publication of the photographs complained of as damages would be an adequate remedy. The Court of Appeal emphasised that while English law had been willing to recognise an enforceable obligation of confidentiality, it had not to date been relied upon to preclude an unwarranted intrusion into an individual's privacy, where the obligation of confidence did not apply. However, while stressing that they were not making a final decision at an interlocutory stage, the Court recognised the importance of Art 8 of the ECHR and determined, in the words of Lord Justice Sedley, that 'Mr Douglas and Ms Zeta-Jones have a powerful prima facie claim for redress for invasion of their privacy as a qualified right recognised and protected by English law'.

The substantive claim was then heard by Lindsay J in the High Court, *Douglas v Hello!* [2003] EWHC 786 (Ch). He found that *Hello!* had breached a duty of confidence they owed to Michael Douglas, Catherine Zeta-Jones and *OK!* Magazine. The wedding had taken place in circumstances importing an obligation of confidentiality on *Hello!* magazine and the publication of surreptiously obtained photographs (in breach of the Press Complaints Commission code) was detrimental to the claimants. Lindsay J held over the issue of damages.

The claimants, however, failed in their claim of privacy under Art 8 of the ECHR. The Judge considered that the claimants were adequately protected by the law of confidence. There was no need for him to attempt to construct a law of privacy and it would be wrong of him to do so. The judgment, however, suggests that some sort of privacy law in the UK is inevitable. Lindsay J cautioned that, in cases where the existing law did not afford protection to individuals whose rights to private and family life were infringed, the courts might have to address inadequacies if Parliament failed to 'grasp the nettle'. He said that a 'glance at a crystal ball of, so to speak, only a low wattage, suggests that if Parliament does not act soon, the less satisfactory course, of the courts creating the law bit by bit at the expense of litigants, and with inevitable delays and uncertainty, will be thrust upon the judiciary'.

In November 2003, Lindsay J awarded damages for the breach of confidence. Ms Zeta Jones and Mr Douglas received £14,600 while the publishers of *OK!* were awarded £1,033,156.

7.8.2 'KISS AND TELL'

An unreported decision of the Court of Appeal on 11 March 2002 laid down guidance for the first time for judges in the UK faced with privacy claims. The *Sunday People* newspaper had obtained interviews with two married women who claimed to have had long-term affairs with a successful footballer, who is married with children. Sex with both women was consensual and in private and continued after both women learned that the footballer was married. It was claimed that one of the women tried to blackmail the plaintiff before going to the newspaper with her story. The second woman, a lap dancer, accepted that she had demanded £5,000 from the married man to keep the affair private.

In November 2001, following a full interlocutory hearing in *A v Sunday People*, Mr Justice Jack granted an injunction against the publication of the details of the relationship. He relied upon the Human Rights Act 2000 in the UK, which had incorporated the ECHR into English law, and the provisions of Art 8 of the ECHR. He ruled that sexual relationships are by definition confidential and that publication by the newspaper of a story revealing the existence of the relationships, or any details of them, would infringe the applicant's right to privacy.

The Court of Appeal overturned this decision, allowing for the identification of the applicant. Lord Woolf said that public figures were entitled to have their privacy respected and were entitled to a private life, but they had to recognise that their public position subjected their actions to closer scrutiny by the media. He said: 'Whether you have courted publicity or not, you may be a legitimate subject of public attention.' He added: 'Footballers are role models for young people and undesirable behaviour on their part can set an unfortunate example.' The plaintiff was 'inevitably a figure in whom a section of the public and the media would be interested.' The Court concluded:

'Any interference with the press has to be justified because it inevitably has some effect on the ability of the press to perform its role in society. This is the position irrespective of whether a particular publication is desirable in the public interest.' and

'In our view, to grant an injunction would be an unjustified interference with the freedom of the press. Once it is accepted that the freedom of the press should prevail, then the form of reporting in the press is not a matter for the Courts but for the Press Council and the customers of the newspapers concerned'.

7.8.3 CELEBRITY ADDICTION

In October 2002, the Court of Appeal decided that supermodel Naomi Campbell's right to privacy had not been breached by an article in the *Daily Mirror* (*Campbell v MGN Limited* [2002] EWCA Civ 1373). The *Daily Mirror* had reported that Campbell was receiving treatment at Narcotics Anonymous for drug addiction. Campbell was also surreptitiously photographed leaving a meeting. She claimed, among other things, that this breached her rights under Art 8 of the ECHR.

The Court of Appeal rejected Campbell's claim. She had courted publicity, had volunteered information to the media about aspects of her private life and behaviour and had averred, untruthfully, that she did not take drugs. The detail which had been published and the photographs were a legitimate if not an essential part of the journalistic package designed to demonstrate that Campbell had been deceiving the public when she said she did not take drugs. Provided that publication of confidential information was justifiable in the public interest, and in this case it was, the journalist had to be given reasonable latitude as to the manner in which that information was conveyed to the public as otherwise his right to freedom of expression under Art 10 of the ECHR would be unnecessarily inhibited.

The photographs of Campbell leaving the Narcotics Anonymous meeting were taken in a public place. They did not contain confidential information and *Douglas v Hello! Limited* was distinguished by the Court of Appeal. Ms Campbell has appealed to the House of Lords.

7.8.4   BALANCE

The difficulty of achieving the correct balance between the rights protected by Arts 8 and 10 of the ECHR is shown by the conflicting approaches taken in these recent cases in England. How the Irish courts strike this balance will be one of the most significant challenges they will face following incorporation of the ECHR into Irish law.

7.9   Article 2, ECHR: The Right to Life

Article 2, ECHR guarantees the most basic human right, the right to life. Perhaps surprisingly, this Article has already had an impact on the media's right to free expression in the UK Article 2 states:

> *'Everyone's right to life shall be protected by law. No one shall be deprived of his life intentionally save in the execution of a sentence of a court following his conviction of a crime for which this penalty is provided by law.'*

The murder of James Bulger by John Venables and Robert Thompson on February 12 1993 was a horrific crime that caused much public outrage and attracted international media attention. At the end of the murder trial, the judge determined, notwithstanding the youth of the accused, that they could be named and their images shown by the media. During the period of their detention, however, injunctions were put in place which restricted the information which the media were entitled to publish. Those injunctions came to an end when Venables and Thompson reached 18. They then applied to the President of the Queen's Bench Division in the UK for injunctions preventing their identification for the rest of their lives. They were supported in their applications by the Home Office. Venables and Thompson had received death threats and the authorities proposed to give them new identifies upon their release. Notwithstanding resistance by lawyers for the print media, the injunctions were granted and made final after a full trial.

The President of the Queen's Bench Division, Dame Elizabeth Butler-Sloss, determined that Venables and Thompson were 'uniquely notorious' and would be for the rest of their lives at serious risk of attacks from members of the public, as well as from relatives and friends of the murdered child. As she put it in *Venables and Thompson v Newsgroup Newspapers and Others* [2001] EWHC QB 32:

> 'If any section of the media decided to give information leading to the identification of either young man, such publication would put his life at risk. In the exceptional circumstances of this case and applying English domestic law and the right to life enshrined in Article 2 of the European Convention, I have come to the conclusion that I am compelled to take steps in the almost unique circumstances of this case to protect their lives and wellbeing.'

While recognising the enormous importance of freedom of expression, she nonetheless granted an open-ended injunction for the rest of the lives of Venables and Thompson. Indeed, one Manchester newspaper has already been convicted and fined for contempt of court for breaching her order by publishing material which could have identified their whereabouts (*A-G-v-Greater Manchester Newspapers Limited* [2001] EWHC QB 451).

7.10   Protection of Journalists' Sources

A question of some importance to freedom of expression is the confidentiality of journalistic sources. The European Court has considered such confidentiality to be a necessary pre-condition for press freedom protected by Art 10.

In *Goodwin v UK* (1996) 22 EHRR 123, the court considered whether an order requiring a journalist to disclose his source contravened Art 10. In finding that it did, a majority of the court stated:

> 'Protection of journalistic sources is one of the basic conditions for press freedom, as is reflected in the laws and professional codes of conduct in a number of contracting states and is affirmed in several international instruments on journalistic freedom. Without such protection, sources may be deterred from assisting the press and informing the public on matters of public interest. As a result, the vital public watchdog role of the press may be undermined and the ability of the press to provide accurate and reliable information may be adversely affected. Having regard to the importance of protection of journalistic sources for press freedom in a democratic society and the potentially chilling effect an order of source disclosure has on the exercise of that freedom, such a measure cannot be compatible with Article 10 of the Convention unless it is justified by an overriding requirement in the public interest.'

In Mr Goodwin's case, there was no such overriding requirement in the public interest.

This decision would appear to fly in the face of Irish law as enunciated in *Re Kevin O'Kelly* (1972) 108 ILTR 97 which held that journalists had no greater or lesser right to refuse to disclose confidential information than any other citizen. However, in an unreported case in the Dublin Circuit Court in early 1996 (*Nicola Gallagher v Garda Representative Association*), both counsel for the Attorney General and the presiding Judge, Judge Carroll, accepted that a journalist could only be asked to reveal a confidential source when it was both necessary and relevant for the administration of justice. This is a considerable change from the position of the authorities in 1972 and appears to reflect a change in the law consequent upon Art 10 of the ECHR and European case-law on it.

7.11   Freedom of Expression in the European Union

7.11.1   INTRODUCTION

In addition to the Irish Constitution and the ECHR, the right to freedom of expression is recognised and protected at a third level, that is, within European Union law.

While a basic Charter governing fundamental rights in the European Union has not yet been given legal status and there are relatively few decisions on the topic, the treatment of fundamental rights by the European Court of Justice (ECJ) is expected to develop as greater opportunities arise to invoke the right of freedom of expression before it.

The situations in which freedom of expression have been considered by the ECJ are very different to those under the ECHR. The ECJ deals with matters of public law and regulation, reflective of the Union's economic foundations and objectives.

7.11.2 RECOGNITION OF FREEDOM OF EXPRESSION UNDER EUROPEAN COMMUNITY (EC) LAW

7.11.2.1 General – the nature of fundamental rights

The recognition of fundamental rights within EC law has largely resulted from judicial activism. The original treaties made no provision for rights for individuals other than those economic rights necessary to achieve the objectives of the common market, such as the right to provide and receive services within the common market (Arts 49–55 EC Treaty; see also Joined Cases 286/82 and 26/83 *Luisi and Carbone v Ministero del Tesoro* [1984] 1 ECR 377) and to establish a business in another Member State (Art 43 EC). Whereas all EU Member States are parties to the ECHR, the EC itself does not have the requisite power to accede to the ECHR (*Opinion 2/94* [1996] ECR I-1759).

The constitutional traditions of the Member States and the ECHR have been the main sources for the ECJ in recognising and protecting fundamental rights, as general principles of EC law. This movement was later enshrined in Art 6 TEU (ex Art F). (see **chapter 5**)

7.11.2.2 Freedom of expression

Measures likely to restrict EC rights such as the freedom to provide services must be interpreted in light of general legal principles and in particular of fundamental rights. This was determined in a series of decisions starting with Case 29/69 *Stauder v City of Ulm* [1969] ECR 419 and finding best expression in Case 4/73 *Nold v Commission* [1974] ECR 491 and Case 5/88 *Wachauf* [1989] ECR 2609.

As it is guaranteed by the ECHR, freedom of expression is one of the rights in light of which the ECJ or national court must appraise any measure restricting EC rights. This was recognised implicitly in Joined Cases 43 and 63/82 *VBVB/VBBB v Commission* [1984] ECR 19 (although the applicants' submission failed on the facts) and made explicit in Case C-260/89 *Elliniki Radiophona Tiléorassi* [1991] ECR I-2925 ('*ERT*') where the ECJ stated as follows:

> 'It is for the national court, and if necessary, the Court of Justice, to appraise the application of those provisions having regard to all the rules of Community law, including freedom of expression, as embodied in Article 10 of the European Convention on Human Rights, as a general principle of law the observance of which is ensured by the Court' (para 44).

However, the protection of freedom of expression under EC law extends only to matters of EC competence – that is, to the institutions of the European Union and to Member States when implementing EC law.

In Joined Cases 60 and 61/84 *Cinéthèque v Fédération Nationale des Cinémas Français* [1985] ECR 2605, the ECJ was asked to examine the compatibility with EC law and, in particular, with freedom of expression, of French legislation which imposed an interval between the exploitation of movies in cinemas and on video. The ECJ found that Art 30 EC (now Art 28 EC), which prohibits measures with equivalent effect to quantitative restrictions on imports, did not apply. The French statute covered all video cassettes, whether imported or domestically produced, and was proportionate to the objective sought, viz to encourage cinema production. Accordingly, the ECJ declined to examine the impact of freedom of expression in an area falling within the jurisdiction of the national legislator.

Likewise, in Case C-159/90 *SPUC v Grogan* [1991] ECR I-4685, the ECJ decided that although Irish students, in distributing information regarding abortion services available in the United Kingdom, were exercising their right to freedom of expression, the lack of an economic link between them and the service providers removed them from the scope of EC law. Accordingly, any limitation on their freedom of expression fell to be determined in accordance with national rules.

These cases illustrate that freedom of expression is rarely considered by the ECJ as a stand-alone right. To come within the jurisdiction of the ECJ, a link with EC law – usually an economic link – must be shown.

7.11.3 CASE-LAW OF THE EUROPEAN COURT OF JUSTICE (ECJ)

Many of the ECJ's decisions touching on freedom of expression centre on regulatory matters.

7.11.3.1 Broadcasting

As Case C-260/89 *ERT* [1991] ECR I 2925, discussed above, shows, broadcasting is heavily regulated in most Member States. ERT, the exclusive franchisee for radio and television in Greece, sought to prevent the broadcasting of television programmes by a rival television station. The defendant claimed that the grant of a television monopoly by the Greek government infringed EC rules on competition and its fundamental rights, including freedom of expression. In response to a preliminary reference from the national court, the ECJ declared that national provisions restricting the freedom to provide services were only justified if they were compatible with fundamental rights – in this instance, with freedom of expression.

Measures designed to promote media diversity have been found by the ECJ to conform to Community law and the promotion of freedom of expression: Case C-353/89 *Commission v Netherlands* [1991] ECR I-4069; Case C-23/93 *TV10 SA v Commissariaat voor de Media* [1994] ECR I-4795. These cases concerned a Dutch law requiring domestic broadcasters to allocate airtime on national radio and television to associations representing different social, cultural, religious or philosophical views. In the first case, the ECJ found that the derogation from Art 59 EC was permissible, insofar as the law in question was intended to establish a pluralist and non-commercial broadcasting system, as part of a cultural policy to safeguard the freedom of expression of various groups in the Netherlands. In *TV10*, a broadcaster established in Luxembourg contested its treatment as a domestic undertaking for the purposes of the Act. The Dutch authorities determined that the company had been established in Luxembourg merely to avoid the obligations imposed on domestic undertakings. Its day-to-day management was in the hands of Dutch nationals, its target audience was the Dutch public and its advertisements were made in the Netherlands. The ECJ rejected submissions that the authorities' decision breached the applicant's right of freedom of expression under Art 10 ECHR. In doing so, it referred to its earlier finding that the maintenance of freedom of expression was the very thing which the legislation sought to guarantee.

The importance of ensuring the proportionality of measures restricting freedom of expression was highlighted in another case regarding broadcasting: Case C-245/01 *RTL Television v NLR* [2003] ECR I-1.

In this case, the ECJ found that restrictions placed on advertising breaks during films broadcast on television did not unduly restrict the broadcasters' freedom of expression as these related only to the frequency of breaks and not to their timing or the content of the advertising. The Court found that the restrictions could be justified as they aimed to protect consumers against excessive advertising and to protect their interest in having access to quality programmes.

7.11.3.2 Publishing

Unsurprisingly, the need for press diversity is viewed by the ECJ as crucial to freedom of expression.

The subject was first broached in Joined Cases 43 and 63/82, *VBVB/VBBB* [1984] ECR 19, discussed above. The European Commission had struck down a system of resale price maintenance in publishing. The applicants challenged this decision before the ECJ. They claimed that the system encouraged the publication of a multiplicity of titles and ensured the availability of works of minority interest. The Commission's actions in restricting the system would make publishing dependent on State subsidies and would fetter freedom of expression. Works of minority interest would no longer be published and the loss of a multiplicity of publications would detrimentally affect free speech. The ECJ recognised the importance of the right to freedom of expression throughout the EU. However, it rejected the applicant's argument on the grounds that they had failed to establish a real link between resale price maintenance and freedom of expression. The Commission had acted to ensure freedom of trade between Member States and the normal conditions of competition would apply. The ability of publishers and distributors to trade would be unaffected by the Commission's decision so freedom of expression was not affected.

The fullest discussion of the freedom of expression in this context is in Case C-368/95 *Familiapress* [1997] ECR I-3689. Austrian law on unfair competition prohibited the sale of certain periodicals containing competitions and promotions. It was hoped to protect small publications unable to offer significant prizes. A company from Germany – where no such provision exists – claimed this was an improper restriction on the free movement of goods. The ECJ's examination of freedom of expression centred on Austria's public policy justification for derogation from its treaty obligations, primarily its claims that the law was intended to safeguard press diversity. The Court referred to its decision in Case C-353/89 *Commission v Netherlands*, [1991] ECR 1 4069 where the maintenance of press diversity was recognised as a noble aim. It also observed that Art 10(2) of the ECHR permitted derogations from freedom of expression to maintain press diversity, provided such derogations were prescribed by law and necessary in a democratic society. Accordingly, it was for the national court to determine whether a prohibition was proportionate to the aim of maintaining press diversity and whether that objective could be attained by less restrictive measures, on the basis of a study of the national press market.

The limits of the right to free expression, as set out in Art 10(2) ECHR, were discussed in a slightly different context in Case C-219/91 *Ter Voort* [1992] ECR I-5485. Here the ECJ held that Directive 65/65/EEC, which instituted a national licensing system for medicinal products, did not restrict the freedom of expression of third parties publishing information ascribing therapeutic effects to those products. The applicant had ascribed medicinal properties to tea produced and distributed by another company. Such publication did not bring the products within the scope of the Directive and so could not infringe the publication rights of persons unconnected with the manufacturer or seller of the product. The ECJ went on to state that even where the freedom of expression of a third party *connected* with the manufacturer/seller of the product (and thus subject to the provisions of the Directive) could be regarded as limited by the Directive, 'it should be borne in mind that the inherent requirements of the exercise of that freedom must be judged against the requirements of the objective of the protection of public health pursued by Directive 65/65' (para 38).

Finally, the conflicting interests of freedom of expression in publication over the Internet and the right to privacy and the protection of personal data were considered by the ECJ in Case C-101/01 *Bodil Lindqvist* [2003] ECR.

7.11.3.3 Freedom of expression and officials of the European Union

The importance of freedom of expression, journalistic integrity and independence from the institutions of the European Union was recognised in Case 100/88 *Oyowe and Traore v Commission* [1989] ECR 4285. The Commission had refused to appoint the applicants, journalists with a Community-funded publication on Africa-Caribbean-Pacific ('ACP') States, as Community officials on the grounds, *inter alia*, that the journalists' work would be incompatible with the duty of allegiance owed by officials under the Staff Regulations. The ECJ found against the Commission. It stated that 'the duty of allegiance to the Communities imposed on officials in the Staff Regulations cannot be interpreted in such a way as to conflict with freedom of expression, a fundamental right which the Court must ensure is respected in Community law, which is particularly important in cases, such as the present, concerning journalists whose primary duty is to write in complete independence of the views of either the ACP States or the Commission' (para 16).

This does not mean that all restrictions on the freedom of expression of officials of the communities are contrary to EC law: see joined Cases T-34 and 163/96 *Connolly v Commission* [1999] ECR II-463. The ECJ held that a requirement that Community officials obtain prior authorisation for the publication of certain articles was justified on the basis that (i) it reflected a legitimate objective that texts dealing with the activities of the Community should not adversely affect its interests or reputation; and (ii) it was not disproportionate to this objective, as prior authorisation was only required where the publication was connected to the activities of the Community and could only be withheld if the publication was likely to jeopardize the interests of the Community.

The ECJ held in the later case of *Commission v Cwik* (Case C-340/P, [2001] ECR I-10269) that, where permission to publish an article is refused, the official is entitled to be given the reasons for such refusal. Furthermore, the mere fact that the official intends to publish an article expressing an opinion differing from the position adopted by the institution is not sufficient to show that it is liable to prejudice the interests of the Communities. To accept such a proposition, and on these grounds restric freedom of expression, would be to negate the purpose of that fundamental right.

7.11.4 FUTURE DEVELOPMENTS

As with the ECHR, freedom of expression under EC law is not absolute. It may be used as a balance to other rights – eg in assessing whether derogations to trade laws are acceptable – and in turn may be subject to the exercise of other rights and policy requirements. In this context, proportionality is the ultimate arbiter: *Familiapress; Connolly,* and Case C-112/00, *Schmidberger v Austria* [2003] ECR I-5659.

The decisions of the ECJ have, to date, been less sophisticated and nuanced than those of the ECt.HR or the Irish courts. However, there are indications that this could change. The right has been pleaded more frequently in recent years, reflecting its growing familiarity within the legal order: see Case C-235/92 *Montecatini v Commission* [1999] ECR I-4539. Further, there have been two significant constitutional developments.

First, the 'treatification' of human rights has introduced the possibility of sanctions against Member States which fail to observe and protect those rights. Article 7 TEU (introduced by the Treaty of Amsterdam) provides a mechanism whereby a majority of Member States can impose sanctions for the persistent disregard of fundamental rights by a Member State. Indeed, a perceived failure to guarantee freedom of expression was one of the grounds on which the fourteen Member States decided to impose sanctions on Austria when the controversial Freedom Party, led by Jörg Haider, entered a coalition government in 2000. (The sanctions were withdrawn when a study of Austria's behaviour concluded that they were unjustified.)

Second, the right to freedom of expression is guaranteed by Article 11 of the Charter of Fundamental Rights of the European Union, proclaimed at Nice in December 2000 and incorporated into the Draft Treaty establishing a Constitution for Europe. Article 11 provides:

> '1.   *Everyone has the right to freedom of expression. This right shall include freedom to hold opinions and to receive and impart information and ideas without interference by public authority and regardless of frontiers.*
> 2.   *The freedom and pluralism of the media shall be respected.'*

It is notable that the Charter, which is addressed to the institutions of the EU and to Member States when implementing European Union law, adopts the language of Art

10(1) ECHR and reflects the jurisprudence of the ECJ, on the need to protect media diversity.

In addition, Art 52 of the Charter provides that insofar as the enumerated rights correspond to rights guaranteed by the ECHR, the meaning and scope of those rights shall be the same as those laid down in the Convention, although EU law may provide more extensive protection. How this will operate in practice will depend to a large extent on the status of the Charter, which is not yet settled, but it is hoped that it will help resolve the thorny problems of jurisdiction sidestepped by the ECJ in accepting the contents of the ECHR, not as binding, but as general principles of EC law.

7.12 Conclusion

While the extent of the impact of Art 10 on freedom of expression has yet to be fully determined by the Irish courts, there is already a considerable body of European case-law which, it can be properly anticipated, will have an impact here. While in many cases, the Irish constitutional and common law protection of freedom of expression coincides with European jurisprudence, there are areas where it is considerably less liberal and changes are likely.

A common theme of Irish and European jurisprudence, even within the presently less developed case-law of the ECJ enforcing European Community law, is the need to balance the right of freedom of expression with conflicting rights. It is not, and cannot be, an absolute right. Yet it is central to a properly functioning democracy. The concepts of balance and proportionality allow for considerable discretion and give scope for judicial activism or retrenchment. With increasingly quick worldwide communication, the challenges for Irish and European judges have never been greater. How they respond to them will determine not just the effectiveness of Art 10, but possibly of the ECHR itself.

CHAPTER 8

FAMILY AND CHILD LAW

8.1 Introduction

The principal source of fundamental rights in the family law arena in Ireland has been the Constitution. Articles 41 and 42 of the Constitution have had a profound impact on the manner in which family legislation has been enacted and family law judgments delivered.

8.2 The Constitution and the Family

Article 41 of the Irish Constitution of 1937 concerns the family and 'recognises the family as the natural and primary unit group of society' and further guarantees 'to protect the family in its constitution and authority'. It is, however, immediately evident from the terms of Art 41.3.1° itself that the family, which the Constitution contemplates as deserving such protection, is that based on marriage alone. The latter-mentioned section speaks, with a somewhat misguided air of self-evidence, of 'the institution of marriage, on which the family is founded . . .'. The pre-eminence of the family based on marriage, in other words, is not so much asserted as assumed. The institution of marriage, enjoys a privileged position in the Irish constitutional order. By virtue of Art 41.3.1° of the Constitution, the State 'pledges to guard with special care the institution of marriage, on which the family is founded, and to protect it against attack.'

The Irish courts have remained steadfast in asserting the exclusivity of the constitutional 'family'. In *State (Nicolaou) v An Bord Uchtála* [1966] IR 567, the Supreme Court definitively affirmed that the family referred to in Art 41 did not include an unmarried couple and their child. The court, moreover, ruled that the applicant, as unmarried father of the child, had no constitutional rights whatsoever in respect of his child.

The courts cannot be accused of inconsistency in this regard. In the early 1990's the Supreme Court reiterated this position in *In Re SW, K v W* (1990) 2 IR 437. (See also *Keegan v Ireland* (1994) 18 EHRR 342, discussed at **8.5.5**). The applicant in this case and his partner, although unmarried, had enjoyed a stable relationship for approximately two years. The couple had decided to have a child together, but some time before the child's birth, they became estranged from each other. The applicant's partner placed the child for adoption without the consent, or even the knowledge, of the applicant. At the time, he had no right under Irish law to challenge a decision to place for adoption either before the Adoption Board or before the courts. The applicant argued that this was a breach of his constitutional rights. The Supreme Court, however, concluded that the failure to consult the father of the child was not a breach of any constitutional right, whether of the family or otherwise, again noting that the applicant was not, and had not been, a member of the family in the sense understood by the Constitution. (See also *WO'R v E.H*, [1996] 2 IR 248, and O'Driscoll J, *'The Rights of Unmarried Fathers'* [1999] 2 IJFL 18).

Within these confines, however, the courts have acknowledged that to be a family enjoying rights under Arts 41 and 42 of the Constitution, a household need not necessarily conform to the stereotype of 'father, mother and children'. It would appear, for instance, that a married couple without children still constitutes a family for the purposes of Art 41. (*Murray v Ireland* [1985] ILRM 542, *per* Costello J at 546). Similar considerations apply to widowed persons and their children (*per* Sullivan CJ in *In re Frost, Infants* [1947] IR 3 at 28) and even, presumably, to orphaned siblings (whose parents had been married prior to their deaths). All of these families, despite their bereavements, continue to enjoy the family rights guaranteed by the Constitution. Similarly, a family headed by persons who, though married, have separated due to irreconcilable differences, nonetheless retains its privileged constitutional status. (*TF v Ireland* [1995] IR 321). It is no small irony that such a family, even in the throes of marital breakdown, will be accorded full family rights under Art 41, while its non-marital but happy and stable contemporaries will not.

The rights guaranteed by Art 41 are recognised as belonging not to individual members of the family but rather to the family unit as a whole. An individual on behalf of the family may invoke them but, as Costello J notes in *Murray v Ireland* [1985] ILRM 542 at 547 they 'belong to the institution in itself as distinct from the personal rights which each individual member might enjoy by virtue of membership of the family'.

Article 41 lacks a child focus. It fails to recognise the child as a juristic person with individual rights. This is in no small measure attributable to the principle of parental autonomy created by Art 41 of the Constitution. This establishes a private realm of family life, which the State can enter only in the exceptional circumstances detailed in Art 42.5 of the Constitution. Article 42 provides as follows:

> *'(1) The state acknowledges that the primary and natural educator of the child is the family and guarantees to respect the inalienable right and duty of parents to provide, according to their means, for the religious and moral, intellectual, physical and social education of their children. . . .*
>
> *(5) In exceptional cases, where the parents for physical or moral reasons fail in their duty towards their children, the state, as guardian of the common good, by appropriate means shall endeavour to supply the place of the parents, but always with due regard for the natural and imprescriptible rights of the child.'*

Clearly, this provides that only in exceptional cases, where parents, for physical or moral reasons, fail in their duty towards their children, can the State as guardian of the common good endeavour to supply the place of the parents.

The Irish Constitution is unique in that whereas most other Western constitutions have a public/private divide, the family unit in Ireland has autonomy over and above that of the individual members of the family. In fact, the individual rights of the constituent members of the family are both directed and determined by the family as an entity in itself. Consequently, membership of the constitutional family in Ireland subordinates the rights of the individual members. This is true specifically of the rights of children and manifests itself glaringly in Supreme Court judgments on the issue.

Focusing on Art 42 of the Constitution, it is true to say that this in fact has more to do with the family than it does with the substantive right to education and, in many respects, is an addendum and subordinate to Art 41. It deals with education in a wider sense than scholastic education. When it refers to education, it is alluding to the upbringing of the child, which it holds not only to be a right but a duty of parents. This article reinforces the decision-making autonomy of the family. This can be observed on examining the intellectual structure of Art 42, which assigns a strong sense of priority to parental autonomy.

Article 42.5 of the Constitution is of particular importance in that it addresses the complete inability of parents to provide for their children's education. It has been interpreted as not being confined to a failure by the parents of a child to provide education for him/her, but extends in exceptional circumstances, to failure in other duties necessary to satisfy the personal rights of the child. This interpretation supports the assertion previously made that the right to education in Art 42 is a mere extension of the concept of 'the family' in Art 41.

Looking at Arts 41 and 42 of the Constitution in unison, it is clear that they render the rights of married parents in relation to their children 'inalienable'. Article 41 of the Constitution alludes to the inalienable and imprescriptible rights of the family. Article 42 refers to the rights and duties of married parents. Only if the circumstances allow the constitutional caveat on inalienability, contained in Art 42.5 of the Constitution, to be satisfied is there then scope for the legal supplantation of the rights of the married parents.

Section 3 of the Guardianship of Infants Act, 1964 makes it abundantly clear that in considering an application relating to the guardianship, custody or upbringing of a child, the court must have regard to the welfare of the child. This, the section states, is 'the first and paramount consideration'. The Supreme Court, however, has determined that the welfare of a child must, unless there are exceptional circumstances or other overriding factors, be considered to be best served by its remaining as part of its marital family. This was dictated, the court considered in a number of cases, by the constitutional preference for the marital family exhibited in Art 41.3 of the Constitution and the requirement therein that it be protected from attack. (See, for example, *Re JH (An Infant)* [1985] IR 375 and *North Western Health Board v HW and CW* [2001] 3 IR 635.) There is an uneasy tension between the provisions of Arts 41 and 42 of the Constitution and the welfare principle outlined in s 3 of the Guardianship of Infants Act, 1964.

The apparent contradiction between Arts 41 and 42 of the Constitution and the principle of the welfare of the child in s 3 of the Guardianship of Infants Act, 1964 has been correctly reconciled by the judiciary by holding that the welfare of the child is to be found within the confines of the Constitution. (*North Western Health Board v HW and CW* [2001] 3 IR 635. See, however, *Southern Health Board v CH* [1996] 1 IR 231, 238 where O'Flaherty J observed, in a case concerning the admissibility of a video-taped interview containing allegations of parental abuse, that: 'it is easy to comprehend that the child's welfare must always be of far graver concern to the court. We must, as judges, always harken to the constitutional command which mandates, as prime consideration, the interests of the child in any legal proceedings'). This is a negative definition of welfare insofar as it impacts on the child. The focus is not on actively promoting the welfare interests of the child, but merely with ensuring that these are not seriously impaired. This approach is attributable to the wording of Arts 41 and 42 of the Irish Constitution of 1937.

8.3   International Obligations

8.3.1   INTRODUCTION

Internationally, the traditional nuclear family is becoming an endangered species. Notwithstanding this, the designation of the family as a private realm in Art 41 of the Constitution, which is virtually impenetrable, still endures in Ireland today as can been seen from the recent Supreme Court case of *North Western Health Board v HW and CW* [2001] 3 IR 635. In the face of such a restrictive interpretation of the 'family', litigants have sought redress under international law through international human rights treaties. However, our dualist approach to international law makes international human rights treaties binding on the State, though not on the courts, as such treaties have not been incorporated into Irish law. (Most of the other Member States of the Council of Europe adopt a monist approach to international law, where international law is automatically applicable in domestic law, without the need for any implementing legislation). This will now change, to a limited extent, with the incorporation of the European Convention on Human Rights and Fundamental Freedoms (ECHR) into domestic law.

8.3.2 UN CONVENTION ON THE RIGHTS OF THE CHILD 1989

Ireland ratified the UN Convention on the Rights of the Child, 1989 without reservation on 21 September 1992. Again, by virtue of Ireland's dualist nature, the provisions do not form part of domestic law. The Convention recognises children's rights in its widest sense. Article 3 of the Convention states, *inter alia*:

'1. *In all actions concerning children, whether undertaken by public or private social welfare institutions, courts of law, administrative authorities or legislative bodies, the best interest of the child shall be a primary consideration.*

2. *State parties undertake to ensure the child such protection and care as is necessary for his or her well-being, taking into account the rights and duties of his or her parents, legal guardians, or other individuals legally responsible for him or her, and, to this end, shall take all appropriate legislative and administrative measures.'*

While this Article requires only that the children's interests be *a* primary consideration, not *the* primary consideration, it must also be read alongside the series of explicit rights which the Convention protects. These include: 'the inherent right to life' (Art 6); 'the right from birth to a name, the right to acquire a nationality and, as far as possible, the right to know and be cared for by his or her parents' (Art 7); 'the right of the child to preserve his or her identity, including nationality' (Art 8); 'the right of the child who is separated from one or both parents to maintain personal relations and direct contact with both parents on a regular basis, except if it is contrary to the child's best interests' (Art 9(3)); 'the right (of a child who has the capacity to form his or her own views) to express those views freely in all matters affecting the child, the views of the child being given due weight in accordance with the age and maturity of the child' (Art 12); 'the right to freedom of expression' (Art 13); 'the right of the child to freedom of thought, conscience and religion' (Art 14(1)); 'the right of the child to freedom of association and to freedom of peaceful assembly' (Art 15); 'the right to the protection of the law against arbitrary or unlawful interference with the child's privacy, family home or correspondence and unlawful attacks on the child's honour and reputation' (Art 16); 'the right of every child to a standard of living adequate for the child's physical, mental, spiritual, moral and social development' (Art 27); 'the right of the child to education' (Art 28); and 'the right of every child alleged as, accused of, or recognised as having infringed the penal law to be treated in a manner consistent with the promotion of the child's sense of dignity and worth' (Art 40). Taking cognisance of the foregoing rights, and in particular Art 12 of the UN Convention on the Rights of the Child, 1989, it can be seen that the UN Convention on the Rights of the Child, 1989, is soundly based on a defensible concept of children's rights. The law in Ireland, however, falls far short of such a concept.

8.3.2.1 Participation

The primary foothold for the separate representation of children in international child law can be found in Art 12 of the United Nations Convention on the Rights of the Child, 1989, which provides that:

'1. *State parties shall assure to the child who is capable of forming his or her own views the right to express those views freely in all matters affecting the child, the views of the child being given due weight in accordance with the age and maturity of the child.*

>   2. *For this purpose, the child shall in particular be provided the opportunity to be heard in any judicial and administrative proceedings affecting the child, either directly, or through a representative or an appropriate body, in a manner consistent with the procedural rules of national law.'*

Article 9 of the same Convention provides for the participation by children in separation and divorce processes:

>   '1. *State parties shall ensure that a child shall not be separated from his or her parents against his or her will, except when competent authorities subject to judicial review determine, in accordance with applicable law and procedures, that such separation is necessary for the best interests of the child. Such determination may be necessary in a particular case such as one involving abuse or neglect of the child by the parents, or one where parents are living separately and a decision must be made as to the child's place of residence.*
>   2. *In any proceedings pursuant to paragraph 1 of the present article, all interested parties shall be given an opportunity to participate in the proceedings and make their views known.'*

The failure of the State to bring into force s28 of the Guardianship of Infants Act, 1964 amounts to a breach of Art 9 of the 1989 Convention. The positive effect of child participation in the separation and divorce process is detailed in the work of the developmental psychology expert, E. Singer. (Singer, 'Kinderen als morele personen: Argumenten vanuit een ontwikkelings-psychologisch perspectief,' in: Van Nijnatten; Sevenhuijsen (eds), *Dubbelleven; Nieuwe perspectieven voor kinderen na echtscheiding*, Thela Thesis, 2001, Amsterdam, 31–40).

8.3.3   EUROPEAN CONVENTION ON THE EXERCISE OF CHILDREN'S RIGHTS 1996

Ireland has signed but not ratified the European Convention on the Exercise of Children's Rights, 1996. (European Treaty Series No. 160. The European Convention on the Exercise of Children's Rights was opened for signature at Strasbourg on 25 January, 1996. It came into force on 1 July 2000 following ratification by Greece (11 September 1997), Poland (28 November 1997) and Slovenia (28 March 2000) in accordance with Art 21(3) of the 1996 Convention). In some respects, it is of more limited application than its 1989 counterpart. It focuses predominantly on procedural rather than substantive rights, the emphasis being on such matters as the right of children to participation in, and information about, cases that concern their welfare. For example, Art 5 of the 1996 Convention states:

>   *'Parties shall consider granting children additional procedural rights in relation to proceedings before a judicial authority offering them, in particular:*
>   (a) *the right to apply to be assisted by an appropriate person of their choice in order to help them express their views*
>   (b) *the right to apply themselves, or through other persons or bodies, for the appointment of a separate representative, in appropriate cases a lawyer*
>   (c) *the right to appoint their own representative*
>   (d) *the right to exercise some or all of the rights of parties to such proceedings.'*

Clearly, the foregoing provisions are aimed primarily at children of sufficient age and maturity to understand the matters under scrutiny. That said, in appropriate cases, a child should have a person to help to express his or her views. Articles 4 and 9 of the European Convention on the Exercise of Children's Rights provide for the appointment of such a special representative. The absence of a facility for children in Ireland to articulate their views, where a case is settled in advance of the hearing, is a serious problem.

8.4 European Convention on Human Rights and Fundamental Freedoms

8.4.1 INTRODUCTION

Of special significance in discussing our international obligations are the relevant provisions of the European Convention on Human Rights and Fundamental Freedoms (ECHR), which have been incorporated into Irish law by way of statute. As a result of incorporation, the provisions of the ECHR have become part of our domestic law. It is now possible to take proceedings in the Irish courts alleging a breach of the ECHR. Previously, to assert any rights under the ECHR, an injured party had first to exhaust all domestic remedies before bringing the case to the European Court of Human Rights (ECt.HR) in Strasbourg with the costs and delays associated with that process.

There is little doubt that inconsistencies will arise between Irish family law and practice and the standards required by the ECHR. That said, the significance of this development has been overstated in the arena of Irish family law. The indirect or interpretative mode of incorporation preserves the domestic primacy of the Constitution. (See s 2 of the European Convention on Human Rights Act, 2003). Consequently, Art 41 of the Constitution will continue to act as an impediment to the effective implementation of the legal entitlements of individuals under the ECHR. In particular, incorporation of the ECHR at sub-constitutional level will ensure that child rights remain subordinate to parental rights. (If there is a conflict between a provision of the Constitution and the ECHR, the Constitution prevails). Therefore, in the family law arena, there will continue to be cases where a remedy for a breach of a ECHR right cannot be procured in the Irish courts, with the only avenue at the disposal of such litigants being an application to the Strasbourg Court.

8.4.2 EUROPEAN CONVENTION ON HUMAN RIGHTS ACT, 2003

The European Convention on Human Rights Act, 2003 (2003 Act) was signed by the President on 30 June, 2003 and came into force on 31 December, 2003. Section 1 of the 2003 Act provides that Arts 2–14 of the ECHR and Protocols 1, 4, 6 and 7 are to be incorporated into Irish law.

A number of issues emerge from a consideration of the provisions of the 2003 Act insofar as they impact on family and child law. The most significant is the fact that no provision has been made for legal aid in the Act, a right established under Articles 6 and 8 ECHR (see *Airey v Ireland* (1979–80) 2 EHRR 305).

The New Regime
Section 2 of the 2003 Act requires the Irish courts to interpret Irish law in a manner compatible with the State's obligations under the ECHR, 'in so far as is possible'. All courts are now obliged to interpret and apply any statutory provision or rule of law in accordance with the ECHR and take judicial notice of the decisions of the institutions of the ECHR. Where this is not possible and where no other legal remedy is adequate and available, the superior courts may make declarations of incompatibility in relation to legislation and awards of damages (and other remedies) against *'organs of the State'* who behave in a manner contrary to the State's obligations under the ECHR.

Every organ of the State, pursuant to s 3(1) of the 2003 Act, is required to perform its functions in a manner compatible with the ECHR. The definition of *'organ of the State'* specifically excludes the courts. (It does however appear to include health boards). Section 3(2) of the 2003 Act states:

> '3.–(2) A person who has suffered injury, loss or damage as a result of a contravention . . . may,

> *if no other remedy in damages is available, institute proceedings to recover damages in respect of the contravention in the High Court (or, subject to subsection (3) [This subsection deals with jurisdiction limitations.], in the Circuit Court) and the Court may award to the person such damages (if any) as it considers appropriate.'*

The effect of this provision is that if a person has suffered injury, loss or damage as a result of a breach of s 3(1), he may take an action for damages but only if no other remedy in damages is available. It excludes proceedings taken in the District Court. This is a matter of particular concern in the child law area, as the District Court has principal jurisdiction for proceedings instituted under the Child Care Act, 1991. Section 3(5) of the Act states that proceedings for violation of a ECHR right must be brought within one year of the contravention. This one year period may be extended by a court order if the court considers it appropriate to do so in the interests of justice.

Section 4 of the 2003 Act requires a court to take judicial notice of both the ECHR provisions and the decisions of the institutions of the ECHR. It further requires a court to *'take due account of the principles laid down by ... decisions'* of the institutions of the ECHR when applying the ECHR provisions.

Section 5 of the 2003 Act provides that where the High Court, or the Supreme Court on appeal, rules that there is an incompatibility between domestic law and the Convention, a declaration of incompatibility may be granted by that court. It should, however, be noted that demonstrating that no other legal remedy is *'adequate or available'* is a condition precedent to invoking this section. Further, legal aid is not available to the applicant seeking a declaration of incompatibility. Where the courts issue a declaration of incompatibility, it is a matter for the Government to consider the steps to be taken to remedy the incompatibility as such a declaration will not, for constitutional reasons, affect the validity, enforcement or continuing operation of the national law in question. Section 5(4) creates a new compensatory scheme for a person who has been granted a declaration of incompatibility by the courts. Such a person may apply to the Government for payment of ex gratia compensation in respect of any injury, loss or damage he/she may have suffered as a result of the incompatibility. This section has been criticised for failing to provide a mechanism whereby the level of compensation awarded can be appealed.

Section 6 of the 2003 Act provides that, before a court decides whether to make a declaration of incompatibility, the Attorney General must be given notice of the proceedings in accordance with the rules of court. In summary, the remedies available to a litigant under the 2003 Act are confined to a declaration of incompatibility (and possible ex gratia compensation) and an action for damages against an 'organ of the State' (ie a health board).

The District Court
Sections 2 and 4 of the 2003 Act apply in the District Court. Consequently, decisions of the ECt.HR are now relevant in public and private law cases dealt with in this court. The District Court must also interpret legislation in a manner harmonious with the State's obligations under the ECHR. This, it must do, however, *'in so far as is possible'* and *'subject to the rules of law relating to interpretation and application'*. No remedy is available in the District Court for breach of a ECHR right. District Court issues likely to be informed by ECt.HR jurisprudence include placing children in care, access issues in respect of children placed in care, the representation of children in proceedings and expert reports in cases involving children.

8.5 Family Law and the European Convention on Human Rights

8.5.1 FAMILY LIFE

One cannot avoid noting the enormous potential of the ECHR to protect and promote the rights of individuals. Article 8(1), ECHR guarantees as a basic right, the right to respect for private and family life, home and correspondence. Article 8(2) sets out the limits of permissible interference with the enjoyment of these rights by the State. The ECHR (unlike the Irish Constitution) makes no distinction between the family life of a marital and non-marital family. (See *Marckx v Belgium* (1979–80) 2 EHRR 330, *Johnston v Ireland* (1987) 9 EHRR 203 and *Keegan v Ireland* (1994) 18 EHRR 341; see also *Berrehab v The Netherlands* (1989) 11 EHRR 322 where the ECt.HR held that the traditional family relationship between a divorced man and his marital child did not cease to exist on the separation or divorce of the parents; *Boyle v UK* (1995) 19 EHRR 179 where family life was held to exist between an uncle and a nephew; *Kroon v The Netherlands* (1994) 19 EHRR 263 where the relationship between a man and a child conceived during an extra-marital affair, which amounted to a long-term relationship wherein the parties had four children by the time of the application, constituted a family within the meaning of Art 8 of the ECHR; and *Boughanemi v France*, ECtHR 24 April 1996, Reports of Judgments and Decisions 1996.II, 594, para 35 where family life was held to exist where the father could show a close relationship to the child. (Also *Elsholz v Germany*, Application No. 25735/94, 13 July 2000).

Family life constitutes not only relations between parents and their children, but also extends to grandparents and grandchildren (*Marckx v Belgium* (1979–80) 2 EHRR 330). For other relationships, it is necessary to produce evidence of a real and close family tie.

In summary, the existence of family life is a question of fact and degree (*X, Y and Z v UK* [1997] 2 FLR 892). Family life, for example, has been held by the ECt.HR to include the relationship between an adopted child and adoptive parents (*X v France* (1982) 5 EHRR 302). Similarly, for a foster parent and a foster child, although the Court has noted that the content of family life may depend on the nature of the fostering arrangement (*Gaskin v UK* (1990) 12 EHRR 36, para 49; *X v Switzerland*, Application No. 8257/78, 10 July 1978; and *Rieme v Sweden* (1992) 16 EHRR 155). The position of a non-marital father lacking a legal filiation link (through marriage or recognition) was considered in *RS Yousef v The Netherlands* [2003] 1 FLR 210.

In *Dudgeon v United Kingdom* (1982) 4 EHRR 149 and *Norris v Ireland* (1991) 13 EHRR 186, the ECt.HR described sexual life as the most intimate aspect of a person's private life for the purposes of Art 8, ECHR (See also *X v UK* (1997) 24 EHRR 143). The ECt.HR has not, however, been prepared to extend the concept of 'family life' to include a same-sex relationship.

It can be seen that the protection to be offered to the *de facto* family as defined within the jurisprudence of the ECt.HR is varied and a wide margin of appreciation is allowed to the Contracting Parties. More than in any other area of law, there is great potential for conflict between the Irish domestic concept of the family and concepts set down by the ECt.HR.

8.5.2 LEGAL AID

In *Airey v Ireland* (1979–80) 2 EHRR 305, the European Court of Human Rights held that Art 6 of the ECHR imposed obligations upon a State which may only be discharged by providing legal representation (See also *Dombo Beheer BV v Netherlands* (1994) 18 EHRR 213 and *P, C and S v UK* (2002) 35 EHRR 1075). This decision does not create a right to free legal aid in all civil cases, but rather imposes a duty upon the State to act, which depends upon the nature of the rights under consideration. (Interestingly, Ireland entered a reservation in respect of legal aid on 3 September 1953. A reservation gives a state certain immunity from challenge on ECHR grounds). It is likely that the requirement to provide free legal aid will arise more frequently in relation to children than to adults.

8.5.3 THE RIGHT TO PARTICIPATE IN LEGAL PROCEEDINGS

Articles 6 and 8, ECHR afford certain procedural safeguards applicable in court proceedings in a contracting state. The right of the individual to participate in legal proceedings is one of those procedural safeguards, a conclusion underlined by the ECt.HR in *T v UK* (Application No. 24724/94) and *V v UK* (December 16, 1999 (Application No. 24888/94)). Both cases concerned whether two eleven-year-old boys who were tried for murder in an adult court had received a fair trial within the meaning of Art 6, ECHR. The cases turned on whether the boys had participated effectively in their own criminal trial and the court held in the circumstances that they had not. The provision of separate and impartial representation to children was, in these cases, deemed to be essential to the conduct of certain criminal proceedings involving children. Considering the far-reaching nature of many public law proceedings involving children, a similar approach is likely in relation to applications by a health board for orders for care or supervision of a child and perhaps even in civil proceedings generally. Failure to hear children, aged four and six years, was a feature of the recent decision in *Kutzner v Germany* (Application No. 46544/99, February 26, 2002), even though expert evidence was obtained by the court in that case prior to its decision to take the children into care.

At best the child's right in Ireland to representation in court applications affecting him or her is discretionary. The net result of such discretion is a chaotic system of representation for children with significant variations as to the operation of the provision of representation throughout the state. The provisions for the separate representation of children in Irish public and private law proceedings are primarily for the children themselves and the entitlement accrues to them under the ECHR, not as some kind of dispensation.

8.5.4 DELAY

The prospects of a fair hearing may be diminished by significant delay in family law proceedings. (In *Eastern Health Board v MK and MK*, [1999] 2 IR 99; [1999] 2 ILRM 321, Denham J expressed her concern at the considerable delay (three years) which had occurred in that case:

> 'Time is of the essence in child custody cases. Childhood exists for only a short and finite time. Custody and care arrangements of themselves create dynamics which have a profound effect on children and their families. The long-term effects can be immense. Consequently, I voice my unease at the length of time, the delay, which exists between the judgment of the High Court and the appeal).'

This may result in a breach of Arts 6 or 8 of the ECHR or, as in *W v UK* ((1988) 10 EHRR 29 at 65), of both. Article 7 of the European Convention on the Exercise of Children's Rights, 1996 requires that:

> '[I]n proceedings affecting a child the judicial authority shall act speedily to avoid any unnecessary delay and procedures shall be available to ensure that its decisions are rapidly enforced.'

Mindful that 'justice delayed' is often 'justice denied', or at least diminished, the jurisprudence of the ECt.HR has tended to lean towards requiring that the national authorities display special diligence in expediting proceedings involving children. Indeed, in *H v UK* (1988) 10 EHRR 95, the ECt.HR stated that exceptional diligence is required where the maxim 'justice delayed is justice denied' is fully applicable. This might arise where custody and access proceedings are initiated by parents of children in the care of health boards as such proceedings are decisive for the parents' future relations with their children and have a 'particular quality of irreversibility'. The ECt.HR in *H v UK* alluded in particular to delay such that the elapse of time has the effect of determining the issue. Denham J expressed a similar view in *M(E) ex parte v M(J)* 9 July 2003, Supreme Court (unreported), a Hague Convention case (ie child abduction case) where time is of the essence.

In *Nuutinen v Finland* (ECt.HR, 27 June 2000) the ECt.HR held that Art 6, ECHR had been violated by custody and access proceedings which had lasted for five years and five months. The current delay in the procurement and completion of s 20 reports in Ireland and the difficulties encountered in retaining guardians *ad litem* must surely fall to be considered in this context. If it transpires that a child is seriously neglected or ill treated due to a delay in the procurement of a s 20 report, for example, a breach of Art 3, ECHR may also arise (*See Z and D v UK*, No. 29392/95, Comm. Rep. 10.9.99). In *Glaser v UK* (ECt.HR, 19 September 2000) the ECt.HR stated that it is essential that custody and access cases be dealt with speedily. The ECt.HR ruled that neither the volume of work nor shortage of resources will justify excessive delay.

8.5.5 RIGHT TO A FAIR TRIAL

One of the procedural safeguards afforded by the ECHR is the right to a fair trial (See *V v UK*, 16 December 1999 (Application No. 24888/94)). Article 6(1) provides:

'In the determination of his civil rights and obligations or of any criminal charge against him, everyone is entitled to a fair and public hearing within a reasonable time by an independent and impartial tribunal established by law. (See also Barbera, Messegue and Jabardo v Spain (2000) 11 ECHR 360.)'

In *Ruiz-Mateos v Spain* (1993) 16 EHRR 505 the ECt.HR stated that 'as a matter of general principle the right to a fair adversarial trial means the opportunity to have knowledge of and comment on the observations filed or evidence adduced by the other party'. The three central requirements of a fair trial are:

(a) a hearing in the presence of the parties;

(b) all evidence should be produced to the parties; and

(c) there should be an opportunity to challenge evidence, including the right to cross-examine witnesses (*X v Austria*, Application No. 5362/72, (1972) 42 CD 145).

In children's cases, however, the Court has determined that some relaxation of the composition of a typical court and its procedures may be required. (See *McMichael v UK* (1995) 20 EHRR 205, though in that case the failure to disclose social reports to the applicants amounted to a violation of Art 6(1), ECHR. Also *L v UK* (2000) 2 FLR 322 ECHR where a breach of Article 6(1), ECHR was held in respect of the provision of documents at case conferences when not all participants see them. This case also considered the obtaining of information from Adoption Agencies and Local Authorities.)

The right to a fair trial mirrors, of course, the explicit obligations under Art 6, ECHR, but it is also arguably a part of the procedural safeguards in Art 8. The inextricable link between the rights expressed in Art 6 and the inherent safeguards of Art 8 is underlined by the decision in *Keegan v Ireland* (1994) 18 EHRR 342. In that case, involving primarily the question of a non-marital father's right to be consulted in relation to the adoption of his child, the court held that the father's rights under Arts 6 and 8, ECHR had been violated. The Court at p. 362, para 51 in particular, noted that:

'[t]he fact that Irish law permitted the secret placement of the child for adoption without the applicant's knowledge or consent, leading to the bonding of the child with the proposed adopters and to the subsequent making of an adoption order, amounted to an interference with his right to respect for family life.'

Article 8, ECHR was applicable, the ECt.HR emphasised, despite the fact that the natural parents of the child were never married to each other. For two years prior to the making of the adoption order, the mother and father had been living in a stable relationship and that essentially, formed a family for ECHR purposes. Alluding to Art 6, ECHR, the ECt.HR held that the father's right to 'a fair and public hearing by an independent and impartial tribunal' had also been violated. Effectively, the father had 'no rights under Irish law' to challenge the decision to place his child for adoption, either before the Adoption Board or before the Courts. In summary, he had 'no standing in the adoption procedure generally' (*ibid* at 364). The applicant was awarded £12,000 in pecuniary and non-pecuniary loss and approximately £38,000 in respect of his domestic and Strasbourg legal costs and expenses. The Adoption Act, 1998, in amending the Adoption Act, 1952, has now introduced consultation procedures for natural fathers in the adoption process and also details the circumstances when such procedures need to be applied.

8.5.6 PUBLIC HEARING

In general, Irish law is committed to the administration of justice in public. This principle is guaranteed by the Constitution. Article 34(1) of Constitution states:

> '*Justice shall be administered in courts established by law by judges, and, save in such special and limited cases as may be prescribed by law, shall be administered in public.*'

By way of exception to this general principle, however, family law cases and cases involving children are among the categories of cases which may by law be shielded from such public and media scrutiny. In general, the public and the media are not admitted to family proceedings. The Courts (Supplemental Provisions) Act, 1961 provides that justice may be administered otherwise than in public in specified circumstances. Section 45(1) of the 1961 Act states:

> '*Justice may be administered otherwise than in public in any of the following cases:*
> (a) *applications of an urgent nature for relief by way of habeas corpus, bail, prohibition or injunction;*
> (b) *matrimonial causes and matters;*
> (c) *lunacy and minor matters;*
> (d) *proceedings involving the disclosure of a secret manufacturing process.*'

Individual family law statutes provide that the 'in camera rule' is mandatory in most family law matters (See s 34 of the Judicial Separation and Family Law Reform Act, 1989, s 38(5) of the Family Law (Divorce) Act, 1996, s 25(1) and (2) of the Family Law (Maintenance of Spouses and Children) Act, 1976, s 29 of the Child Care Act, 1991, s 38(6) of the Family Law Act, 1995 and s 16(1) of the Domestic Violence Act, 1996. There is no mandatory provision in the Guardianship of Infants Act, 1964 or Family Home Protection Act, 1976. That said, the discretionary provision of s 45 of the 1961 Act applies to such applications).

Of special significance in discussing the 'in camera rule' is Art 6, ECHR. In *Werner v Austria* (judgment of 24 November 1997) the ECt.HR stated that 'the holding of court hearings in public constitutes a fundamental principle enshrined in paragraph 1 of Article 6', save where there is 'a pressing social need' and the reasons advanced for the restriction are 'relevant and sufficient'. The right to a public hearing mirrors, of course, the explicit obligations under Art 6, ECHR, but it is also a right that arises under the guarantee of freedom of expression enshrined in Art 10, ECHR.

The decision of the ECt.HR in *B and P v UK* (judgment of 24 April 2001) states that a rigid interpretation of a mandatory 'in camera rule' may be in breach of the ECHR if it is disproportionate. This case related to two fathers who wanted their residence applications concerning their sons to be heard in public, with a public pronouncement of the judgment. They pleaded breach of Arts 6 and 10, ECHR. The ECt.HR noted the existence of a judicial discretion in English domestic law to hear Children Act proceedings in public, if merited by the special features of the case. As both cases were routine and 'run of the mill' in their nature, the hearings 'in camera' did not give rise to a violation of Art 6(1) of the ECHR. Neither was there a breach of Art 10, ECHR on the ground that the fathers could not share information revealed in the cases with others, as the restrictions imposed were to protect the rights of others, to prevent the disclosure of information received in confidence and to maintain the authority of the judiciary. The restriction of disclosure was proportionate to these aims. In the Irish context, the absolute and mandatory nature of the 'in camera rule' in the 1989 and 1996 Acts is clearly inconsistent with the requirements of Art 6(1), ECHR. This shortcoming has been addressed in the recently published Civil Liability and Courts Bill, 2004. Section 31(2) of the Bill, as published, allows for the publication of reports of family law proceedings so long as the report does not identify the parties or any child to which the proceedings relate. It provides as follows:

> '31(2) Nothing contained in a relevant enactment shall operate to prohibit:
>
> (a)   the preparation and publication of a report of proceedings to which the relevant enactment relates; or
>
> (b)   the publication of the decision of the Court in such proceedings, provided that the report or judgment does not contain any information which would enable the parties to the proceedings or any child to which the proceedings relate to be identified.'

A number of concerns arise in relation to the proposed reform of the 'in camera rule'. There is a serious absence of detail in the section. For example, no individual has been identified for the purposes of the preparation and publication of family law proceedings. A code of practice has been promised but this will be of little assistance to the client whose privacy has been breached, perhaps through inadvertence.

Reform of the 'in camera rule' involves a sensitive balancing act between the right to privacy and the right to a fair, transparent and accountable system of justice. Legislation that omits both to identify persons permitted to report on family law proceedings, and provide for prohibitive sanctions for those who breach the anonymity of the parties at a time of intense emotional family upheaval, fails to achieve this balance.

8.5.7   THE RIGHT TO MARRY

The right to marry is guaranteed by Article 12 of the ECHR:

> '*Men and women of marriageable age have the right to marry and to found a family, according to the national laws governing the exercise of this right.*'

In the past, this right has been held to refer to a traditional marriage between a heterosexual couple. Particular difficulty has arisen in the case of a person who is transsexual, especially where such a person has undergone gender reassignment surgery. The ECt.HR initially rejected the proposition that the failure to recognise such gender reassignment was a breach of Art 12 of the ECHR (See, for example, *Rees v UK* (1987) 9 EHRR 56 and *Cossey v UK* (1991) 13 EHRR 622). More recent cases, however, indicate a growing recognition of the right to marry as a member of the sex with whom one psychologically identifies (provided that the party has undergone a 'sex change'). In *Christine Goodwin v UK* (Application No. 28957/95, [2002] 2 FLR 487) the ECt.HR, in a unanimous decision, held that the United Kingdom was in breach of Arts 8 and 12, ECHR by refusing to allow a post-operative male to female transsexual the right to marry under any circumstances. The ECt.HR justified its departure from the *ratio* in *Rees* and *Cossey* in the following manner:

'Reviewing the situation in 2002, the Court observes that Article 12 secures the fundamental right of a man and woman to marry and to found a family . . . There have been major social changes in the institution of marriage since the adoption of the Convention as well as dramatic changes brought about by developments in medicine and science in the field of transsexuality . . . While it is for the Contracting State to determine *inter alia* the conditions under which a person claiming legal recognition as a transsexual establishes that gender re-assignment has been properly effected or under which past marriages cease to be valid and the formalities applicable to future marriages (including, for example, the information to be furnished to intended spouses), the Court finds no justification for barring the transsexual from enjoying the right to marry under any circumstances.' (See also *I v UK*, Application No. 25680/94, [2002] 2 FLR 518).

The unanimous decision of the ECt.HR in the *Goodwin* case is interesting in the Irish context in that it was issued in the same week as the rejection by the High Court of the application by Dr Lydia Annice Foy to have her birth certificate amended to reflect the fact that, though registered at birth as male, she had undergone gender-reassignment procedures to allow her to appear as a woman (See *Foy v The Registrar of Births, Deaths and Marriages*, McKechnie J., 9 July 2002, High Court, (unreported)). This case is currently on appeal to the Supreme Court.

8.5.8   DISCRIMINATION

Article 14 ECHR, the right not to be discriminated against, has been less effective than some of the other ECHR provisions in that it can only be pleaded in conjunction with another article in the ECHR. (This is likely to change when Protocol 14 to the ECHR comes into force). It has, on occasion, been used to challenge the substantive outcome of child custody/access disputes. (See *Keegan v Ireland* (1994) 18 EHRR 34 and *Hoffman v Austria* (1994) 17 EHRR 293.) Article 14 states:

'*The enjoyment of the rights and freedoms set forth in the Convention shall be secured without discrimination on any ground, such as sex, race, colour, language, religion, political or other opinion, national or social origin, associated with a national minority, property, birth or other status.*'

In the case of *Hoffman v Austria*, the ECt.HR found a violation of Article 14, ECHR as the legislation under consideration provided a blanket ban on awarding custody to a person who had changed his/her religion (See also *Salgueiro da Silva Mouta v Portugal* (2001) 31 EHRR 1055, which directly follows the *Hoffman* case). It should be noted that the non-discrimination protocol (Protocol 12) has not yet been ratified by Ireland.

8.6   Child Law and the European Convention on Human Rights

8.6.1   INTRODUCTION

The civil and political rights enshrined in the ECHR emphasise individual and familial freedom and autonomy and protection from excessive state interference. The ECHR is not child focused as such in the same way as the United Nations Convention on the Rights of the Child, 1989. It does not recognise children as a special group requiring particular protection, because of their inherent vulnerability in a world of adults. The rights contained in the ECHR are as available to children as to adults, however, and there is an increasing awareness that the ECHR has potential as an important resource in the promotion of child rights. While it must be acknowledged that only a small body of ECHR case-law deals with cases from the perspective of the child, it has been utilised very effectively to protect children within their family life with their parents.

8.6.2 CARE ORDER

The right to family life cannot be interfered with, unless such interference is in accordance with law and has an aim or aims that is or are legitimate. (Art 8(2), ECHR). The interference must also be shown to be 'necessary in a democratic society'. As a core principle, then, the ECHR requires that the Contracting Parties refrain from arbitrary interference in the lives of individuals in the State. Where the State intervenes in the life of a family, for instance by taking a child into care, the State must show that its intervention is in accordance with the law, for the furtherance of a legitimate aim or aims and necessary in a democratic society.

In a case against Finland, the ECt.HR held that as the care order was not the only option available to the local authority, in that case for securing the children's protection, the reasons used to justify it were insufficient and amounted to a violation of Art 8, ECHR (*K and T v Finland*, judgment of 27 April 2000). The impact of the judgment is that where health boards fail to use a care order as a measure of last resort, a violation of a core provision of the ECHR may arise (See also *EP v Italy* (2001) 31 EHRR 17).

8.6.3 THE RIGHT TO LIBERTY AND SECURITY

Article 5, ECHR guarantees the right to liberty and security, though this right is not an absolute right. It has been invoked in cases involving disturbed children, for whom there are at present insufficient high support units in Ireland and where, in many cases, they are held in penal institutions for want of appropriate accommodation. Ireland has recently been held to be in breach of Art 5, ECHR in *DG v Ireland* (judgment of 16 May 2002). The case challenged the legality of detaining in St Patrick's Institution a 16 year-old non-offending child with serious behavioural problems. The ECt.HR held that the detention of the child in St Patrick's Institution was in contravention of rights guaranteed under Art 5(1), ECHR. The ECt.HR ruled that the State acted unlawfully in failing to provide the disturbed child with a safe, suitable therapeutic unit and upheld the claim that the child's human rights were violated and his right to compensation denied. (See, however, *Koniarska v UK*, judgment of 12 October 2000, where the court held that placing a child in secure accommodation was not contrary to the ECHR as it amounted to 'educational supervision' within the meaning of Art 5 of the ECHR.)

8.6.4 ACCESS

Where a child is validly taken into care, Art 8 of the ECHR guarantees that parents and children have access to each other. Any restriction on access must be justified by reference to Art 8(2), ECHR (See for instance, *Hendriks v Netherlands* (1983) 5 EHRR 223; *W v UK* (1988) 10 EHRR 29; *R v UK* (1988) 10 EHRR 74; *O v UK* (1988) 10 EHRR 82; *H v UK* (1988) 10 EHRR 95; *Olsson v Sweden* (1989) 11 EHRR 259 and *McMichael v UK* (1995) 20 EHRR 205). There is, in addition, a positive duty on the health board to facilitate access between the parent and child (See *Eriksson v Sweden* (1990) 12 EHRR 183). The ECt.HR has taken the view that as the mutual enjoyment by a child and a parent of each other's company constitutes a fundamental element of family life, access should only be denied where there is clear evidence that it is contrary to the best interests of the child. This approach now forms part of Article 9(3) of the UN Convention on the Rights of the Child 1989 which provides for:

'the right of the child who is separated from one or both parents to maintain public relations and direct contact with both parents on a regular basis, except if it is contrary to the child's best interests.' (See also **8.3.2**).

The ECt.HR has also stated access to be the right of the child. (See *Hoppe v Germany* (2003) 1 FLR 384.) In protecting individual rights, the State is under an obligation to prevent interference by others with a view to undermining these rights (See *Airey v Ireland* (1979–80) 2 EHRR 305, *X and Y v Netherlands* (1985) 8 EHRR 235; *Johnston v Ireland* (1987) 9 EHRR 203; *Keegan v Ireland* (1994) 18 EHRR 342 and *Hokkanen v Finland* (1994) 19 EHRR 139). This is a positive duty placed on the State. In *Hokkanen v Finland*, for instance, the ECt.HR ruled that the Finnish government had a positive obligation to facilitate parental access to a child, including ensuring that third parties (in this case the maternal grandparents) did not impede the child's right to access ((1994) 19 EHRR 139. See, however, *Nuutinen v Finland*, ECt.HR, 27 June 2000, Reports of Judgments and Decisions (2001)).

The ECt.HR has held that a care order is intended to be temporary in nature and that its implementation must always be guided by the ultimate aim of family reunion. Contact between parents and children in care is vital to maintain the family relationship. In *Olsson v Sweden* (1989) 11 EHRR 259, the ECt.HR noted that there was a positive obligation on each State to take appropriate measures to facilitate a reunion between children and their parents. In that case, three children from one family (the Olssons) had been placed in foster care with different foster parents living a considerable distance from each other and from the parents of the children. As a result of the geographical distance between them, contact between the children themselves and between the parents and the children was made virtually impossible. This, the ECt.HR concluded, constituted a breach of Art 8, ECHR, the State having failed to make adequate provision for intra-familial contact. The administrative difficulties (such as the apparent shortage of appropriate foster families) asserted in a defence by the State, were deemed not to be of sufficient weight to prevent a ruling against it (See *Implementation Handbook for the Convention on the Rights of the Child*, prepared for UNICEF by Rachel Hodgkin and Peter Newell, New York, 1998, 152). Little guidance is given, however, as to what is an acceptable distance by which children and their parents can be separated.

In *Elsholz v Germany* (ECt.HR, 13 July 2000) the ECt.HR considered the hearing of children in access proceedings. The court held that an expert should have been appointed to interpret the child's evidence:

'Moreover, taking into account the importance of the subject-matter, namely, the relations between a father and his child, the Regional Court should not have been satisfied, in the circumstances, by relying on the file and the written appeal submissions without having at its disposal psychological expert evidence in order to evaluate the child's statements.'

Elsholz is an important ruling by the ECt.HR that emphasises the need to obtain psychological analysis of children's evidence. In *Sommerfeld v Germany* (Application No. 31871/96, 11 October 2001), the ECt.HR criticised the German national court for not obtaining a psychological report, to assess the apparently entrenched views of a thirteen year-old child not to see her father. The Chamber's decision was overturned by the Grand Chamber, who held that the national court could rely on the directly expressed views of a thirteen year-old ((2003) 2 FCR 619). The decision of the ECt.HR in *Sahin v Germany* (2002) 1 FLR 119 is also worthy of particular note. In that case, a father's application for access (in respect of his five-year-old child) was rejected on the basis that expert evidence supported the termination of access. The domestic court did not hear the child as it relied on the experts' view that hearing the child in court would impose a psychological strain on her, as she could gain the impression that her statements would be decisive. The ECt.HR, however, held that the domestic court should only have considered the best interests of the child after having direct contact with her. In particular, the European Court stated that complete information on the relationship between the father and the child was an indispensable prerequisite for establishing a child's true wishes, thereby striking a fair balance between the interests at stake. This case was later referred to the Grand Chamber where the Chamber's decision was overturned. The Grand Chamber held that the Regional Court had not overstepped the margin of appreciation in relying on the expert's statements 'about the risks inherent in questioning a child' ((2003) 2 FLR 671).

8.6.5 THE RIGHT OF THE CHILD TO INITIATE LEGAL PROCEEDINGS

The child's right to initiate proceedings is implied in the right of access to a court under Art 6, ECHR. In *Golder v UK* (ECt.HR, 21 February 1975, series A Vol. 18, para 39), the ECt.HR explicitly refers to the right of the child to bring proceedings, although in the later case of *Ashingdane v UK* (ECt.HR, 28 May 1985, series A Vol. 93), the ECt.HR held that the right of access to court could be restricted.

8.6.7 PROTECTION

There is an obligation, imposed by Art 3, ECHR, to protect children from harm and ill-treatment. In *Z and Ors v UK* (2001) 2 FLR 612, the ECt.HR called into question the approach of the English courts to the liability of public authorities. It held that a local authority has a positive duty to see that measures are taken to protect a child at risk. The ECt.HR noted, in particular, the local authority's failure to assign a senior social worker or guardian *ad litem* for the child at the centre of that case. In *KL v UK* (1998) 26 EHRR CD 113 (a case now before the ECt.HR), the Commission on Human Rights declared admissible a case in which children, placed in care following abuse by their parents, argued a breach by the local authority of its duty to comply with its positive obligations under Art 3 to take steps to protect them. (See also *E v UK* (2003) 1 FLR 348 where the ECt.HR held that there had been a breach of Art 3 where there had been no effective remedy for the continuous assaults suffered by four children at the hands of their stepfather due to maladministration by a local authority).

In *A v UK* (1999) 27 EHRR 611, the ECt.HR, considering the caning of a nine year-old boy by his stepfather and the defence of 'reasonable chastisement' in the law of the UK, concluded that the State had failed to protect the applicant from punishment amounting to inhuman or degrading treatment within the meaning of Art 3, ECHR. The Court held that cognisance should be taken of the following criteria when considering whether the punishment is reasonable:

- the nature and context of the child's behaviour

- the duration of the behaviour

- the physical and mental consequences of the behaviour of the child and

- the age and personal characteristics of the child.

It is clear from the judgment of the ECt. HR in this case that the State has a positive duty to take measures to ensure that no one private individual is subjected to torture, inhuman or degrading treatment at the hands of other private individuals. On this point, the court held that States are:

'[r]equired to take measures designed to ensure that individuals within their jurisdiction are not subjected to torture or inhuman or degrading treatment or punishment, including such ill-treatment administered by private individuals. Children and other vulnerable individuals, in particular, are entitled to State protection, in the form of effective deterrence against such serious breaches of personal integrity.'

(See, however, *Costello-Roberts v UK* (1993) 19 EHRR 112, where three 'whacks' on the bottom administered by a headmaster to a seven year-old boy was not found to amount to a violation of Art 3 ECHR).

8.6.8   CONSULTATION AND ACCESS TO REPORTS

Parents should be adequately consulted about and informed of all matters pertaining to their children. Failure to do so will amount to a breach of Art 8, ECHR, unless the exempting provisions of Art 8(2) apply. In *McMichael v UK* (1995) 20 EHRR 205, the ECt.HR ruled that a parent cannot, without good reason, be denied access to reports or documents relating to his/her child. To do so would be to deny the parent his right to participate in the decision-making process relating to his child.

Denying a parent access to reports or documents may also constitute a breach of Art 6, ECHR, which guarantees the right to a 'fair and public hearing'. This necessarily involves the right of access to reports or documents, save where this is otherwise than in the best interests of the child. In *TP and KM v UK* ((2001) 2 FLR 549, for example, the ECt.HR held that parents, defending serious allegations regarding children, should be afforded full access to information as to their factual basis.

8.6.9   CONCLUSION

The ECHR has been criticised as being too conservative. Much of the early jurisprudence suffers from the now dated assumption that shielding 'the family' from state interference automatically protects children. There is, however, a clear power imbalance between adults and children in cases of conflict (See for example *Nielson v Denmark* (1989) 11 EHRR 175 where the majority of the ECt.HR held that the rights of a twelve year-old boy under Art 5, ECHR had not been infringed by his detention and placement in a psychiatric ward at the request of his mother). Recent jurisprudence of the ECt.HR has unambiguously recognised and addressed the power imbalance inherent in disputes between parents and children. (See *Hokkanen v Finland* [1996] 1 FLR 289 and *A v UK (human rights: punishment of child)* [1998] 2 FLR 959.) The net result of this development is that the ECHR is now proving to be a potent instrument in the promotion of child rights, a fact borne out by recent statistics from England and Wales indicating that the majority of Convention cases in family law involved children. There is no doubt that the European Convention on Human Rights Act, 2003 which came into force on 31 December 2003 will have a positive impact on family law in Ireland.

8.7   The Charter of Fundamental Rights of the European Union

The Charter of Fundamental Rights of the European Union was adopted on 7 December, 2000, with its principal aim being the maintenance of the human rights protection currently afforded by European Union law, national law and international law (OJ C 364 Vol. 43, 18 December 2000). In s 4 of the preamble to the Charter, it is stated that:

> '[i]t is necessary to strengthen the protection of fundamental rights in the light of changes in society, social progress and scientific and technological developments by making those rights more visible in a Charter.'

Significantly, the Charter is declaratory rather than legally binding, rendering it of little direct assistance to the individual litigant. That said, the case-law of the European Court of Justice (ECJ) is certain to be affected by this development (see, for example, *Carpenter v Secretary of State for the Home Department*, 13 September 2001).

The Charter does not create new family and child rights, but is generally confined to re-stating rights available under existing international instruments. Chapter II guarantees the right to respect for private and family life (Art 9) and the right to marry and found a family. Equality between men and women and the protection of children (see also Arts 24 and 31 of the Charter) are covered in Chapter III. Chapter V protects the right of access to documents. The right to a fair trial is provided for in Chapter VI. Chapter VII explains the relationship between the Charter of Fundamental Rights of the European Union and the ECHR. This Chapter allows the ECJ to depart from the interpretation afforded by the ECt.HR of a right protected by the ECHR. Article 51 of the Charter, however, provides:

> *'Nothing in this charter shall be interpreted as restricting or adversely affecting human rights and fundamental freedoms as recognised, in their respective fields of application, by international law and international agreements to which the Union, the Community or all Member States are party, including the European Convention for the Protection of Human Rights and Fundamental Freedoms, and by the Member States' constitutions.'*

With the adoption of the Charter of Fundamental Rights of the European Union, we see the emergence of two separate systems of human rights protection in Ireland. The Irish courts are bound by EU law to follow the jurisprudence of the ECJ, but are also bound under international law to follow the jurisprudence of the ECt.HR. To which system should the domestic courts defer? This growing tension between EU law and international law can be seen in the cases of *Pellegrini v Italy* (Application No. 30882/96, 20 July 2001) and *Sahin v Germany* (2003) 2 FLR 671. (See also Case C-60/00 *Carpenter v Secretary of State for the Home Department*, 13 September 2001, Case C-459/99 *Mouvement contre le racisme, l'antisémitisme et la Xénophobie ASBL v The Belgian State*, 25 July 2002 and the opinion of A-G Geelhoed in Case C-413/99 *Baumbast and R v Secretary of State for the Home Department*, 5 July 2001). The issues raised in *Pellegrini* and *Sahin* are especially important for the Member States of the European Union who are obliged by virtue of Art 19 of Council Regulation 1347/00 to give effect to each other's judgments in civil proceedings relating to divorce, legal separation or marriage annulment and parental responsibility on the occasion of those proceedings. The importance derives from the fact that individuals may seek to invoke the provisions of the ECHR to prevent the automatic recognition of a judgment under Council Regulation 1347/00. The time is now ripe to clarify the position by establishing a hierarchy of courts.

8.8 Overview and Conclusion

Irish family law is unique in that it has resisted the steady erosion of parental rights that has characterised international family law systems. By ratifying the 1989 United Nations Convention on the Rights of the Child on 21 September 1992, without reservation, Ireland accepted its international obligations towards children. Article 41 of the Irish Constitution, however, continues to act as an impediment to the effective implementation of children's legal entitlements under the 1989 Convention.

The European Convention on Human Rights Act, 2003 is likely to create a significant paradigm shift in legal culture in family law. In relation to the law on children, it will consolidate the four main aims of the UN Convention on the Rights of the Child, 1989, the standard-setter on children's rights, which have been identified as prevention, protection, provision and participation. Where family law and child law issues conflict in terms of rights, it will be necessary to balance the rights of different family members. The approach when Art 8, ECHR is invoked in relation to private family law will be to balance the rights of all family members, with the interests of the child being decisive where the way is not clear. (See *Yousef v The Netherlands* (2003) 1 FLR 210).

CHAPTER 9

THE RIGHT TO LIFE AND THE RIGHT TO BODILY INTEGRITY

9.1   Introduction

This chapter discusses the right to life in the context of Irish and international law. It seeks to examine the 'right to life' in all of its aspects from the rights ascribed to the unborn to those rights that are ascribed at the time approaching death and how the courts have balanced this right against other rights. The chapter examines the value that law has placed on 'life' as it impacts on the individual throughout his life, and looks at the ramifications of the constitutional issues for medical practitioners, the implications for maternal autonomy, the potential implications on refugee law and touches on issues such as extradition and the death penalty. The right to bodily integrity is examined as an expanding right and issues such as the prevention of torture are taken into account.

Article 40.3.2° of the Irish Constitution provides the primary guarantee of the right to life. It states:

> 'The State shall, in particular, by its laws protect as best it may from unjust attack and, in the case of injustice done, vindicate the life, person, good name, and property rights of every citizen.'

It should be noted that the European Convention on Human Rights Act, 2003, s 2, states that:

> 'In interpreting and applying any statutory provision or rule of law, a court shall, in so far as is possible, subject to the rules of law relating to such interpretation and application, do so in a manner compatible with the State's obligations under the Convention provisions.'

The right to life is an almost universally recognised right – for example, the EU Charter of Fundamental Rights declares at Art 2(1) that 'Everyone has the right to life'.

The right is also recognised by other common law jurisdictions. It has been stated in Re *J (a minor)* [1990] 3 All ER 930 at 945 *per* Taylor LJ that:

> 'The court's high respect for the sanctity of human life imposes a strong presumption in favour of taking all steps capable of preserving it, save in exceptional circumstances.'

9.2   Hierarchy of Rights

Various views have been expressed about the status of the right to life. It has been stated in relation to the right on an international basis:

> 'One might be forgiven for expecting that the right to life would have some kind of

primacy in the international code; that in some way it would be ranked before the others. After all to have any human rights one must be a living individual . . . But in fact one finds nothing of the kind. The right to life is like any other human right. Like others, it has its own peculiar characteristics – the state obligation is absolute and immediate, for instance, and there can be no derogation from it even in times of war or public emergency – but it enjoys no special pre-eminence. Indeed, in its treaty formulations it even admits of quite a few exceptions.' (Sieghart, 'The Lawful Rights of Mankind', 1986, OUP, 107.)

However, in Ireland, there is no doubt whatsoever that the right to life ranks as the highest right within the hierarchy of fundamental human rights, which receives protection by the law. The right to life will take priority when balanced with other fundamental rights. In The *People (DPP) v Shaw* [1982] IR 1, the detention by the Gardaí of an individual, who was accused of having kidnapped two women, in excess of the time permitted by law, was held to be justified by the Supreme Court, since the Gardaí held as an honest belief that the life of one of the women was in imminent danger. The detention was for the purpose of finding out where this woman was and saving her life. The right to life took precedence and was superior to the detainee's right to personal liberty.

The right to life has as Casey notes '. . . been held superior to other constitutional rights, such as those to personal liberty, to travel, to disseminate or receive information or to the inviolability of the dwelling' (Casey, 'Constitutional Law in Ireland', 3rd edn, 2000, Roundhall, Sweet and Maxwell, 343).

The Supreme Court has recently reiterated the superiority of the right to life stating *per* Hamilton CJ, in *In the matter of a Ward of Court* [1995] 2 ILRM 401, at 425:

'. . . if there was an interaction of constitutional rights . . . the right to life would take precedence over any other rights'.

The common law courts of other jurisdictions have also made it clear that they will afford such high protection to the right to life. (See the dicta of Taylor LJ in *J (a minor)* cited at **9.1** above.

However, the superiority of the right to life will depend on the circumstances at hand. As stated by Egan J in *Attorney General v X* [1992] 1 IR 1, 92:

'The right to life of one person (as in *Shaw's* case) was held to be superior to the right to liberty of another but, quite clearly, the right to life might not be the paramount right in every circumstances. If, for instance, it were necessary for a father to kill a man engaged in the rape of his daughter in order to prevent its continuance, I have no doubt but that the right of the girl to bodily integrity would rank higher than the right to life of the rapist'.

Also, notwithstanding the common law and constitutional protection of the right to life, it is not the case that the law regards the right to life as absolute in every circumstance. In *The Matter of a Ward of Court* [1995] 2 ILRM 401, Denham J stated at 457, 'The requirement to defend and vindicate the life is a requirement "as far as practicable," it is not an absolute. Life itself is not an absolute'. In certain circumstances, an individual's right to bodily integrity might rank higher in value than his right to life. In the instant case, the ward was in a 'near-PVS' (ie near Permanent Vegetative State, a condition where the individual has a minimal state of cognitive capacity and minimal awareness. In this condition, the patient is alive. The condition is distinguished from 'brain death' where the patient is legally dead). The family of the ward sought to seek permission to discontinue her artificial nutrition and hydration. The High Court granted the orders sought and this was upheld by the Supreme Court on appeal.

Notwithstanding the high status of the right to life, remarkably little is written about it in mainstream academic texts. This no doubt stems from the fact that the right in itself has not often found itself the sole subject of judicial scrutiny. Most of the literature tends to concentrate on the right to life in the context of abortion. However, a closer examination reveals that in reality the right is invoked at the various stages of life.

While Ireland has little case-law on the topic, other jurisdictions have examined the issue in various scenarios, which at some stage inevitably will present themselves before the Irish courts. The right to life has most often been invoked in the following situations, each of which merit individual consideration: (i) Before birth in relation to right to life of the unborn (*Attorney General (SPUC) v Open Door Counselling* [1989] ILRM 19; *AG v X* [1991] 1 IR 1; *In Re Article 26 of the Constitution and the Regulation of Information (Services outside the State for the Termination of Pregnancies) Bill*, 1995 [1995] 1 IR 1; *Society for the Protection of the Unborn Child v Grogan* [1998] 4 IR 343. (ii) In post-birth situations pertaining to the right to life of the gravely ill very young child (the 'malformed neonate'). The courts in the UK have examined this scenario in the following cases (*Re C (1989)* 2 All ER 782; *Re B* [1990] 3 All ER 927; *Re J* [1990] 3 AER 930). (iii) Also in relation to the protection of one's life during and at any stage of life (*McGee v AG* [1974] IR 284) and (iv) in relation to the gravely ill and/or near death situation (*In the matter of a Ward of Court* [1995] 2 ILRM 401).

9.3 The Right to Life of the Unborn

The right to life of the unborn has special status in Irish constitutional law. (For an in-depth review of this issue in the legal and political forum, see further: Kingston *et al.*, 'Abortion and the Law', 1997, Roundhall, Sweet and Maxwell, and Hogan and Whyte 'JM Kelly: The Irish Constitution', 3rd edn, 1994, Butterworths, 790–810.)

9.4 Judicial Dicta Prior to the Eighth Amendment

Notwithstanding that, prior to the eighth amendment to the Constitution, no express provision existed which guaranteed the life of the unborn, the courts nevertheless recognised such a right. In the case of *McGee v Attorney General* [1974] IR 284, the right to marital privacy was established. While the protection of the right to life itself was promoted (as will be examined in a later section), Walsh J, stated at 312.

'... any action on the part of either the husband and wife or of the State to limit family sizes by endangering or destroying human life must necessarily not only be an offence against the common good but also against the guaranteed personal rights of the human life in question'.

In *G v An Bord Uchtála*, [1980] IR 32 Walsh J. stated at p. 69:

'[A child] has the right to life itself and the right to be guarded against all threats directed to its existence whether before or afterbirth ... The right to life necessarily implies the right to be born, the right to preserve and defend (and to have preserved and defended) that life ...'

9.5 Eighth Amendment and Thereafter

Article 40.3. 3°, introduced by virtue of the eighth amendment to the Constitution in 1983, states:

'The State acknowledges the right to life of the unborn and, with due regard to the equal right to life of the mother, guarantees in its laws to respect, and, as far as practicable, by its laws to defend and vindicate that right.'

9.6 THE 'X CASE'

On the issue of the right to life of the unborn, the judiciary were faced with what '. . . must surely qualify as the most controversial case ever to come before an Irish court' (Hogan and Whyte 'JM Kelly: The Irish Constitution', 3rd edn, 1994, Butterworths, 796). In *Attorney General v X* [1992] 1 IR 1, or the 'X case' as it came to be known, the courts were faced with a dilemma in which they had to attempt to interpret a constitutional provision which equates '. . . two rights which, on those rare occasions when they come into conflict, cannot be reconciled' (Hogan and Whyte, 802). The defendant was a fourteen year-old girl who had been raped and had become pregnant. The High Court had granted an injunction prohibiting the defendant from leaving the State for the purposes of obtaining an abortion. She however, had stated that if she had to go through the pregnancy, she would commit suicide. The Supreme Court decided that in certain limited circumstances an abortion would be permitted. Finlay CJ stated at 53:

'. . . the proper test to be applied is that if it is established as a matter of probability that there is a real and substantial risk to the life, as distinct from the health, of the mother, which can only be avoided by the termination of her pregnancy, such termination is permissible, having regard to the true interpretation of Art 40, s.3(3) of the Constitution.'

As the law now stands an abortion may be permissible in this jurisdiction in certain circumstances. Such an abortion will only be permissible if there is a real and substantial risk to the life of the mother which only a termination could avoid. Such a risk includes the risk of suicide by the mother.

Allied to this issue, were the issues of individuals being permitted to travel for the purposes of undergoing a termination and the dissemination of information relating to abortion.

9.7 The Thirteenth Amendment: The 'Travel Amendment'

In the *X* case, the Supreme Court had difficulties in relation to the issue of travel for the purpose of undergoing a termination. The matter has now been resolved by virtue of the thirteenth amendment to the Constitution, which amended Art 40.3.3° by adding:

'This subsection shall not limit freedom to travel between the State and another state.'

In *A & B v Eastern Health Board & C* [1998] 1 ILRM 460, the High Court explored this amendment in the context of a minor who also, as a result of rape, had become pregnant. The Eastern Health Board, which had taken the girl into care had applied to the District Court for orders allowing it to take the girl abroad for an abortion and to make all necessary arrangements for the abortion. In a judicial review application relating to the interim care order under the Child Care Act, 1991, the High Court examined the thirteenth amendment, Geoghegan J. stating as follows:

'This amendment is framed in negative terms and must, in my view, be interpreted in the historical context in which it was inserted. There was, I think, a widespread feeling in the country that a repetition of *The Attorney General v X* [1992] 1 I R 1, should not occur in that nobody should be injuncted from actually travelling out of the country for the purpose of an abortion. It must be remembered that three out of the five judges of the Supreme Court took the view that in an appropriate case a travel injunction could be granted. It was in that context, therefore that the amendment was made and I do not think it was ever intended to give some new substantial right. Rather, it was intended to prevent injunctions against travel or having an abortion abroad. A court of law, in considering the welfare of an Irish child in Ireland and considering whether on health grounds a termination of pregnancy was necessary, must, I believe, be confined to considering the grounds for termination which would be lawful under the Irish Constitution and cannot make a direction authorising travel to another jurisdiction for a different kind of abortion. The amended Constitution does not now confer a right to abortion outside of Ireland. It merely prevents injunctions against travelling for that purpose ... the fact that there may be different views as to the importance of the constitutional right to travel does not in my view affect the issue of whether the District Court under the Child Care Act, 1991, can actually exercise a jurisdiction authorising travel for a particular purpose, namely, for an abortion in circumstances where the proposed abortion would not be allowed under Irish law. I think that the court would be prevented from doing so by the terms of the right to life of the unborn expressed in the Constitution and as the Supreme Court have held, unaffected by "the travel amendment".'

The court made it clear that a court would not have any jurisdiction to *authorise* travel for the purpose of obtaining an abortion outside the grounds of the *X* case, since the amendment was drafted in negative terms – ie an individual could not be injuncted from travelling to another country, but a court would not have the jurisdiction to authorise travel to another country for an abortion beyond the grounds envisaged in the *X* case.

9.8 The Fourteenth Amendment: The Provision of Information

From the time of the eighth amendment, the courts had been concerned with the matter of the advertising of information relating to abortion services. The Irish courts in *The Attorney General (SPUC) v Open Door Counselling Ltd* [1988] IR 593; *SPUC v Coogan* [1989] IR 734; *SPUC v Grogan* [1989] IR 753 seemed relatively content to restrict such information. However, in Case C-159/90 *SPUC v Grogan* [1991] ECR 1 4685, the European Court of Justice (ECJ) ruled that there was a right to advertise abortion services lawfully available in another EC State once it was for economic profit. The position was clarified by the addition of the fourteenth amendment to the Constitution, which states at Article 40.3.3°:

'*This subsection shall not limit freedom to obtain or make available, in the State, subject to such conditions as may be laid down by law, information relating to services lawfully available in another state.*'

The conditions laid down by law are contained in the Regulation of Information (Services Outside the State for the Termination of Pregnancies) Act, 1995, which the Supreme Court in *Re Article 26 and the Regulation of Information (Services Outside the State for the Termination of Pregnancies) Bill, 1995* [1995] 1 IR 1 found was not repugnant to the Constitution. The Act provides for the provision of non-directive information in relation to terminations, which does not promote or advocate it and where such information relates to lawful abortions in the state in which they are carried out.

9.9 The Proposed Twenty-Fifth Amendment: Restricting the Parameters of the *X* Case

Those unhappy with the decision in the *X* case felt particularly aggrieved by the fact that suicide as distinct from medical complications which arise in cases of pregnancy could be regarded as factor that could be regarded as a real and substantial risk to the life of the mother. Government efforts to evaluate the aftermath of the *X* case by means of the report of the Constitutional Review Group in 1996 and a substantial initiative which resulted in an All-Party Oireachtas Committee on the Constitution producing a large document entitled the *Fifth Progress Report: Abortion*, (Dublin, 2000) led the Government to draft a proposed Amendment to the Constitution contained in the twenty-fifth amendment of the Constitution (Protection of Human Life in Pregnancy) Bill, 2001 which stated at s 1(2):

> '. . . *abortion does not include the carrying out of a medical procedure by a medical practitioner at an approved place in the course of which or as a result of which unborn human life is ended where that procedure is, in the reasonable opinion of the practitioner, necessary to prevent a real and substantial risk of loss of the woman's life other than by self-destruction.*'

A majority of those who voted in the referendum rejected the proposal to introduce this Bill and the law remains as set out in the *X* case.

9.10 Implications for Healthcare Professionals

Sections 58 and 59 of the Offences Against the Person Act, 1861 prohibit the administering of drugs or the use of instruments to procure abortion or the supplying of drugs or instruments to procure abortion.

After the *X* case, the Medical Council made its policy clear in the Medical Council's *A Guide to Ethical Conduct and Behaviour* 5th ed (Medical Council, Dublin, 1998) para 26.5 of which states:

> 'The deliberate and intentional destruction of the unborn child is professional misconduct. Should a child *in utero* suffer or lose its life as a side effect of standard medical treatment of the mother, then it is not unethical. Refusal by a doctor to treat a woman with a serious illness because she is pregnant would be grounds for complaint and could be considered to be professional misconduct.'

This clearly did not take into account the ruling of the *X* case, but rather remained in line with traditional medical opinion that should the child in utero, by no action on the part of the medical practitioner, lose its life due to standard medical procedure, then that was not unethical. This is of course a classic invocation of the doctrine of double effect. The Guidelines did not touch on the issue of the *X* case. In effect, a medical practitioner, who carried out an abortion if it came within the ambit of the *X* case grounds, notwithstanding the ruling of the Supreme Court, could still have faced a charge of professional misconduct. This did not ever happen and was unlikely to happen, since under the provisions of the Medical Practitioner's Act, 1978, a practitioner found guilty of professional misconduct by the Medical Council has a right of appeal to the High Court. It is unlikely that the High Court would uphold a charge of professional misconduct by the Medical Council when such conduct would be covered by the Supreme Court judgment. Nevertheless, the medical profession were unhappy that their guidelines left them in an ethically uncomfortable predicament.

The Medical Council, after much debate, published its first amendment to its fifth edition in December 2001, which practitioners received in 2002. The amendment replaces the previous guidelines above and now states:

'The Council recognises that termination of pregnancy can occur when there is a real and substantial risk to the life of the mother and subscribes to the views expressed in Part 2 of the written submission of the Institute of Obstetricians and Gynaecologists to the All-Party Oireachtas Committee . . .'

Part 2, however, only states that rare complications do sometimes occur when therapeutic intervention is required when there is no prospect of survival of the baby and where failure to intervene could cause death to mother and baby. The paragraph goes on to state:

'We consider that there is fundamental difference between abortion carried out with the intention of taking the life of the baby, for example for social reasons, and with the unavoidable death of the baby resulting from essential treatment to protect the life of the mother.'

Effectively, the guidelines seek to come to a compromise between the X case (by adjusting the words of the guidelines to adopt the words of the Supreme Court in the X case) and the Council's views. The effect of this amendment remains to be seen. However, it seems that the lack of complete clarity might still result in a doctor defending himself against a charge for professional misconduct even though his/her actions come within the current status of the law. It is:

(a) likely that the court will be involved in any such decisions for the foreseeable future; and

(b) unlikely that a medical council's finding of misconduct (once such conduct is within the parameters of the X case) would stand on appeal to the High Court, if such court finds that the conduct was indeed within the realms of the X case.

9.11 Implications of Foetal Protection for Maternal Autonomy

In other common law jurisdictions, in a situation where a 'maternal-conflict' occurs, for example, where a competent adult woman does not wish to receive medical treatment (a common example being caesarean section) and that non-treatment will result in the death of her child *in utero*, the rights of the woman have been held to be paramount. In the UK case of *Re MB* (1987) 8 Med LR 217, 224 the Court of Appeal clarified English law on this controversial issue:

'. . . we are . . . sure that however desirable it may be for the mother to be delivered of a live and healthy baby, on this aspect of the appeal it is not a strictly relevant consideration. If therefore the competent mother refuses to have the medical intervention, the doctors may not lawfully do more than attempt to persuade her. If that persuasion is unsuccessful, there are no further steps towards medical intervention to be taken. We recognise that the effect of these conclusions is that there will be situations in which the child may die or may be seriously handicapped because the mother said no and the obstetrician was not able to take the necessary steps to avoid the death or handicap. The mother may indeed later regret the outcome, but the alternative would be an unwarranted invasion of the right of the woman to make the decision.'

This rationale was reconfirmed in the case of *St George's Healthcare NHS Trust v S; R v Collins, ex parte S* [1998] 3 WLR 936 where Judge LJ stated:

'In our judgment while pregnancy increases the personal responsibilities of a woman it does not diminish her entitlement to decide whether or not to undergo medical treatment. Although human, and protected by the law in a number of different ways . . . an unborn child is not a separate person from its mother. Its need for medical assistance does not prevail over her rights. She is entitled not to be forced to submit to an invasion of her body against her will, whether her own life or that of her unborn child depends on it. Her right is not reduced or diminished merely because her decision to exercise it may appear morally repugnant . . . Of themselves the perceived needs of the foetus did not provide the necessary justification.'

In the United States, this is also the case as was made clear in the case of *Re AC* (1990) 573 A 20l 1235, where the Court of Appeals stated:

'We hold that in virtually all cases the question of what is to be done is to be decided by the patient – the pregnant woman – on behalf of herself and the foetus. If the patient is incompetent or otherwise unable to give an informed consent, to a proposed course of medical treatment, then her decision must be ascertained through the procedure known as substituted judgment.'

In Ireland, it does not seem that these stances could represent the law. In *Attorney General v X* [1992] ILRM 401, 422, Hederman J stated:

'. . . the termination of pregnancy other than a natural one has a legal and social dimension and requires a special responsibility on the part of the State . . . Therefore no recognition of a mother's right of self-determination can be given priority over the protection of the unborn life. The creation of a new life, involving as it does pregnancy, birth and raising the child, necessarily involves some restriction of a mother's freedom but the alternative is the destruction of the unborn life. The termination of pregnancy is not like a visit to the doctor to cure an illness. The State must, in principle, act in accordance with the mother's duty to carry out the pregnancy.'

It is quite clear that an Irish court would not give a woman the overriding power of self-determination when a foetus can be saved and it does not represent a real and substantial risk to the life of the mother. In Ireland, it seems that if a mother wished to refuse a caesarean section, which if not carried out would result in the death of the foetus, she would probably be compelled to have this treatment, unless it carried a real and substantial risk to her life as opposed to just her health. In effect and reality, such treatment would have to be forced on the woman and here her rights to bodily integrity would be compromised in favour of the right to life of the foetus.

9.12 Implications for Refugee Law

The position of the rights of the unborn child have not been examined in relation to whether such rights could apply to a non-national. Various views have been expressed by the courts in relation to the application of fundamental rights to non-citizens. None can be said to have given any definitive view on this matter.

The High Court and on appeal, the Supreme Court have recently touched on the matter in *Baby O v Minister for Justice, Equality and Law Reform* [2002] 2 IR I69. (At the time of writing the High Court decision remains uncirculated and this report has come from a newspaper article. 'High Court Challenge by Nigerian Woman is Dismissed' (2002) *Irish Times*, 19 January). The facts pertained to a pregnant Nigerian national who had failed in an asylum application and who was to be deported. In November 2001, the woman obtained an order preventing deportation on a number of grounds the underlying basis of which was her pregnancy. The rights to birthright and the right to life of the unborn were invoked by the applicant. In the High Court, Smyth J seemed to distinguish this case from the *X* case, since the woman in the *X* case was a national whereas in this case, the woman was not. Also, the court seems to have stated that the birthright provided for in Art 2 of the Constitution is an entitlement of a person born in Ireland. In relation to Art 40.3.3°, the court stated that in the absence of any adverse medical decision, the right to life was not an issue in the case and a threat to the life of the unborn had not been proffered. Keane CJ, in the Supreme

Court, agreed and stated that the issue of termination of the unborn was irrelevant since the State was not seeking to terminate the pregnancy. Keane CJ stated that had the applicant arrived with a young child that would not affect the decision to deport and neither would the decision to deport differ in the case of a pregnant woman. He stated that 'it is obvious that the rights of the born in this context, cannot be less than those of the unborn' (at p 82) It is difficult to predict the full impact of this judgment.

9.13 The Right to Life and the Gravely Ill

The Courts in Ireland have not yet been called upon to deal with the issue of the right to life in relation to the 'malformed neonate' or those just born who are very seriously ill. The Irish courts have, of course, examined the range of medico-legal and constitutional dilemmas that would arise in such cases as the *Ward* case. It is quite likely that the law as analysed and set down in the *Ward* case would apply in some degree to most such cases. In these cases, the courts have granted permission to allow patients to die, where it was considered that any other option was not in the patient's best interests. With the very seriously malformed neonate (*Re C (a minor)* [1989] 2 All ER 782, and *In Re J (a minor)* [1990] 3 All ER 930) the PVS patient, *(Airedale NHS Trust v Bland* [1993] 1 All ER 821) the near-PVS patient and patients in very low awareness states, (*Re R (Adult: Medical Treatment)* (1996) 2 FLR 99) the courts have sanctioned actions to withdraw medical treatment, such that these patients' lives were allowed to 'come to an end peacefully and with dignity'. (*Re C (a minor)* [1989] 2 All ER 782, *per* Lord Donaldson of Lymington MR).

9.13.1 THE MALFORMED NEONATE

The courts in the UK have been called upon to opine on a number of controversial issues, which dealt with the right to life at the early stages of life.

In *Re C* [1989] 2 All ER 782, an infant was born with a condition (congenital hydrocephalus) which had caused irreparable brain damage. The brain structure was severely and poorly formed and there was no chance of the child having a meaningful life span. The question then to be asked was whether the infant should receive 'treatment appropriate to a non-handicapped child' or treatment 'appropriate to her condition', subject to the fact that, as the court stated *per* Lord Donaldson of Lymington, MR at 783, 'Baby C is dying and nothing the court can do, nothing that the doctors can do and nothing known to medical science can alter that fact'.

At this point, the judge referred back to the *dicta* of Ward J, the trial judge, who directed that it was foremost in the best interests of the child that 'the hospital authority . . . be at liberty to allow her life to come to an end peacefully and with dignity.'

His reason for this direction was, as he stated at 787, that he was:

'. . . quite satisfied that the damage is severe and irreparable. Insofar as I can assess the quality of life, which as a test in itself raised [as] many questions as it can answer, I adjudge that any quality of life has already been denied to this child because it cannot flow from a brain incapable of even limited intellectual function. Inasmuch as one judges, as I do, intellectual function to be a hallmark of our humanity, her functioning on that level is negligible if it exists at all. Coupled with her total physical handicap, the quality of her life will be demonstrably awful and intolerable . . . Asking myself what capacity she has to interact mentally, socially, physically, I answer none. This is her permanent condition.'

Soon after this case, the same court developed the rationale laid down in *Re C* in its landmark decision of *Re J (a minor)* [1990] 3 All ER 930. J was born very prematurely, suffering irreparable brain damage. The medical evidence showed that he was likely to develop serious spastic quadriplegia, be blind, deaf and unlikely to ever be able to speak or develop even limited intellectual abilities, but would probably feel pain to the same extent as any normal baby, since pain was such a basic response. His life expectancy was uncertain, but he was expected to die before late adolescence. He had been ventilated twice before for long periods, a procedure which was both hazardous and painful. However, he was neither dying nor on the point of dying. The question thus arose that if he suffered a further collapse, should he be re-ventilated? The trial judge stated that he should be given antibiotics in the case of infection, but should not be re-ventilated, unless the doctors thought otherwise. The case was appealed.

In dismissing the appeal, all three judges made important comments as to the status quo of the law. Lord Donaldson of Lymington, examining when to consent to a procedure to prolong the life of a patient stated at 938:

> 'As this court recognised in *Re B*, account has to be taken of the pain and suffering and the quality of life which the child will experience if life is prolonged. Account has also to be taken of the pain and suffering involved in the proposed treatment itself.'

The court, asserting its belief in the sanctity of human life, stated:

> 'We all believe in and assert the sanctity of human life . . . even very severely handicapped people find a quality of life rewarding which to the unhandicapped may seem manifestly intolerable. People have an amazing adaptability. But in the end there will be cases in which the answer must be that it is not in the interests of the child to subject it to treatment which will cause increased suffering and produce no commensurate benefit, giving fullest possible weight to the child's and mankind's desire to survive . . .'

Balcome LJ, rejected the 'absolute' submission, which states that the court must respect the sanctity of life, regardless of any other considerations. He stated at 942:

> 'In my judgment there is no warrant, either on principle or authority, for the absolute submission. There is only the one test: that the interests of the ward are paramount . . . I say that there should be no such rule because it could in certain circumstances be inimical to the interests of the ward that there should be such a requirement: to preserve life at all costs, whatever the quality of life to be preserved, and however distressing to the ward may be the nature of the treatment necessary to preserve life, may not be in the interests of the ward.'

Taylor LJ, in agreeing with the other two judges stated at 945:

> 'The court's high respect for the sanctity of human life imposes a strong presumption in favour of taking all steps capable of preserving it, save in exceptional circumstances. The problem is to define those circumstances . . . I am of the view that there must be extreme cases in which the court is entitled to say: "The life which this treatment would prolong would be so cruel as to be intolerable." If for example, a child was so damaged as to have negligible use of its faculties and the only way of preserving its life was by the continuous administration of extremely painful treatment such that the child either would be in continuous agony or would have to be sedated continuously as to have no conscious life at all . . . In those circumstances . . . I consider the court is entitled in the best interest of the child to say that deliberate steps should not be taken artificially to prolong its miserable life span. . . . I consider that the correct approach is for the court to judge the quality of life the child would have to endure if given the treatment and decide whether in all the circumstances such a life would be so inflicted as to be intolerable to that child. . . . the test must be whether the child in question, if capable of exercising sound judgment, would consider the life intolerable. . . . The circumstances to be considered would, in appropriate cases, include the degree of existing disability and any additional suffering or aggravation of the disability which the treatment itself would superimpose.'

Subsequently, in *Airedale NHS Trust v Bland* [1993] 1 All ER 821, 870 *per* Lord Goff, the House of Lords agreed with this reasoning.

It is clear, according to this line of reasoning, that the common law, while acknowledging the sanctity and the right to life, (now in the UK by virtue of the Human Rights Act 1998 which incorporates Art 2 of the European Convention on Human Rights, protecting the right to life, into its national law). See also the recent conjoined twins case: *Re A (children) (conjoined twins: surgical separation)* [2000] 4 All ER 961 generally and at 1016–1018 *per* Ward LJ recognises that there is a threshold below which the maintenance of life may be so intolerable that the court will allow such a life not to be prolonged. It is interesting to note the courts' fluctuating criteria. In *Re C*, the court emphasised the importance of 'intellectual function', mental, physical and social interaction and the fact that in this case the infant was dying. In *Re J*, it mattered not whether the individual involved was dying or on the point of death but whether the quality of life would be full of pain and suffering, intolerable, and a life where the use of the patient's faculties were negligible. Clearly, the degree of pain and mental impairment played an important part in the decisions. It could be said that in such cases the rights of bodily integrity outweighed the right to life.

9.13.2 PATIENTS LACKING AWARENESS AND IN STATES OF MINIMAL AND LOW AWARENESS

In the case of *Airedale NHS Trust v Bland* [1993] 1 All ER 821, where a young patient who suffered a severe crushed chest injury following the events of the Hillsborough disaster and lapsed into a Persistent Vegetative State (PVS), the question of the withdrawal of artificial nutrition and hydration from an insensate patient came to be considered by the English Courts.

From the outset, the House of Lords stated emphatically *per* Bingham MR at 334:

> 'There are certain important principles relevant to this case which both parties accept. (1) A Profound respect for the sanctity of human life is embedded in our law and moral philosophy . . .'

The Court *per* Butler-Sloss LJ at 344 went on to state that in this case 'there is a conflict between the principle of self-determination . . . and another basic principle of our society, the preservation of life.'

Lord Goff at 367 (and *per* Lord Musthill at 395) citing various articles from various international codes including Article 2 of the European Convention of Human Rights stated:

> 'Here, the fundamental principle is the principle of the sanctity of life . . . But this principle, fundamental though it is, is not absolute.'

The House of Lords, looking at the totality of the treatment given and to the principles of self-autonomy and dignity (*per* Hoffman LJ at 351) and looking at the factors of:

(a) the reality of irrecoverability to a sapient state;

(b) the fact that there was no cure or improvement;

(c) the treatment was invasive; and

(d) was non-therapeutic/non beneficial

held that the withdrawal of artificial nutrition and hydration was lawful and in the best interests of the patient.

The Irish courts also had an opportunity to examine the issue in the case of *In the Matter of a Ward of Court* [1995] 2 ILRM 401 where the adult patient was in a 'near-PVS', but was neither dead nor dying. Her condition was described by the High Court as follows:

'Over two decades ago the ward, who was then 22 years old, underwent a minor gynaecological operation under general anaesthetic. During the procedure she suffered three cardiac arrests resulting in anoxic brain damage of a very serious nature. Since that catastrophe the ward has been completely dependent on others, requiring total nursing care. She is spastic as a result of the brain damage. Both arms and hands are contracted. Both legs and feet are extended. Her jaws are clenched and because she had a tendency to bite the insides of her cheeks and her tongue, her back teeth have been capped to prevent the front teeth from fully closing. She cannot swallow. She cannot speak. She is incontinent . . . The ward is, of course, bedridden. She is in a condition which is nearly, but not quite, what in modern times has become known as persistent or permanent vegetative state (PVS) . . . In the present case the ward's heart and lungs function normally. Assuming that she is adequately furnished with nutrition and hydration (nourishment), her digestive system operates normally as do her bodily functions, although bowel movements require some assistance, but as she cannot swallow and as her teeth are spastically clenched together, she cannot receive nourishment in the normal way and as already stated, is and has had to be tube-fed since the catastrophe. Assuming that she continues to be nourished by tube, she could live for many years but of course she might also die in the short term if she developed some infection such as pneumonia, unless it were treated aggressively with antibiotics. The ward has no capacity for speech or for communicating. A speech therapist failed to elicit any means of communication. She has a minimal capacity to recognise, for example, the long established nursing staff and to react to strangers by showing distress. She also follows or tracks people with her eyes and reacts to noise, although the latter is mainly, if not indeed, wholly reflex from the brain stem and a large element of reflex eye tracking is also present in the former which, however, also has some minimal purposive content . . . I am satisfied that although the ward is not fully PVS, she is very nearly so and such cognitive capacity as she possesses is extremely minimal. A fully PVS person cannot feel pain and has no capacity for pleasure or displeasure even though they may groan or grimace or cry, especially in response to painful stimuli, nor have they any realisation whatever of their tragic situation. This is probably the ward's state but if such minimal cognition as she has includes an inkling of her catastrophic condition, then I am satisfied that that would be a terrible torment to her and her situation would be worse than if she were fully PVS there is no prospect whatsoever of any improvement in the condition of the ward.'

Echoing the words of other courts in relation to the limit of the right to life, the Supreme Court stated *per* Denham J at 457:

'The requirement to defend and vindicate the life is a requirement "as far as practicable", it is not an absolute. Life itself is not an absolute.'

In relation to the right to life, Hamilton CJ stated at 426:

'As the process of dying is part, and an ultimate, inevitable consequence, of life, the right to life necessarily implies the right to have nature take its course and to die a natural death and, unless the individual concerned so wishes, not to have life artificially maintained by the provision of nourishment by abnormal artificial means, which have no curative effect and which is intended merely to prolong life.'

Denham J, stated:

'The primary constitutional concept is to protect life within the community. The State has an interest in the moral aspect of society – for the common good. But, balanced against that is the person's right to life – which encompasses a right to die naturally and in the privacy of the family and with minimum suffering.'

The Supreme Court, allowed withdrawal of artificial nutrition and hydration stating *per* Hamilton CJ at 429 that it '. . . was intrusive and burdensome and of no curative effect . . .'

The effect of this decision was to analyse and place the right to life not only in balance with other rights, such that the right to bodily integrity could outweigh the absolute right to life, but also to state that the right to die a natural death was in fact, very much a part of the right to life itself.

As can be seen from the above examination, the right to life exists and is invoked at various different times and stages of life itself. The right, while ranking as the highest in the hierarchy of rights, and from which all other rights stem, is not absolute, and when invoked by those who rely on them, the courts will engage in a careful exercise of balance to ensure that above and beyond all other things, the constitutional dignity of an individual is protected. It could be said that this right, which Denham J, recognised at 466 'as an unspecified right' is perhaps greater than the sum of all of the rights and in many respects is what the courts in one manner or another are seeking to protect.

9.14 International Obligations: The European Convention for the Protection of Human Rights and Fundamental Freedoms

9.14.1 THE RIGHT TO LIFE

A number of international treaties now provide articles that deal with the right to life and what may be deemed the protection of bodily integrity. The European Court of Human Rights (ECt.HR) has dealt with the rights to life and bodily integrity in various ways. Because of the high eminence afforded to the right to life in Irish law, it is doubtful that the incorporation of the European Convention on Human Rights (ECHR) would add any particularly new dimension to the right. Such eminence is reflected in the jurisprudence of the ECt.HR.

9.14.2 THE EUROPEAN CONVENTION FOR THE PROTECTION OF HUMAN RIGHTS AND FUNDAMENTAL FREEDOMS

Article 2 ECHR states that:

'1. *Everyone's right to life shall be protected by law. No one shall be deprived of his life intentionally save in the execution of a sentence of a court following his conviction of a crime for which this penalty is provided by law.*

2. *Deprivation of life shall not be regarded as inflicted in contravention of this article when it results from the use of force which is no more than absolutely necessary:*
    (a) *in defence of any person from unlawful violence;*
    (b) *in order to effect a lawful arrest or to prevent the escape of a person lawfully detained;*
    (c) *in action lawfully taken for the purpose of quelling a riot or insurrection'.*

In *McCann v United Kingdom* (1996) 21 EHHR 97, the ECt.HR stated:

'It must also be borne in mind that, as a provision (art. 2) which not only safeguards the right to life but sets out the circumstances when the deprivation of life may be justified, Article 2 (art. 2) ranks as one of the most fundamental provisions in the Convention ... it also enshrines one of the basic values of the democratic societies making up the Council of Europe ... As such, its provisions must be strictly construed.'

This has been reiterated very recently in *McKerr v United Kingdom* (04/5/01, ECHR).

Recently, the ECt.HR made it clear that the right to life did not extend to the right to die. The court in the case of *Pretty v United Kingdom* (29/4/02, ECHR) stated:

'The Court's case-law accords pre-eminence to Article 2 as one of the most fundamental provisions of the Convention . . . It safeguards the right to life, without which enjoyment of any of the other rights and freedoms in the Convention is rendered nugatory . . . The text of Article 2 expressly regulates the deliberate or intended use of lethal force by State agents. It has been interpreted however as covering not only intentional killing but also the situations where it is permitted to "use force" which may result, as an unintended outcome, in the deprivation of life . . . The Court has further held that the first sentence of Article 2 § 1 enjoins the State not only to refrain from the intentional and unlawful taking of life, but also to take appropriate steps to safeguard the lives of those within its jurisdiction . . . This obligation extends beyond a primary duty to secure the right to life by putting in place effective criminal-law provisions to deter the commission of offences against the person backed up by law-enforcement machinery for the prevention, suppression and sanctioning of breaches of such provisions; it may also imply in certain well-defined circumstances a positive obligation on the authorities to take preventive operational measures to protect an individual whose life is at risk from the criminal acts of another individual . . . More recently, in the case of *Keenan v. the United Kingdom*, Article 2 was found to apply to the situation of a mentally ill prisoner who disclosed signs of being a suicide risk . . . The consistent emphasis in all the cases before the Court has been the obligation of the State to protect life. The Court is not persuaded that "the right to life" guaranteed in Article 2 can be interpreted as involving a negative aspect . . . To the extent that these aspects are recognised as so fundamental to the human condition that they require protection from State interference, they may be reflected in the rights guaranteed by other Articles of the Convention, or in other international human rights instruments. Article 2 cannot, without a distortion of language, be interpreted as conferring the diametrically opposite right, namely a right to die; nor can it create a right to self-determination in the sense of conferring on an individual the entitlement to choose death rather than life. The Court accordingly finds that no right to die, whether at the hands of a third person or with the assistance of a public authority, can be derived from Article 2 of the Convention. The Court finds that there has been no violation of Article 2 of the Convention.'

9.14.3 THE DEATH PENALTY

Protocol No. 6 ECHR concerning the abolition of the death penalty states at Article 1 'The death penalty, shall be abolished. No-one shall be condemned to such penalty or executed'.

The Criminal Justice Act, 1990 abolished the death penalty in Ireland, s 1 stating that 'No person shall suffer death for any offence.'

Subsequent to this Act, an amendment to the Constitution was passed, in 2001, which resulted in the Constitution Act, 2001, which inserted Art 15.5.2. This states that:

'The Oireachtas shall not enact any law providing for the imposition of the death penalty.'

Article 2 of the ECHR regarding the death penalty in time of war states:

'A State may make provision in its law for the death penalty in respect of acts committed in time of war or of imminent threat of war; such penalty shall be applied only in the instances laid down in the law and in accordance with its provisions. The State shall communicate to the Secretary General of the Council of Europe the relevant provisions of that law.'

It should be noted that the status quo of a nation's death penalty will have ramifications for the issue of extradition law (see the *Soering* case below). In Ireland, the Extradition Act, 1965 at s 19 states that:

'Extradition shall not be granted for an offence which is punishable by death under the law of the requesting country but is of a category for which the death penalty is not provided for by the law of the State or is not generally carried out unless the requesting country gives such assurance as the Minister considers sufficient that the death penalty will not be carried out.'

9.15 European Law Obligations

It should be noted that the European Court of Justice (ECJ) does not seem to have dealt with the rights to life or bodily integrity. The EU Charter of Fundamental Rights reflecting the terms of the ECHR, states at Article 2:

'1. Everyone has the right to life.
2. No one shall be condemned to the death penalty, or executed'.

9.16 The Right to Bodily Integrity

9.16.1 AN UNENUMERATED RIGHT IN IRISH CONSTITUTIONAL LAW

This unenumerated right will be explained in terms of an individual's right to be protected against violation by the State and by private individuals (eg in medical treatment). This was the first unenumerated right to be recognised by the Irish courts. In *Ryan v Attorney General* [1965] IR 294, the plaintiff sought to allege that the State's fluoridation of water endangered her and her family's health.

In the High Court, Kenny J., stated:

'I think that the personal rights which may be involved to invalidate legislation are not confined to those specified in Article 40 but include all those rights which result from the Christian and democratic nature of the State. It is however, a jurisdiction to be exercised with caution. None of the personal rights of the citizen are unlimited.'

The Court went on to state:

'In my opinion, one of the personal rights of the citizen protected by the general guarantee is the right to bodily integrity. I understand the right to bodily integrity to mean that no mutilation of the body or any of its members may be carried out on any citizen under authority of the law except for the good of the whole body and that no process which is or may, as a matter of probability, be dangerous or harmful to the life or health of the citizens or any of them may be imposed (in the sense of being made compulsory) by an Act of the Oireachtas.'

The Supreme Court upheld this finding.

The scope of this right is vast in terms of the protection of one's health by the State and others, but like every other right, it is not absolute. In *McGee v Attorney General* [1974] IR 284, the Supreme Court held that the plaintiff's right to bodily integrity was breached in effect, as Walsh J put it, the plaintiff had '. . . a right to be assisted in her efforts to avoid putting her life in jeopardy.'

In *The State (C) v Frawley* [1976] IR 365, it was alleged that a prisoner who was suffering from a mental condition, which caused him *inter alia* to swallow metal objects, should be released on the grounds that his bodily integrity was not being protected by the State. This was rejected by Finlay P at 373 who stated that there could not be '. . . an obligation to provide for prisoners in general the best medical treatment . . .' nor a duty to '. . . build, equip and staff . . .' the specialised unit of the prison. However, Finlay P at 372 did state of the right that he could not see any:

> '. . . reason why the principle should not also operate to prevent an act or an omission of the Executive which, without justification, would expose the health of a person to risk or danger.'

In the *State (Richardson) v The Governor of Mountjoy Prison* [1980] ILRM 82, the court accepted the evidence of a woman prisoner in relation to lax standards of hygiene and stated that the State had failed in it duty to protect the applicant's health.

As has been examined, the right to bodily integrity has been relied on in relation to an individual's right to refuse medical treatment and in balancing such a right with the artificial maintenance of life in the *Ward* case. The right to bodily integrity operates to ensure that the State fulfils its duty not to endanger the health of its citizens but the right also operates to ensure that individuals' rights are not breached within a private sphere. There is no doubt that certainly, in the sphere of healthcare, this right is likely to appear many times, as a topic of review before the courts, in future when attempts are made to impose medical treatment on individuals when medical professionals believe it is in the individual's best interests. The right may also be invoked along with the right to life and with the many other unenumerated rights now outlined by the courts in the gravely-ill cases and indeed in cases where the healthcare sector seeks to argue the inability to provide health by virtue of a scarcity of resources. What is almost inevitable is that these rights, whilst now somewhat explored, have much to offer by way of future judicial interpretation and application.

9.16.2 THE EUROPEAN CONVENTION FOR THE PROTECTION OF FUNDAMENTAL RIGHTS AND FREEDOMS

Article 3 on the 'Prohibition of torture' states:

> *'No one shall be subjected to torture or to inhuman or degrading treatment or punishment.'*

Article 3 has been utilised in a number of settings. The difference between the three terms torture, inhuman or degrading treatment lies in '. . . a difference in the intensity of the suffering inflicted' (*Ireland v United Kingdom* (1980) 2 EHRR 25). In relation to torture in the arena of police custody, in the *Ireland v United Kingdom* decision, 'interrogation in depth' techniques (namely, deprivation of sleep, food and drink, subjection to noise and hooding) were inhuman or degrading treatment but not torture. In *Aksoy v Turkey* (1997) 23 EHRR 553, electrocution of a detainee was described by the court as '. . . of such a serious and cruel nature that it can only be described as torture.'

In *Herczegfalvy v Finland* (1993) 15 EHRR 437, it was not inhuman or degrading treatment to force-treat and feed a hunger striking prisoner with a history of psychiatric problems since '. . . a measure which is a therapeutic necessity cannot be regarded as inhuman or degrading.'

The UN Convention against Torture and Other Cruel Inhuman or Degrading Treatment or Punishment (1984) describes torture as *'any act by which severe pain or suffering, whether physical or mental, is intentionally inflicted . . .'.*

Another important point to consider is that of contracting States extraditing or deporting individuals to a non-contracting State where a breach of Art 3 may occur. It has been held by the ECt.HR that such an action may breach the Convention when if an individual is extradited, there is a 'real risk of being subjected to torture or to inhuman or degrading treatment or punishment in the requesting country' and where there are substantial grounds to show this (*Soering v United Kingdom* (1989) 11 EHRR 439).

A similar bar from deportation may be a consideration in refugee law under the principle of *non-refoulement*.

9.16.3 THE CHARTER OF FUNDAMENTAL RIGHTS OF THE EUROPEAN UNION, 2000

The Charter states at Art 3, entitled 'Right to the integrity of the person':

> '1. *Everyone has the right to respect for his or her physical and mental integrity.*
> 2.   *In the fields of medicine and biology, the following must be respected in particular:*
>   – *the free and informed consent of the person concerned, according to the procedures laid down by law,*
>   – *the prohibition of eugenic practices, in particular those aiming at the selection of persons,*
>   – *the prohibition on making the human body and its parts as such a source of financial gain,*
>   – *the prohibition of the reproductive cloning of human beings.'*

The rights in Art 3 of the EU Charter are a reaffirmation of the provisions of the Convention on Human Rights and Biomedicine (ETS 164 and additional protocol ETS 168).

Thus, at international level, whilst the protection of the right to life is similar to national protection, the right to 'integrity' is wide ranging and encompasses protections ranging from protection against torture and *non-refoulement* of asylum seekers to informed consent in medicine and a prohibition on reproductive human cloning. The rights to bodily integrity are ripe for further exploration by our courts.

Article 4, entitled *'Prohibition of torture and inhuman or degrading treatment or punishment'*, states *'No one shall be subjected to torture or to inhuman or degrading treatment or punishment'*.

9.17 Conclusion

At national and international level, the right to life is regarded as the most fundamental right in the hierarchy of human rights. It is not however, an absolute right, and the courts will balance it by taking into account other rights such as the developing right of human dignity. With advances in medical technology in areas of reproduction, genetics and end of life care the right to life will no doubt continue to be considered by the courts. Constitutional lawyers need to remain aware of developments in international jurisprudence when formulating arguments and advice in cases where the right to life will be carefully balanced and proportioned to ensure that what is achieved in every case is a respect for the human person.

CHAPTER 10

EQUALITY

10.1 Introduction

This chapter begins by exploring the concept of equality as there are different perceptions of what the right to equality or equal treatment means. In this jurisdiction, protections for the right are sourced from a number of bases: EC law, Bunreacht na hEireann, domestic legislation and various international treaties. The guarantee of equality will be examined in these various spheres. It is worth noting at the outset that much of our domestic protection of the right to equality stems from the implementation here of EC law and because of the hierarchies of law in operation this is an important consideration.

10.2 Competing Ideas of Equality

The right to equality is one of the more difficult human rights to conceptualise, meaning different things to different people. It is an idea that carries as much political significance as legal challenge and is applicable to such diverse conceptual and practical subjects as the exercise of civil rights and the distribution of resources. The right has been mentioned in all basic human rights instruments, both national and international, since the French Revolution.

Early formulations made the idea applicable to civil and political rights and, in that sense, it was sometimes said that the right to equality did not guarantee any right in particular, but guaranteed to all that which was available. The right was usually expressed as the notion of equality before the law, which in reality demanded that states did not put any person above the law. This liberal conception of equality was perversely ascendant even in times when slavery was legal and wives were regarded as their husband's property. In fact, the task of defining equality is one of the more elusive philosophical objectives and competing theories differ widely in the values articulated and in the means proposed to achieve equality. Some of the most fundamental ideological debates have revolved around competing notions of economic equality, with left wing politics favouring more substantive redistributative economic policies and neo-liberal politicians preferring the application of the marketplace's rules to all, without special intervention. At this broad level, the arguments on equality are bound up with a range of other factors that shape public choices and values.

Debates concerning equality are not confined to economics and go to the philosophical and, ultimately legal, content of the idea. On one analysis, the right may be seen as equality of treatment, which underlies the legal notion of equality before the law, ie that all persons are entitled to the application of the same rules. This formal notion of equality has had a particular importance in the application and enforcement of laws. Allowing for the fact that personal characteristics vary, it led to the Aristotelian idea of treating like alike, but differences differently. This model of equality is perhaps the most widely accepted in the judicial and legal context and can be seen in the formulation in Article 40.1 of the 1937 Constitution, which provides:

> *'All citizens shall, as human persons, be held equal before the law. This shall not be held to mean that the State shall not in its enactments have due regard to differences of capacity, physical and moral, and of social function.'*

Such uniformity of treatment may seem appealing, but without a recognition that innate characteristics or circumstance can affect one's effective participation in society, this goal may be empty. To guarantee equal access to the law does not mean that all can have access equally, particularly if a person cannot afford legal representation. It also raises problems of comparison to determine who are alike and for what purpose. More fundamentally, formal equal treatment protection cannot guarantee any better treatment because to treat all similarly-characterised persons equally corresponds badly with the rationale and crucially cannot redress long-standing inequalities.

This exclusion was felt by certain persons most often excluded, especially in employment. While the initial impetus to introduce equality laws came from women's groups, other groups, especially racial minorities, including Travellers and the disabled, have also championed ideological change to the notion of equality. Initially, the focus was on equality of outcome, which sought to guarantee a certain equal result and not just uniform treatment. The aim goes beyond procedural fairness to secure substantive changes in conditions. For example, imposing a requirement for all potential employees to have a third level qualification will exclude those unable to go to college, just as requirement to work full-time may exclude women who remain the primary caregivers for young children.

To overcome these structural inequalities, there has been some focus on measures of positive action to increase the representation of traditionally marginalised groups in various sectors of society, most notably the workplace. Theorists who favour this approach are committed to the aim of equality of outcome, not just equality of opportunity. Such special measures are typically justified by reference to ongoing or structural differentials in the participation of disadvantaged minorities and groups. Generally, Irish law has eschewed such measures, though there are some exceptions. Examples in law include the reservation of a certain number of places for women on State boards and positive duties to make reasonable accommodation for persons with disabilities.

These measures have on occasion proved controversial, attracting the criticism that they sacrifice individual ability to a utopian ideal. Often criticised as unwieldy State attempts to restructure the marketplace, such measures are sometimes, often superficially, themselves condemned for failing to treat persons equally. The theory most often espoused by such critics and others seeking a middle ground between formal equality and equality of outcome is that of equality of opportunity, whereby certain protections are designed to ensure an equality of starting point, but that the personal characteristics determine the finish, particularly in the marketplace. This approach can itself be questioned because it in no way guarantees that everyone can compete equally for resources in that marketplace.

10.3 Equality Laws in Ireland

In many ways, the manner in which the right to equality is treated in Irish law reflects the different ideals of equality as set out above. The Constitution has been used to prevent invidious or capricious discrimination by the State, though criticised for being too weak and focused on formal equality. More particularly, specific laws requiring equality in the workplace were introduced in the 1970's. The Anti-Discrimination (Pay) Act, 1974 and the Employment Equality Act, 1977 were the first pieces of legislation on the matter in

Ireland. These Acts, rooted in the directives from the then EEC, banned discrimination on the ground of sex and marital status. They have since been repealed and replaced by the Employment Equality Act, 1998, which adds seven other protected categories to the list and introduced some measures enabling positive action. The 1998 Act applies to employment only but the Equal Status Act, 2000 bans discrimination in the provision of goods and services and in other non-employment situations.

These laws demonstrate a particular feature of modern equality law whereby specific characteristics are protected, chosen from traditionally discriminated against groups. There are nine such characteristics in the main legislation and a comparative categorical approach is used in that claiming discrimination means claiming to be a member of a class that is treated less favourably than others outside that class. Claiming discrimination, eg. as a disabled person, necessarily involves proving different but less favourable treatment from others without that disability. It is difficult to escape such an approach when dealing with equality rights. The basic idea is to make these characteristics factors to be ignored or specially provided for when considering the availability of employment or goods and services. In that way equality is achieved, not because everyone is treated the same, but because certain characteristics are protected. To be successful, a claimant must not only show less favourable treatment but also that that treatment was as a result of his or her connection to a protected characteristic. In that regard, it may be more accurate to describe Irish legislation as being anti-discrimination law rather than equality law.

The theoretical approach adopted by Irish legislation is generally that of formal equality, in that less favourable treatment of an individual is outlawed if that treatment is based on the protected characteristic, though no special treatment of the characteristic is mandated. There are a number of specific rules that add to this formal approach and go to a version of substantive equality. Some positive action is permitted by Irish legislation, eg s 14(b) of the Equal Status Act, 2000 permits positive measures to cater for persons with special needs. Similarly, discrimination on the disability ground is recognised in domestic legislation as occurring where a person's disability is not reasonably accommodated. Finally, the banning of indirect discrimination outlaws seemingly neutral rules that have an adverse effect on certain groups.

10.4   A Note on the Hierarchies of Law

Given that the right to equality does not guarantee any specifically tangible entitlement or service (as opposed, for example, to the right to liberty or freedom of expression), it is peculiarly susceptible to being outweighed by more substantive considerations. This is associated with the traditional reluctance of the judiciary to engage with social and economic rights, seeing such matters as being the preserve of other branches of the State, especially the executive. The right to equality has often been seen in contrast to, and as being trumped by, substantive rights, particularly property rights, and by economic factors.

Perhaps the most famous example of such a clash was *In re Article 26 and the Employment Equality Bill 1996* [1997] 2 IR 321. This proposed a requirement that employers make reasonable accommodation for disabled employees unless this caused undue hardship. The Supreme Court held that the Bill was unconstitutional as it was felt that obliging employers to bear the costs involved was an infringement of their property rights. In the redrafted legislation which became the 1998 Act, the duty to make provision was limited to accommodation involving no more than a nominal cost.

Because of the involvement of the EC in equality rights, a new level was added to the hierarchy. Sex discrimination has always been a concern of the EC and is now a fundamental part of the treaties. Because of the paramount status of EC law in Ireland, no domestic law can trump its provisions. Because of the centrality of equal pay and equal treatment provisions, these equality rules are placed above others and are treated differently to the other grounds.

10.5 International Law

There are a wealth of references to the notion of equality in international human rights conventions. In the Universal Declaration of Human Rights and the International Covenant on Civil and Political Rights, the equality guarantees are recognised as central to the delivery of the other protected rights to individuals. However, equality was not seen as a right in itself guaranteeing substantive improvement in conditions for individuals. At this international level, there were competing theories of rights in that the former Eastern Bloc countries preferred a focus on substantive economic and social rights, which came to be protected in the International Covenant on Economic, Social and Cultural Rights.

There have also been a number of specific conventions designed to promote equality with respect to particular groups. Foremost among these are the Convention on the Elimination of Discrimination Against Women (often called CEDAW) and the Convention on the Elimination of Racial Discrimination (called CERD). These conventions, while not being as enforceable as domestic or EC law, can be important as they are evidence of the public policy of the State and can be used to campaign for change.

10.6 European Convention on Human Rights (ECHR)

As one of the most successful human rights treaties ever signed and one that can be enforced against the State, the ECHR's statements on equality will have a particular importance. Similar to the other international treaties, equality is guaranteed in terms of the delivery of the other rights under the convention. Article 14 provides:

> 'The enjoyment of the rights and freedoms set forth in this Convention shall be secured without discrimination on any ground such as sex, race, colour, language, religion, political or other opinion, national or social origin, association with a national minority, property, birth or other status.'

Such a formal view of equality renders the right contingent on other rights for activation. A claimant must seek some substantive redress and show that there was discrimination against him or her on the ground of one of the protected categories. In *Belgian Linguistics* (*No. 2*) (1979) EHRR 252, the European Court of Human Rights (ECt.HR) stated that Art 14 operated as if it were an integral part of each of the articles laying down rights and freedoms. In that case, the court also stated that under Art 14 the principle of equal treatment would be breached if a distinction was drawn between persons which had no objective and rational justification or where the means employed was unreasonably disproportionate to the aim of the measure.

10.7 European Community Law

For matters within the competence of the European Community, EC law enjoys the paramount status of constitutional law in each Member State, thereby guaranteeing that its provisions trump any other conflicting law; see Art 29.4 of Bunreacht na hÉireann (see **1.4.2**). That has proved useful in the development of equality legislation and will continue to do so as the competence of the EC develops. Given the weak nature of the right to equality in the Constitution, many who favour the strengthening of equality law look to EC developments.

Because the original aim of the EU was to create a common market within Member States, it is not surprising that the Treaty of Rome outlawed discrimination on the grounds of nationality. This is now contained in Art 12 of the EC Treaty which states that any discrimination on the ground of nationality shall be prohibited.

The EC Treaty as amended now gives greater competence to the EC in relation to discrimination issues. Article 13 permits the Council, acting unanimously, to take appropriate action to combat discrimination based on sex, racial or ethnic origin, religion or belief, disability, age or sexual orientation.

The Council has adopted a new Directive 2000/43/EC of 29 June 2000, the Race Directive. Member States had three years to implement its provisions, which outlaw discrimination on the ground of racial and ethnic origin in employment and in the provision of goods and services. A second directive, called the framework Directive 2000/78/EC of 27 November 2000, has been adopted to ban discrimination in employment on the grounds of religion or belief, age, sexual orientation and disability. It should be noted that, while these grounds of discrimination are covered by the Employment Equality Act, 1998 and the Equal Status Act, 2000, some changes may be required to ensure the directives are transposed properly into Irish law. As of the time of publication the Equality Bill 2004 was being debated in the Oireachtas. The Bill, if enacted, will implement changes to transpose both Directives, and introduce other changes to equality law.

Aside from nationality, EC law was traditionally concerned only with sex and marital status as grounds for protection against discrimination. The roots of EC equality law lie in the creation of the common market. France, which had developed measures to outlaw sex discrimination, was concerned that it would be at a competitive disadvantage if other States were not obliged to introduce similar rules. Thus, former Art 119 (now Art 141) of the EC Treaty guaranteed the principle of equal pay for equal work on the ground of sex. In the landmark case of *Defrenne v Sabena* [1976] ECR 455, the European Court of Justice (ECJ) held that the right was directly effective. It also suggested that the provision formed part of the social objectives of the then EEC. This has now been bolstered by the inclusion of gender discrimination in Art 13 of the EC Treaty. The general definition of discrimination as adopted by the ECJ is that 'discrimination involves the application of different rules to comparable situations, or the application of the same rules to different situations' (see Case C-342/93 *Gillespie v Northern Health and Social Services Board* [1996] ECR I-475).

Council Directive 75/117/EEC, the Equal Pay Directive, was designed to implement this principle of equal pay more fully. Council Directive 76/207/EEC followed, which broadened the application of sex discrimination law to more general employment concerns, including working conditions and the recruitment process. These directives were first implemented into Irish law by the Anti-Discrimination (Pay) Act, 1974 and the Employment Equality Act, 1977 respectively and are now enforced through the Employment Equality Act, 1998. The particular rules are dealt with when considering in the Employment Equality Act, 1998, though it must be noted that the decisions of the European Court of Justice (ECJ) on the interpretation of the Treaty and directives are binding on Irish administrative and judicial authorities charged with the implementation of the rules.

More recently, EU Council Directive 97/80/EC of 15 December, 1997 on the burden of proof in sex discrimination cases has come into force by SI 337 of 2001, the EC (Burden of Proof in Gender Discrimination Cases) Regulations, 2001. These provide that in any proceedings where facts are established from which direct or indirect discrimination may be presumed, it shall be for the other party to prove the contrary.

The substantive law on the right to equality shall be examined under the following headings, though other topics of relevance will be dealt with later when dealing with domestic legislation.

10.7.1 EQUAL PAY

The notion of equal pay for equal work was fundamental to the Treaty of Rome and led to the enactment of the first specific piece of anti-discrimination law in Ireland, the Anti-Discrimination (Pay) Act, 1974. Article 141(1) of the EC Treaty provides that *'[e]ach member state shall ensure that the principle of equal pay for male and female workers for equal work or work of equal value is applied.'* For these purposes, pay is defined in Art 141(2) EC as meaning the ordinary or basic minimum wage or salary or other commission, whether in cash or in kind, which the worker receives directly or indirectly in respect of his employment from his employer.

The ECJ has given the concept of 'pay' a broad meaning and in *Garland v British Rail* [1982] ECR 359, the ECJ held that travel concessions for employees after retirement constituted pay. The fact that there was no specific entitlement to the concession in the contract of employment was held not to be relevant as the benefit was referable to the employment, which was all the Treaty required. Contributions by employers to occupational pension schemes, whether internal to the enterprise or contracted out, have also been recognised as constituting pay, see *Barber v Guardian Royal Exchange* [1990] ECR I-1889. (The difficulties arising from occupational pension schemes led to the adoption of specific rules for pensions.)

A decision on whether work is equal or equal in value is for national authorities. In *Murphy v Bord Telecom Eireann* [1988] ECR 673, the ECJ stated that there is an entitlement to equal pay where a worker carries out work of greater value to that of her comparator.

Differences in pay have also been condemned as being indirectly discriminatory by the ECJ. In *Enderby v Frenchay Health Authority* [1993] ECR I-5535 a speech therapist sought to compare herself with a male pharmacist in circumstances where most speech therapists were female and most pharmacists were male, who were paid at a higher rate. The ECJ held that where statistics show that pay differentials are based on a grading that is polarised on gender grounds, a prima facie case of discrimination is made out and it is for the employer to show that there are objective reasons unrelated to sex for the difference in pay.

The ECJ has adopted an approach based on the shifting burden of proof in relation to taking equal pay cases. Where an enterprise operates a pay system that disadvantages one sex and is wholly lacking in transparency, it is for the employer to prove that the pay practice is not discriminatory; see *Danfoss* [1989] IRLR 532.

10.7.2 EQUAL TREATMENT

The phrase equal treatment refers to aspects of equality law in employment situations other than equal pay. Before the Treaty of Amsterdam amended the EC Treaty, the sole basis for these rules was Council Directive 76/207/EEC. The core of this Directive was expressed in Article 2(1) which provides:

> *'For the purposes of the following provisions, the principle of equal treatment shall mean that there shall be no discrimination whatsoever on grounds of sex either directly or indirectly by reference in particular to marital or family status.'*

Article 141(3) EC now places a legal obligation on the EC to adopt measures to ensure this principle of equal treatment of men and women in employment. Being mentioned specifically in the Treaty ensures that such equality is a fundamental aim of the EC.

Article 3 of the Directive specifies that the principle of equal treatment applies to access to employment, Article 4 makes it applicable to vocational training and Art 5 to conditions of work and dismissals. While the specific rules on equal treatment are discussed below, the approach of the ECJ, which is binding on national authorities, sets the parameters of our law so cannot be overlooked.

One of the areas where the ECJ has been active relates to pregnancy discrimination. In the case of Case C-177/88 *Dekker v Stichting Vermingscentrum voor Jong Volwassenen* (*VJV – Centrum Plus*) [1990] ECR I-3941 the ECJ held that the refusal to employ a woman because she was pregnant was direct sex discrimination, contrary to Art 3, as only women can suffer such discrimination. That led to another important finding that, because of the uniqueness, there was no need for a male comparator. It was also held that financial loss incurred by an employer because of hiring a pregnant woman could not be an excuse for discrimination.

Following this, the ECJ decided the case of Case C-32/93 *Webb v EMO Air Cargo (UK) Ltd* [1994] ECR I-3567. Ms Webb was employed to replace an employee on maternity leave but to remain permanently with the company. Soon after beginning work she informed her employer of her pregnancy. She was dismissed. The employer sought to justify the dismissal by stating that a man would be similarly treated if he were also unavailable for the work he was hired to undertake.

Holding for Ms Webb in an important decision, the ECJ rejected any comparison between a pregnant woman and a sick man. Drawing on the rules contained in the Pregnancy Directive, the Court stated that EC law protections for pregnant workers could not be circumvented by arguments based on the essential presence of an employee at work.

In reaching its decision, the ECJ relied on the fact the Ms Webb was employed in a permanent capacity. This led to much debate as to whether the protections also applied to a pregnant employee employed on a fixed term contract. The ECJ recently resolved this issue, again in favour of the protection of pregnant women in the cases of Case C-438/99 *Jimenez Melgar v Ayuntamiento de Los Barrios* [2001] ECR I-6915 and C-109/00 *Tele Danmark A/S v HK* [2001] ECR I-6993.

The ECJ has also held that less favourable treatment on the ground of a pregnancy-related illness is also unlawful gender discrimination. In *Hertz v Aldi marked K/S* [1991] IRLR 31, the ECJ stated that the dismissal of a pregnant woman for absences caused by a pregnancy-related illness during the period of maternity leave was unlawful direct discrimination on the ground of gender. However, after the maternity leave ceases, an ill woman is not protected, even if the illness has its origin in pregnancy or confinement. In Case C-394/96 *Brown v Rentokill* [1998] ECR I-4185, the ECJ held that dismissal at any time during pregnancy because of absences caused by a pregnancy-related illness was unlawful. It should be noted that dismissals for such absences after the maternity leave ends might, depending on the circumstances, be unlawful discrimination on a standard comparison with male workers.

These cases are applied by domestic adjudicators when considering gender discrimination by reasons of dismissal during or because of pregnancy. In deciding whether a dismissal was discriminatory, the Labour Court has taken a strict approach. In *Emmerdale Ltd v A Worker* (EED-025; 30 May 2002), the Court stated that an employer should have given serious consideration to a work-share arrangement where the pregnant employee desired less hours on medical grounds. In that case, the employer advertised the pregnant employee's position the day after she informed them of her pregnancy and a posited defence that this was to replace the employee when she was on maternity leave was rejected as the advertisement seriously undermined the employee's position and led to a loss of trust and confidence in her employers, which justified her resignation.

In *Parcourt Ltd v A Worker* (EED0211; 15 November 2002), the claimant was held to have been dismissed because of her pregnancy. The employee had taken leave because of a pregnancy-related illness. The employer knew of her pregnancy but claimed that it was not informed of the illness and concluded that she had abandoned her employment. The

Court stated that the employer should have been alert to the fact that the absence was pregnancy-related and held that a prudent employer would attempt to ascertain the facts of a situation. Both of these case impose clear duties on employers to ensure that well regarded pregnant employees are secure in their situation at work and that an employer cannot let a pregnant employee drift away from work.

10.7.3   INDIRECT DISCRIMINATION

In developing the principles of discrimination the ECJ has always made a distinction between direct and indirect discrimination and this has now become a standard feature of anti-discrimination law. Direct discrimination occurs when a person is treated less favourably because he or she possesses a protected characteristic, eg because she is a women. Indirect discrimination, sometimes called adverse effect discrimination, focuses on the effects of what are not ostensibly discriminatory rules. The ECJ had applied the principles of direct and indirect discrimination for both the equal pay provisions and the equal treatment rules.

The leading case regarding equal pay is *Bilka-Kaufhaus v Weber von Hartz* [1986] 2 CMLR 701. This concerned an employer's refusal to make pension contributions to part-time employees, on the basis that it was in its financial interest to discourage part-time employment. The ECJ reasoned that where such an exclusion adversely affected a much greater number of women than men it was unlawful unless an employer could show that the rule was based on objectively justifiable factors unrelated to sex. The court continued and said that if it was found that the justification proffered (a) met a genuine need of the enterprise (b) was suitable for attaining the objective pursued by the enterprise and (c) was necessary for that purpose, then the rule would not be discriminatory, even though it had a disparate impact. (This shows that, unlike cases of direct gender discrimination, there is a defence to indirect discrimination.)

The application of indirect discrimination substantially broadens the scope of EC anti-discrimination rules and permits an analysis of the effects of an otherwise neutral provision. Both the Employment Equality Act, 1998 and the Equal Status Act, 2000 have provisions that bring a similar approach into Irish law.

The leading Irish case on indirect discrimination is the Supreme Court decision in *Nathan v Bailey Gibson* [1998] 2 IR 162. The Court set out the terms of indirect discrimination by saying that a requirement relating to employment, which is not an essential requirement for such employment and in respect of which the proportion of persons of one sex or (as the case may be) of a different marital status but of the same sex able to comply is a substantially higher number may amount to indirect discrimination. The Court said that in such a case it was sufficient for a worker:

> 'to show that the practice complained of bears significantly more heavily on the complainant's sex than on members of the other sex. At that stage the complainant had established a *prima facie* case of discrimination and the onus of proof shifts to the employer to show that the practice complained of is based on objectively verifiable factors which have no relation to the complainant's sex'.

10.7.4   POSITIVE ACTION

As part of their efforts to promote equality, some Member States introduced measures of positive action, or affirmative action as it is sometimes called, to counteract the effect of historical or structural inequalities. Given that such rules are discriminatory in their operation, there has always been controversy regarding their legality. The Equal Treatment Directive contains a provision, Art 2(4), that permits some measures to promote such equality.

After some wavering (see C-450/93 *Kalanke v Freie Hansestadt Bremen* [1995] ECR I-3051), the ECJ in Case C-409/95 *Marschall v Land Nordrhein-Westfalen* [1997] ECR I-6363 sanctioned a law whereby women were to be appointed to a post where, after a fair competition, they were equal with a male candidate. The law was saved because of an exception whereby women would not get priority if there were specific reasons why an individual male ought to get it. The ECJ justified the rule by reference to historical factors and stereotypes against women, which it stated, meant that the fact that a man and a woman ended up equal following a competition, did not mean they had the same chances.

The legitimacy of such positive action measures was further strengthened by the Treaty of Amsterdam which incorporated a new Art 141(4) into the EC Treaty to permit States to adopt measures *'providing for specific advantages in order to make it easier for the under-represented sex to pursue a vocational activity or to prevent or compensate for disadvantages in professional careers'*.

10.7.5 PREGNANCY AND MATERNITY

In addition to the anti-discriminatory aspects of pregnancy, the EC has also adopted other measures to protect pregnant women and women on maternity leave. These rules come from the Pregnancy and Maternity Directive 92/85/EEC. The Directive goes beyond the formal equal treatment approach of equality law by introducing specific benefits to pregnant women and women on maternity leave. Many of the provisions of the Directive relate to the protection of the health of such women, but Arts 8 to 11 protect their employment rights, eg the right not to be sacked during pregnancy and maternity leave. This Directive also introduced the right to maternity leave and the right to return to work after that time. The provisions of the Directive have been transposed into Irish law by the Unfair Dismissals Acts, 1977 and 1993 and the Maternity Protection Act, 1994 as amended.

10.7.6 SOCIAL SECURITY

The Social Security Directive 79/7 implements the principle of equal treatment between men and women in the field of social welfare. The Directive is aimed at legislation that creates social welfare entitlements for workers. It only applies to certain benefits. Article 3(1) sets out the type of scheme covered as:

> '(a) *Statutory schemes which provide protection against the following risks:*
> *Sickness; invalidity; old age; accidents at work and occupational diseases; unemployment;*
> (b) *social assistance, in so far as it is intended to supplement or replace the schemes referred to in (a)'.*

The Directive bans direct and indirect discrimination on the ground of sex and indirect discrimination on the basis of marital and family status. Article 4 of the Directive is one of the more important provisions as it provides that there shall be no discrimination in relation to the scope of the schemes and the conditions of access thereto; the obligation to contribute and the calculation of contributions and the calculation of social welfare benefits.

10.8   Bunreacht na hÉireann 1937

Equality appears in the Constitution under the heading 'Fundamental Rights' and is contained in Article 40.1. The addressee of the right is the State which is prevented from engaging in what is often called invidious discrimination. However, the right is one of the weaker of the fundamental rights. The terms of Article 40.1 amount to a guarantee of equality before the law, not equality as such, and it is designed to ensure that the laws of the State are enforced and apply to all equally.

The protection that stems from Art 40.1 was seen as limited to the essential attributes of human personality, and not persons in other capacities. This severely limited the scope of the protection provided. In one of the most famous explanations of this idea, Walsh J in *Quinn's Supermarket v Attorney General* [1972] IR 1 said:

> 'The provision is not a guarantee of absolute equality for all citizens in all circumstances, but it is a guarantee of equality as human persons and . . . is a guarantee related to their dignity as a human beings and a guarantee against any inequalities grounded on an assumption . . . that some individual . . . by reason of their human attributes or their ethnic or racial, social or religious background, are to be treated as the inferior or superior of other individuals in the community.'

In their analysis of Art 40.1, Hogan and Whyte question whether the human personality doctrine still reflects the actual approach of the judiciary (Hogan and Whyte, 'JM Kelly: The Irish Constitution', 4th edn, 2003, Butterworths, chapter 7.2). The doctrine never applied to cases concerning the administration of justice nor democratic processes. In recent times the judiciary have been willing to discuss a wider principle of equality as a concept that tempers the exercise of power. In *McKenna v An Taoiseach (No. 2)* [1995] 2 IR 10, public financing of one side of a referendum campaign was ruled unconstitutional on the basis that neither side in a democratic exercise should be unequally favoured by government.

Article 40.1 is not a guarantee that all persons shall be treated identically as Walsh J made clear in *State (Nicolaou) v An Bord Uchtala* [1966] IR 567:

> 'Article 40.1 is not to be read as a guarantee or undertaking that all citizens shall be treated by that law as equal for all purposes, but rather as an acknowledgement of the human equality of all citizens.'

This approach gets support from the wording of Art 40.1, which in the second sentence, often called the proviso, allows certain differences to be taken into consideration. Even if there is a differential treatment by the State, it, may be justified if it corresponds with some difference of capacity or social function. This was used in the *Nicolaou* case to deny equal treatment to unmarried fathers, as the court felt there was such a difference in social function between them and their married counterparts.

In fact there have been relatively few cases where the Courts have ruled some State provision unconstitutional on the equality ground. This is in part accounted for by the reluctance to expand the scope of the equality provision, and in part by the preference to develop substantive rights.

In *O'G v Attorney General* [1985] ILRM 61, a widower challenged a rule in the Adoption Act, 1952 that required him to have another child in his custody before an adoption order could be made in his favour. No such requirement was placed on widows. The State sought to defend the law on the basis of differential function between the two, but the courts rejected this, with McMahon J stating he was satisfied that the law was:

> 'founded on an idea of difference in capacity between men and women which has no foundation in fact and . . . is therefore an unwarranted denial of human equality.'

Where the State does make distinctions between groups for the purpose of differential treatment on the ground of different function or capacity, it must not be excessive in the manner in which the distinction is made. In other words, when a statute uses what might be called a suspect classification, the rules adopted must serve a legitimate legislative purpose and the classification must be rationally related to that purpose. *An Blascaod Mór Teo v Commissioners of Public Works (No. 3)* [2000] 1 IR 1, concerned a law imposing compulsory purchase of land, except lands owned by certain persons including descendants of owners/occupiers from a certain date. In declaring the provision invalid Barrington J said of the requirement, at p.19, that:

> 'It is hard to see what legitimate legislative purpose it fulfills. It is based on a principle – that of pedigree – which appears to have no place . . . in a democratic society committed to the principle of equality. This fact alone makes the classification suspect. This court agrees . . . that a constitution should be pedigree blind just as it should be colour blind or gender blind except when those issues are relevant to a legitimate legislative purpose.'

The weakness of the Constitutional guarantee of equality can be seen cases such as *Dennehy v Minister for Social Welfare*, Barron J, 26 July 1984, High Court, (unreported), where a man claimed that the lack of an equivalent payment to men of a deserted wives allowance was unconstitutional. The claim failed as it was felt that there was a difference of function between men and women. A challenge to a similar welfare provision the lone parents allowance, which received a less favourable rate of payment than deserted wives allowance was turned down by both the High Court and the Supreme Court in *Lowth v Minister for Social Welfare* [1998] 4 IR 321. The male plaintiff clamed such differential treatment was unlawfully discriminatory on the ground of sex. The reasons for these decisions lie in the statement of O'Hanlon J in *Madigan v Attorney General* [1986] ILRM 136, where he said:

> 'It has been well recognised . . . that tax laws are in a category of their own, and that very considerable latitude must be allowed to the legislature in the enormously complex task of organising and directing the financial affairs of the State.'

It appears that these, and other, considerations, can easily trump the right to equality.

Those other considerations include other provisions of the Constitution. *O'B v S* [1984] IR 316 concerned a rule of interpretation which had the effect of excluding children born outside marriage from succeeding to the intestate estate of their father under the Succession Act, 1965. The Act was challenged for breaching the child's right to equality with other children, but the Supreme Court refused the claim. In doing so the court stated that this seemingly suspect provision was saved from unconstitutionality because of the protection given to the family based on marriage by Art 41, which justified discrimination against a child born outside marriage. (As a footnote this case went to the European Court of Human Rights and was settled when the State agreed to change the law, which it did in the Status of Children Act, 1987. This also demonstrates how international human rights treaties can be effective.)

10.9   Domestic Legislation

The Employment Equality Act, 1998 and the Equal Status Act, 2000 are the two statutes that particularise anti-discrimination laws within Ireland. The 1998 Act is the principal domestic code dealing with equal treatment at work, while the 2000 Act caters for situations outside the workplace.

10.9.1   THE EMPLOYMENT EQUALITY ACT, 1998

The Employment Equality Act, 1998 extends the grounds of employment-related discrimination beyond the previous bases of sex and marital status. Those two grounds were the only bases for seeking equality under the Anti-Discrimination (Pay) Act, 1974 and the Employment Equality Act, 1977. The 1998 Act replaces those and puts in place a comprehensive list of discriminatory grounds to include, among others: gender; marital status; disability; and family status. There were certain problems with the two former statutes that necessitated reform, not least the limited nature of discriminatory grounds, but also some other matters, including the absence of a definition of sexual harassment.

EQUALITY

The Act is a comprehensive code for dealing with discrimination and harassment in the workplace and one that provides its own enforcement mechanisms, mainly through the Office of the Director of Equality Investigations. It ought to be noted that the Act is not retrospective and only discrimination occurring after its entry into force is covered.

10.9.1.1 The discriminatory grounds

Nine discriminatory grounds are contained in the statute. Gender discrimination is treated separately under the Act and is stronger in effect than the rules applicable to the other grounds, which reflects its root in EC law. As with most equality provisions there is a comparative approach used in that claiming discrimination means claiming to be a member of a class that is treated less favourably than others along preordained lines. Claiming discrimination, eg, as a disabled person, necessarily involves showing different treatment from others without that disability or with a different disability.

The nine grounds upon which discrimination is banned are, in a comparative sense:

(a) the gender ground, ie one is a woman and the other is a man;

(b) the marital status ground, ie they are of different marital status and 'marital status' means being single, married, separated, divorced or widowed;

(c) the family status ground, ie one has family status and the other does not;

(d) they are of different sexual orientation, which is defined as having a heterosexual, homosexual or bisexual orientation;

(e) one has a different religious belief from the other or that one has a religious belief and the other has not, with 'religious belief' being defined as including a religious background or outlook;

(f) that they are of different ages (for the purposes of age discrimination, discrimination is banned for those between 18 and 65 only);

(g) that one is a person with a disability and the other either is not, or is a person with a different disability;

(h) that they are of different race, colour, nationality or ethnic or national origins;

(i) that one is a member of the traveller community and the other is not (referred to as 'the traveller community ground').

In this context, family status is defined in the statute as having responsibility as a parent:

(a) or as a person in *loco parentis* in relation to a person who has not attained the age of 18 years; or

(b) or the resident primary carer in relation to a person of, or over, 18 with a disability which is of such a nature as to give rise to the need for care or support on a continuing, regular or frequent basis.

Disability is defined broadly as:

(a) the total or partial absence of a person's bodily or mental functions, including the absence of a part of a person's body;

(b) the presence in the body of organisms causing, or likely to cause, chronic disease or illness;

(c) the malfunction, malformation or disfigurement of a part of a person's body;

(d) a condition or malfunction which results in a person learning differently from a person without the condition or malfunction; or

(e) a condition, illness or disease which affects a person's thought processes, perception of reality, emotions or judgment or which results in disturbed behaviour and shall be taken to include a disability which exists at present, or which previously existed but no longer exists or which may exist in the future or which is imputed to a person.

The Act deals with discrimination in different ways. Firstly, there are general provisions on discrimination. Part III contains specific provisions relating to discrimination between men and women, while Part IV deals with discrimination on the other grounds. Part V established the Equality Authority, Part VI established Equality Reviews and Action Plans and Part VII deals with remedies and enforcement.

10.9.1.2 Discrimination generally

Discrimination, as defined in s 6, exists where one person is treated less favourably than another is, has been, or would be treated. The Act covers not just discrimination in relation to pay, but also other terms and conditions of employment. Its purpose is to equalise the employment playing field, but not necessarily to improve the quality of the field as such (other than ensuring the worthy aim of a discrimination-free workplace).

The general discrimination prohibition is set out in s 8(1) and provides that in relation to:

- access to employment
- conditions of employment
- training or experience for or in relation to employment
- promotion or re-grading or
- classification of posts

an employer shall not discriminate against an employee or prospective employee and a provider of agency work shall not discriminate against an agency worker. (It should be noted that, throughout the Act, agency workers can only use other agency workers as comparators for discrimination.)

Section 8 also provides that an employer shall not, in relation to employees or employment, have rules or instructions which would result in discrimination against an employee or class of employees in relation to any of the matters specified in points (2) to (5) above or otherwise apply or operate a practice which results, or would be likely to result, in any such discrimination.

In relation to access to employment, eg a job spec, the interview or the criteria for employment, specific rules are provided and the employer will be guilty of discrimination if he or she discriminates in any arrangements made for the purpose of deciding to whom employment should be offered, or by specifying, in respect of one person or class of persons, entry requirements for employment which are not specified in respect of other persons or classes of persons, where the circumstances in which both such persons or classes would be employed are not materially different. (If there are material differences in the circumstances of employment, different specifications can be made.)

Other non-exhaustive but specified discriminations include where the employer does not offer or afford to an employee or prospective employee the same

- terms of employment (other than pay and pensions)
- working conditions and
- treatment in relation to overtime, shift work, short time, transfers, lay-offs, redundancies, dismissals and disciplinary measures

as the employer offers or affords to another person or class of persons, where the circumstances in which both such persons or classes are, or would be, employed are not materially different.

Other provisions include those in s 10 that ban discriminatory job advertisements. This was found to have been breached in *The Equality Authority v Ryanair* [2001] ELR 107 where a job advertisement stated that the respondent needed a 'young and dynamic professional' and that 'the ideal candidate will be young, dynamic . . .' The respondent was found to have discriminated on the ground of age.

Section 11, which covers employment agencies, provides that they cannot discriminate against persons who seek to use the services of the agency to obtain employment (unless the employer in question could lawfully discriminate for that job). Section 12 concerns the provision of vocational training and outlaws discrimination in respect of how courses are offered, by refusing or omitting access to the course or generally, in the manner in which the course is provided. Professional bodies that control the entry to or carrying on of a profession or occupation cannot discriminate in relation to membership of the body or other benefits.

The basis for non-discrimination continues for as long as the employee is willing and able to do the job in question, though care should be taken to ensure that the bases for the incapability or unwillingness are not themselves based on a discrimination, such as making the employment impossible by imposing conditions which themselves are unlawful. The relevant provision in the Act is s 16 and reads in part:

> '(1)   Nothing in this Act shall be construed as requiring any person to recruit or promote an individual . . . if the individual –
>
> (a)   will not undertake . . . the duties attached to that position or will not accept . . . the conditions under which those duties are, or may be required to be, performed, or
>
> (b)   is not . . . fully competent and available to undertake, and fully capable of undertaking, the duties attached to that position, having regard to the conditions under which those duties are, or may be required to be, performed.'

It should be noted that disabled persons have the benefit of reasonable accommodation in the application of this section, see below.

10.9.1.3   Provisions between men and women

Part III of the Act continues the old areas of discrimination in a new context. This Part is mostly a re-enactment of the law as it applied under the 1974 and 1977 Acts in relation to sex. Both of those were based originally on Directive 75/117/EEC and Directive 76/207/EEC and the provisions of the new Act are also so based, which preserves continuity and the jurisdiction of the ECJ. There are three main concerns in this part. The first is to re-enact the entitlement to equal pay, the second to cater for indirect discrimination and the third is to outlaw sexual harassment.

The Act implies a mandatory equal pay clause into all contracts of employment, which is given a broad meaning in this part and includes some contracts for services. Common to all equal pay claims, there are a number of conditions to be established. Firstly, both the employee and the comparator must work for the same or an associated employer. They must both be employed on 'like work', a phrase defined in s 7, and covers situations where they both do the same work, or similar work or work of equal value for an employer or associated employer.

The concept of indirect discrimination has been explicitly extended to cover equal pay claims in s 19(4), which was amended by the EC (Burden of Proof in Gender Discrimination Cases) Regulations, 2001 (SI 337/2001). Where a criterion is applied to all members of a class and results in higher pay for those who satisfy the criterion but where the proportion of one sex who are disadvantaged by the criterion is substantially higher and is not appropriate and necessary and cannot be justified by objective factors unrelated to sex, then the person disadvantaged shall be treated as satisfying, or not (as the case may be), the criterion, whichever results in higher pay.

One recognised example of such indirect discrimination concerns part-time employees. Such workers are often paid less than their full-time counterparts and are often predominantly female. Such was the case in *St Patrick's College, Maynooth v 19 Female Employees* (EP4/84) and, as it was held that working full-time was not an essential requirement unrelated to sex, the pay practice was held to be discriminatory.

Different rates of pay that are not based on any discriminatory ground are permitted. In the past there have been a few generally recognised exceptions. These include 'red-circling', which occurs where an employee is retained on an individually preferential rate of pay, collective bargaining and market forces.

Section 21 concerns direct discrimination, other than pay, and implies an equality clause into all contracts of employment that will override any express contractual stipulation to equalise the positions of the claimant and his or her comparator. The equalisation is by raising the standard of the discriminated person to that of the advantaged person, thus raising the overall standards. The clause does not operate if the difference of treatment is genuinely based on grounds other than gender (and of course discrimination on other grounds will be covered by a similar provision in Part IV of the Act). If the employer claims this, the burden of proof may shift to him or her to prove it.

Cases on non-pay discrimination cover many aspects of the employment relationship, from hiring to firing. Questions at interview, such as asking a woman who will look after her children, have been held to be discriminatory as they would not be asked of a man; see *Gough v St Mary's Credit Union* (EE15/2000). This also applies to statements made outside the formal interview, see *Rodmell v TCD* (EE31/2000) where the claimant was identified as a 'lady electrician.'

In *Rotunda Hospital v Gleeson* (DEE-003/2000, 18 April 2000), the claimant was discriminated against on the ground of gender in relation to the appointment to the post of consultant obstetrician/gynaecologist. The Labour Court noted that unfavourable comments had been made during the interview that identified the claimant by her sex, a male-dominated interview panel was used and that the claimant was more qualified for the post than the appointed male. The court awarded the claimant £50,000, one of the highest awards made.

Indirect discrimination on grounds other than pay is covered by s 22, which was amended by the EC (Burden of Proof in Gender Discrimination Cases) Regulations, 2001 (SI 337/2001) and now provides:

'(1) Where a provision (whether in the nature of a requirement, practice or otherwise) which relates to any of the matters specified in paragraphs (a) to (e) of section 8(1) or to membership of a regulatory body —
(a) applies to both A and B,
(b) is such that the proportion of persons who are disadvantaged by the provision is substantially higher in the case of those of the same sex as A than in the case of those of the same sex as B, and
(c) is not appropriate and necessary and cannot be justified by objective factors unrelated to A's sex,
then, for the purposes of this Act, A's employer or, as the case may be, the regulatory body shall be regarded as discriminating against A on the gender ground . . .'

In assessing the disparate impact a provision has, a statistical or numerical analysis is often used. In *Wilson v The Adelaide and Meath Hospital* (DEC-E2002–025) a female ward attendant applied for the post of permanent porter. A requirement for the post was to have previous experience as a porter. In considering a claim that the requirement constituted indirect discrimination, the equality officer held that the appropriate pool of people within which to analyse the claim were the 13 interviewees, made up of nine males and four females. All four females and one male could not fulfil the requirement of experience. The practice disadvantaged 100 per cent of females but only eleven per cent of males, which was held to be 'substantially higher' within the meaning of s 22. The onus fell on the respondent to justify the requirement, which in this case it was unable to do.

10.9.1.4 Sexual harassment

Sexual harassment is for the first time given a statutory definition. Before the 1998 Act, sexual harassment was dealt with as discrimination and was unlawful on that basis. In *A Garage Proprietor v A Worker* (EE2/1985) the Labour Court stated that 'freedom from sexual harassment is a condition of work which an employee of either sex is entitled to expect.' Although commentators were generally pleased with the manner in which the Labour Court dealt with sexual harassment, specific provision was necessary. In addition, there were issues relating to the vicarious liability of employers for sexual harassment, which stemmed from the absence of a statutory definition.

That definition now states:

> 'If, at the workplace or otherwise in the course of A's employment, B sexually harasses A and either —
>
> (a)   A and B are both employed at the same workplace or by the same employer, or
>
> (b)   B is A's employer, or
>
> (c)   B is a client, customer or other business contact of A's employer and the circumstances of the harassment are such that A's employer ought reasonably to have taken steps to prevent it, then, for the purposes of this Act, the sexual harassment constitutes discrimination by A's employer, on the gender ground, in relation to A's conditions of employment'.

Without prejudice to the above, it is provided that if, in a case where one of the conditions in paragraphs (a) to (c) above is fulfilled —

(a)   B sexually harasses A, whether or not in the workplace or in the course of A's employment; and

(b)   A is treated differently in the workplace or otherwise in the course of A's employment by reason of A's rejection or acceptance of the sexual harassment or it could reasonably be anticipated that A would be so treated,

then, for the purposes of the Act, the sexual harassment constitutes discrimination by A's employer, on the gender ground, in relation to A's conditions of employment.

For the purposes of the Act —

(a)   any act of physical intimacy by B towards A;

(b)   any request by B for sexual favours from A; or

(c)   any other act or conduct of B (including spoken words, gestures or the production, display or circulation of written words, pictures or other material);

shall constitute sexual harassment of A by B if the act, request or conduct is unwelcome to A and could reasonably be regarded as sexually or otherwise on the gender ground, offensive, humiliating or intimidating to A.

In this, 'A' is the victim of sexual harassment, and 'B' is the perpetrator. It can be noted that the test encompasses a mixed subjective and objective test but does not explain how they are to be measured. One other difficulty to be noted is that sexual harassment is seen as a form of gender discrimination, which would rule out same-sex sexual harassment, though this will most likely be covered by the anti-harassment provisions concerning the other eight grounds of discrimination in Part IV. The sexual harassment must occur in the workplace (and note the coverage of environmental harassment) or during a course of employment, for the employer to be liable. There is a defence for employers under s 23(5) if they took reasonable steps to prevent the conduct and, where it has occurred, reverse its effects.

10.9.1.5　Discrimination on other grounds

Part IV covers discrimination on the other eight grounds. In many ways, the provisions here mirror those in Part III in that there are bans on direct and indirect discrimination in relation to pay and other matters. The methods of enforcement are also similar in that the mechanism of contract modification is used. In this part, the claimant and comparator are called 'C' and 'D' respectively, which makes the statute difficult to read. Thus, if the claimant 'C' is married then 'D' will be single, widowed or divorced; if 'C' is disabled, 'D' will not be or will have a different disability.

The right to equal pay on grounds other than sex is covered by s 29, which covers both direct and indirect discrimination. One difference is that instead of justification by 'objective factors unrelated to sex', the indirect pay discrimination on non-sex grounds 'cannot be justified as being reasonable in all the circumstances of the case', which is more open-ended. In *Langan v C-Town Ltd* (DEC-E2003–010) a claim for equal pay was successful where it was found that a worker who was nineteen years younger than his comparator performed like work.

Section 30 concerns direct discrimination, other than pay, and implies an equality clause that will override any express contractual stipulation to equalise the positions of the claimant and the comparator. Section 31 deals with indirect discrimination on the non-gender grounds. Section 32 bans harassment in the workplace on the basis of the relevant characteristic, ie being of a particular sexual orientation, being disabled, etc. The ban is in the same terms as sexual harassment. However, it is not strong enough to comprehensively deal generally with bullying in the workplace as the harassment suffered by a person must be because of his or her possession of a protected characteristic.

10.9.1.6　Reasonable accommodation for disabled workers

Section 16 of the Act introduces an important special provision for disabled workers. This is a recognition that such workers may require material changes to the workplace and to the manner in which work is structured to ensure they are capable of undertaking the task. Without such a provision, the general terms of s 16 that relate to an employee's competence to work could operate against disabled workers.

It is provided that, for the purposes of the Act, a person who has a disability shall not be regarded as other than fully competent to undertake, and fully capable of undertaking, any duties if, with the assistance of special treatment or facilities, such person would be fully competent to undertake, and be fully capable of undertaking, those duties. More importantly, the Act imposes an obligation on employers to do all that is reasonable to accommodate the needs of a person who has a disability by providing such special treatment or facilities.

However, the amount of such provision is limited as s 16 further provides: 'A refusal or failure to provide for special treatment or facilities . . . shall not be deemed reasonable unless such provision would give rise to a cost, other than a nominal cost, to the employer.' This is known as the 'nominal cost' exception and may operate to seriously restrict the provision of special treatment. The Bill as originally formulated proposed a cost exception based on undue hardship, but that was deemed unconstitutional by the Supreme Court in *Re Article 26 and the Employment Equality Bill 1996* [1997] 2 IR 321.

From the early case-law under the Act, it seems clear that an employer must explore the options available to accommodate the needs of a disabled employee and that discrimination is committed by such a failure; see *Kehoe v Convertec Ltd* (DEC-E – 2001–034). In *A Computer Component Company v A Worker* (EED-013/2001), the Labour Court was dealing with a case of discriminatory dismissal where the employee was dismissed because of her epilepsy. The respondent defended the action by claiming that the employee was, because of her disability, not fully competent and capable of performing her duties, and that her need could not have been accommodated. However, the court held that if the employer concluded that she could not do her job, it had done so precipitously as it did not undertake, nor did it even consider undertaking, any safety assessment to assess any danger level from her disability or how to ameliorate any such danger. The Court stated, in finding for the claimant, that:

> 'On the evidence, the Court does not accept that the respondent could reasonably and objectively have come to the conclusion that the complainant was not fully competent or capable of performing the duties of her employment. Even if the respondent did reach such a conclusion, it is abundantly clear that it did not give the slightest consideration to providing the complainant with reasonable special facilities which would accommodate her needs and so overcome any difficulty which she or the respondent might otherwise experience.'

In *An Employee v A Local Authority* (DEC-E2002/4) the equality officer held that in assessing the size of a nominal cost, all employers are not to be treated in an identical fashion. It would appear that more will be expected of large employers.

The EC framework Directive 2000/78/EC of 27 November, 2000, contains protections for disabled workers and includes a more onerous obligation of reasonable accommodation. The proper transposition of that Directive into Irish law will require an amendment to the 1998 Act, to the benefit of disabled workers. The Equality Bill 2004 will, if passed, impose an obligation of reasonable accommodation to take appropriate measures, unless the measures would impose a disproportionate burden on the employer.

10.9.1.7 Positive action

Section 24 of the Act contains some provisions catering for positive discrimination, but is merely permissive of steps to promote equal opportunities between men and women and does not demand any measures in particular. In effect, it permits an employer to take positive steps to remove existing inequalities which affect women's opportunities at work. Section 26(1) permits treatment which confers benefits on women in connection with breast-feeding and maternity or adoption.

In relation to the non-gender grounds, some positive action is permitted by s 33. Measures to reduce or eliminate discrimination against certain workers are permitted to facilitate their integration into the workplace. The particular workers permitted this special treatment are:

(a) persons who have attained the age of 50 years;

(b) persons with a disability or any class or description of such persons; or

(c) members of the Traveller community.

Section 35(2) permits, again without demanding, positive action for disabled workers by providing that nothing in the Act shall make it unlawful for an employer or any other person to provide, for a person with a disability, special treatment or facilities where the provision of that treatment or those facilities –

(a) enables or assists that person to undertake vocational training, to take part in a selection process or to work; or

(b) provides that person with a training or working environment suited to the disability; or

(c) otherwise assists that person in relation to vocational training or work.

10.9.1.8 Exceptions

The Act contains exceptions that permit some discrimination. In relation to the gender ground, s 25 permits certain discrimination where a person's sex amounts to an occupational qualification for the post in question. Such discrimination is permitted where, for example, it is required by reason of physiology (other than strength or stamina) or on the grounds of authenticity for entertainment or where a post involves personal services and it is necessary to have persons of both sexes employed or where the employment necessarily involves the provision of sleeping and sanitary accommodation for employees on a communal basis and it would be unreasonable or impracticable to expect the provision of separate accommodation.

Under s 26(2), the Act does not apply to employment which consists of the performance of personal services, such as the care of an elderly or incapacitated person, in that person's home, where the sex of the employee is a determining factor.

The exceptions for the non-gender grounds are contained in s 34. Section 34(1), which applies to the eight non-gender grounds, permits an employer to provide a benefit to:

(a) an employee in respect of events related to members of the employee's family or any description of those members;

(b) or in respect of a person as a member of an employee's family;

(c) an employee on or by reference to an event occasioning a change in the marital status of the employee; or

(d) an employee who has family status, intended directly to provide or assist in the provision, during working hours, of care for a person for whom the employee has responsibility.

While these rules have been lauded as helping to engender a family-orientated workplace, they may have some serious downsides, foremost among which is caused by the marriage-based definition of family in the Act. It would appear that benefits given to a spouse do not have to be given to a cohabitee, despite being prima facie discriminatory on the grounds of marital status. In fact, this rolls back the law as such discrimination was banned under the old law. In *Eagle Star Insurance Co v A Worker* [1998] ELR 306, a scheme whereby staff and their spouses received discounted insurance was found to discriminate against a cohabitating employee. Under the 1998 Act, it is unclear whether a similar rule would be unlawful as it may be permitted by the exception.

Section 34(3) provides that nothing in the Act shall make unlawful discrimination on the age or disability ground in circumstances where it is shown that there is clear actuarial or other evidence that significantly increased costs would result if the discrimination were not permitted in those circumstances. It is also provided in s 34(4) that it shall not constitute discrimination on the age ground to fix different ages for the retirement (whether voluntarily or compulsorily) of employees or any class or description of employees. Section 34(5) states that it shall not constitute discrimination on the age ground to set a maximum age for recruitment which takes account of:

(a) any cost or period of time involved in training a recruit to a standard at which the recruit will be effective in that job; and

(b) the need for there to be a reasonable period of time prior to retirement age during which the recruit will be effective in that job.

Section 34(7) provides that it shall not constitute discrimination on the age ground for an employer to provide for different persons different rates of remuneration or different terms and conditions of employment if the difference is based on their relative seniority (or length of service) in a particular post or employment.

These age provisions have caused concern as it seems that what the Act gives with one hand, it takes away with another. It also perpetuates notions that the elderly should not be re-trained as they might not stay long enough in the employment for the employer to benefit. Of course, the legal regime does not itself facilitate workers who do in fact wish to work beyond retirement age. The same is true for disabled persons. However, clear actuarial or other evidence is required before those sub-sections can operate to the detriment of the aged or disabled and it would follow that it is for the employer to provide and prove that.

Disabled workers face more difficulties from s 35 with regard to equal pay. The pay provision allows a difference in pay if disabled workers cannot work the same hours or do the same amount of work because of the disability but without reference to different number of hours. The ethos would again appear to view the disabled worker as having a lower work ability.

Finally, s 37 allows a religious, educational or medical institution to preserve their ethos, as they will not be taken to discriminate by preferring one employee over another where reasonable to protect that ethos. The section itself is very unclear as to when this exception applies and as to its scope and fears have been expressed that it could allow discrimination. The section appears to be a kind of a statutory replication of the decision in the case of *Flynn v Power* [1985] ILRM 336, where an unmarried teacher was sacked while pregnant. The school was run by a Roman Catholic order which had demanded, before the applicant became pregnant, that she terminate her extra-marital relationship. The High Court held that this did not constitute dismissal on the grounds of pregnancy, but was because the applicant's behaviour was a rejection of the school's religious tenets.

10.9.1.9 The Equality Authority

Part V establishes the Equality Authority which takes over from the former Employment Equality Agency. Its functions are to work towards eliminating discrimination in employment, promote equality of opportunity and provide information to the public on the workings of this and other Acts. The Authority is empowered to draw up codes of practice for the promotion of equality and ending discrimination. A code can be approved by the Minister and if this is done it becomes admissible in evidence in proceedings under the Act and 'shall be taken into account in determining' the issue. The Authority gives general advice on discrimination law and can sponsor cases under discrimination law.

The Authority can also conduct inquiries into certain matters and employ others for that purpose, once a term of reference has been set. This shows the pro-active nature of the Authority's role. The inquiry is given information-gathering powers in relation to the investigation, which can result in reports and recommendations being made. If a breach of the Act is found during the investigation the Authority can serve a non-discrimination notice, calling on the employer, etc., to cease the matter in question. The Authority must hear representations made by the employer, who can also appeal to the Labour Court against the findings. The notices can be enforced by High Court or Circuit Court injunction. Failure to comply with the notice is a criminal offence.

10.9.1.10 Remedies

The Act establishes a Director of Equality Investigations. All claims, other than dismissal or gender discrimination, must be referred first to this office. Hearings will take place before an Equality Officer appointed by the Director. The forum is now called the Equality Tribunal. Cases of dismissal on a discriminatory ground must go to the Labour Court. Gender discrimination cases may be taken to the Circuit Court, where it should be noted there is no monetary limit on awards.

In pursuing claims, the claimant is given a right to information from the respondent, though some exceptions are allowed regarding confidential information. In particular, no information can be given concerning a particular individual without his or her consent, which will be important in equal pay claims.

A limitation period of six months applies to making a complaint from the date of the most recent occurrence of the act of discrimination, which can be extended in exceptional circumstances.

would amount to discrimination. Discrimination by association is an important matter for a law of this nature to cover as the nature of discrimination is to base exclusion on matters of irrelevance. The exact nature of association is a matter that should be clarified, but a standard definition would limit the concept to availing of a service together with a person with the characteristic. This would be a conservative approach and a broader meaning should be considered to ensure proper protection.

The final definition of discrimination caters for indirect discrimination and occurs where a person is a member of a protected category and is required to comply with a condition that substantially more people outside the category can comply with, where the obligation to comply with the condition cannot be justified as reasonable in the circumstances. The inclusion of indirect discrimination is vital because discrimination often occurs in covert ways, as service providers are unlikely to directly discriminate, especially when they learn of the consequences of so doing. The ban on indirect discrimination means that supposedly neutral criteria cannot be used to cloak what in reality amounts to unlawful unequal treatment. For a bar to have a requirement of living in a house would amount to indirect discrimination on the Traveller community ground as substantially more non-Travellers can comply with it and it would appear difficult to justify it as a reasonable requirement for being provided with a service otherwise available to the 'general public'.

10.10.1 ACTIVITIES COVERED

One of the central provisions of the Act, contained in s 5, is to ban discrimination in the disposal of goods or the provision of services that are available to the public generally or a section of the public. It is irrelevant that the service or goods are given for consideration or not. The State is not specifically included in the definition of service provider and this was a cause for criticism among interested groups, but the law will cover the State regardless. Service is defined more particularly, but without prejudice to generality, as access to and the use of any place; facilities for banking, insurance, loans, etc., entertainment, cultural activities and transport; services provided by a club and professional or trade services.

For the first time in Irish law a business cannot refuse to serve a person simply because he or she falls into one of the categories. A black person cannot be refused service on the basis of being black nor a woman because she is a woman. In this regard, the nature of the law must be understood. It is not a demand that everyone in a protected class be served at all times, but just that they be treated the same as anyone else in relation to that service. To the extent that the provision of any service is discriminatory of someone else who cannot thereby avail of the service the Act will require an equality of discrimination.

In *O'Reilly v Q Bar* [2003] ELR 35, a 72-year-old was discriminated against on the ground of age when he was refused admission to a bar that catered predominantly for younger persons. In *Gallagher v Merlin's Night Club* (DEC-S2002–133), the claimant was successful in a gender discrimination case where he was refused admission to a nightclub because he was wearing sandals. A woman in the claimant's company was admitted while wearing similar sandals and the claimant was told by a doorman that women were permitted wear sandals in the club.

In *Maughan v The Glimmerman* (DEC-S2001–020) a blanket ban on children being present on a licensed premises with their parents was found to be discriminatory of those parents on the basis of their family status.

As a result of changes introduced by Part 4 of the Intoxicating Liquor Act, 2003 all claims for discrimination against licenced premises are now referred to the District Court. That Act also permits a measure of age discrimination in pubs, in that a policy of not serving persons below a specified age is permitted as long as the policy is displayed on the premises and is implemented in good faith.

There are some exceptions in s 5(2) where this principle of equal treatment is abrogated. Differences on the gender ground in relation to services of an aesthetic or cosmetic nature where the services require physical contact are excluded. For example, a women's hairdresser need not serve men and vice versa. Other permissible differences of treatment include that in relation to the provision of pensions, insurance policies and other matters related to the assessment of risk, where there is clear actuarial evidence to justify the difference, disposals of goods by will or gift and there is also an exception relating to sporting events. Age requirements for a person to be an adoptive or foster parent are specifically excluded as are cultural performances where persons can be treated differently on gender, age and disability for reasons of authenticity. While the list of exceptions is long they appear necessary as otherwise some peculiar consequences would follow. Indeed this reflects the true notion of equality of treating similar things the same but differences differently.

Section 6 deals with the provision of accommodation and provides that nobody shall discriminate in the disposal of any estate or interest in premises or in providing accommodation or any services relating thereto. This does not apply to disposals by gift or will. Neither does it apply where the provision of accommodation or disposal is in respect of a small premises (which is defined as accommodation for not more than three households (in relation to accommodation for more than one such) or, as the case may be, six persons in addition to the resident person), when the person making the disposal, a near relative or other person with an interest in the property intends to reside there. Grounds of privacy in relation to accommodation of one gender is included as an exemption. Overall, this provision will be a marked improvement for many people seeking accommodation. Landlords will have to be particularly careful to ensure that only objective factors are used to decide to whom to let premises. For example, in the past many pregnant women have had difficulties securing rented accommodation. Discrimination on that basis will now be unlawful.

The admission and access to courses of education are covered by s 7, which also bans discrimination in relation to the punishment and sanction of students. This is a welcome addition to the notion of service provision and demonstrates the broad nature of the Act in the remit of activities covered. Again, some discrimination is permitted, eg if a non-third level establishment admits students of one gender only then it is not unlawful to exclude members of the opposite gender, and schools which promote religious values are entitled to prefer students of that religion, so long as a refusal to admit a student is essential to maintain the ethos of the school. This latter test is very stringent, as it will be difficult to prove that the exclusion of a potential student is essential for the ethos in question. Other equality related obligations are placed on universities by s 36 of the Universities Act, 1997.

One particularly notorious form of discrimination in Ireland has been the refusal of some golf and tennis clubs to admit women. This, along with discrimination on the other protected grounds, is unlawful under s 8 of the Act, which draws discrimination widely in this regard as having a rule, policy or practice which discriminates against a member or applicant for membership, or where a person involved in management so discriminates. By covering not just rules and policies, but extending the provisions to practices, clubs that operate subtle forms of making certain persons unwelcome are in danger of breaching the law. Section 9 allows certain clubs to discriminate, for example if its purpose is to provide for a particular religion, age, nationality or national origin.

The sanction against discriminating clubs is somewhat different to those generally under the Act. When a club is accused, by an individual or the Equality Authority, of discrimination the matter goes to the District Court for determination and if found to be discriminating, no certificate of registration can issue or be renewed under the Registration of Clubs Acts, 1904 to 1995, in other words the club will lose its drink license. This is a proper sanction as such a license is a benefit given by the State and there is no reason to allow it continue to benefit a discriminating club. It appears that other remedies under the Act can also be pursued by persons discriminated against.

10.10.2 REASONABLE ACCOMMODATION FOR THE DISABLED

One group that requires more than just formal equality is the disabled. Often, because of the disability, such persons need special provision to ensure their right to full participation in society. In this regard, ss 17, 18 and 19 cater for public transport and the disabled. Section 17 permits the Minister to make regulations to ensure that new road and rail passenger vehicles are equipped so as to be readily accessible to, and usable by, persons with a disability. Section 18 applies similar rules to bus and rail stations while s 19 provides that local authorities shall provide dipped footpaths near pedestrian crossings, etc., to facilitate disabled users. The Act does not extend its provisions to taxis and hackneys.

Throughout the Act, there are provisions that allow some special rules for promoting special interests of certain groups. Without such an express rule, special provision might itself be discriminatory, and in effect they allow for the unequal treatment of some groups, including the disabled. However, these provisions do not demand special treatment. For disabled people, s 4 is of crucial importance in this regard by providing that failure by a service provider to do all that is reasonable to accommodate a disabled person by providing special treatment or facilities, if without such it would be impossible or unduly difficult for a disabled person to avail of the service, amounts to discrimination under the Act. Section 4(2) says that a failure to provide special treatment will not be reasonable unless the provision would give rise to a cost, other than a nominal cost, to the service provider.

In *Roche v Alabaster Associates Ltd* [2002] ELR 343, a visually impaired person was refused permission to bring his guide dog into a pub. The respondent claimed that this was due to food hygiene regulations. The equality officer held that the respondent knew of the disability, did not do all that was reasonable to accommodate the needs of the claimant and that the food hygiene regulations did not compel the dog's exclusion. The pub was ordered to pay the maximum compensation under the Act to the claimant.

10.10.3 MISCELLANEOUS

Sexual and other harassment has been recognised as a serious problem in the workplace, but it may also happen in other environments. Section 12 of the Act outlaws both of these. Sexual harassment occurs where one person subjects the victim to an act of physical intimacy, requests sexual favours from the victim or subjects that person to conduct with sexual connotations or displays, in circumstances where the conduct is unwelcome and could be reasonably regarded as offensive, humiliating or intimidating to him or her. This is a broad definition that mirrors that under the Employment Equality Act, 1998. For instance it covers not just direct sexual harassment, but also environmental harassment, eg where a club is decked with lewd pictures of naked women. Harassment is treatment akin to sexual harassment, but caters for the other discriminatory grounds. An example would be racist posters in a shop or abusive name-calling by a service provider to a member of the Traveller community.

Mention should also be made of s 15, reputedly introduced at the behest of publicans. The section provides, for greater certainty, that nothing requires a service provider to provide service in circumstances which would lead a reasonable individual to the belief, on grounds other than the discriminatory grounds, that the provision of services would create a substantial risk of criminal or disorderly conduct or behaviour or damage to property.

Section 15(2) provides that actions taken in good faith by a liquor license holder for the sole purpose of complying with the Licensing Acts, 1833 to 1999 shall not amount to discrimination. In *Maughan v The Glimmerman* (DEC-S2001–020), the claimant was refused service in a bar, which attempted to rely on this provision in its defence. The equality officer held that the respondent could not do so in circumstances where it had no previous knowledge of the claimant or his associates so a refusal could not have been made 'in good faith' for fear of breach of the licensing Acts. In *Conroy v Costello* (DEC-S2001–014), it was held that: 'In order to take an action in good faith it has to be free of any discriminatory motivation.' In *Collins v Drogheda Lodge Pub* (DEC-S2002–097/100), it was held that the issue of good faith was to be judged subjectively.

10.10.4 ENFORCEMENT

The enforcement procedures under the Act are similar to those under the Employment Equality Act and the same offices are to be used. The Equality Authority and the Director of Equality Investigations will have a role in all Irish anti-discrimination cases. A person who claims to have suffered prohibited conduct must first raise the matter with the service provider within two months (in exceptional cases this time can be extended by a further two months by the Director of Equality Investigations.) If the claimant gets an unsatisfactory response or if there is no response after one month, he or she can refer the case to the Director within six months of the incident, which can be extended in exceptional cases. The complainant must be the person who suffered the discrimination. The Equality Authority can also refer cases to the Director, where the conduct is of a general nature or where the person who suffered discrimination would not reasonably be expected to take a case.

As noted above, claims of discrimination against pubs are now referred to the District Court; see Part 4 of the Intoxicating Liquor Act, 2003.

It should also be noted that equality officers have adopted the shifting burden of proof in making Decisions under the Act in similar manner to that employed to the non-gender grounds under the 1998 Act. In several cases, it has been stated that a claimant must prove three matters to establish a prima facie case of discrimination and thereby shift the burden of proof to the respondent. These are:

(a) membership of a discriminatory ground;

(b) evidence of specific treatment of the claimant by the respondent;

(c) evidence that the treatment received by the claimant was less favourable than the treatment someone not covered by that ground did or would have received in similar circumstances.

The Director is given wide powers of investigation under the Act and if satisfied that the claim is made out, can order damages up to the District Court limit, €6,348.69 (£5,000). The Director can also order that specified persons take a certain course of action designed to stop the discriminatory activity. An appeal lies from the determination of the Director to the Circuit Court, and from there to the High Court on a point of law. A decision of the Director can be enforced by the Circuit Court where a person fails to comply with it.

10.11 Conclusion

Given the recent enactment of much of the core domestic equality legislation, this area of law is still in a state of development in Ireland. The exact scope of many of the provisions of those laws remain to be adjudicated upon. Other changes may also have an impact on the development of equality law. The long-awaited incorporation of the European Convention on Human Rights may deepen the protection given to the right to equal treatment. The transposition of the new EC equality directives will also strengthen the protection afforded to the right to equality in this country.

CHAPTER 11

CIVIL RIGHTS: THE NORTH AMERICAN EXPERIENCE

11.1   Introduction

This chapter takes a comparative look at civil rights in North America, specifically Canada and the United States. Although neighbours, both have had separate histories and have undergone very different paths, with some civil liberties having more of an impact in one country than in the other. The Constitution is seen as the supreme instrument in Canada and in the United States for guaranteeing fundamental rights, affording the utmost protection to individuals, and the Supreme Court in both countries is seen as the ultimate guarantor of those rights, affording a legal recourse of redress to citizens.

The Canadian Constitution, which includes the Canadian Charter of Rights and Freedoms, was proclaimed into force on 17 April 1982, with its purpose to protect and safeguard the rights and freedoms enumerated, and to contain governmental action within reasonable limits. Section 52(1) provides:

> '52(1) The Constitution of Canada is the supreme law of Canada and any law that is inconsistent with the provisions of the Constitution is, to the extent of the inconsistency, of no force or effect.'

The American Constitution was signed on 17 September 1787, with several Amendments added over the years in order to guarantee citizens additional protection of their rights. The seminal case of *Marbury v Madison*, 1 Cranch 137 (1803), underscored the important principle that the Constitution is the supreme law of the land. The Supremacy Clause of the Constitution is contained in Article VI, which states:

> 'VI. This Constitution, and the laws of the United States which shall be made in pursuance thereof; and all treaties made, or which shall be made, under the authority of the United States, shall be the supreme law of the land; and the judges in every state shall be bound thereby, anything in the Constitution or laws of any State to the contrary notwithstanding.'

The five substantive areas covered in this book will be examined in this chapter from the North American perspective: due process of law – civil and criminal – including the burden of proof; freedom of expression; the right to life – abortion and the death penalty; family law; and equal rights and equal protection. The important elements of the respective Constitutions along with seminal cases in the areas will be examined according to their peculiar and interesting impacts on Canadian and American society.

11.2 Due Process of Law

11.2.1 CIVIL DUE PROCESS

In examining civil due process, one must also examine the important concept of the burden of proof. In looking at civil due process in Canada, the Supreme Court, in interpreting the Constitution, uses the purposive approach, whereby the underlying purpose of the legislative provision and the nature of the interest are identified. It is important to note that fundamental freedoms can be subjected to several constitutional opting-out clauses. Section 33 of the Constitution is the infamous notwithstanding clause, allowing the Canadian provinces to opt out of the Constitution for successive and infinite five-year periods, providing:

> '33. Parliament or the legislature of a province may expressly declare in an act of Parliament or of the legislature . . . that the act or a provision thereof shall operate notwithstanding a provision included in . . . Section . . . 15 of this Charter.'

Further, s 1 of the Constitution is the infamous overriding clause, stating:

> '1. The Canadian Charter of Rights and Freedoms set out is subject only to such reasonable limits prescribed by law as can be demonstrably justified in a free and democratic society.'

When examining the burden of proof, a two-step procedure is utilised by the Canadian Supreme Court to see whether the limit contained in s 1 can uphold an infringement of a right: Firstly, has the right been violated? Secondly, can the violation be justified under s 1? The burden of proof is such that the onus of establishing a prima facie infringement of the Charter is on the person alleging it, while the onus of justifying a reasonable limit on the protected right is on the party invoking s 1, and the standard is a preponderance of probabilities. To come within s 1 of the Charter, two criteria must be satisfied. Firstly, the objective of the limiting measure must be sufficiently important, and the concerns must be pressing and substantial to justify overriding a constitutionally protected right. Secondly, the means must be reasonable and demonstrably justified according to a proportionality test, which balances the interests of society against those of individuals. There are three components to the test:

(a) the measure must be carefully designed to achieve the stated objective, and must not be arbitrary, unfair or irrational;

(b) the measure should impair the right as little as possible; and

(c) proportionality must exist between the effect of the limiting measure and its objectives (*R v Oakes*, [1986] 1 SCR 103).

In looking at civil due process in the United States, the Fifth and Fourteenth Amendments of the Constitution, enacted in 1791 and 1868 respectively are of paramount importance in the fight for civil rights. With the due process clause of the Fifth Amendment including an equal protection component and applying to both civil and criminal due process, the Fifth and Fourteenth Amendments provide due process of law and equal protection to citizens from federal and state actions, respectively. The due process clauses state:

> 'Amendment V
> No person shall be . . . deprived of life, liberty, or property, without due process of law. . . .'

> 'Amendment XIV
> 1. . . . No state shall . . . deprive any person of life, liberty, or property, without due process of law.'

In examining the burden of proof, the United States Supreme Court has developed three different levels of review, depending upon the type of action brought in a legal proceeding.

The Court will examine the legislative purpose of the governmental action alleged to be contrary to the constitutional amendments, and will choose among the three levels of scrutiny in evaluating a case.

The *strict scrutiny level* is applied where the classification is suspect, affecting fundamental rights, such as in racial discrimination cases. This test is the highest level of review, where the defendant government must show a compelling interest for the restriction – a hard burden to meet. It requires a precisely tailored objective to a compelling government interest, with no less drastic means available (*Plyler v Doe*, 457 US 202 (1982)), and is used where there has been 'a history of purposeful unequal treatment . . . and a position of political powerlessness' (*San Antonio Independent School Dist v Rodriguez*, 411 US 1 (1973)).

The *heightened scrutiny level* applied to quasi-suspect cases, such as in gender discrimination cases, which will be examined later in the right to equality. This test is the intermediary level of review, where the defendant government must show that the restriction has a substantial relationship to an important government interest. The equal protection clause and the due process clause of the Fifth and Fourteenth Amendments confer a consti-tutional right to be free from discrimination, which does not serve an important govern-ment objective or is not substantially related to the achievement of the objective (*Davis v Passman*, 442 US 228 (1979)).

The *minimum rationality level* applied to see the rational basis for the means to the ends. This test is the lowest level of review, where the plaintiff must show that there is no rational basis for the State restriction – a hard burden to meet as the State has a legitimate interest in regulating an activity within its jurisdiction. The governmental classification will not offend the Constitution's equal protection clause 'simply because it is not made with material nicety or because in practice it results in some inequality' (*Dandridge v Williams*, 397 US 471 (1970)), but will fail if the unequal distinction 'rests on grounds wholly irrelevant to the achievement of the State's objective' (*McGowan v Maryland*, 366 US 420 (1961)).

11.2.2   CRIMINAL DUE PROCESS

In looking at criminal due process in Canada, the Canadian Constitution guarantees vari-ous criminal law rights vital to every stage of a prosecution. Section 7 is important and states:

> '7.   *Everyone has the right to life, liberty and security of the person and the right not to be deprived thereof except in accordance with the principles of fundamental justice.'*

Prior to arrest, ss 8 and 9 enumerate the rights guaranteed:

> '8.   *Everyone has the right to be secure against unreasonable search or seizure.'*

> '9.   *Everyone has the right not to be arbitrarily detained or imprisoned.'*

Upon arrest, s 10 lists a number of rights, among them the fundamental right to counsel:

> '10.   *Everyone has the right on arrest or detention:*
>   *(a)   to be informed promptly of the reason therefor;*
>   *(b)   to retain and instruct counsel without delay and to be informed of that right; and*
>   *(c)   to have the validity of the detention determined by way of habeas corpus and to be released if the detention is not lawful.'*

Once charged with an offence, s 11 guarantees certain rights, among them the double jeopardy clause and important right to be tried within a reasonable time:

> '11.   *Any person charged with an offence has the right:*
>   *(a)   to be informed without unreasonable delay of the specific offence;*

(b)   to be tried within a reasonable time;

(c)   not to be compelled to be a witness in a proceeding against that person in respect of the offence;

(d)   to be presumed innocent until proven guilty according to law in a fair and public hearing by an independent and impartial tribunal; . . .

(f)   except in the case of an offence under military law tried before a military tribunal, to the benefit of trial by jury where the maximum punishment for the offence is imprisonment for five years or a more severe punishment;

(g)   if finally acquitted of the offence, not to be tried for it again and, if finally found guilty and punished for the offence, not to be tried or punished for it again.'

In looking at criminal due process in the United States, several Amendments to the American Constitution were enacted in 1791, to guarantee important rights essential in the criminal law process. Amendments IV and V outline important rights, including the double jeopardy clause and of course the due process clause already mentioned:

'Amendment IV
The right of the people to be secure in their persons, houses, papers, and effects, against unreasonable searches and seizures, shall not be violated, and no warrants shall issue, but upon probable cause, supported by oath or affirmation, and particularly describing the place to be searched, and the persons or things to be seized.'

'Amendment V
No person shall be held to answer for a capital, or otherwise infamous crime, unless on a presentment or indictment of a grand jury . . .; nor shall any person be subject for the same offense to be twice put in jeopardy of life or limb; nor shall be compelled in any criminal case to be a witness against himself, nor be deprived of life, liberty, or property, without due process of law.'

Amendment VI guarantees the vital right to counsel and the right to a speedy trial:

'Amendment VI
In all criminal prosecutions, the accused shall enjoy the right to a speedy and public trial, by an impartial jury of the state and district wherein the crime shall have been committed . . ., and to be informed of the nature and cause of the accusation; to be confronted with the witnesses against him; to have compulsory process for obtaining witnesses in his favor, and to have the assistance of counsel for his defense.'

The importance of these Amendments was underlined in *Miranda v Arizona*, 384 US 436 (1966), where suspects were questioned by police officers and prosecuting attorneys in rooms without prior warnings of rights at the outset of the interrogation. The Court considered whether the police practice of interrogating individuals without having notified them of their right to counsel and their protection against self-incrimination violated the Fifth Amendment? The Supreme Court held that prosecutors could not use statements stemming from custodial interrogation of defendants, unless they demonstrated the use of procedural safeguards effective to secure the privilege against self-incrimination, the right to remain silent and the right to have counsel present during interrogations – the famous Miranda warnings. With regard to the fundamental right to counsel and the right to a speedy trial, the 11 September 2002 (9-11) attack on the United States has raised an important constitutional question: what rights does a United States citizen detained by his government have when the citizen is alleged to be allied with an enemy group? An American Bar Association Task Force examined the issue of American citizens detained on American soil as enemy combatants in the nation's war on terrorism, stressing their right of access to judicial review and to legal counsel. Noting that the United States has struggled since its inception to find the proper balance between protection of liberty and individual rights, the ABA stressed that 'in time of war or threat of war, the balance may shift appropriately toward security, but from past experience we know that such a shift carries with it a danger of government overreaction and undue trespass on individual rights'.

CHAPTER 12

REFUGEE LAW

12.1 Introduction

12.1.1 GENERAL INTRODUCTION

According to the United Nations High Commissioner for Refugees, there are between 15 and 25 million refugees in the world. The majority are women and children. This does not include those who are internally displaced, forced from their residences, but who remain within their own countries. The rich industrialised countries including western European countries, receive less than ten per cent of the world's refugees but have the most elaborate system for dealing with each claim on an individual basis. In contrast, the poorer countries in the South, which are nearest the conflicts that give rise to refugee flows, are host to the remaining ninety per cent of the world's refugees.

By virtue of Art 14 of the Universal Declaration of Human rights, every person has the right to apply for and to enjoy asylum as a fundamental human right recognised by all member states of the United Nations. Those who recognise the right to seek asylum recognise that their right to control migrants in their country is tempered by their obligations under international law to permit a person to apply for asylum and to give shelter (asylum) to those whom they find in need of protection.

The basic international law document, ratified by over 130 countries, is the United Nations 1951 Geneva Convention relating to the Status of Refugees, amended by its 1967 Protocol. For the sake of brevity, the Convention and Protocol will be called the '1951 Geneva Convention' for the remainder of this chapter. The 1951 Geneva Convention was ratified by Ireland in 1956 and the 1967 Protocol in 1968. The Convention is legally binding on Ireland but, by virtue of Ireland's 'dualist' system of law, does not form part of Ireland's domestic law.

Some world regions have extended protection to categories of refugees beyond those recognised in the 1951 Geneva Convention. The 1974 Declaration of the Organisation of African Unity and the 1984 Cartagena Declaration on Refugees include protection for other categories of people at risk. While the Council of Europe has recommended extension of those who should be recognised as refugees the binding rights obligations for European nations are still those contained in the 1951 Geneva Convention.

The core protection concepts in the 1951 Geneva Convention are the internationally agreed description of who is a refugee (Art 1) and a re-statement of the customary law prohibition on *refoulement* (Art 33), which is defined in **12.1.2**. The Convention also stipulates minimum conditions for refugees and those claiming asylum. The 1951 Geneva Convention does not provide for any international tribunal to enforce compliance or to interpret its terms. Instead, one of the functions of the international agency charged with overseeing the application of the 1951 Geneva Convention, known as the United Nations

High Commissioner for Refugees (UNHCR), is to promote refugee protection. The UNHCR Executive Committee (ExComm) and secretariat issue guidelines, recommendations and conclusions by way of non-binding guidance to states on refugee protection.

Each state makes its own arrangements for the examination of asylum claims. Recognition criteria can vary, depending on the state examining the claim. What countries regard as 'persecution' can vary, even within similarly minded states, such as those of the EU.

State policy in relation to refugee protection may also change from time-to-time. Depending on factors as diverse as world war and the employment needs of the receiving state, the entry and examination process for refugees making a claim for asylum may be easier or more difficult. This tension between the right of a state to control migration and the state's obligation to comply with international human rights law is a continual one and can result in a person who would be recognised as a refugee in one period of time being refused in another or vice versa.

The practice of refugee law in Ireland involves the application of an internationally recognised human right – the right to apply for and to enjoy asylum – in an Irish context. The law relating to refugees and asylum is closely linked to, but is separate from, the laws of migration control.

Until the 1990s, the numbers in Ireland applying for asylum were minuscule. In 1993, the number was under one hundred. By the year 2000, the number of applications had increased to almost 11,000 coming from persons from ninety-eight different countries. The change in numbers in Ireland is consistent with trends throughout Europe. A variety of reasons contributed to the change. It is generally accepted that they include the massive increase in armed conflicts in the world and their ferocity, the fall of the Berlin Wall, conflicts in and near Europe, increased access to Ireland and Ireland's increased profile in world affairs from economics through politics to sport.

12.1.2   TERMS IN COMMON USE

'Refugees' are those who have fled their own country in fear. Some refugees will be recognised by the international community as deserving of international protection. 'Convention Refugees' is a common name for those refugees who are recognised as coming within the 1951 Geneva Convention. Such refugees are entitled to the specific protections of that Convention and also to such additional protection as is available under the law of the country where their status is recognised. Convention refugees are those who have a well-founded fear of persecution in their country of origin, because of their race, religion, nationality, membership of a social group or political opinion, who are unable or owing to such a fear, are unwilling to get protection in their own country and who are not otherwise disqualified from protection.

'Asylum seekers' are those who want to be recognised as Convention refugees.

'Refoulement' is prohibited by the 1951 Geneva Convention and by customary international law. *'Refoulement'* is the expulsion of a person to the borders of a country where the life or freedom of the person would be threatened on account of his or her race, religion, nationality, membership of a particular social group or political opinion.

'Programme Refugees' are those victims of war or persecution who have been invited by the Irish State to leave their own country and to live in Ireland. These people are pre-selected to come to Ireland, in groups, from a particular country and do not undergo any approval process after they arrive.

'Temporary Protection' is a newly emerging concept, particularly within the European Union. The term has been applied where countries within the EU gave protection to groups of people on the basis that their country was in severe crisis, rather than on the the basis of individual entitlement, but on the understanding that the protection was likely to be withdrawn when the protecting country perceived a reduced level of risk in the home country.

'Family reunification'. Those recognised as refugees within the 1951 Geneva Convention may apply to the Minister for Justice Equality and Law Reform for permission to have their close family members join them.

'Leave to remain'. This can be called 'exceptional' or 'temporary' or 'humanitarian' leave to remain. It is a permission given by the Minister for Justice Equality and Law Reform to people who are not recognised as refugees. It may be given to comply with Ireland's obligations to protect human rights beyond the 1951 Geneva Convention. Other legal obligations stem from treaties such as the European Convention on Fundamental Protections and Human Rights, treaties against torture and those against violations of specific rights or the rights of specific categories of people. This leave to remain may also be granted where it is recognised that it would be inhumane to require someone to leave, whether because of personal and family reasons, the person's contribution to Ireland or the general situation in their home country.

'Illegal immigrants' are those who are in Ireland without proper authorisation. Although many asylum seekers arrive without prior notice or authorisation and may arrive in an irregular way, they cannot be deemed illegally in the state while they exercise their international human right to apply for asylum.

'The Minister' and 'The Department of Justice Equality and Law Reform'. An asylum seeker applying for recognition as a convention refugee makes an application for a declaration to the Minister for Justice Equality and Law Reform through two agencies known as the 'Office of the Refugee Applications Commissioner' and the 'Refugee Appeals Tribunal'. The implementation of the decisions of each of these and the application for leave to remain are ultimately matters for the Minister for Justice Equality and Law Reform who makes the final order. The Department of Justice Equality and Law Reform is the primary one dealing with issues relating to immigration.

12.1.3   APPLICATION OF THE 1951 GENEVA CONVENTION IN IRELAND

Until the late 1990s, asylum seekers were processed under purely administrative schemes, the most significant of which were commonly called the 'von Arnim' and 'Hanlan' procedures. Ireland has now put a domestic statutory structure in place to examine the claims of asylum seekers who wish to be recognised as refugees and to deal with associated matters. The basic Act is the Refugee Act, 1996. This was substantially amended by s 9 of the Immigration Act, 1999, by the Illegal Immigrants Trafficking Act, 2000, the Immigration Act, 2003 and the Immigration Act, 2004. The bulk of the Refugee Act, 1996, came into effect in November 2000, with the remaining sections becoming operative in September 2001. The very extensive amendments to the Refugee Act, 1996, which were contained in later acts, make for difficult reading. At the time of writing, the Department of Justice Equality and Law Reform website www.justice.ie has a helpful publication, entitled 'Refugee Act 1996 incorporating amendments to be made by the Immigration Act, 2003', which is an unofficial consolidation of the Refugee Act as amended up to and including the 2003 Act.

The definition of a refugee in Irish law follows that contained in Article 1 of the 1951 Geneva Convention.

Section 2 of the Refugee Act, 1996 defines a refugee as:

> 'In this Act "a refugee" means a person who, owing to a well-founded fear of being persecuted for reasons of race, religion, nationality, membership of a particular social group or political opinion, is outside the country of his or her nationality and is unable or, owing to such fear, is unwilling to

avail himself or herself of the protection of that country; or who, not having a nationality and being outside the country of his or her former habitual residence, is unable or, owing to such fear, is unwilling to return to it, but does not include a person who—

(a) *is receiving from organs or agencies of the United Nations (other than the High Commissioner) protection or assistance;*

(b) *is recognised by the competent authorities of the country in which he or she has taken residence as having the rights and obligations which are attached to the possession of the nationality of that country;*

(c) *there are serious grounds for considering that he or she—*

   (i) *has committed a crime against peace, a war crime, or a crime against humanity, as defined in the international instruments drawn up to make provision in respect of such crimes;*

   (ii) *has committed a serious non-political crime outside the State prior to his or her arrival in the State, or*

   (iii) *has been guilty of acts contrary to the purposes and principles of the United Nations'.*

Section 1 of the Refugee Act, 1996 provides that:

' *"membership of a particular social group" includes membership of a trade union and also includes membership of a group of persons whose defining characteristic is their belonging to the female or the male sex or having a particular sexual orientation'.*

Section 5 of the Refugee Act, 1996 reflects the prohibition on *refoulement* in Article 33 of the 1951 Geneva Convention. It sets out the commitment of the Irish State not to expel persons whose life or freedom might be at risk as follows:

'(1) *A person shall not be expelled from the State or returned in any manner whatsoever to the frontiers of territories where, in the opinion of the Minister, the life or freedom of that person would be threatened on account of his or her race, religion, nationality, membership of a particular social group or political opinion.*

(2) *Without prejudice to the generality of subsection (1), a person's freedom shall be regarded as being threatened if, inter alia, in the opinion of the Minister, the person is likely to be subject to a serious assault (including a serious assault of a sexual nature).'*

12.2 Criteria for Determining Refugee Status

12.2.1 GENERAL INTRODUCTION TO THE ELEMENTS OF THE DEFINITION OF A REFUGEE

The definition of a 'refugee' as articulated in s 2 of the Refugee Act, 1996 contains various elements or criteria. To qualify for recognition, an applicant must meet all of the criteria. In the analysis of a claim, the refugee applicant must prove:

(a) a well-founded fear;

(b) that the fear is of persecution;

(c) that the fear of persecution is for the reasons specified in the 1951 Geneva Convention and s 2 of the Refugee Act, 1996; race, religion, nationality, membership or a social group o r political opinion;

(d) that he or she is outside the country of his or her nationality;

(e) that he or she is unable or, because of the fear, unwilling, to avail of state of origin protection or that the state has failed to protect the person; and

12.2.4.4 Membership of a particular social group

This is the vaguest of the various 1951 Geneva Convention grounds. Section 1 of the Refugee Act, 1996 notes that this includes membership of a trade union and those groups *'whose defining characteristic is their belonging to the female or the male sex or having a particular sexual orientation.'* In 1999, the House of Lords found that Pakistani women, victims of domestic violence, whose spouses were not subject to State sanction constituted 'a particular social group' in the UK (*R (ex p Shah & Islam) v Home Secretary* [1999] 2 WLR 1215). In general, claims on this basis relate to some shared characteristic of the group which is fundamental to the refugee's identity and which the refugee either cannot change or should not be asked to change. Persecution alone cannot be used to define the group. Paragraphs 77–79 of the UNHCR Handbook are particularly relevant.

12.2.4.5 Political opinion

The test is 'opinion' not 'activity'. On occasion, the applicant may not even hold the political opinions which would give rise to the persecution but rather the opinions may be imputed to the refugee by the authorities in the country of origin because of the person's family, connections or address. Paragraphs 80–86 of the UNHCR Handbook are relevant.

12.2.5 OUTSIDE COUNTRY OF NATIONALITY

Internally displaced persons, who have not passed outside their country's borders, cannot qualify for Convention Refugee status. Within the EU, a Protocol to the Amsterdam Treaty prohibits an application from an EU national to any other EU state. Belgium has not signed the Protocol.

Some people are not refugees when they leave their own countries but because of changes in the home country, they have a well-founded fear of persecution if they return. Others become fearful of persecution because their activities abroad are, or become, unacceptable to the authorities of the home country. Such refugees, whose claim originates after they leave their country are commonly called *'refugees sur place'*.

Some countries penalise refugees who do not make asylum applications within a short time of arrival. Even where there is no obligation to apply within a time period, s 11B(d) of the Refugee Act, 1996 provides that the credibility of an applicant's claim may be doubted because of a failure to provide a reasonable explanation as to why he or she did not claim asylum immediately on arriving at the frontiers of the State.

Nationality in this part of the definition refers to citizenship. The refugee must fear persecution from the country of nationality, because that is the country with the primary obligation to extend protection to its citizens.

Paragraphs 87–107 of the Handbook apply to 'outside country of nationality'.

12.2.6 UNABLE OR UNWILLING TO AVAIL OF STATE PROTECTION/ STATE FAILURE TO PROTECT

An applicant must show that either the applicant is:

(a)   actually unable to return to the country of origin because of the genuine risk of persecution; or

(b)   unwilling to return because of the fear.

Inability may be the physical impossibility of getting protection in a situation of conflict in the home country. Unwillingness will arise in circumstances where the refugee is unwilling to accept what appears to be a state offer of protection. The unwillingness to accept available protection will have to be on foot of a 'well-founded fear' of persecution.

Having protection in theory, such as laws governing the situation, is useless if the laws do not protect the refugee in reality. The protection available must be effective and durable. For some applicants, the source of the danger is the seeking of state protection. In some situations of conflict, there may be no effective state, hence no possibility of state protection. The apprehended persecution may be from some agency from which the State will not or cannot protect the applicant.

The applicant must also show that there is no possibility of re-location within the home state; that there is no internal flight alternative. As Professor James Hathaway states in his 'Law of Refugee Status', 1991, Butterworths, 133), '[a] person cannot be said to be at risk of persecution if she can access effective protection in some part of her state or origin. Because refugee law is intended to meet the needs of only those who have no alternative to seeking international protection, primary recourse should always be to one's own state'. Paragraphs 97–100 of the UNHCR Handbook deal with failure of state protection.

12.2.7   EXCLUSION CLAUSES

In addition to stipulating who should be entitled to recognition as a refugee, the 1951 Geneva Convention and s 2 of the Refugee Act, 1996 set out criteria by which individuals may be excluded from international protection. The list of those who may be excluded is definitive and is to be interpreted narrowly. According to s 2 of the Refugee Act, 1996 a person may be excluded if:

(a)   he or she 'is receiving protection or assistance from organs or agencies of the United Nations (other than the UNHCR).' This applies only to a limited group of Palestinian refugees in particular refugee locations in the Middle East.

(b)   the person 'is recognised by the competent authorities of the country in which he or she has taken residence as having the rights and obligations which are attached to the possession of the nationality of that country' A strong guarantee of continuous protection from the state of residence will be required before this clause is applied.

(c)   there are serious grounds for considering that the person 'has committed a crime against peace, a war crime, or a crime against humanity, as defined in the international instruments drawn up to make provision in respect of such crimes' Such crimes are defined in the international instruments, ranging from the 1945 Charter of the International Military Tribunal to the Statute of the International Criminal Court and the ad hoc Tribunals for the former Yugoslavia and Rwanda.

(d)   there are serious grounds for considering that he or she 'has committed a serious non-political crime outside the State prior to his or her arrival in the State' This clause is to protect the host state from the danger of admitting someone who has committed a serious common crime. The crime must be serious by the standards of the home and of the receiving state. A crime committed out of genuine political motives will be considered political and will not be subject to the exclusion clause.

(e)   there are serious grounds for considering that the applicant 'has been guilty of acts contrary to the purposes and principles of the United Nations'. United Nations resolutions relating to the 2003 Iraq war have indicated what might be meant by this phrase.

Paragraphs 140–163 of the UNHCR Handbook and UNHCR Guidelines on the use of the exclusion clauses apply.

12.2.8   CESSATION/REVOCATION

Once a person has been declared a refugee, that status is maintained unless one of the cessation clauses applies or the Minister for Justice Equality and Law Reform revokes the declaration. It may only be revoked without consent in the limited circumstances set out in the Refugee Act, 1996, s 21 of which provides:

'(1)   Subject to subsection (2), if the Minister is satisfied that a person to whom a declaration has been given—

(a)   has voluntarily re-availed himself or herself of the protection of the country of his or her nationality,

(b)   having lost his or her nationality, has voluntarily re-acquired it,

(c)   has acquired a new nationality (other than the nationality of the State) and enjoys the protection of the country of his or her new nationality,

(d)   has voluntarily re-established himself or herself in the country which he or she left or outside which he or she remained owing to fear of persecution,

(e)   can no longer, because the circumstances in connection with which he or she has been recognised as a refugee have ceased to exist, continue to refuse to avail himself or herself of the protection of the country of his or her nationality,

(f)   being a person who has no nationality is, because the circumstances in connection with which he or she has been recognised as a refugee have ceased to exist, able to return to the country of his or her former habitual residence,

(g)   is a person whose presence in the State poses a threat to national security or public policy ("ordre public"), or

(h)   is a person to whom a declaration has been given on the basis of information furnished to the Commissioner or, as the case may be, the Tribunal which was false or misleading in a material particular.

The Minister may, if he or she considers it appropriate to do so, revoke the declaration.

(2)   The Minister shall not revoke a declaration on the grounds specified in paragraph (e) or (f) where the Minister is satisfied that the person concerned is able to invoke compelling reasons arising out of previous persecution for refusing to avail himself or herself of the protection of his or her nationality or for refusing to return to the country of his or her former habitual residence, as the case may be.'

Because the revocation of a declaration removes protection, these provisions must be interpreted restrictively. Therefore, a 'voluntary' return must be truly voluntary, intentional, informed as to the consequences to the refugee status and must actually have taken place. The Minister should only form an opinion that the circumstances giving rise to the refugee status no longer exist after the refugee has an opportunity to explain why the refugee is not prepared to accept the protection of the state of origin.

The UNHCR Handbook addresses the cessation of refugee status at paragraphs 111–139.

12.3   The Case of Patrick Francis Ward

A leading Canadian case, *Ward v Canada* (1993) 2 SCR 689 which has persuasive precedent in Irish refugee law, addressing several elements of the refugee definition, concerns the claim for asylum of Patrick Francis Ward, born in Northern Ireland. For reasons of political conviction, Mr Ward had been a member of the illegal republican organisation called the Irish National Liberation Army (INLA). In the course of his activities for this organisation, he had taken hostages. He had released the hostages for reasons of conscience when he learned that they were to be shot and he had renounced his membership of the INLA. He was imprisoned in Ireland for the hostage taking. He was apprehensive that on his release from prison, he would be at risk of very serious harm from his former colleagues in the INLA and fled to Canada, where he claimed asylum.

The court found as a fact that Mr Ward's apprehension of serious risk to his most fundamental human rights was well-founded. It also found that police in Ireland had conceded that they were unable to protect him from this risk. In fact, the State had assisted Mr Ward in obtaining an Irish passport and airline tickets to Canada. While the court did not find the INLA to be a 'particular social group', it did find that Mr Ward was exercising a political opinion within the meaning of the 1951 Geneva Convention.

It also found that Mr Ward was entitled to dual British and Irish nationalities and on this ground, his claim must fail. He had failed to seek the protection of the UK authorities against the persecution. This failure meant he was unable to prove that a State that was obliged to protect him had failed to do so. The court concluded that international refugee law is a surrogate protection, which should serve as a back-up to the protection owed to a national by his or her state. It comes into play only in situations where that protection is unavailable and then, only in certain situations.

12.4   Complementary Protection

The State's obligations to protect non-nationals is not limited to those it recognises as refugees. Under Art 33 of the 1951 Geneva Convention and s 5 of the Refugee Act, 1996, the State is obliged not to expel someone if the Minister is of the view that the life or freedom of that person would be threatened by such expulsion on account of his or her race, religion, nationality, membership of a particular social group or political opinion. This applies whether the person is to be directly expelled to the country or is to be sent to an intermediate country where he or she will not obtain durable, effective protection from expulsion.

Section 4 of the Criminal Justice (United Nations Convention Against Torture) Act, 2000 specifically prohibits refoulement where there is a substantial danger of torture. In addition to that Act and to any protection which may be available at Irish law or under the Constitution, other international human rights standards may also oblige the State to extend protection to non-nationals on grounds which are not connected with refugee status. Customary law and Art 3 of the European Convention on Human Rights and Fundamental Freedoms prohibit the expulsion of anyone to a serious risk of torture, cruel, inhuman or degrading treatment – no matter who is inflicting it or for what reason (*Soering v United Kingdom* (1989) 11 EHRR 439). In addition, international law obligations under the International Bill of Rights, the Conventions against Torture, the Conventions on the Rights of the Child etc. may be relevant in considering the protection needs of the applicant and the obligations of the State.

The agencies which examine refugee claims are mandated only to consider whether the definition of 'refugee' applies. They have no mandate to examine complementary protection needs. An application can be made to the Minister for Justice Equality and Law Reform at any time for protection on grounds of complementary protection but there is no particular process or time frame for the making or determination of such a claim. Normally, such claims are made following the unsuccessful conclusion of a claim for recognition as a refugee. Alternatively, or additionally, the claimant may have a right to a remedy under one of the other human rights treaties by which Ireland is bound, including the right to apply to the European Court of Human Rights under the European Convention on Human Rights and Fundamental Freedoms or the Human Rights Committee of the International Covenant on Civil and Political Rights.

12.5 Procedure for Examination of Claims in Ireland

While there will be variations from case to case and while each stage is open to court challenge, mainly by judicial review, a claim for asylum generally proceeds as follows:

First Instance

1   An applicant makes a claim for asylum in Ireland at the border or within the State.

2   The applicant is interviewed by an immigration officer, if the claim was made at the border. If made within the State, the interview may be by an immigration officer or by an official of the Office of the Refugee Applications Commissioner.

3   If the interview was by an immigration officer, the papers are transferred to the Office of the Refugee Applications Commissioner. The applicant gives personal details to that office which normally issues a temporary residence certificate. Applicants over fourteen years old will be fingerprinted. Those under 14 may also be fingerprinted. The Commissioner's office will give the applicant a detailed questionnaire to complete.

4   At the same time as personal details are being processed by the Commissioner's office, the Reception and Integration Agency of the Department of Justice Equality and Law Reform allocates accommodation.

5   The Refugee Applications Commissioner usually decides at this stage (although the decision can be made later) whether it wishes to deal with the claim in Ireland or whether, because of the applicant's links with another EU state, it should transfer the applicant to that other EU country to have the case heard there. There is a right of appeal against a determination to transfer the case but making an appeal may not suspend deportation to that other EU state.

6   If the case is to be dealt with in Ireland, the applicant will be called for a substantial interview by the Office of the Refugee Applications Commissioner.

7   The Commissioner will make a recommendation, which will be notified to the applicant. If the recommendation is that the person should be recognised as a refugee, the Minister for Justice Equality and Law Reform will also be notified. There is a right of appeal against a negative decision.

8   A negative decision will be given where an application is refused or withdrawn. In some cases the authorities will deem an application withdrawn.

Appeal

9   All appeals to transfer the case to another country or against a refusal are made to a member of the Refugee Appeals Tribunal. There is no appeal against a decision that an application is withdrawn or deemed to be withdrawn.

10   The format and time limit for the appeal depends on the type of refusal against which the appeal is made. The result of the appeal is communicated to the applicant. The results of appeals are submitted to the Minister.

11   If the Minister receives a recommendation from the Commissioner or a decision of the Tribunal that the person should be recognised as a refugee, the Minister must make a declaration to this effect. Even without such recommendation, the Minister may permit the person to remain in the State anyway. The usual next step is for the Department of Justice Equality and Law Reform to notify an unsuccessful applicant that the Minister proposes to make a Deportation Order.

Application for leave to remain

12   The applicant must then present reasons in writing to the Department of Justice Equality and Law Reform as to why no deportation should occur.

13   If the applicant's representations to remain are successful, the person will be given leave to remain. If the applicant is unsuccessful, the person will be notified and sent a copy of the Deportation Order.

14   An unsuccessful applicant must co-operate in the arrangements for the deportation. Persons may be detained pending deportation.

15   Most court challenges, made during or at the end of the procedure, are brought by way of Judicial Review application to the High Court.

A more detailed discussion of each of these elements now follows.

12.5.1   APPLICATION FOR ASYLUM

Section 8 of the Refugee Act, 1996 states:

> '(1)(a) A person who arrives at the frontiers of the State seeking asylum in the State or seeking the protection of the State against persecution or requesting not to be returned or removed to a particular country or otherwise indicating an unwillingness to leave the State for fear of persecution . . . may apply to the Minister for a declaration'.

Seeking asylum is a request to the Minister for Justice Equality and Law Reform for a declaration that the person's refugee status is recognised by the Irish State. An applicant must ask for asylum or otherwise make it known that he or she wants to be recognised as a refugee. No specific form of words has to be used. The person must then be given leave to land in the State (Refugee Act, 1996 s 9) and, unless transferred to another EU state, remain pending the determination of their asylum claim.

Many asylum seekers arrive without papers or with false ones. EU countries require pre-clearance visas from the nationals of most refugee generating countries and asylum seekers normally do not have the requisite visa. Article 31 of the 1951 Geneva Convention forbids States from penalising asylum seekers for their unauthorised presence provided that such people present themselves without delay to the authorities and show good cause for the illegal entry or presence.

Such illegal entry is discouraged by legislation affecting those who assist or carry non-nationals without acceptable papers. The Illegal Immigrants (Trafficking) Act, 2000 and the Immigration Act, 2003 create offences of assisting or carrying those without valid papers, with associated powers of search and arrest. Substantial fines encourage carriers to scrutinise the papers of their passengers rather than risk commission of an offence.

12.5.2   INITIAL INTERVIEW

When the application for asylum is made, the applicant is interviewed to establish details of the person's identity, why the person is in the State and how the applicant arrived (Refugee Act, 1996 s 8(2)). If the claim was made directly to the Office of the Refugee Applications Commissioner, that office will conduct the interview. Otherwise, an immigration official will carry it out. Any identity or travel papers that the applicant has are handed over to the authorities and will be retained for the duration of the application. The applicant is entitled to interpretation and to consult a solicitor and the UNHCR (Refugee Act, s 8(1)(b)).

12.5.3   REGISTRATION OF THE APPLICANT

The office of the Refugee Applications Commissioner registers the applicant's claim. Personal information, name, address, date of birth, etc. will be sought. The applicant will be photographed and, if over fourteen years old, fingerprinted. Minors under fourteen may also be fingerprinted. Those fingerprints may be submitted to a Europe-wide database or to another EU Member State. The prints may be retained for up to ten years. (Refugee Act, 1996, s 9A). The applicant is issued with a temporary residence certificate and a Personal Public Service number.

The applicant is also given a detailed questionnaire to complete and return within a specified time; often a week. The questions seek information on the applicant's identity, family and status in the home country, particulars of how the person got to Ireland and details of why the person seeks protection in Ireland.

This questionnaire is very important. It forms a basis for the applicant's later interview. Any omissions or inaccuracies in this document may affect the applicant's credibility or lead to a conclusion that the applicant has failed in the duty to co-operate imposed by s 11C of the Refugee Act, 1996. All relevant additional information available to the applicant about the claim should be submitted with the form.

12.5.4   ACCOMMODATION AND WELFARE SERVICES

Asylum seekers who need housing and sustenance are housed through the Department of Justice, Equality and Law Reform's Reception and Integration Agency. Current government policy is to send asylum seekers to hostel accommodation throughout the State where the applicant will receive full board. While in the hostel, applicants receive a small weekly sum for any supplementary needs. They are notified of their entitlement to apply for a medical card and legal aid. If they leave the accommodation assigned to them, they are usually not entitled to any accommodation at all.

12.5.5   TRANSFER OF AN ASYLUM APPLICATION TO ANOTHER EU STATE

As part of the overall policy of establishing a common policy on asylum within the European Union, its Member States, together with Iceland and Norway, have agreed procedures to permit an asylum seeker to only make one asylum claim throughout the territory of the EU, Iceland and Norway and to determine which country is the correct one to hear the claim. Arrangements have been made to permit the transfer of an asylum seeker from one state to another if the mechanisms determine that the asylum claim should be heard in another state.

The first EU-wide agreement, the so-called Dublin Convention now applies only to transfer applicants from another EU state to or from Denmark. All of the other countries use the mechanisms in Council Regulation (EC) 343/2003, the so-called 'Dublin II' regulation or mechanism. Pursuant to s 22 of the Refugee Act, 1996, statutory instruments have provided for the implementation of the EU legislation in Irish law in the Dublin Convention (Implementation) Order 2000 (SI 343 of 2000) and the Refugee Act, 1996 (Section 22) Order 2003 (SI 423/2003).

Article 4.1 of EC Council Regulation 343/2003 states:

> 'The process of determining the Member State responsible under this Regulation shall start as soon as an application for asylum is first lodged with a Member State.'

Therefore from the time that the application is made, particularly from the short initial interview, the Refugee Applications Commissioner may consider whether or not to transfer the applicant. There may or may not be a separate interview to determine the issue. An applicant is entitled to make written submissions to the Refugee Applications Commissioner as to why a transfer should or should not take place but it should be noted that applicants may not even know that the question is under consideration until they are informed of the decision to transfer. The hierarchy of criteria used to decide the appropriate state to hear the application are contained in Chapter III, Articles 5–14 of the Regulation and include consideration of an applicant's family connections and any residence of the applicant in a Member State. There is a right to appeal a decision to transfer the case out of Ireland, but an appeal will not necessarily suspend transfer to that other EU state. Even where there is a right by Ireland to transfer a case to another state, Ireland has a discretion to accept and hear such a case.

12.5.6   SUBSTANTIAL INTERVIEW

The applicant will be notified in writing to attend an interview with an official of the Office of the Refugee Applications Commissioner. The purpose of the interview is to investigate the applicant's claim, following which the Commissioner will prepare a report and recommend recognition or refusal. For the interview, the Commissioner's office will supply an interpreter, if so required by the applicant (Refugee Act, 1996, s 11(2)). On a non-statutory basis, it is the practice for the Commissioner to permit the applicant's solicitor to attend if necessary and, if so requested in time by an applicant, to arrange for the authorised officer and interpreter to be of the same sex as the applicant. Applicants should ensure that they supply all of their information and documents at or in advance of the interview.

The interview is recorded by the interviewer. This is done by writing down all the questions and either the full answer or a summary of the answer depending on its length and the style of both interviewer and interviewee. While it is helpful to have a record, the method of recording can lead to interruptions in the presentation of the case. Some answers are hard to summarise accurately. The interviewer and interviewee will sign each page to signify that the record is accurate. The applicant is entitled to a copy of the interview notes at the end of the interview. Interviews vary in length, depending on how long it takes the interviewer to obtain the information he or she considers necessary to understand and decide on the claim. The lawyer is usually asked not to intervene in the interview but to save any submissions until the end.

12.5.7   RECOMMENDATION OF THE REFUGEE APPLICATIONS COMMISSIONER

The Refugee Applications Commissioner's task is to investigate whether the applicant has demonstrated a well-founded fear of persecution for the reasons given in the definition of a refugee. The facts of the case are to be tested against the Convention criteria. In addition, the investigator has to decide if the applicant is credible.

For the investigation, the Commissioner will consider the information given by the applicant. It will also use its own sources to examine such matters as conditions in the country of origin. It may make enquiries from other Departments, such as the Department of Foreign Affairs including its consulates abroad, from the UNHCR or from other countries. The confidentiality of the asylum application should not be compromised in those enquiries without the applicant's full consent.

The report on the findings of the authorised officer and the assessment of the applicant then form the basis of the Commissioner's recommendation which, in due course, is notified to the applicant. The Commissioner will recommend that the applicant should or should not be declared a refugee. In a recommendation to refuse status as a refugee, the Commissioner may further include a finding under s 13(6) of the Refugee Act, 1996. Section 13(6) states:

'The findings . . . . are –

(a)   *that the application showed either no basis or a minimal basis for the contention that the applicant is a refugee;*

(b)   *that the applicant made statements or provided information in support of the application of such a false, contradictory, misleading or incomplete nature as to lead to the conclusion that the application is manifestly unfounded;*

(c)   *that the applicant, without reasonable cause, failed to make an application as soon as reasonably practicable after arrival in the State;*

(d)   *the applicant had lodged a prior application for asylum in another state party to the Geneva Convention (whether or not that application had been determined granted or rejected); or*

(e)   *the applicant is a national of, or has a right of residence in a safe country of origin for the time being so designated by order under section 12(4)'.*

The countries currently designated as 'safe countries of origin' are set out in statutory instrument SI 422/2003. They are all of the countries which acceded to the EU in May 2004, Bulgaria and Romania.

Where the Commissioner recommends that the applicant should be recognised as a refugee in Ireland, the recommendation is sent to the applicant, his or her solicitor and to the Minister for Justice Equality and Law Reform, who must then declare that the person is a refugee.

Where the applicant is not recognised, but there is no finding under s 13(6) Refugee Act, 1996, the applicant may appeal to the Refugee Appeals Tribunal. There is a right of oral appeal in such cases.

Where the claim is not recognised and there is a s 13(6) finding, there is also a right of appeal, but the time limit is more restrictive and a written appeal only is allowed.

12.5.8   REFUGEE APPEALS TRIBUNAL

The Tribunal is established pursuant to s 14 and Sch 2 of the Refugee Act, 1996. It hears appeals against determinations of the Commissioner to transfer an applicant under the Dublin Convention or Regulation and against negative recommendations of the Commissioner. The Tribunal has a full time chairperson. The rest of its members, who sit alone to hear appeals, are lawyers, practising or retired who sit part-time with the Tribunal. The bulk of the provisions in relation to appeal are set out in s 16 of the Refugee Act, 1996, the Refugee Act, 1996 (Appeals) Regulations 2003 (SI 424/2003) and the Refugee Act, 1996 (Section 22) Order 2003 (SI 423/2003).

Usually, at the same time as he or she is notified of the negative decision, the applicant will be given a copy of that part of the Commissioner's file on which the negative recommendation was based. This information is also furnished by the Commissioner to the Tribunal secretariat and is available to the Tribunal member at the case hearing.

If the applicant does not appeal within the statutory time, the negative recommendation is sent to the Minister and the applicant will pass out of the refugee determination process.

Before deciding an appeal against a negative recommendation, s 16(16) of the Refugee Act, 1996 (which does not apply to Dublin Convention or Regulation Appeals) specifies that the Tribunal must consider:

(a)   the Notice of Appeal;
(b)   the report of the Refugee Applications Commissioner;

(c) any observations made to the Tribunal by the Commissioner or the UNHCR;

(d) the evidence adduced and any representations made at an oral hearing, if any; and

(e) any documents, representations in writing or other information furnished to the Commissioner prior to making the negative recommendation.

Following the hearing, the Tribunal member gives a written decision which, in due course is notified to the Applicant, the applicant's lawyer and the Minister for Justice Equality and Law Reform.

12.5.9 DIFFERENT TYPES OF APPEAL

12.5.9.1 Dublin Convention/Dublin Regulation mechanism

Appeals against determinations to transfer an applicant's application for asylum to another EU state are regulated by the Refugee Act, 1996 (Section 22) Order 2003 (SI 423/2003). That Order includes the format for the notice of appeal and specifies a time limit of 15 working days from the date of the determination for the appeal to be lodged. All relevant information must be included with the notice of appeal. Art 8(3) of the Order provides that:

> '(t)he making of an appeal under paragraph (2) shall not suspend the transfer of an applicant to a Council Regulation country on foot of a transfer order under Article 7.'

The transfer procedures assume that the appeal will be decided on technical formal grounds. They do not refer to the danger of indirect *refoulement*, which may occur as a result of the transfer. Indirect *refoulement* could occur if the EU State to which the applicant is transferred is not a safe place for the applicant's claim to be considered. The Court of Appeal of England and Wales has refused to permit Dublin Convention deportations to Germany and France on this basis, *R v Secretary of State for the Home Department, ex p Gashi* [1991] Imm. A.R. 415 *and R v Secretary of State for the Home Department, ex p. Adan* [1991] 3 WLR 1274. In *Gashi*, the applicant, a Kosovar Albanian, successfully contested the order made under the Dublin Convention to transport him back to Germany. He argued that it was statistically proven that Kosovar Albanians were very often refused asylum and deported from Germany. It was held that the Home Secretary was required to ensure that a third country would deal with the applicant in accordance with the provisions of the 1951 Geneva Convention. In *Adan*, the court concluded that, as France and Germany did not recognise persecution by non-state agents, they could not be considered safe third countries. The Somalian applicants successfully appealed the Secretary's order to transport them back to France and Germany under the Dublin Convention on the basis that these countries would not accept persecution from non-state agents, which they feared they would face on their return, as adequate grounds for asylum.

Concerns relating to safety or *refoulement* should be notified to the Minister for Justice, Equality and Law Reform as they form part of the protection extended by the State's obligations of complementary protection.

If the Dublin Convention appeal succeeds, the case is re-submitted to the Commissioner's office for consideration and the applicant, if transferred already, must be brought back to Ireland. If unsuccessful, the applicant is liable to deportation to the other EU state, provided that the time limits specified in the Convention Dublin II regulation are observed. There is no requirement that the accepting State guarantee a substantial hearing to the applicant.

12.5.9.2 Negative recommendations

An appeal against a negative recommendation, which does not include any finding listed in s 13(6) Refugee Act, 1996, must be made within fifteen working days of the issue of the recommendation, in the format of Form 1 of the First Schedule to the Refugee Act, 1996 (Appeals) Regulations, 2003 (SI 424/2003). An oral hearing may be requested. The applicant may seek the attendance of witnesses, although it is the Tribunal's decision as to whom it will direct to attend. There is no power to compel attendance of witnesses. The applicant's submissions for the appeal, together with the authorities and documents on which the applicant intends to rely, must, pursuant to the regulations, be submitted with the appeal form.

There is no set formula for oral hearings before the Tribunal. The Commissioner and the applicant must have an opportunity to be heard. The Tribunal schedules the hearing date. Any application for adjournments must be made to the Tribunal itself. Evidence to the Tribunal is not sworn. An interpreter will be provided by the Tribunal, if one is required. The applicant is usually heard first, followed by any witnesses sanctioned. The representative of the Commissioner's office, the presenting officer, will normally respond by defending the negative decision and perhaps questioning the applicant. The presenting officer for the Commissioner is not the person who investigated the case or prepared the recommendation.

12.5.9.3 Negative recommendations with a s 13(6) finding

Where the appeal is against a negative recommendation where the Commissioner has also made a finding under s 13(6) Refugee Act, 1996, the applicant has ten working days from the sending of the notice to lodge an appeal. The appeal form is set out in Schedule 1, Part 2 of Refugee Act, 1996 (Appeals) Regulations 2003 (SI 424/2003). As stated in s 16(5)(a) Refugee Act, 1996, such appeal will be determined without an oral hearing. All information and submissions must be filed with the form of appeal.

Sections 12 and 13(7) of the Refugee Act, 1996 allow the Minister for Justice, Equality & Law Reform to make orders prioritising and classifying certain groups of claims. If the Minister makes an order under s 13(7), an applicant may only have four working days to appeal a negative recommendation to which s 13(6) findings are attached. As of February 2004, no such order was made.

The results of all appeals are notified to the applicant in writing. Section 16(16A) of the Refugee Act, 1996 provides that:

> 'The Tribunal shall affirm a recommendation of the Commissioner unless it is satisfied, having considered the matters referred to in subsection (16) that the applicant is a refugee.'

12.5.10 ROLE OF MINISTER FOR JUSTICE EQUALITY AND LAW REFORM

If the Minister receives a recommendation from the Commissioner or a decision of the Tribunal that the person should be recognised as a refugee, the Minister will make a declaration to this effect. Even without such recommendation, the Minister may pursuant to s 17(6) of the Refugee Act, 1996, permit the person to remain in the State 'for such period and subject to such conditions as the Minister may specify in writing'. The more usual next action of the State in respect of an unsuccessful applicant, is to send the applicant a notification that the Minister proposes to make a Deportation Order.

12.5.11 LEAVE TO REMAIN

By virtue of s 9(2) of the Refugee Act, 1996, an asylum seeker's leave to remain lasts until transferred to another country under the Dublin Convention or Regulation or until the applicant is notified that the Minister for Justice Equality and Law Reform has refused to make a declaration of refugee recognition or the application is withdrawn or deemed withdrawn.

When the applicant is notified of the Minister's proposal to make a Deportation Order, he or she will also be told that submissions may be made to the Department of Justice Equality and Law Reform within fifteen working days of the issue of the letter of notification as to why no deportation should take place. All relevant issues relating to the applicant's protection, his or her links with the State and any special circumstances should be included as should any documents, including references, which might vouch the application. By way of guidance, s 3(1) and s 3(6) of the Immigration Act, 1999, set out matters which the Minister must take into account. Section 3(1) requires that the prohibition on *refoulement* be taken into account.

Section 3(6) of the Immigration Act, 1999, requires the Minister to consider:

'(a) the age of the person;
(b) the duration of residence in the State of the person;
(c) the family and domestic circumstances of the person;
(d) the nature of the person's connection with the State, if any;
(e) the employment (including self-employment) record of the person;
(f) the employment (including self-employment) prospects of the person;
(g) the character and conduct of the person both within and (where relevant and ascertainable) outside the State (including any criminal convictions);
(h) humanitarian considerations;
(i) any representations duly made by or on behalf of the person;
(j) the common good; and
(k) considerations of national security and public policy, so far as they appear or are known to the Minister.'

The list is not conclusive. It is for the applicant to point out any information which should inform the Minister's decision. The publicly stated policy of the Minister is that each case will be considered on its own merits.

The age of the person may be particularly relevant for children. The family and domestic circumstances may include asserting the right to residence of a non-national spouse of an EU citizen or a person's role in a family unit based in the State. In *Fajujono v Minister for Justice* [1990] ILRM 234, the Supreme Court identified a constitutional right of an Irish citizen child to assert a right to live in the State with the care and company of its parents. In *A.O. & D.L v The Minister for Justice, Equality & Law Reform* [2003] 1 IR 1, the Supreme Court has elaborated on that right, placing it in a context of the State's need to preserve the common good and the integrity of the asylum process and, in those cases, refusing permission to remain to the families of the Irish citizen children.

The employment record and prospects of an applicant may include the right to a business permission of a third country national under the 'Association Agreements' (also called 'Europe Agreements') between the EU and some of its neighbours. The business permission issued by the State normally requires applicants to make their applications from outside the Irish jurisdiction so that the residence comes after the business permission, rather than the other way around. In its decision in *G.A.G. & V.S. v The Minister for Justice, Equality & Law Reform* 30 July 2003, Supreme Court (unreported), the Supreme Court endorsed the State's approach by deciding that those asserting rights under these agreements could be obliged to make their applications from outside the State if the authorities so require. However, the State is at liberty to consider an application from someone who is in the State in advance of the application for permission.

The application should highlight any of the applicant's rights that might be breached by deportation. Reference should be made to any relevant domestic law, constitutional or international human rights law obligations of the State. Some of Ireland's international law commitments have been incorporated into domestic law, notably in the Criminal

Justice (United Nations Convention Against Torture) Act, 2000 and the European Convention of Human Rights Act, 2003. Other human rights treaties remain as obligations which may be relevant in the context of a proposed deportation. The application for leave to remain is the common way to avail of complementary protection. Such complementary protection is the protection offered by a state to protect those whose reasons for flight are outside the strict limits of the Refugee Convention, but who nevertheless require international protection.

12.5.12 RESULT OF LEAVE TO REMAIN APPLICATION

The application for leave to remain is considered within the Department of Justice Equality and Law Reform and in due course, the applicant is informed of the outcome. The Minister is not obliged to specify the reasoning behind a decision to refuse or grant permission to remain, *P B & L v Minister for Justice Equality and Law Reform* [2002] 1 ILRM 16. If the application is successful, the applicant will normally be told that he or she is given leave to remain on 'an exceptional' basis, for a specific period of between one and five years, renewable at the Minister's discretion. The conditions on which the leave is given will be given in the letter. If the application is unsuccessful, the applicant will be notified.

12.5.13 DEPORTATION

At the end of the procedure, the unsuccessful applicant who has remained in the State will have a Deportation Order made against him or her. The decision from the Department of Justice Equality and Law Reform refusing leave to remain is usually accompanied by a copy of the Deportation Order.

As with the Refugee Act, 1996, there is an unofficial but useful consolidation of recent Immigration legislation on the website of the Department of Justice Equality & Law Reform (www.justice.ie). The procedures for deportation are set out in the Immigration Act, 1999, particularly ss 3, 5 and 6. The notice to the proposed deportee will include instructions to report to a specified Garda Station at a specified time, with travel documents, for the purpose for arranging his or her deportation. A deportee must co-operate with the garda and immigration authorities in obtaining all necessary tickets and travel documents. Obstruction or failure to co-operate is an offence which may be punished by fine or imprisonment (ss 8 and 9 of the Immigration Act, 1999). The cost of deportation will be borne by the State but the Minister for Justice Equality and Law Reform may make regulations to recoup the expenditure from the deportee. The person may be detained pending removal (Immigration Act, 1999, s 3(1)(A) and Immigration Act, 2004). A person may consent to the making of a deportation order.

Ireland has concluded international agreements with Romania, Poland and Nigeria known as 're-admission agreements' to facilitate the deportation from Ireland and readmission to those countries of their nationals whose permission to remain in Ireland has expired. Government policy is to conclude such agreements with other countries in the future.

12.5.14 JUDICIAL REVIEW OF ASYLUM DECISIONS

Section 5(1) of the Illegal Immigrants (Trafficking) Act, 2000, as amended by s 10 of the Immigration Act, 2003 states that:

> 'A person shall not question the validity of:
>
> (a)   a notification under section 3(3)(a) of the Immigration Act, 1999,
>
> (b)   a notification under section 3(3)(b)(ii) of the Immigration Act, 1999,
>
> (c)   a deportation order under section 3(1) of the Immigration Act, 1999,
>
> (d)   a refusal under Article 5 of the Aliens Order, 1946 (S.R and O. No. 395 of 1946),
>
> (e)   an exclusion order under section 4 of the Immigration Act, 1999,
>
> (f)   a decision by or on behalf of the Minister to refuse an application for refugee status or a recommendation of an Appeal Authority referred to in paragraph 13 of the document entitled "Procedures for Processing Asylum Claims in Ireland" which, as amended, was laid by the Minister for Justice, Equality and Law Reform before the Houses of the Oireachtas in March 1998,
>
> (g)   a recommendation under section 12 (as amended by section 11(1)(h) of the Immigration Act, 1999) of the Refugee Act, 1996,
>
> (h)   a recommendation of the Refugee Applications Commissioner under section 13 (as amended by section 11(1)(i) of the Immigration Act, 1999) of the Refugee Act, 1996,
>
> (i)   a decision of the Refugee Appeals Tribunal under section 16 (as amended by section 11(1)(k) of the Immigration Act, 1999) of the Refugee Act, 1996,
>
> (j)   a determination of the Commissioner or a decision of the Refugee Appeals Tribunal under section 22 (as amended by section 11(1)(p) of the Immigration Act, 1999) of the Refugee Act, 1996,
>
> (k)   a refusal under section 17 (as amended by section 11(1)(l) of the Immigration Act, 1999) of the Refugee Act, 1996,
>
> (l)   a determination of an officer appointed under section 22(4)(a) of the Refugee Act, 1996,
>
> (m)   a decision of an officer appointed under section 22(4)(b)of the Refugee Act, 1996, or
>
> (n)   a decision under section 21 (as amended by section 11(1)(o) of the Immigration Act, 1999) of the Refugee Act, 1996,
>
> otherwise than by way of an application for judicial review under Order 84 of the Rules of the Superior Courts (S.I. 15/1986)'.

This list includes the usual decisions, notifications and orders which arise in the course of a refugee's claim to be recognised in Ireland, from refusal of leave to land through decisions about Dublin Convention Transfer to decisions about deportation.

Section 5 of the Illegal Immigrants (Trafficking) Act, 2000, also provides that any application for leave for judicial review must comply with the usual requirements for judicial review set out in Order 84 of the Rules of the Superior Courts and in addition, must be made on notice to the State (rather than the more usual judicial review procedure of making the application for leave ex parte) and demonstrate 'substantial grounds' (rather than the more general requirements, elaborated in *G v DPP* [1994] 1 IR 374 that the applicant have a sufficient interest in the matter and an arguable case). It is to be made within 14 days of the notification of the decision mentioned at s 5(1) and can only be appealed to the Supreme Court in those cases where the High Court certifies that its decision involves a point of law of exceptional public importance and that an appeal should be taken.

The constitutionality of s 5 of the Illegal Immigrants Trafficking Act, 2000 was considered by the Supreme Court by way of reference under Art 26 of the Constitution (*In re Article 26 and the Illegal Immigrants (Trafficking) Bill, 1999* [2000] 2 IR 360). In the course of its judgment that the section was not unconstitutional, the Court commented:

> 'Subsection (1) of s 5 [of the Illegal Immigrants Trafficking Bill] specifies judicial review as the only procedure by which a person may question the validity of any decision or other matters referred to at paragraphs (a)–(n) of the subsection. All of those matters fall to be decided in an administrative process by persons authorised by law to decide them. It is not the function of the courts to decide such matters anew on their merits but

to determine the validity of the decisions taken as a question of law. Should a person seek to challenge the validity of any of the matters covered by the subsection, he or she will not be limited as to the grounds upon which the validity of a decision may be attacked by virtue of being confined to judicial review as the only form of remedy. Given that the jurisdiction of the courts is limited to reviewing whether any such matter has been decided in accordance with law, the grounds for challenging such validity would not be any more extensive under other procedures such as proceedings commenced by plenary summons.'

Judicial review is concerned with the decision-making process. In refugee and immigration cases, the Irish courts have accepted that the appropriate standard is that set out in *O'Keeffe v An Bord Pleanala* [1993] 1 IR39 where the test was stated by Finlay CJ (at p. 72) as follows: 'I am satisfied that in order for the applicant for Judicial Review to satisfy a Court that the decision-making authority has acted irrationally in the sense that I have outlined above so that the court can intervene and quash its decision, it is necessary that the Applicant should establish to the satisfaction of the Court that the decision-making Authority had before it no relevant material which would support its decision.'

In the High Court judgment of *Meadows v The Minister for Justice Equality and Law Reform*, 19 November 2003, High Court (unreported) Gilligan J has certified that the question of whether it is correct to apply that standard in determining the reasonableness of an administrative decision which affects or concerns constitutional rights or fundamental rights as one fit for appeal to the Supreme Court. The appeal is pending at the time of writing.

12.5.15 CLAIMS WITHDRAWN AND DEEMED WITHDRAWN

If an asylum seeker withdraws a claim for asylum at first instance or on appeal, a negative recommendation will be made by the Refugee Applications Commissioner. An application may be deemed withdrawn in the circumstances set out in s 11(10)–(11), s 16 2A–2B Refugee Act, 1996 and Article 8(7) of SI No 423/2003 dealing with the Dublin Regulation on transfer of claims. There is no appeal mechanism against a decision that an application is deemed withdrawn. This will happen when the applicant:

(a) fails to attend for interview without an explanation which the examiner finds reasonable;

(b) appears to the examining authority to be failing in a duty to co-operate or to furnish relevant information;

(c) leaves or attempts to leave the State;

(d) engages in or seeks work;

(e) fails to notify the authorities of an address or change of address (s 11(11)(b) Refugee Act, 1996;

(f) fails to report to immigration authorities or to reside at a specific address.

12.5.16 RECOGNITION AS A REFUGEE

If the Refugee Applications Commissioner or the Refugee Appeals Tribunal reports to the Minister that a person should be recognised as a refugee, the Minister must make a declaration that the person be so recognised. The notification to the applicant will set out the rights granted to the recognised refugee as a result of the declaration. These are mentioned below. Even where the Minister for Justice Equality and Law Reform recognises the refugee's status, he or she reserves the right not to extend all usual protections if circumstances of national security or public policy apply.

12.6   Issues Arising in the Determination of a Claim

12.6.1   GENERAL

As the UNHCR Handbook says:

> 'Determination of refugee status is a process which takes place in two stages. Firstly it is necessary to ascertain the relevant facts of the case. Secondly the definitions in the 1951 Convention and the 1967 Protocol have to be applied to the facts thus ascertained.' (para 29);

and

> 'It should be recalled that an applicant for refugee status is normally in a particularly vulnerable situation. He finds himself in an alien environment and may experience serious difficulties, technical and psychological in submitting his case to the authorities of a foreign country, often in a language not his own.' (para 190).

12.6.2   ASCERTAINING THE RELEVANT FACTS OF THE CASE

For both the decision maker and the applicant's lawyer, ascertaining the relevant facts is crucial. The facts will normally be ascertained by gathering information from the applicant by way of interview, researching the objective information on the country of origin from known sources and vouching where possible any facts capable of being proved in the applicant's claim.

12.6.2.1   Interview

Getting instructions or information from a refugee involves an investigation of matters that may be extremely personal to the applicant and which may be traumatic. The trauma may not be obvious, particularly to an interviewer from another country or culture. In all refugee cases, at the very least, the applicant is in a foreign country. He or she may be trying to communicate in a foreign language and to explain events or customs which are unknown to the person conducting the interview. Even when translated, words can mean different things in different cultures.

Quite regularly, the refugee lawyer will find that one interview is insufficient to gain the history or perhaps even the confidence of the client, who may treat the lawyer as another authority figure to be distrusted.

12.6.2.2   Interpretation and translation

Where an interpreter is needed, translation will delay responses. However, an interpreter should always be used, unless lawyer and client are sure that the applicant's command of the language of the interview is sufficient not only to tell the story but also to deal with an explanation of refugee law and procedures. It is crucial that at all stages of representation, the applicant must have such translation and interpretation facilities as he or she needs to fully participate in the application, to understand the nature of the application and to allow communication between all relevant parties. The Refugee Act, 1996 provides for interpretation at various official stages of the procedure. In the initial interview with the immigration officer, the officer must inform a person of their right to apply for recognition as a refugee and their right to a solicitor *'where possible in a language that the person understands'*. The interview with the Refugee Applications Commissioner is to be interpreted *'where necessary and possible'*. The Refugee Appeals Tribunal is to use its *'utmost endeavours'* to produce an interpreter.

12.6.2.3 Country of origin information

A claim for recognition as a refugee and for complementary protection involves, inter alia, a decision by an official in Ireland or by an Irish government minister in relation to the level of human rights' protection available to the applicant in his or her own country. In addition to the applicant's own account, the decision-maker will look for outside information on the country of origin. The Commissioner's and Tribunal's office both have their own country of origin sources. However, it is a matter for the applicant and the applicant's lawyer to ensure that in coming to a decision, the decision-maker has whatever country of origin information is appropriate and relevant to properly examine the case.

There are a number of sources of information. The best sources are credible, informative and comprehensive. It should be borne in mind that many events which take place will never make it to international news or human rights reports, because they were overshadowed by more significant events in the international world of news or reports. Among recognised sources of information are:

- UN documents and country reports, particularly those of the UNHCR and the UN High Commissioner for Human Rights and the Human Rights Committee.

- Other intergovernmental reports on human rights abuses in countries or by themes. The EU and OSCE carry out such assessments.

- Government assessments. These are done by many countries including Denmark, Canada, Switzerland, the UK and the USA.

- Reports of international non-governmental organisations, such as Amnesty International, European Council on Refugees and Exiles, Human Rights Watch, Lawyers Committee for Human Rights.

- Special Interest Group reports, focusing on particular groups or human rights breaches, eg PEN/Write net on freedom of speech, Church groups on freedom of religion, organisations representing groups such as trade unions, Roma people etc.

- News reports from the country of origin as well as international news reports.

There are many sources. It must be remembered that an international report, focusing on the law in theory may not reflect the practice on the ground from which the applicant is fleeing and the aim is to furnish the information that is appropriate to assist a determination of the facts. Each report is written for a particular audience, with a particular mandate and this should also be borne in mind when assessing the information.

12.6.2.4 Vouching facts capable of being proved

Where corroborating information is available or can be obtained without danger to the applicant or other people in the home country, it should be obtained.

Medical reports, including psychological reports, may support a claim of torture or persecution. Unless a doctor is appropriately trained or properly briefed, they may not be able to identify injuries incurred through torture nor associate the marks or trauma found with the treatment sustained. Many torturers leave no physical marks.

12.6.2.5 Special categories including children and trauma victims

Children, particularly those who are not accompanied by parents or guardians, pose a special challenge. Section 8(5) of the Refugee Act, 1996, requires that the local Health Board be alerted to the arrival of an unaccompanied minor. There is no special determination procedure for a child's claim. Under the general provisions of Irish law, the 'best interests of the child' must be taken into account. This will normally include dealing with the claim expeditiously. Under s 12(1) Refugee Act, 1996, the Minister may direct the examining bodies to accord priority to certain classes of claims. One of those is the class of applicants under 18. Interviewing a child and assessing the child's claim can pose special challenges and the detailed guidelines issued by the UNHCR and others relating to Separated Children should be consulted in advance. If an applicant arrives as a child but achieves majority in the course of the claim, special note should be taken of the fact that the applicant was a child at the time that he or she fled.

Those who have experienced physical or mental trauma or shock may be particularly reluctant to explain their case. As with any client, a refugee lawyer who finds evidence of trauma must examine whether it is safe for the investigation or interview of a refugee client to proceed without expert assistance and must bear the trauma in mind and, with the consent of the applicant, bring it to the attention of the examining authority.

12.6.3 APPLICATION OF CONVENTION CRITERIA TO THE FACTS

12.6.3.1 Standards and guidelines

While the criteria for determining refugee status are internationally agreed, it is for each State to decide on what it perceives as a 'well-founded fear' or what constitutes 'persecution'. Each State decides on who should receive complementary protection. While there is no international court to set specific standards, the international nature of refugee law means that there are a number of very valuable, if non-binding, sources of 'soft law' and guidance available. These include:

- The UNHCR Handbook, a basic guide, is used by both lawyers and examiners in the asylum process in Ireland. The UNHCR also issues Notes, Conclusions and Guidelines to assist governments and lawyers in assessment of specific claims such as those relating to women refugees and children, in interviewing and in application of the exclusion clauses. UNHCR publications tend to be particularly persuasive, issuing as they do from an inter-governmental agency.

- State jurisprudence on elements of the definition of a refugee. The decisions of the refugee determination procedures and the courts of Canada, the USA, the UK, Australia and New Zealand are published. In due course, the Irish Tribunal expects to publish at least some of its decisions.

- Expert writings. These may be basic texts on refugee law or studies by interest groups who focus on specific issues.

12.6.3.2 Assessing credibility

'The relevant facts of the individual case will have to be furnished in the first place by the applicant . . . It will then be up to the . . . examiner to assess the validity of any evidence and the credibility of the applicant's statement'. (UNHCR Handbook, para 195). The examiner has to decide whether he or she believes the applicant's statement. An assessment will be made as to the 'internal consistency' of the applicant's history and as to its 'external credibility' to establish how the case matches what is known of the country of origin.

In line with normal rules of evaluation, credibility must not be prejudged. Each applicant is entitled to an individual hearing and the applicant's credibility must be assessed in the context of his or her case. Credibility may be damaged by an applicant failing to tell the entire story as much as by telling an untruth. While contradictions, discrepancies and omissions will affect credibility, minor discrepancies should not be over emphasised, particularly where they are not central to the claim, and the entirety of the evidence should be assessed together. Section 11(B) Refugee Act, 1996 lists 13 factors which the examiner should take into account in assessing credibility.

Because refugee law protects those at real risk of serious harm, decision makers must still assess the credible evidence to see if the applicant fulfils the criteria even in a case where some evidence is found not to be credible.

12.6.3.3 The burden of proof and the standard of proof

The 1951 Geneva Convention is silent on the burden and the standard of proof. A claim to refugee status is, in effect, an assertion that the applicant has a well-founded fear of being persecuted based on one or more of the convention grounds. The UNHCR Guidelines on the determination of claims provide that:

> 'Although the burden of proof rests on the applicant, the applicant and the interviewer share the duty to ascertain and evaluate all the relevant facts' (para 196).

Section 11A, Refugee Act, 1996 shifts the burden of proof onto an applicant if the applicant:

(a) is a national of or has a right to reside in a stipulated safe country of origin (designated by SI 422/2003);

(b) made a prior application for asylum;

(c) seeks to remain in Ireland rather than be transferred to another EU state; or

(d) appeals against a negative recommendation of the Refugee Applications Commissioner.

The standard of proof is the sufficiency of the evidence that an applicant must provide to prove a point. It is recognised within the Irish determination process that the correct standard of proof is that of a 'reasonable likelihood' or a 'reasonable probability' of persecution. This standard of proof is considered to be lower than the 'balance of probabilities' standard applied by the civil courts and well below the criminal standard of 'beyond reasonable doubt'. This lower standard is in recognition of the difficulties in gathering evidence in refugee cases.

12.7 Rights and Obligations of an Asylum Seeker

The asylum seeker has the following specific rights and obligations, apart from any rights and obligations arising from his or her status as a non-national living in the State:

- The right to remain in the State pending the determination of the asylum claim or its transfer to another EU state or Norway or Iceland. (Refugee Act, 1996, s 9) and the right to apply for leave to remain.

- A right to information (Refugee Act, 1996, s 8(1)(b) and s 11(8)). If information is supplied to an examining agency on the basis that it is to remain confidential, it will not be furnished to the applicant.

- A right to consult a solicitor. Subject to eligibility under the means test, this includes a right to free or assisted legal aid from the Refugee Legal Service, a branch of the Legal Aid Board.

- Housing and Subsistence through the Reception and Integration Agency of the Department of Justice Equality and Law Reform but not to the normal supplementary welfare allowances available to destitute people in the State.

- Free interpretation and translation facilities at official examinations of the claim.

- Health and education. There is no right for adults to access training or education but asylum seeking children are, as a matter of practice, accommodated in schools pending determination of their claims. Asylum seekers may access health services on a means tested basis. There is no right to interpretation or translation to assist medical care providers.

- The asylum seeker has the right to notify the UNHCR of the claim. The UNHCR may attend any interview or appeal hearing or may make written submissions. Given the limited resources of the UNHCR, this will only happen in very particular circumstances.

- Confidentiality. Under s 19(1) of the Refugee Act, 1996, all those concerned with the examination of a refugee claim must *'take all practicable steps to ensure that the identity of applicants is kept confidential'*. This does not affect the sharing of information between EU states. Section 16(14) of the Refugee Act 1996 requires an Appeal to be heard in private. Section 19(2) of the Refugee Act, 1996 prohibits publication of material *'likely to lead members of the public to identify a person as an applicant'* without the consent of that person. This does not apply to someone who is the subject of a s 4 Immigration Act, 1999 Exclusion Order.

- Applicants' fingerprints may be taken. Section 9A(3) Refugee Act, 1996 prescribes restrictions on when fingerprints can be taken from a child under fourteen. Records are likely to be submitted to the EU database of prints to check the applicant's identity.

- An applicant may not leave the State without the consent of the Minister for Justice Equality and Law Reform and must notify the authorities of any change of address (s 9 of the Refugee Act, 1996). Failure to observe this may result in the claim being deemed withdrawn.

- Unaccompanied child asylum seekers have the right to access to the health boards, and, if necessary, to have a person appointed by the health board make their application (s 8(5) of the Refugee Act, 1996).

- Asylum seekers are obliged not to work or seek work. If they do so, their claims may be deemed withdrawn.

- Section 11C of the Refugee Act, 1996 imposes a duty to co-operate:

  '(1)   It shall be the duty of an applicant to co-operate in the investigation of his or her application and in the determination of his or her appeal, if any.

  (2)   In compliance with subsection (1), an applicant shall furnish to the Commissioner or the Tribunal, as may be appropriate, as soon as reasonably practicable, all information in his or her possession, control or procurement relevant to his or her application.'

12.8   Rights of a Recognised Refugee

The rights to which a refugee are entitled are those stipulated in the 1951 Geneva Convention and those articulated in s 3 of the Refugee Act, 1996, as follows:

  '(1)   Subject to section 17(2), a refugee in relation to whom a declaration is in force shall be entitled to the same rights and privileges as those conferred by law on persons generally who are not Irish citizens (as distinct from such rights or privileges conferred on any particular person or group of such persons).

  (2)   (a) Without prejudice to the generality of subsection (1), a refugee in relation to whom a declaration is in force –

  (i)   shall be entitled to seek and enter employment, to carry on any business, trade or profession and to have access to education and training in the State in the like manner and to the like extent in all respects as an Irish citizen,

(ii) *shall be entitled to receive, upon and subject to the terms and conditions applicable to Irish citizens, the same medical care and services and the same social welfare benefits as those to which Irish citizens are entitled,*

(iii) *shall be entitled, subject to section 4(2), –*
    (I) *to reside in the State, and*
    (II) *to the same rights of travel in or to or from the State as those to which Irish citizens are entitled,*

(iv) *shall have the same freedom to practise his or her religion and the same freedom as regards the religious education of his or her child as an Irish citizen,*

(v) *shall have access to the courts in the like manner and to the like extent in all respects as an Irish citizen, and*

(vi) *shall have the right to form and be a member of associations and trade unions in the like manner and to the like extent in all respects as an Irish citizen'.*

There is also a right to hold land in the same manner as an Irish citizen (Refugee Act, 1996, s 3(2)(c)) and to obtain a travel document in lieu of a national passport pursuant to Article 28 of the 1951 Geneva Convention.

A refugee may apply to the Minister for Justice Equality and Law Reform for permission for family members to join the refugee in the State. The application is examined by the Refugee Applications Commissioner. Only spouses of subsisting marriages, dependent children under eighteen or the parents of an unmarried refugee who is under eighteen are recognised as 'member of the family'. Other dependent family members may be permitted but on a discretionary basis. An application for reunification may be refused pursuant to s 18 of the Refugee Act, 1996, on the grounds of national security or public policy ('*ordre public*').

12.9   Detention

Section 9(8) of the Refugee Act, 1996, provides for detention of asylum seekers over 18 years of age in a number of circumstances. The text provides:

'Where an immigration officer or a member of the Garda Síochána, with reasonable cause, suspects that an applicant –
(a) poses a threat to national security or public order in the State;
(b) has committed a serious non-political crime outside the State;
(c) has not made reasonable efforts to establish his or her true identity,
(d) intends to avoid removal from the State in the event of his or her application for asylum being transferred to a convention country pursuant to section 22, or a safe third country (within the meaning of that section);
(e) intends to leave the State and enter another state without lawful authority, or
(f) without reasonable cause has destroyed his or her identity or travel documents or is in possession of forged identity documents;
he or she may detain the person in a prescribed place (referred to subsequently in this Act as "a place of detention")'.

The Immigration Act, 1999 provides for the detention of a person against whom a deportation order has been made:

(a) to ensure his or her deportation from the State (s 3(1A));

(b) where the immigration authorities or gardai suspect with reasonable cause that the person:

(i)   failed to comply with instructions relating to the deportation;
(ii)   intends to leave and enter another country without permission;
(iii) has damaged or forged identity documents; or
(iv)   intends to avoid removal from the State.

Provisions in relation to detained asylum seekers are set out in s 10 of the Refugee Act, 1996, and recognise the right of detained persons to information and interpretation.

Those detained must be brought before the District Court as soon as practicable. The District Court may order the release of the person on terms as to place of residence or reporting or on other conditions. Alternatively, the court may order the detention of the person for up to twenty one days and may repeat the order for further periods of twenty one days pending the determination of the applicant's claim. Section 10(4) of the Refugee Act, 1996 requires the Refugee Applications Commissioner and Appeals Tribunal to ensure that the application of a detained person is dealt with as soon as possible and, if necessary is given priority.

12.10   Conclusion

As will be seen from this chapter, the practice of refugee law in Ireland is a mixture of international and domestic law. The domestic law framework, mainly set out in the Refugee Act, 1996, the Immigration Acts, 1999–2004 and the Illegal Immigrants (Trafficking) Act, 2000, controls the procedures for administration of the determination procedure. For the substantive law on what it means to be a refugee or to need protection, the practitioner has to look to international law. This chapter can only skim the surface of a very extensive and expansive area of law. A refugee lawyer will have to read further.

The law of refugees is also highly political and constantly evolving. Each time a country goes into crisis, new protection issues and groups emerge. Much is being done at EU level pursuant to the Treaty of Amsterdam to attempt to harmonise the substance and practice of law across the EU Member States and in accession states. There are extensive sanctions against carriers to try to stop people arriving irregularly at the borders. Refugee rights are part of the debate on integration of groups within the state, as well as in relation to racism. The tensions between state protection of borders and universal human rights obligations to extend protection to those at risk will keep the topic on the political agenda and will require the refugee lawyer to keep up to date not only with law, but also with current affairs.

APPENDIX

Further Reading

CHAPTER 1

Aziz, Sovereignty Lost, Sovereignty Regained? The European Integration Project and the Bundesverfassungsgericht, Robert Schuman Centre Working Paper, EUI 2001/3

Byrne and McCuthcheon, *The Irish Legal System*, 3rd edn, 1996, Butterworths.

Casey, *Constitutional Law* 2nd edn, 1992, Sweet and Maxwell.

Collins, *European Community Law in the United Kingdom*, 4th edn, 1990, Butterworths.

Craig and de Búrca, *EU Law: Text, Cases and Materials*, 3rd edn, 2003, Oxford University Press.

Craig and de Búrca (eds), *The Evolution of EU Law*, 1999, Oxford University Press.

Dickson, (ed), *Human Rights and the European Convention: The Effects of the Convention on the United Kingdom and Ireland*, 1997, Sweet and Maxwell.

Handoll, 'The Nice Treaty', Paper for the Diploma in Applied European Law, Law Society of Ireland, 27 April 2002.

Hogan and Whelan, *Ireland and the European Union: Constitutional and Statutory Texts and Commentary*, 1995, Sweet and Maxwell.

Hogan and Whyte, *J M Kelly: The Irish Constitution*, 3rd edn, 1994, Butterworths.

Hogan and Whyte, *J M Kelly: The Irish Constitution*, 4th edn, 2003, Butterworths.

McMahon and Murphy, *European Community Law in Ireland*, 1989, Butterworths.

O'Connell, 'Ireland' in Blackburn and Polakiewicz, (eds) *Fundamental Rights in Europe: The ECHR and its Member States, 1952–2000*, 2001, Oxford University Press.

O' Reilly, (ed) *Human Rights and Constitutional Law: Essays in Honour of Brian Walsh*, 1992, Colour Books Ltd.

Phelan and Whelan, 'National Constitutional Law and European Integration' *Irish Journal of European Law* 24.

Reid, 'The Impact of Community Law on the Irish Constitution' ICEL, No.13 1990.

Report of the Constitutional Review Group, May 1996, Government Publications.

Temple Lang, 'The Sphere in which Member States are Obliged to Comply with the General Principles of Law and Community Fundamental Rights Principles' *Legal Issues of European Integration* 1991/2 23.

Tompkin 'Implementing EC Directives into National Law: The Demands of a New Legal Order' (to be published shortly).

CHAPTER 2

Brownlie, *Principles of Public International Law*, 5th edn, 1998, Oxford University Press.

Casey, *Constitutional Law in Ireland*, 3rd edn, 2000, Round Hall, Sweet and Maxwell.

Hogan and Whyte, *J M Kelly: The Irish Constitution*, 3rd edn, 1994, Butterworths.

Hogan and Whyte, *J M Kelly: The Irish Constitution*, 4th edn, 2003, Butterworths.

FURTHER READING

CHAPTER 3

Clements, *European Human Rights: Taking a Case Under the Convention*, 2nd edn, 1998, Sweet and Maxwell.

Grosz, Beatson and Duffy, *Human Rights: The 1998 Act and the European Convention*, 2000, Sweet and Maxwell.

Harris, O'Boyle and Warbrick, *Law of the European Convention on Human Rights*, 1995, Butterworths.

Leach, *Taking a Case to the European Court of Human Rights*, 2001, Blackstone.

O'Connell, 'Ireland' in Blackburn and Polakiewicz, (eds) *Fundamental Rights in Europe: the ECHR and its Member States 1950–2000*, 2001, Oxford University Press.

Overy and White, *Jacobs and White: the ECHR*, 3rd edn, 2002, Oxford University Press.

Reid, *A Practitioner's Guide to the ECHR*, 1998, Sweet and Maxwell.

Van Dijk and Van Hoof, *Theory and Practice of the ECHR*, 3rd edn, 1998, Kluwer.

Websites

Council of Europe: http://www.coe.int
European Court of Human Rights: http://www.echr.coe.int

CHAPTER 4

Buergenthal, *International Human Rights in a Nutshell*, 2nd edn, 1995, Oxford University Press.

McGoldrick, *The Human Rights Committee*, 1994, Oxford University Press.

Newman and Weissbrodt, *International Human Rights: Law, Policy and Process*, 3rd edn, 2001, Anderson.

O'Flaherty, *Human Rights and the United Nations: Practice before the Treaty Bodies*, 2nd edn, 2002, Sweet and Maxwell.

O'Flaherty and Heffernan, *The ICCPR: International Human Rights Law in Ireland*, 1997, Brehon Publishing.

Steiner and Alston, *International Human Rights in Context*, 2nd edn, 2000, Oxford University Press.

Websites

United Nations: http://www.un.org
UN High Commissioner for Human Rights: http://www.unhchr.ch

CHAPTER 5

Alston, (ed) *The EU and Human Rights*, 1999, Oxford University Press.

Canor, 'Primus Inter Pares. Who is the Ultimate Guardian of Fundamental Rights in Europe?', (2000), 25 *European Law Review*, 3.

Coppel and O'Neill, 'The European Court of Justice: Taking Rights Seriously?', (1992), 29 *Common Market Law Review*, 669.

Craig and de Búrca, *EU Law: Text, Cases and Materials*, 2nd edn, 1998, Oxford University Press.

Craig and de Búrca, *EU Law: Text, Cases and Materials*, 3rd edn, 2002, Oxford University Press.

Craig and de Búrca, *The Evolution of EU Law*, 1997, Oxford University Press.

de Búrca, 'The Drafting of the European Union Charter of Fundamental Rights', (2001), 26 *European Law Review*, 126.

de Witte, 'Community Law and National Constitutional Values', 1991/2, *Legal Issues of European Integration* 1.

Foster, 'The European Court of Justice and the European Convention on Human Rights', (1987), 8 *Human Rights LJ*, 245, 270.

Goldsmith, 'A Charter of Rights, Freedoms and Principles', (2001), 38 *Common Market Law Review*, 1201.

Hartley, *Foundations of European Community Law*, 3rd edn, 1994, Clarendon Press.

Jacobs, 'Human Rights in the European Union: the Role of the Court of Justice', (2001), 26 *European Law Review*, 331.

Lawson and de Bloijs, (eds), *The Dynamics of the Protection of Human Rights in Europe: Essays in Honour of Henry G. Schermers*, 1994, Nijhoff.

Lenaerts, 'Fundamental Rights in the European Union', (2000), 25 *European Law Review*, 575, 581.

Lenaerts and Van Nuffel, *Constitutional Law of the European Union*, 1999, Sweet and Maxwell.

Lenaerts and De Smijter, "A Bill of Rights for the European Union", 38 *Common Market Law Review*, 273.

Moriarty, 'EC Accession to the ECHR', (2001), *Hibernian Law Journal*, 13.

Oliver, 'Fundamental Rights in European Union Law after the Treaty of Amsterdam', in O'Keefe, and Bavasso, (eds), *Liber Amicorum in Honour of Lord Slynn of Hadley: Judicial Review in European Union Law*, 319, 2000, Kluwer.

O'Dowd, 'Boston or Berlin? EU Charter of Fundamental Rights: Some Irish Perspectives', (2002), 14 *European Public Law Review*, 427.

O'Neill, 'The Expansion of the ECJ's Fundamental Rights Jurisdiction: a Recipe for Tensions with Strasbourg?', (1995) 13 *Irish Law Times*, 168.

Schermers, 'The European Community Bound by Fundamental Human Rights', (1990), 27 *Common Market Law Rev*, 249.

Weatherill and Beaumont, *EU Law*, 3rd edn, 1999, Penguin.

Weiler, 'Does the European Union Truly Need a Charter of Rights?' (2000) 6 *European LJ*, 95.

CHAPTER 6

Alston (ed), *The European Union and Human Rights*, 1999, Oxford University Press.

Archbold, *Criminal Pleading, Evidence and Practice*. Richardson (ed), 2002 published annually, Sweet and Maxwell.

Berger, *Case Law of the European Court of Human Rights* – (Various Volumes), 1989 and onwards, Roundhall Press.

Brownlie and Goodwin-Gill (eds), *Basic Documents on Human Rights*, 4th edn, 2002, Oxford University Press.

Bunreacht na hÉireann (The Irish Constitution).

Charter of the United Nations, 1945.

Dickson (ed), *Human Rights and the European Convention: The Effects of the Convention on the United Kingdom and Ireland*, 1997, Sweet and Maxwell.

European Convention on Human Rights and Fundamental Freedoms, 1950.

International Covenant on Civil and Political Rights, 1966.

Lester and Pannick (eds), *Human Rights – Law and Practice*, 1999, Butterworths.

O'Flaherty and Heffernan, *International Covenant on Civil and Political Rights: International Human Rights Law in Ireland*, 1995, Brehon Press.

Universal Declaration of Human Rights, 1948.

CHAPTER 7

Quill, 'Jury Instructions on the Quantum of Damages in Defamation Cases in the wake of De Rossa', delivered at a conference in Trinity College Dublin entitled 'Recent Developments in Defamation and Contempt of Court: A Practical Update' 22 January 2000.

CHAPTER 8

Hodgkin and Newell, *Implementation Handbook for the Convention on the Rights of the Child*, 1998, prepared for UNICEF, New York.

O'Driscoll, 'The Rights of Unmarried Fathers' (1999) 2 *IJFL* 18.

Singer, 'kinderen als morele personen: Argumenten vanuit een ontwikkelings-psychologisch perspectief,' in: Van Nijnatten and Sevenhuijsen (eds), *Dubbelleven; Nieuwe perspectieven voor kinderen na echtscheiding*, Thela Thesis, Amsterdam, 2001, 31–40.

CHAPTER 9

All-Party Oireachtas Committee on the Constitution, *Fifth Progress Report: Abortion*, 2000, Dublin.

Cusack, Sheikh & Hyslop-Westrup. ' "Near-PVS": A New Medico-Legal Syndrome?' (2000) *Med. Sci. Law*, Vol. 40, No. 2: 133.

Hogan and Whyte (eds), *J M Kelly: The Irish Constitution*, 3rd edn, 1994, Butterworths.

Kingston, *Abortion and the Law*, 1997, Round Hall, Sweet and Maxwell.

Medical Council, *A Guide to Ethical Conduct and Behaviour*, 5th edn, 1998, Medical Council.

Sheikh & Cusack, 'Maternal Brain Death, Pregnancy and the Foetus: The Medico-Legal Implications', (2001) *Medico-legal Journal of Ireland*, Vol. 7, No. 2, 75.

CHAPTER 10

Barnard, *EC Employment Law*, 2000, Oxford University Press.

Bolger and Kimber, *Sex Discrimination Law*, 2000, Round Hall.

Curtain, *Irish Employment Equality Law*, 1989, Round Hall.

Ellis, *EC Sex Equality Law*, 2nd edn, 1998, Oxford University Press.

Fredman, *Discrimination Law*, 2002, Oxford University Press.

Hervey and O'Keeffe, *Sex Equality Law in the European Union*, 1996, Wiley.

Hogan and Whyte, *J M Kelly: The Irish Constitution*, 3rd edn, 1994, Butterworths.

Hogan and Whyte, *J M Kelly: The Irish Constitution*, 4th edn, 2003, Butterworths.

McColgan, *Discrimination Law*, 2000, Oxford-Portland.

O'Connell, *Equality Now*, 1999, SIPTU.

Websites

The Equality Tribunal: www.odei.ie
The Equality Authority: www.equality.ie
The Labour Court: www.labourcourt.ie

CHAPTER 11

Act to Amend the Indian Act, Bill C-31, 1985.

American Declaration of Independence, 1776.

Attorney General of Canada v Lavell; Isaac et al v Bedard, [1974] S.C.R. 1349.

Baker v State of Vermont (98–032)

Bradwell v State, 16 Wall. 130 (1873).

Brown v Board of Education, 347 U.S. 483 (1954).

Canadian Constitution, 1982.

Canadian Criminal Code, 1892.

Canadian Bill of Rights, 1960.

Charte de la langue française, Bill 101, 1977.

Craig v Boren, 429 U.S. 190 (1976).

Dandridge v Williams, 397 U.S. 471 (1970).

Davis v Passman, 442 U.S. 228 (1979).

Devine v Quebec (Attorney General), [1988] 2 S.C.R. 790.

Dred Scott v Sandford, 19 How. 393 (1857).

Eisenstadt v Baird, 405 U.S. 438 (1972).

Engel v Vitale, 370 U.S. 421 (1962).

Extradition Treaty, 1976.

Flag Protection Act, 1989.

Ford v Quebec (Attorney General), [1988] 2 S.C.R. 712.

Frontiero v Richardson, 411 U.S. 677 (1973).

Furman v Georgia, 408 U.S. 238 (1972).

Gregg v Georgia, 428 U.S. 153 (1976).

Griswold v Connecticut, 381 U.S. 479 (1965).

Halpern et al. v Attorney General of Canada et al. (ONCA 10 June 2003).

Harper v Canada (Attorney General) (ONSC 68400; 392001).

Indian Act, 1876.

International Covenant on Civil and Political Rights, 1976.

Loving v Virginia, 388 U.S. 1 (1967).

Marbury v Madison, 1 Cranch 137 (1803).

Martin Luther King Jr., March on Washington, Aug. 28, 1963.

McGowan v Maryland, 366 U.S. 420 (1961).

Miranda v Arizona, 384 U.S. 436 (1966).

Missouri Compromise, 1820.

Plessy v Ferguson, 163 U.S. 537 (1896).

Plyler v Doe, 457 U.S. 202 (1982).

Re Manitoba Language Rights, [1985] 1 S.C.R. 721.

Reed v Reed, 404 U.S. 71 (1971).

R. v Morgentaler, [1988] 1 S.C.R. 30.

R. v Oakes, [1986] 1 S.C.R. 103.

Roe v Wade, 410 U.S. 113 (1973).

San Antonio Independent School Dist. v Rodriguez, 411 U.S. 1 (1973).

Sandra Lovelace v Canada, Communication No. R.6/24 (29 December 1977), U.N. Doc. Supp. No. 40 (A/36/40) at 166 (1981).

Separate Car Act, 1890.

Singer v Canada, Communication No. 455/1991, U.N. Doc. CCPR/C/51/D/455/1991 (1994).

Texas v Johnson, 491 U.S. 397 (1989).

United States Constitution, 1776 and Amendments.

United States v Burns, [2001] 1 S.C.R. 283.

United States v Eichman, 496 U.S. 310 (1990).

Vermont Civil Union Law (H.847), 2000.

Vermont Constitution.

CHAPTER 12

Brownlie, *Principles of Public International Law*, 5th edn, 1998, Oxford University Press.

Cullen, *Undercurrents. Refugees and Asylum Seekers in Ireland*, 2000, Cork University Press.

Goodwin-Gill, *The Refugee in International Law*, 2nd edn, Clarendon.

Hathaway, *The Law of Refugee Status*, 1991, Butterworths.

Heffernan (ed), *Human Rights: A European Perspective*, 1994, Round Hall.

Hogan and Morgan, *Administrative Law in Ireland*, 3rd edn, 1998, Round Hall, Sweet and Maxwell.

Nicholson & Twomey, (eds), *Refugee Rights and Realities: Evolving International Concepts and Regimes*, 1999, Cambridge University Press.

FURTHER READING

UNHCR publications. The Handbook on Procedures and Criteria for determining Refugee Status; EXCOMM conclusions, UNHCR guidelines (Available from offices of the UNHCR and can also be downloaded from the UNHCR website).
Any standard compilation of texts of International Human Rights Treaties.
Gender Guidelines for the Determination of Asylum Claims in the UK, 1998, Refugee Womens Legal Group, London.
International Journal of Refugee Law, (issued quarterly), Oxford University Press.

Websites

Amnesty International: www.amnesty.org
British Home Office Immigration & Nationality Division: www.homeoffice.gov.uk/ind
Department of Justice Equality and Law Reform: www.justice.ie
European Council on Refugees and exiles: www.ecre.org
Michigan Refugee case law site: www.refugeecaselaw.org
UN High Commissioner for Human Rights: www.unhchr.ch
UN High Commissioner for Refugees: www.unhcr.ch

Index

INDEX

INDEX